FOOD, FEAST AND FAST

*The Christian Era from Ancient World
to Environmental Crisis*

Praise for *Food, Feast & Fast*

"In prose that is always clear, considered, and insightful, Lyons weaves together an impressive body of historical and theological literature to argue that 'the role of food, feast and fast in the Christian life' must now speak to what he calls 'the looming environmental crisis', with answers that are both spiritual and political."

Dr. Richard J. Butler
School of History, Politics and International Relations
University of Leicester.

* * *

"Many of us would not label our daily meal a feast. In fact, we probably take eating for granted unless we are food insecure or live in poverty. We fast out of necessity for health reasons, not religiously. Moreover, for many eating is something that is just done, with little thought and no fanfare. Unfortunately the same can probably be said for the way that many Christian believers approach the Holy Eucharist – we take it for granted and do not even think of it in terms of food or sustenance, much less a feast. Fintan Lyons, OSB challenges these attitudes towards food, feasting and fasting in this wide-ranging yet accessible introduction that is, in the end, a theology of eating."

Professor Greg Peters
Professor of Medieval and Spiritual Theology
Biola University, La Mirada, CA 90639.

* * *

"Lyons invites us to reflect upon the connectedness between what we profess and how we act in relation to our consumption of the fruits of the earth, the value we place upon shared meals as opportunities for deepening friendships and building community, and what can at times be an over-casual approach to celebrating the liturgy and especially the Eucharist. He is very much on the same page as Pope Francis in his demand of an integral ecology that is attentive to the plight of our planet and of the poor. It has been said that no one should be entrusted with a leadership role in the Christian community unless s/he can throw a good dinner party. This book explains why."

Father Eamonn Conway,
Professor of Systematic Theology,
Mary Immaculate College, University of Limerick, Ireland.

food, FEAST & FAST

The Christian Era from Ancient World to Environmental Crisis

P. FINTAN LYONS O.S.B.

columba
BOOKS

First published in 2020 by

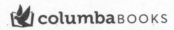 columbaBOOKS

23 Merrion Square North
Dublin 2, Ireland
www.columba.ie

ISBN: 978-1-78218-371-6

Set in Adobe Garamond Pro 11/15
Cover and book design by Alba Esteban | Columba Books
Printed by Jellyfish Solutions

In memory of my brother, Liam,
who had a deep understanding
of what this book endeavours to describe.

CONTENTS

CHAPTER THREE

The Greco-Roman world

51

CHAPTER FOUR

The toleration of Christianity and consolidation of its position

71

CHAPTER FIVE

The demands of Christian living.
From Augustine Benedict

91

CHAPTER SIX

The Carolingian era. Civilising a tribal world

107

CHAPTER SEVEN

The social effects of Eucharistic theology

123

CHAPTER EIGHT

An urban culture and its way of celebrating

139

CHAPTER NINE

The Protestant Reformation: a new epoch

153

CHAPTER TEN

Christian freedom and enforcing virtue. The Swiss Reformation

169

CHAPTER NINETEEN

Food, Feast and Fast

349

CHAPTER TWENTY

General Conclusion

365

BIBLIOGRAPHY
373

INDEX
385

LIST OF ILLUSTRATIONS

Page

Foreword

This book came about from my observation that fasting from religious motives has declined greatly in Western Christianity, while holding up reasonably well in the Orthodox world. At the same time, restraint in eating for health reasons and in dietary programmes is on the rise. The decision of many Catholic Bishops' Conferences to remove the obligation to abstain from meat on Fridays in the years after the Vatican Council was a move away from external observances towards a more internal penitential practice in reaction to a situation of near non-compliance. Also, Friday abstinence from meat could be presented as an anachronistic way of doing penance, when the traditional substitute for meat was no longer seen as a lesser form of food. For quite some time, fish has been promoted as an attractive, healthy, and often expensive item for fine dining. The banquet served to Sir Gawain – see Chapter Seven – could be replicated today nearly a thousand years later.

The accent in official documents has been on other ways of doing penance on Friday and during Lent. In fact, it has to be admitted that the alternatives have been worthy of serious engagement and the success of aid programmes associated with Lent has been a fruit of the policy. However, even though 'Fish on Friday' can no longer be associated with real hardship, no alternative forms of penance can have the impact on people's consciousness as the deprivation of food.

Looking at these issues, I began to realise that a subject worth examining in the context of the Christian life was eating itself, rather than abstaining from it, especially as today's culture places huge emphasis on enjoying food, as the supplements to the Sunday newspapers and the TV shows amply demonstrate.

Examining the role of food in our lives inevitably raises the issue of the food that is the most important, the Eucharist, if we are to live a life that anticipates true fulfilment as sharers in the Supper of the Lamb. The meal that was at the origin of the Christian life has as a result become the most engaging subject of this work, and the way the church celebrates it will emerge as the key to dealing with the looming environmental crisis of our time.

Feast of Corpus Christi
June 2018

Introduction

Christian theology and ethics, framed by belief in the goodness
of creation and the incarnation of the word of God, need to
be attentive to the implications of embodiment and to the giv-
en constraints and possibilities of embodied life. This requires
theologians and ethicists to attend to a range of ways of understanding embodied life, including variety of perspectives on
why people do what they do and eat what they eat.[1]

This book is not a comprehensive history of the eating practices of Christians, much less a history of food, but a journey through the centuries
stopping here and there to look at food culture in its socio-political setting and at individuals with contrasting views on food matters, whether involving excess or deprivation. Though there is for the most part a
chronological sequence, and some chapters lead into the one following,
dipping into the text here and there should be possible.

Individuals and dynasties, authorities both secular and ecclesiastical,
have all contributed to setting the standard for the rest of the population in
how food and fasting, and feasting both religious and of the secular kind,
are to be perceived. Many who are sincere Christians get by without reflecting much on these influences or engaging in independent thinking about
the quotidian issue of eating, while health conscious people of no faith may
devote much attention to reflection and to action by way of dieting.

From a common sense point of view, feasting and fasting considered
at the material level are opposing though related ideas, implying gourmet
delights on the one hand and lean times on the other. This is the way in
which many publications deal with these prominent aspects of contemporary living, from the ever-popular, ever-new, recipe books to ubiquitous programmes for achieving weight reduction using special diets and

exercises. Experience shows that over-indulgence in food or fasting gen-erates a felt need for compensation by means of the other – with bulimia and anorexia unfortunate situations involving issues far more complex as well as extreme. To reflect to any profound degree together on these two aspects of life and their opposites is to reflect on human nature itself. It is to draw attention to the fact that underneath mental attitudes and physical activities of the human person there is necessarily a view of life itself, a philosophy, in grander terms, an anthropology. Further, the use or deprivation of food is indicative not only of the attitude towards one's own life but also of one's relationship with society, in that the views of society, the social body, constrain the way the physical body is perceived and this is true also the other way around. The sociologist, Mary Doug-las, expressed it this way:

> The physical experience of the body ... sustains a particular view
> of society. There is a continual exchange of meanings between the
> two kinds of bodily experience, so that each reinforces the catego-
> ries of the other.[2]

This is of particular importance when the social context is that of reli-gion as is the case here; the aim of this work is to establish how feasting in quite a broad sense and fasting have a significant but often insufficiently appreciated role in the Christian life. The claim is that the enjoyment of food and the cultivation of fasting are relevant to the creation and furthering of the Christian identity, though it is recognised also that the Eucharist is the fundamental food of the Christian life.[3]

The idea of feasting will therefore include but go beyond the simple understanding represented by a meal or banquet. It will extend to the li-turgical idea of a feast, which may or may not involve a celebration of the Eucharist. In liturgical terms a feast encompasses the Liturgy of the Hours or Divine Office as well as the Eucharist. Given that this Liturgy involves several such 'hours' and therefore is celebrated over a longer period than the Eucharistic liturgy, the concept of feast can mean much more than might at first appear when there is no meal element involved; a well celebrated Vespers can be a feast for the senses by the use of good music, vestments and incense. In itself, the celebration of the Eucharist could be that and more, as there is food and drink at the heart of it, though as will be seen later, that meal dimension became less and less obvious over the centuries.

The focus of interest is the Christian life today. However, Christianity has a strong element of tradition in its makeup because of its organic, continuing growth, the incorporation of traditions which in some cases have a normative role. Over the centuries, Christians have acquired their own insights, prejudices and preferences, always in need of critical examination, but at some times in history accepted complacently by church authorities, as well as by the larger body of believers. Since the sixteenth-century Protestant Reformation, a critical attitude has been to the fore and has focused very much on structures and official beliefs and practices, if not on the experiences and attitudes of ordinary people. Today, because of progress in the human sciences, there is greater awareness of the human person in its physicality and psychology, its need to celebrate, its relationship with the environment as well as with others. From that perspective, inherited attitudes towards food, feasting and fasting are of significance for the Christian life today, and that inheritance goes back a long way.

Rather than comprehensively analysing that inheritance, this work will focus on snapshots of significant people and events in history in order to identify the various inherited elements that brought about the situation that obtains today – a looming environmental crisis.

The inheritance from Jewish history is quite significant; throughout the Old Testament text, food and dietary laws were given much attention and served to distinguish the Hebrew people from other tribes and nations. When the people of the Exodus rebelled against Moses, their complaint was given added bitterness from the contrast between their meagre diet of manna and the food they had eaten at a time when in reality they were deprived of their identity as a people. 'Think of the fish we used to eat free in Egypt, the cucumbers, melons, leeks, onions and garlic.' (Nb 11:5) Now their meagre food, rather than being a mark of identity, was used as a way of repudiating it. As the story developed a covenant was established with God which gave them their identity as his people; the leaders were commanded to go up the mountain with Moses and there they 'saw the God of Israel, beneath whose feet there was, it seemed, a sapphire pavement pure as the heavens themselves. He laid no hand on these notables of the sons of Israel: they gazed on God. They ate and they drank'. (Ex 24:10-11)

A shared meal from there on was one of the important markers of their identity. But just as 'food was one of the most important languages in which Jews expressed the relationship among human beings and God'[4], so too it continued to be for the early Christians, though now with a universalist symbolism rather than the exclusivist one of the Jewish tradition: 'every day …they devoted themselves to meeting together in the temple area and to breaking bread in their homes. They ate their meals with exultation and sincerity of heart, praising God and enjoying favour with all the people' (Ac 2:46). This text of the Acts of the Apostles expresses the new covenantal relationship foreshadowed by the meal in God's presence of the text of Exodus.

This is one example of how attention will need to be given to the food culture of various periods in history and the possible connection or disconnection with religion. It will become clear that both food and fasting have never been matters of indifference in relation to things of the spirit. An indication of how some authors have judged the relationship between the two to have been perceived by Christians of a particular era can be seen in the intriguing title, *From Feasting to Fasting, The Evolution of a Sin*. The book had the explanatory subtitle, *Attitudes to Food in Late Antiquity*.[5] As will be seen when that period is discussed, a central issue was the motivation of those who cultivated asceticism, how the relationship between body and soul was understood when the dominant philosophy was Neo-Platonism, and Manichaeism influenced the religious culture. The perception of the relationship between food and the Christian life was perhaps unique to the period, but evidence will be presented in relation to its persistence in later centuries.

24

The old conception of the Eucharist as a meal was never completely lost, but when attention turned to the nature of the Eucharistic elements at the end of the first millennium, controversy arose concerning the notion of eating flesh. This was one of the factors leading to de-emphasising the meal element in favour of the idea of the Eucharist as sacrifice. It is, however, worthy of note that the term banquet was applied to the Eucharist in the liturgy composed by Thomas Aquinas for Corpus Christi in the thirteenth century, though this was long after the term banquet had come to mean something much more evocative of earthly bread than of the bread of angels. The reasons for this change will be discussed in the course of this work. Fasting, too, can be taken in a less or more material sense and over the centuries has ranged in meaning from simple deprivation of food to having a more mystical import. Further, when considered here, whether in a material sense or otherwise, the overall perspective will be of feast and fast in relationship with each other and not just singly.

The medieval period saw its own philosophical and religious movements flourish, with consequences in particular for the understanding of the Eucharist as food for the soul. The Eucharistic devotion of religious, in particular of religious women, was one where consumption evolved into contemplation, and fasting took on a mystical meaning. Subsequently, Renaissance humanism created new celebratory attitudes to food as well as to the idea of the human, and Erasmus pointed to the obsession with food on the part of religious as well as laypeople and the means adopted to avoid the rules on fasting.[6] The way of life of clergy and religious was close to that of the aristocracy, while the class structure of the time meant that monotonous frugality was the lot of the great majority of the population, who became spectators at the banquets of the nobility. Yet in the towns of late medieval Europe it was possible to speak of the 'social miracle of the Eucharist'[7], of how the feast of Corpus Christi could unite for a day a socially divided society, 'integrating the disparate efforts of the guilds into a single whole … echoed in the neighbourhood conviviality of the evening'.[8]

The sixteenth century Reformation was a movement which questioned traditional religious practices in radical ways. Laws concerning fasting were seen as an example of unevangelical restrictions and oppressive impositions on the faithful on the part of a corrupt ecclesiastical institution. A new approach promoted emphasis on the freedom of the Christian and so brought about a repudiation of a whole regime of Lenten and other seasonal fasts along with the mechanism of dispensations used to mitigate their rigour.

Modernity and the coming of the Industrial Age brought new attitudes to both food and fasting. The possibility and soon the commercial necessity to engage for long hours in repetitive work meant that fasting was perceived as an unacceptable, even impossible burden. Frugality did not need to be chosen but was the undesired and unintended result of the dominance of an industrial economy with its low wages and ever higher demands for production. In industrial countries such as Britain and the U.S.A., festivals of the predominant Protestant churches with their rather reduced rituals, could hardly nourish those whose hunger was of a physical nature. Arguably, Catholic ritual in similar situations was more successful; Benediction of the Blessed Sacrament gave an emotional uplift at a time when the jejune character of the Low Mass was the habitual experience of most people. The ritual of Friday abstinence had its own importance; Mary Douglas in *Natural Symbols* drew attention to the loyalty of Irish labourers in London to the practice, their devotion to things Catholic, in the midst of the strenuous manual work. [9]

Today's post-industrial world is no less demanding on workers. Sedentary work patterns, involving less strenuous effort, drain energy in less obvious ways and often involve tension caused by demand for real though less physical output. This can leave workers more tired than actual manual labour. In such a situation, some create a carefully planned work-life balance by combining a regime of physical exercise with an appropriate diet, but obesity is an increasingly common condition. A well-chosen diet does allow for occasional indulgence and often requires periods of abstinence, but to maintain that balance is difficult when there is no motivation beyond the material. Binge drinking is often the result among younger people. When there is no religious affiliation, and no motivation to link fasting with donations to help the needy, the effective self-identity lacks the communitarian dimension of a truly human identity. It creates very often feelings of isolation that the camaraderie of a pub or gym cannot overcome.

All of these developments present challenges to the Catholic Church. Clearly, the ethos of the church was changed greatly by the decisions of the Second Vatican Council, though it has to be said that changes in the liturgy and in the rules of fasting connected with the celebration of the Eucharist had already occurred in the decade or so preceding it. The sense of obligation, and of its extent, associated with all the regulations in the minds of most Catholics, did change radically as a result of the Council. Attitudes to the liturgy also changed and again the questions about obligation were significant. The issue for the church today, however, is principally in the area of understanding of the liturgy by the generality of the faithful. If feasting and fasting are to be the foundations of a new Catholic spirituality, one, that is, which reflects a genuine Christian anthropology, much formation will be needed in both areas. The present situation is that many practising Catholics sit lightly to the regulation requiring a fast of an hour before receiving Holy Communion, as well as the obligation to be there at all. From the evidence of how they see the Eucharistic liturgy actually celebrated many would find it very difficult to associate a festal character with it. The challenges involved here in relation to the development of a new vision of the Christian life for the present time will be the focus of the final part of this work.

ENDNOTES

1   David Grumett and Rachel Muers, *Theology on the Menu. Asceticism, Meat and the Christian Diet* (London: Routledge, 2010) 143-4

2   Mary Douglas, *Natural Symbols* (London: Barrie and Jenkins, 1973²) 93

3   The word Eucharist, meaning thanksgiving, will be used throughout this book as the oldest and most expressive term for the mass

4   Gillian Feeley-Harnik, *The Lord's Table. The Meaning of Food in early Judaism and Christianity* (Washington: Smithsonian Institution Press, 1994²) 165

5   Author: Veronika Grimm. London: Routledge, 1996.

6   Erasmus, *In Praise of Folly* (Harmondsworth, Penguin Classics, 1966) 204-5

7   John Bossy, *Christianity in the West. 1400 -1700* (Oxford: O.U.P., 1985) 57-75

8   Ibid. 72

9   Mary Douglas, *Natural Symbols* 24

CHAPTER ONE

Food, feast and fast in the ancient world

The truth at length broke into his slow understanding, that it was the pig that smelt so, and the pig that tasted so delicious; and surrendering himself to the new-born pleasure, he fell to tearing up whole handfuls of the scorched skin with the flesh next to it. [1]

Fodder becomes food

Charles Lamb's fanciful narrative concerning the origins of cooked food underlines the fact that little is known about the early history of eating, a time when the fodder of animals became the food of humans. In the early stages of humanity's existence, the era of hunter gatherers, when people lived by hunting and fishing and the gathering of wild herbs and fruits, it can be assumed that feeding and fasting succeeded each other according to the fortunes of the hunt. Uncertainty about future prospects would mean taking full advantage to the point of satiety of game or edible plants discovered, as wild animals still do, followed by a period of deprivation until the next opportunity to find food presented itself. There was no question of choice, but simply the acceptance of the natural order of things. Fasting in this situation had not the overtones it has for us today; it was factual but without a purpose, part of a natural rhythm to which human metabolism had adapted in its evolution. Such a rhythm of feeding and fasting has arguably some continuing inherent value.

At the end of the Neolithic age, between 30,000 and 10,000 B.C., human colonisation ranging from Siberia to Alaska began to move southwards and hunted some species, the mammoth, for example, to extinction. Later, climate change opened up land previously protected by ice mountains to a wind direct from the arctic.

In the prairie provinces the giant bison, the mastodon and the camel fell victim to the sudden drop in temperature. As a result of all this, the descendants of the first Americans had little choice but to rely on the primitive forerunners of vegetables like the potato, the cush-cush yam and the sweet varieties of manioc, which, protected by the soil, survived even the arctic wind. It is impossible to know when human beings first began to dig for their food as well as gathering surface plants, but in Europe the wild ancestors of turnips, onions and radishes were used in prehistoric times.[2]

The beginnings of agriculture

Gradually, people began to domesticate available animals, and agriculture was introduced. A certain regularity of feeding became possible and life according to days and seasons became the norm. The regular pattern of eating according to the diurnal cycle originally centred on a single daily meal towards the middle of the day and left a long period of abstinence which accorded on a daily basis with the fundamental cycle of feeding and fasting. Agriculture was seasonal and involved also a cycle of plenty and scarcity. This was in the distant unreachable past, but it is worth noting today that it was the beginning of land use which, as will be discussed later, is by now creating potential disaster for the planet.

Given enough of tilling agriculture, people would gradually erode and thus render relatively lifeless vast stretches of the world (recall that the 'Fertile Crescent' is now mostly a desert landscape).[3]

The invention of the plough has been described as 'the most significant and explosive event to appear on the face of the earth, changing the earth even faster than did the origin of life'.[4]

The invention of cooking was of similar but less harmful significance as cooking increases the nutritive value of many foods and makes some edible that would otherwise be inedible. Raw flesh may not have been in this latter category for primitive people, but in some unknown period, cooking developed, perhaps by accident in China as Charles Lamb's imaginary tale suggested.

Early religion

Primitive people saw themselves surrounded by a myriad of unseen forces.[5] In some instances, this gave rise to a belief in a supreme being oriented between sky and earth, as the importance of sunshine and rain came to be seen as vital for life, while an alternative belief in a mother earth figure arose among those who began to cultivate crops. In both cases divinities were to be acknowledged and now the element of choice, and motivation for the choice, in relation to the use of food could enter. The gods were to be placated on a group as well as an individual level because of the social nature of humanity and this gave rise to cultic ceremonies.[6] The pre-historic story of Cain and Abel in Gen. 4:1-8 hinges on the distinction between those who acknowledged the gods above and those who related to mother earth. In both types of religion, the gods were gods of fertility to whom offerings needed to be made to ensure food supply.

Fasting arose only as the voluntary deprivation of the source of nutrition which was sacrificed to the deity. In that sense it had meaning, but only as manipulation, lacking motivations such as purification or repentance, which could only come with revealed religion. The emergence of the inter-personal relationship between God and humanity would bring about these new forms of motivation. Nonetheless, the element of giving in order to receive has been present throughout the history of religion and has to be kept in mind in all discussions of the relation between feast and fast.

The civilisations that emerged in the then Fertile Crescent (the area including the Levant, Mesopotamia and Ancient Egypt, now largely desert) developed cultic religions and with local variations these were still practised in the early stages of Old Testament history. Their male and female gods, the Baals and Baalaths (or Ashtarts) of the religion of the Canaan region, are referred to in the Book of Judges (2:13) and in I Samuel (7:4). Israel would in due course be warned against the influence of this older religion (Deut 23:18) and in fact there was a tendency for the two religions to coalesce in for example the use of the Canaanite calendar for the Jewish festivals and in the naming of offspring. David and Saul both gave Baal names to their children.[7]

In another part of the Crescent, Mesopotamia, consisting of today's Iraq, Kuwait and part of Saudi Arabia, a highly stratified civilisation developed on a pyramidal model, with kings and nobles on the apex of society. The Mesopotamian monarchs apparently 'staged stupendous banquets for important events such as military victories or the arrival of an embassy, the inauguration of a new palace or temple'.[8] A feature of this urbanised culture with its concentration of the rich and powerful was that it drew to itself the food resources of large surrounding areas, leaving the rural population with a penurious and poorly nourished way of life; they fasted while their betters feasted. Even in today's globalised economy this imbalance remains in some countries, exacerbated in fact in parts of the world.

The kind of deprivation described here arose in situations which included natural cycles as well as the desire to manipulate nature, with celebratory feasting as the outcome. It is not the same as the deprivation of food normally thought of in the case of religiously motivated or health motivated fasting of modern times. However, as human nature has remained basically unchanged in the course of millennia, it does show that even in these cases today there may be hidden, unacknowledged motives.

The Old Testament

The emergence of revealed religion could be expected to introduce new motivation for both feasting and fasting, as it would now be a case of responding to an initiative from a superior being, a revelation, and no longer express unilateral action. The Old Testament clearly includes this approach to feasting and fasting, based on a covenant relationship with God, who had revealed himself to Abram, as he was then called, and as recounted in the evidently historical section of the Book of Genesis, beginning in Chapter 12. The covenant is sealed by a change of name to Abraham. The story of the covenantal relationship is continued in Genesis by the account of Abraham's descendants up to the eventual liberation from slavery in Egypt and enters a new phase, a renewal of the covenant, under the leadership of Moses, as recounted in Exodus.

The introduction of fasting

In the Book of Deuteronomy, Moses described how he went up the mountain of Horeb to receive the stone tablets of the covenant and how he fasted forty days and forty nights, his purification in preparation for his role as intermediary (Dt 9:9). This is the first mention of fasting in the context of the relationship between God and the people and it will become a significant factor in the celebration of the feasts marking that relationship. The climatic phenomena, thunder and lightning, light and darkness, attendant on Moses' encounter with God on Mount Sinai, the dire warnings to the people not to set foot on the mountain, have a surprising outcome when, after the offering of holocausts and the immolation of bullocks (Ex 24:5-6), Moses and a group of elders go up the mountain at God's command.

The first feast

There they 'saw the God of Israel, beneath whose feet there was, it seemed a sapphire pavement pure as the heavens themselves. He laid no hand on these notables of the sons of Israel: they gazed on God. They ate and they drank' (Ex 24:10-11). This was a feast but it was the climax to a period of preparation. There was an earlier injunction relayed by Moses from God to the people that they must purify themselves. They were to wash their clothes and 'not go near any woman' (Ex 19:11,15) as well as offering holocausts and blood sacrifice.

Fasting becomes embedded in the religion

The feast in this case is preceded by purification, but there is no mention of wrongdoing or of penitential fasting. The situation soon changes, however, as the people take to the worship of a golden calf, and when Moses discovers this lapse into idolatry on their part he again fasts for forty days and nights, according to the Book of Deuteronomy (9:18-19), because of the 'great wrong' they had done and because he was in great dread of the Lord's anger against them. Throughout the Old Testament story, fasting will be associated with repentance for sin; there are several prominent instances recorded. The story of King Ahab of Samaria and his notorious wife, Jezebel, involves several episodes of fasting. When Naboth refused to sell him his vineyard, he went home and refused to eat in what can only be described as an expression of frustration, fasting with no positive motivation. Elijah, the prophet, caught up with him after Jezebel's scheming had brought about the death of Naboth and the passing of the vineyard into Ahab's hands. Elijah's message of condemnation from Yahweh causes Ahab to 'tear his garment, put on sackcloth and fast, sleep in sackcloth and walk with slow steps' (I Kings 21:27). This had the effect of appeasing God's anger.

An apparently similar situation arose in the case of King David, though here fasting had a different motive. After his adultery with Bathsheba, he conspired to have her husband Uriah killed in battle (2 Samuel 11:1-27). Confronted by the prophet, Nathan, who tells him that the child of his sinful liaison will die, David fasts and lies in sackcloth on the ground. His actions however do not denote repentance – he has already acknowledged his sin, and has been told by Nathan that he has been forgiven (2 Sam 12:13). It is rather an attempt to plead for the child's life. When told he has been unsuccessful, he ends his fast. This is a return to the manipulative motivation characteristic of the primitive religions and a reminder that such a temptation, however odd from today's standpoint, may be present in a fasting regime.

Public fasting is sometimes mentioned in the Bible. When Samuel was judge over the Israelites at Mizpah, he called on them to put aside foreign gods and set their hearts on Yahweh, serving him alone. 'They fasted that day and declared "We have sinned against Yahweh"' (I S 7:6). In the Book of Judges, the Israelites had been defeated by the Benjaminites and reacted by going up to Bethel where 'they wept and sat all day in Yahweh's presence; they fasted all day until evening and offered holocausts and communion sacrifices before Yahweh'(Jg 20:26). The object of the exercise was to get advice from Yahweh whether they should fight against 'the sons of our brother Benjamin', so guidance in a situation of moral dilemma seems to have been a motive for fasting.

Isaiah warned against fasting from unworthy motives in a passage which deserves to be cited at length.

> Look, you seek your own pleasure on your fast days and you exploit all your workmen; look, the only purpose of your fasting is to quarrel and squabble and strike viciously with your fist. Fasting like yours today will never make your voice heard on high. Is that the sort of fast that pleases me, a day when a person inflicts pain on himself? Hanging your head like a reed, spreading out sackcloth and ashes? Is that what you call fasting, a day acceptable to Yahweh? Is not this the sort of fast that pleases me: to break unjust fetters, to undo the thongs of the yoke, to let the oppressed go free, and to break all yokes? Is it not sharing your food with the hungry, and sheltering the homeless poor; if you see someone lacking clothes, to clothe him, and not to turn away from your own kin? (Is 58:3-7)

Fasting to achieve an objective from a pure motive is also to be found in the Old Testament. In the story of Queen Esther, Haman plotted to bring about the destruction of the Jews and was authorised by King Ahasuerus to issue a decree to that effect. As a result, among the Jews in every province 'there was great mourning, fasting, weeping and wailing, and many lay on sackcloth and ashes' (Esther 4:3), thus introducing an element of petition as well as a traditional note of penitence. Esther is instructed by her uncle Mordecai to do the same in the royal palace. Her weak and pale condition because of her fast achieves the desired result of causing the king to revoke the edict and condemn Haman. The campaign for justice on the part of Mordecai and Esther leads to the rehabilitation of the Jews and the destruction of their enemies which reached its climax of slaughter on the fourteenth day of the month Adar, after which 'they rested and made it a day of feasting and gladness'(Esther 9:17).

The Jewish feasts

Mordecai, now in a position of authority, sent letters to the Jews through-out the provinces of King Ahasuerus, enjoining them to celebrate the fourteenth and fifteenth days of Adar every year 'as days of festivity and gladness when they were to exchange portions and make gifts to the poor' (Esther 9:22). This is the origin of one of the Jewish feasts, the Feast of Purim. Like most Jewish feasts, it does not involve fasting in anticipation but is simply an occasion for enjoying special food items, in this case a con-fection which is said to have been inspired by Haman's three-cornered hat.

But a fast can also be the central feature of a feast. Among the seven major feasts listed in the Bible, Yom Kippur, the Day of the Atonement, has its origin, according to Lev. 16:1 in the death of two sons of Aar-on because of offering an unlawful sacrifice. It has therefore a special penitential character and is a feast only in the sense of being a religious occasion.[9] As laid down there and in Num 29:8 and observed today, it is a day of rest, of fasting and of reconciliation with God and one another. The day is marked by a prolonged service with prayers of repentance and readings and ends in the evening with the blowing of a long note on the *shofar*, or ram's horn. The fast from sunset of the previous evening to dusk of the day ends in the evening with a light meal which excludes meat. 'We do not fast in order to punish our bodies, but to enable us to concentrate on the meaning of Yom Kippur.'[10]

The feast of Tisha b'Av commemorates the destruction of the first and second Temples in Jerusalem and is therefore a day of lamentation and fasting still observed today. Apart from these two, the practice of fasting is not usually prominently associated with a feast. The multiple dimensions of a feast and the practices it required need to be kept in mind when the Christian liturgy, which Christians regard as the fulfilment of what was foreshadowed in Jewish worship, is considered. As will be seen, Christian worship too is multi-dimensional and the practice of fasting has its role.

It is interesting that with the exception of the Feast of Passover, Jewish feasts tend to be meat-less. The Passover, of course, centres on the sacri-fice of a lamb and its ritual eating, as laid down in Ex. 12:1-4 and elsewhere. Today, the Seder meal celebrating the Passover includes a token sheep's roasted shankbone as part of the table decoration and emphasis is laid on the various herbal confections.[11] The logic behind the choice of foods for feasts was that they commemorated first fruits, and as Passover celebrated the first fruits of the flock, the choice of a lamb for sacrifice was appropriate, whereas the feasts of Pentecost and Tabernacles related to the harvest of wheat and fruit respectively.

Clean and unclean animals
For feasts and for the Jewish food culture through the centuries, animals were categorised as clean or unclean. Lambs were considered clean beasts as they were herbivorous, being among those brought directly into existence at the creation and given 'every green plant for food' (Gn1:30).

> The herbivorous animals most important to nomad pastoralists were, of course, sheep and cows, and the Mosaic Law took these for prototypes. All the beasts that ate grass *and* chewed the cud *and* had cloven hooves were assumed to be clean. Not the horse camel or ass, whose hooves were not cloven. Not the pig, which had cloven hooves, but did not chew the cud. ... Since animals with claws were mainly carnivorous, they were obviously unclean.... The groundbound chicken seems to have escaped the net of un-cleanliness either because it was more ready to fly then than now, or because it had not yet been introduced from India.[12]

Birds flying in the air – except those like eagles which had talons and assumed to be carnivorous - and fish swimming in the waters belonged to the pristine fifth day of creation and were thus considered clean, as long as they behaved accordingly; there were birds such as the swan and ostrich that rarely flew and inhabitants of the deep, such as shellfish, that could not swim, and therefore lost their 'clean' status.

The result of not having meat as a central element in festal meals is that in all Jewish feasts there was and is particular emphasis on fruit and fruit-filled confections of very imaginative kinds and bread in symbolic shapes. This seems to have had an effect in subsequent centuries on the approach to festal meals in the Christian era, as will be seen later. While rejecting Jewish culture, the aristocracy of the Middle Ages and Renaissance era devoted great attention to what is nowadays simply called 'dessert', going to extraordinary lengths to create interesting confections, often full of surprises.

Overall, the themes of Jewish feasts related to past, present and future. They commemorated God's great acts of the past: creation was recalled in the Sabbath ceremonies, while the release from slavery in Egypt was the basis for the Passover. The covenant God made with them was celebrated in the feast of Pentecost. The present entered into the feast in calling the people to the motivation required, ranging from thanksgiving to repentance. They also looked to the future. 'The commemoration of the Exodus foretells and guarantees a new exodus.' [13] The Book of Isaiah prophesies in several places that the reign of God will one day extend to all nations - they will go up in pilgrimage to Jerusalem.

> On this mountain the Lord of hosts will make for all peoples a feast of fat things, a feast of wine on the lees, of fat things full of marrow, of wine on the lees well refined (Is 25:6).

This dimension of future fulfilment is integral to the Christian liturgy as participants declare: 'Blessed are those called to the Supper of the Lamb'.

Conclusion

In conditions where starvation and plenty could succeed each other unpredictably, it may well have taken many thousands of years for humanity to progress from the earliest practice of gathering food in order to remain alive to a culture where both restraint and feasting were both voluntary and possible. The transition came with the emergence of religion, first in primitive forms expressing instinctive attempts to placate forces on which survival depended. Later a cult developed as the result of revelation from a transcendent source, which first communicated with Abram. It reached a highly developed state with the revelation to Moses and became the religion of a chosen people. Both feast and fast were now hedged in by detailed requirements, with the exclusion of some animals as 'unclean' being singularly important. One result was the emergence of a food culture less dependent on meat and particularly rich in dessert confections to provide attractive substitutes. Overall, food had become one of the most important 'languages' in which Jews expressed the relationship between human beings and God. The culinary feast accompanying the religious feast established a tradition which Christianity adopted in its turn.

ENDNOTES

1   Charles Lamb, 'A Dissertation on Roast Pig' in Essays of Elia and Elana (London: Bell and Dandy, 1871) 157

2   Reay Tannahill, Food in History (London: Headline Publishing, 20023) 11

3   Norman Wirzba, Food and Faith. A Theology of Eating (Cambridge: C.U.P., 20192) 54

4   Wes Jackson, New Roots for Agriculture (Lincoln: University of Nebraska, 19852) 2, cited in Norman Wirzba, Food and Faith, 54

5   Ninian Smart, The Religious Experience of Mankind (London: Fontana Library, 1969) 48

6   Raffaele Pettazoni, 'The Supreme Being: Phenomenological Structure and Historical Development' in Mircea Eliade et al., eds, The History of Religions. Essays in Methodology (Chicago: Chicago University Press, 1959) 64-5

7   Ibid. 108

8   Roy Strong, Feast. A History of Grand Eating (London: Jonathan Cape, 2002) 8

9   Cf. Acts 27:9, which refers to 'the time of the Fast', meaning the time of the Feast of the Atonement.

10 Morris Epstein, All About Jewish Holidays and Customs (New York: KTAV Publishing House, 1970) 25

11 Ibid. 61

12 Reay Tannahill, Food in History 57-8

13 Xavier Leon-Dufour, Dictionary of Biblical Theology (London: Geoffrey Chapman, 1973²) 176

CHAPTER TWO

New Testament insights on fasting

So, whether you eat or drink, or whatever you do, do everything for the glory of God. (I Cor 10:31)

Jesus' teaching

The gospels bring new insights into the relation between food, feast and fast. As in the case of Jewish religion, fasting is present in the story of Jesus and his disciples and in the Acts of the Apostles, but is not featured prominently. While Jewish contemporaries had a tradition of fasting on two days of the week, Mondays and Thursdays, Jesus appears to have had a detached or even a critical attitude towards that aspect of the religion to which he belonged. Matthew's gospel recounts the incident of the disciples picking ears of corn and eating them as they passed through the cornfields on the Sabbath (Mt 12:1ff). Luke's account brings out the breach of the Sabbath prohibition of manual work; they were rubbing the heads of grain in their hands. (Lk 6:1). The important detail, only in Matthew, is that they were hungry, it was not a casual violation of the Sabbath law against work. So Jesus defends them against the criticism of the Pharisees by referring to the precedent of David who, when he was hungry, took the sacred 'bread of the presence', which was forbidden to all except the priests. Jesus - who in Matthew's gospel was a defender of the Law – now reformed it by quoting the example of the breaking of an important law by those who were hungry.

In so doing he relativised also the practice of fasting. It appears that his attitude towards fasting was in contrast with what was expected of the devout Jew. The fact that his disciples did not fast like those of John the Baptist implies that he did not require them to do so. Luke's account of the charge of the Pharisees that his disciples did not fast, which follows the story of the 'great banquet' given by Levi, is put in stark terms: 'John's

41

disciples, like the disciples of the Pharisees, fast and pray, but your disciple eat and drink' (Lk 5:33). When this objection was advanced, Jesus' defence led to a teaching which will be of crucial importance when considering the Eucharistic feast and fast. His presence, he implies, effectively produces the conditions of a wedding feast and consequently precludes fasting. But a time would come when they would fast (5:35).

Motivation

His teaching in Matthew did not question the custom of fasting, but called for the proper motivation; it was not to be a hypocritical observance but a secret pact between the person and God, with no external signs: 'When you fast, do not put on a gloomy look as the hypocrites do'. (Mt 6:16) When he referred to fasting it was not to denigrate it but principally to point to the importance of pure motives and the dangers of hypocrisy. He implied that this was a flaw in the Pharisees' practice and in one of his parables describes a contrast between the Pharisee who fasted twice a week and the tax collector who probably did not (Lk 18:9-14). He showed the importance of fasting in the right circumstances by his own fast in the desert at the beginning of his ministry. As recounted in the gospels, it is modelled on the archetypal fast of Moses on Sinai and on Elijah's walk of forty days and forty nights to Horeb. In these two cases the fast precedes an encounter with God, a preparation for a mission. Jesus' fast had its origin in the urging of the Spirit. 'Led' by the Spirit according to Matthew, 'driven' for Mark, but for Luke 'filled with the Spirit', Jesus fasted for forty days. In Luke's view it was a time to ponder the nature of his mission rather than a period of purification.

After the calling of Levi (Lk 5:27-32) he went to his house where a number of tax collectors and sinners came and ate with him and his disciples, in what was clearly a celebratory feast. This was at a time when pious Jews, and especially the Pharisees, had extended the sense of sacredness associated with the ritual eating of daily sacrifices in the Temple to all shared meals, which consequently demanded ritual purity. Eating with the outcasts of religion would make all impure.[1] He was therefore criticised by the ever-watchful Pharisees. The perception of a meal being for the elite is overturned by Jesus's response to his critics, when he says that 'it is not those who are well who need the doctor, but those who are sick' (5:31). The incident illustrates the theme of Luke's gospel, where Jesus' entire ministry is portrayed as one to the poor and the marginalised. 'As Luke develops this theme in his gospel, the imagery of the meal serves as one major means for conveying it.'[2]

He seemed more at home in that company than at the meals to which Pharisees invited him. He made it clear that he preferred to be with those who needed his company and he instinctively recognised their need. The gospels record his dining with friends as well as with these others with sufficient frequency to indicate that he was not regarded as an ascetic, unlike his relative, John the Baptist. He praised John the Baptist, 'of all the children of women, there is no one greater than John' (Lk 7:28) and showed approval of his asceticism when some ('the crowds' in Mt 11:7) condemned him for it – 'you say he is possessed'. He realised that he himself was also condemned: 'The son of man comes, eating and drinking, and you say, "Look, a glutton and a drunkard, a friend of tax collectors and sinners"'.

Throughout the gospel text there is emphasis on the importance of the shared meal; Jesus appears to be preparing the ground for the custom of meal-sharing by Christians in anticipation of a future great feast. This reaches a new phase of revelation when the gospels record the special meal Jesus celebrated with his disciples on the occasion of the feast of Passover.[3] During it Jesus re-interpreted the Jewish feast and all of the Jewish religion in terms of his own doctrine and mission; the paschal meal was to become a meal in memory of him, as Paul will come to express it later (I Cor 11:25). To the other accounts, Mark adds the important detail: 'I shall not drink any more wine until I drink the new wine in the kingdom of God' (Mk 14:25). There will be an 'already and not yet' dimension to the shared meals of his followers. This new understanding underlies the incident described in Lk 24:13-35 when the risen Lord explains the scriptures to the two disciples on the road to Emmaus, who then recognise him in the breaking of bread and Jesus immediately disappears. When he appeared to his disciples after the resurrection it was in the context of a meal on at least two occasions. In the Acts of the Apostles 10:41, Peter draws attention to this, in a sentence that seems to evoke the event on Sinai: 'We ate and drank in his presence' (Cf. Dt 24:10-11).

The Apostolic Church

This is the period of the Church's life from its inception as a visible community at Pentecost until the death of the last apostle, John, at the end of the first century of the Christian era. The Jerusalem community seems to have been small enough to meet in one room (Acts 2:1) and on the day of Pentecost at least they were there in the morning. After a large number of conversions had taken place at Pentecost, the new Christians, the Parthians, Medes, Elamites and others, spread out into their many areas of origin. The members of the Jerusalem community continued to live together, sharing their resources and going as a body to the Temple every day. The significant information is given that they 'remained faithful to teaching if the apostles, to the brotherhood, to the breaking of bread and to the prayers' (Acts 2:42).

To what extent the early community retained Jewish practices, whether in relation to feasts or fasts cannot be established clearly. There is evidence in the Acts of the Apostles of a relatively early move away from the Jewish dietary regime. Peter had a powerful experience of the need to do so as he was on his way to visit the centurion, Cornelius, in Caesarea at his request. It would seem to have been one of Peter's early encounters with the Gentile world and that he was not quite prepared for it. While on his way he stayed at Jaffa and there had a vision in which he was given a clear lesson on the need to abandon the fundamental law calling some foods unclean. He was hungry and was looking forward to having his meal at midday. Meanwhile he was praying and fell into a trance and 'saw something like a big sheet being let down to earth ... (I)t contained every possible sort of animal and bird' (Ac 10:12). Having been reproved from on high for his refusal to eat the officially unclean foods, he went with a newly opened mind to encounter the Gentile world at the home of the God-fearing Cornelius.

Council of Jerusalem

This experience of Peter, and the opposition from Jews which Paul and Barnabas encountered on their mission described in subsequent chapters, form the background to the Council of Jerusalem (Ac 15:6-21), which freed pagan converts from Jewish observance, though it retained the important rule of abstention from blood and the meat of strangled animals, the reason for the latter prohibition being the presence of the blood after the strangling. There was no mention of unclean foods, but freedom from that restriction can be presumed. As there was no mention of fasting either, it seems logical that this Jewish observance was also not mandatory. There were, however, previous references in Acts to fasting, in the context of community prayer. It was in such a situation, as they kept a fast, that the Holy Spirit instructed the church at Antioch to set aside Saul and Barnabas for their mission (Ac 13:2-3). As these two undertook their task, they appointed elders in towns where they had been received 'and with prayer and fasting they commended them to the Lord in whom they had come to believe' (Ac 14:23). And there are references to the disciples 'persevering with one accord in the prayer' (Ac 1:14) or 'persevering in ... the prayers' (2:42). This seems to refer to praying in community but whether individuals followed the Jewish custom of praying twice a day – or it may have been three times – cannot be known. A document from the end of the first century or a little later and addressed to Gentiles by Jewish Christians, the *Didache,* gave instructions to pray the Lord's Prayer three times a day and fast twice a week, on Wednesdays and Fridays (and not Mondays and Thursdays, the days Jews fasted).[4]

The early Christians had an expectation about the imminent return of Christ and this was the underlying rationale for the combined practice of prayer and fasting. Christ had spoken about the fasting that would result from the absence of the bridegroom and there were gospel passages about the need to be awake and watch for the return of the master (Cf. Lk 12:35-40). The community in this first period lived in readiness for this final outcome, though that atmosphere of expectation would fade with time, and with it presumably the emphasis on fasting, while prayer would become influenced by existential need during the centuries of persecution.

Gathering as a community to celebrate a meal together is recorded in the Acts of the Apostles and in the letters of St Paul and in some cases at least it is clear that the meal is in memory of Christ and takes a ritual form involving the breaking of bread first mentioned in Acts 2:42. That it took place on the first day of the week is clear in one case, at least, the occasion at Troas recorded in Acts 20:7-12 when 'on the first day of the week' Paul spoke at length to the community, broke bread with them after he had restored to life the young man who had fallen from a height, and continued his discourse until dawn. There is no reference at this point to a practice which will become normative in subsequent centuries, a fast on Saturday before the Sunday feast.

The context here is that of a Christian community in the Greco-Roman world and there is a reference also to a Jewish plot against Paul, but little can be known about the extent to which Jewish religious tradition concerning feasts, for example, obtained there. Nonetheless, the text notes that Paul and his companion sailed for Troas 'after the days of unleavened bread' (Ac 20:6). It is possible that this indicates, not simply a calendar reference, but that Paul respected this Jewish feast and this seems borne out by the statement at the end of the passage: 'he was eager to be in Jerusalem, if possible, on the day of Pentecost'. But Paul's missionary career shows a gradual growth in alienation between him and the Jewish communities where he preached on Sabbath days, leading to his decision after his rejection by Jews in Corinth to 'go to the pagans with a clear conscience' (18:6).

Most commentators favour a Eucharistic meaning for the expression, 'the breaking of bread'. It was clearly so at Troas. One commentator summed up the understanding of the term:

> In Jewish circles the 'breaking of bread' was a term for a religious action which included the prayer of praise, the breaking and distribution of the bread at the beginning of a meal.

It was likewise understood by the primitive Christian as the rite which introduced the meal. But nowhere is it used to describe a whole meal. For the Jews it was a ritual related to a meal which followed, while for the Christians it became a technical term for the Eucharist. [5]

The question of the cup

More recently, discussion has focused on the issue of the cup in the Eucharist, and the evangelist Luke's reference or non-reference to it. The standard text of Luke's gospel gives an account of the Last Supper (22:14-21) that includes the words, 'This cup is the new covenant in my blood'. But some old versions of the text (for example, the Codex Bezae and some of the Old Latin and Syriac versions [6]) omit the reference to the cup. It is also omitted in the text above recording Paul's final meeting with the community at Troas, in the account in Luke's gospel of the meal the two disciples had with the risen Christ at Emmaus (Lk 24:25) and in a further text in Acts 27:35. The point at issue is why Luke may have avoided mentioning this part of what would become the normative presentation of the rite of the Eucharist. Diverse views among researchers who have examined other aspects of the life of the early Christian community, especially the strongly ascetical groups, have led to no agreed opinion as to why Luke seems to avoid mentioning wine. One recent view expresses a 'seems likely' position:

> Taken as a whole, it seems likely that Luke knows a bread-only or bread-and-water Eucharistic practice and that his rejection of the culture of sacrifice that dominated the Greco-Roman world of his time leads him to avoid applying 'blood' language to Christian meals.[6]

It is a view not shared by another recent author:

> It would be difficult to argue for a clear or substantial connection between Luke-Acts and the bread-and-water tradition. It is possi-

47

ble in theory that the 'breaking of the bread' is a different tradition again, not marked by refusal of wine ... but simply by indifference to the presence of wine.[7]

The centuries after the Apostolic Church

While in later centuries the Eucharist is clearly a rite involving bread and wine, the situation is not so simple with regard to early centuries practice. Ascetics who would not approve of wine drinking, as well as unorthodox groups who subscribed to esoteric ideas about diet and beliefs, might well look for different ways of celebrating the memory of Christ including the use of bread and water. The Ebionites were a group of this kind, described by Irenaeus and other early writers like Tertullian and Origen.[8] As the overall context is the offering of sacrifice during a meal, it is not surprising that a somewhat ambiguous reference to the offering of oil, cheese and olives can be found in *On the Apostolic Tradition,* a third-century document produced by a Roman community, and traditionally attributed to Hippolytus. The text says:

> If anyone offers oil, he (the bishop) shall render thanks in the same manner as for the offering of bread and wine, not saying it word for word, but to the same effect. ... In the same way, if anyone offers cheese and olives, let him say thus: 'Sanctify this milk which is congealed and congeal us with your love. Let this fruit of the olive which is an example of your richness, not depart from your sweetness, which you poured from the tree into the life of those who hope in you'.[9]

Commentators have noted a similarity here to the rite of a heretical group, the Artotyrites, who unambiguously used cheese (perhaps yoghurt) alongside bread at the Eucharist. But a distinction has been noted between offering and blessing, which was not apparent when texts reached their final redaction, and it is likely that the bishop (the context was the ordination rite for a bishop) offered bread and wine in the Eucharistic rite, while the faithful brought gifts of food, which were to be blessed for the meal.[10]

There will be further discussion of the nature of the offerings made by early Christians, specifically animal sacrifice, in the chapter on the Orthodox Church's worship.

Conclusion

Jesus' teaching on the partaking of food embraced both feasting and fasting. About fasting he clearly taught by his words, echoing Isaiah 58; by his lifestyle he taught more subtly the place of feasting and fasting in human life. The significance of the shared meal was understood by all, but the inclusivity of his choice of table companions radically challenged the exclusivity required by the rules of religious observance. His choice has remained a challenge to Christians ever since. It took time for his early disciples to realise the freedom they now had from the restrictions in relation to Jewish laws concerning the categorisation of clean and unclean foods, the circumcised and the uncircumcised, fasting or not-fasting. It took time also for the ritual commemoration of Jesus' sacrifice as a distinct rite to emerge when the community gathered to express their new identity as Christians by prayer, the teaching of the apostles and the breaking of bread. Some ascetic groups may have chosen to use bread and water and the more extreme and heretical ones even bread and cheese.

ENDNOTES

1 Paul Bradshaw, *Early Christian Worship* (London: S.P.C.K., 2010) 39

2 Dennis E. Smith, *From Symposium to Eucharist. The Banquet in the Early Christian World* (Minneapolis: Fortress Press, 2003) 269

3 It was certainly the time of that Feast, whether it was the day, as the Synoptic gospels assert, or the eve as John's gospel relates, cannot be established with certainty.

4 *Didache* 8.11; 8.2. Translation in http://www.sacred-texts.com/chr/did/did03.htm

5 Edward Kilmartin, 'The Eucharistic Cup in the Primitive Liturgy', *Catholic Biblical Quarterly*, Vol. 24, No. 1, 1962, 32, n.1

6 Stephen Shaver, 'A Eucharistic Origins Story', Part 2, in *Worship*, Vol. 92, July 2018, 298-317

7 Andrew McGowan, *Ascetic Eucharists. Food and Drink in Early Christian Ritual Meals* (Oxford: Clarendon Press, 1999) 234

8 Ibid. 144-5

9 *On the Apostolic Tradition*, Translation with Introduction and Commentary by Alistair Stewart-Sykes (Crestwood N.Y.; St Vladimir's Seminary Press, 2001) 76-8

10 Ibid. 79-81

CHAPTER THREE

The Greco-Roman world

The grand dinner party was a defining event in first-century Roman society.[1]

How the Christian communities related to society generally is of interest; did their social structure reflect the highly stratified nature of the Greco-Roman world? Paul's assertion that that there is neither Jew nor Greek in Galatians 3:28, but that all are one in Christ, reflects perhaps an ideal more than a reality. Scholarly assessment of the language of the New Testament writers has supported the view that they belonged to the lower classes, though the linguistic evidence has also been shown to be ambiguous. There is no consensus among scholars on how socially stratified the communities were. 'To one observer the mixture of classes in the church simply shows that the Christian movement inevitably conforms to the social structure of society as a whole; to another, it reveals a fundamental conflict between the values of the Christian group and those of the larger society'.[2] There has been difficulty in situating Paul himself. As a Roman citizen, 'his family cannot have lived in absolutely humble circumstances'.[3] According to one writer: 'As a missionary working chiefly among the unliterary masses of the great cities, Paul did not patronizingly descend into a world strange to him: he remained in his own social world'.[4]

The Corinthian community

Nevertheless, his account of the Eucharist tradition in I Cor 11 may throw light on the makeup of the Corinthian community. The text has proved helpful in discerning the belief of the community in relation to the Eucharist, but it also throws some light on how the community was structured. There would seem to have been better off and poorer people within it. Paul's concern is that their meetings do more harm than good because of the divisions among them. He accepts that such divisions are inevitable 'for only so will it become clear who among you are genuine' (I Cor 11:19). The divisions show up because when it come to the time to eat (after a period of instruction), some go ahead with their own supper rather than sharing with those who lack. Given this pessimistic assessment, he prefers that people would eat at home, rather than being a source of division. His concern in the end is how the Lord's Supper, what he calls the concluding part of the meeting, is to be celebrated. It is as a united community: 'wait for one another. If you are hungry, eat at home'. (11:33) The significance of this is that the Eucharist is a ritual meal of profound meaning and can be distinguished from the earlier part of the meal shared by the community. In fact, in Chapter 13 of this letter, Paul devotes much attention to love (*agapé*) as of the greatest importance in building up the community at their meetings, and it would seem that the practice grew of having meetings for this purpose which were distinct from the celebrations of the Eucharist or held in conjunction with it, as in the case of the event described in chapter eleven.

The house church

The setting for the community meetings at this early stage was domestic, giving rise to the idea of the 'house church' and gatherings around the dining table. As the number of communities increased, it is not clear whether they came together on occasion, thus creating the need for a larger assembly area than could be accommodated in one house, though it is significant that Justin in the mid-second century says in *First Apology* [5] that 'an assembly is held in one place of all who live in town or country' to celebrate the Eucharist, indicating a larger than domestic setting. (In the second century this would not refer to the 'basilica' building which came into use in the fourth century, the era of Constantine, as will be seen later.) It would be understandable that, in addition to the larger assembly, gatherings of a more intimate type would be held, described as an *agapé*.

It is unclear when the two became separate strands of tradition.... In Jude 12, however, and in Ignatius (of Antioch) ...
the *agapé* is already being mentioned, so that by the end of the
first century C.E. we know that there was such a meal, though it
is still unclear in what way it was related to the still developing
forms of the Eucharist.[6]

The larger assembly

In the larger assembly, where intimacy was lessened and ritual inevitably
increased, the ceremony found meaning primarily in the Passover meal
of Jesus with his disciples, as the community now gathered for a ritual
commemoration of Jesus' sacrifice. How long, the tradition of the *agapé*
itself continued is not known but, Clement of Alexandria referred to it at
the beginning of the third century in his treatise on *Christ the Educator*,
mainly in his criticism of his contemporaries' lavish banquets:

> If anyone dares mention the *agapé* with shameless tongue as he
> indulges in a dinner exhaling the odours of steaming meats and
> sauces, then he profanes the holy *agapé*, sublime and holy creation
> of the Lord, with his goblets and servings of soup; he desecrates its
> name by his drinking and self-indulgence... [7]

To outsiders, the gatherings of the Christians were like other associations of like-minded people or of shared occupations, who met regularly
for conversation and food. There were also more secretive groups who
belonging to imported cults, such as the Eleusinian mystery cult or the
Mithraic cult. The clubs were unlike the guilds of medieval times in that
they 'seem to have been purely social bodies, unconcerned with the business activities of their members'.[8] Clubs whose members shared a common avocation did emerge at the time of the early Christians; the church
which gathered around the tentmakers Paul and Prisca and Aquila in
Corinth about 50 A.D. could have seemed an example of such a club.

For the surrounding population, the Christian groups in their exclusivity might be reckoned a club or a cult and little was known about them. Their distinguishing characteristics can be known mainly from what can be gathered from the New Testament writings and the rather incidental comments of pagan writers, especially a well-known reference by Pliny the Younger writing from Bithynia to the Emperor Trajan early in the second century of the Christian era.

Relations with the larger society

Despite their exclusivity, the Christians were part of the Greco-Roman world and apart from the values by which they lived, and the restrictions their faith imposed in comparison with their neighbours, must have merged into that society in their lifestyle on a superficial level. They were certainly in fundamental ways distinct from society generally, as were other communities, such as the Jewish - in both cases by their repudiation of civil religion and of the honouring of household gods. The divinising of the emperors brought an added contrast, one which resulted in persecution of the Christians as divinity came to be conferred on the emperors themselves.

The Roman world's religious environment

The conflict of the Christians with the culture of the larger society was most evident at the level of worship. What had been the traditional religion of the household gods had been challenged by movements that either rejected or ignored religious belief. The Epicureans, for example, flourished in the century before Christianity but still had influence when Christianity began to spread in the Greco-Roman world. They had a certain amount in common with the Christian communities in that they strove to create a family-like atmosphere as there were both male and female members, slaves and free, and there was no rigid hierarchy among them, as was the case in the typical Greco-Roman household of the time with its dominant male head. All were dedicated to a philosophy of the pursuit of happiness, through the avoidance of pain to oneself or to another. Epicurus, the fourth century B.C. philosopher from whom the movement originally derived, believed such an approach to life was possible because there were no plans of gods or fate ruling the world, or destiny awaiting people, so that human freedom enabled one to decide on and create a way of life. The poems of Lucretius and Horace were powerful expressions of this ideal. Virgil extolled the virtues of the bucolic way of life. However, by the early Christian period the high ideals of Epicurean culture were becoming less influential. Removing belief in gods or an after-life, effectively removed suasions towards moral living and to the unenlightened populace amounted to an invitation to a hedonistic way of life.[9] This debased Epicureanism with its lack of belief in an after-life was presumably in Paul's mind in his teaching on the resurrection of the dead (I Cor 15) when he quoted Is 22:13, 'Let us eat, drink and be merry, for tomorrow we die'.

The Roman world had come to be influenced by another philosophical movement during the first century B.C., Stoicism, a school of philosophy founded by Zeno in Athens in the third century B.C.. Unlike Epicureanism, it blended well with belief in the gods of the late Republic and early Empire, though it 'considered the trappings of religion, such as temples, statues, sacrifices, prayers, unimportant'.[10] This was a philosophy which extolled reason as a faculty shared with the gods and enabled contact and harmony with a universal divine mind, without the need for religious rites. It was a moral philosophy emphasising virtue; the truly wise person lived a self-sufficient life free of all passions, free of fear but also of love and forgiveness. It implied detachment from worldly goods, a state of contentment, of self-sufficiency, not excluding kindness to others, but a strangely aloof form of the practice of charity towards the needy. It suited the Roman temperament and became the cultural foundation of the educated Roman classes, the support of the famous Roman *gravitas*. With its emphasis on virtue, it was to an extent attractive to the Christians when they began to infiltrate Roman society. In the late second century of the Christian era, Justin Martyr, an apologist for Christianity on philosophical grounds, declared, 'In moral philosophy the Stoics have established right principles, and the poets too have expounded such, because the seed of the Word was implanted in the whole human race'.[11]

San Clemente

Early Christianity also came up against the Mystery Religions which had come into the Roman world. Within a couple of centuries, Christianity will come to borrow some of the culture – though not the beliefs - of these religions, but at the early stages the challenge for Christianity was to replace rather than blend with them. This is well symbolised by the Basilica of San Clemente in Rome, which was built over the remains of a Mithraic Temple. It is an archaeologically complex situation in that a church was built in the early twelfth century over the remains of a fourth century church, which in turn was built over a private residence. It had served as a church in the first century, but had already been built over by a Mithraeum, a building devoted to a syncretistic cult, which, according to Justin Martyr even parroted the basic Christian rite of the Eucharist.[12]

Food in the Roman world

The culture of the Roman world at the time Christianity established itself was one where morally upright and hedonistic tendencies competed in the lifestyle of its citizens. Historians who take account of diet and mealtimes point to opposing tendencies in regard to the consumption of food arising from a traditional frugality inspired by the philosophical movements on the one hand and the rise of extravagant hospitality on the other, as the expanding Empire grew richer and could gather in exotic foods from remote territories. 'As the empire reached its height, the delicacies of the known world flowed towards Rome.'[13]

The Roman day, with its rhythmic pattern of work and leisure, *negotium* and *otium*, had a corresponding dining regime: *prandium,* a snack at midday to provide necessary energy and often using left-overs from the previous day, eaten standing up, and *cena,* the evening meal, a leisurely and sometimes lavish affair, especially when there were guests. In such a situation it was called a *convivium,* and marked the way of life of the upper classes, in a highly stratified society. Most of what is known about the food regime of that time, and in fact of succeeding centuries down to modern times, centres on the upper classes, whose way of life was elaborate enough to be worth recording, along with the menus and recipes describing their banquets. There is a collection of such menus, *De re coquinaria*, 'a compilation of Roman and classical Greek cookery during the reigns of the Caesars', [14] attributed to Apicius, though the first century figure of that name was not its author. The collection stretches back to classical Greece, includes meat and fish dishes, and gives evidence of the expanse of imperial Rome by the use of expensive imported spices. The dishes were elaborate but do not show signs of excess; how these recipes were used on any occasion is another matter.

Trimalchio's banquet

As it happens, much information is available about the banquets enjoyed by the rich. Some of it is by way of critical comments from the satirists of the time, in particular, the first century *Satyricon* of Petronius, a courtier during the reign of Nero, which describes a notorious banquet given by a man called Trimalchio at his house, probably near Naples. As a satire it may have fictional aspects, though it has also been suggested that it 'is far closer to reality than a first reading would suggest'. [15] The story line is really concerned with the adventures of two of the guests, but incidentally gives a detailed account of the stages and contents of the banquet. There is a great amount of ceremony involved, including washing of the guests' hands with water by slaves on entry and a repeat with wine at a later stage. As will be seen throughout history up to the middle ages the food items on offer included delicacies which would today be considered repulsive, in this case 'dormice dipped in honey and sprinkled with poppy seed'. [16] The two aristocratic guests were not impressed by the 'plebeian' food which first appeared such as kidneys, chick-peas and a barren sow's womb, but were surprised by the sudden appearance of dishes with fowl, a hare and fish, with wineskins pouring out peppered gravy. This course was outdone by a subsequent one featuring a boar surrounded by piglets made of pastry. There were many following courses, the number not specified in this case.

But it is clear, at least for medieval times, that the amount of food consumed during each course would be quite small, corresponding to today's concept of 'finger food'. Whatever may have been the quantity, it would literally have been finger food, as guests used the only tool available, a knife (provided or the guest's own), to cut a portion and then take it in their fingers.[17] This was still true for Renaissance era banquets; for example, the menu for a feast given by the city of Paris for Catherine de Medici in 1549 lists twenty four sorts of animals, many kinds of cakes and pastry and a mere four vegetable dishes. How many shared the food is not known but it was a civic as well as a royal occasion and thronged with guests, perhaps including uninvited ones.[18]

The *vomitorium*

The myth of the *vomitorium* has been associated with Roman banquets of Trimalchio's era. This was said to be a room to which guests repaired to relieve feelings of over-fullness by vomiting. The associated verb appears to have originated in the writings of a fifth-century author, Macrobius, who in his *Saturnalia* used the expression of an earlier author, Quintus Ennius (239-169 B.C.), about the Tiber 'spewing' (*vomitans*) water into the sea to describe people pouring though passages to their seats in the stadium. The term *vomitorium* went from being associated with his description of a passage to being described as a room to which overly sated guests went to relieve themselves of the contents of their stomachs.

This development is evident in the two-volume work, *Walks in Rome*, by Augustus Hare. In the original 1871 edition, Hare mistook a room opening off the state dining hall, the Triclinium, of the Flavian Palace for a room which he called the *vomitorium*. 'Beyond the Triclinium is a disgusting memorial of Roman imperial life, in the *vomitorium*, with its basin, whither the feasters retired to tickle their throats with feathers, and come back with renewed appetite to the banquet.' By the sixteenth, 1903, edition (just after his death), or in some intervening edition, this had been altered and now gave the name *Nymphaeum* to the room, describing it as a room with a fountain and open windows so that 'the banqueters might be lulled by the splash of the fountain and the cooled air'.[19] How the author came to create or consolidate the myth is not clear but two references in *The Twelve Caesars* of Suetonius (69-126) may have contributed to this further development:

> (The Emperor Vitellius) banqueted three and often four times a day, namely morning, noon, afternoon and evening – the last meal being mainly a drinking bout – and survived the ordeal well enough by taking frequent emetics.[20]
> It was seldom that Claudius left a dining-hall except gorged and sodden; he would then go to bed and sleep supine with his mouth wide open – thus allowing a feather to be put down his throat, which would bring up the superfluous food and drink as vomit.[21]

The final course in Trimalchio's banquet consisted of fruits and nuts enclosed in pastry, and, typically of such banquets, made to look like various animals, birds and fish. This kind of dessert course will persist in the banquets of the rich through the ages up to the Renaissance and beyond.

Another significant feature of this banquet, again to be found throughout history, was the inclusion of singing and instrumental music and processional entries bringing in the many courses. There were scurrilous songs and various vulgar activities, while the host also introduced a note of pretended erudition, in imitation of the customs of the more serious nobility and of the original Greek banquet.

Cicero, in his day, about a hundred years earlier, enjoyed evening meals with his friends following the Greek custom:

> I indeed enjoy the ancestral fashion of appointing a master of ceremonies for the feast, and the rules for drinking announced from the head of the table, and cups, as in Xenophon's *Symposium*,

not over large, and slowly drunk, and the cool breeze for the din-ing-hall in summer, and the winter's sun or fire. Even on my Sa-bine farm I keep up these customs, and daily fill my table with my neighbours, prolonging our varied talk to the latest possible hour. But it is said that old men have less intensity of sensual enjoyment. So I believe; but there is no craving for it. You do not miss what you do not want.[22]

Plutarch's biography of Cicero paints a somewhat different picture, saying that he was very thin and had such poor digestion that he could only take a light meal late in the day.[23]

How true the account of Trimalchio's banquet is cannot be known but the courses and their contents, the number of slaves in attendance, would necessarily reflect reality in order to give the story credibility. This was a satire on the kind of banquet which did exist in Roman society and was an essential feature of its way of ordering affairs and maintaining class divisions. The banquet was a way of indicating who did and who did not belong and of maintaining a power structure.

The elaborate ceremonial of Trimalchio's vulgar banquet will be found in more respectable form throughout history and must be taken into account when considering the place of the 'feast' in Christian culture, where class division will also assert itself. It will be found that throughout Christian history, in a world of class consciousness, the elaborate banquet was characteristic of the upper classes, while frugality was the lot of the poor, thus challenging Christian principles and effecting the understand-ing and performance of the Eucharistic rite.

Emperor Nero

Having Petronius as its author, Trimalchio's banquet would have to be dated about the time of the Emperor Nero (r54-68). Tacitus in *The An-nals of Imperial Rome* gives factual details of the environment in which Nero's social life was lived:

In the wood which Augustus had planted round his naval lake, places of assignation and taverns were built, and every stimulus to vice was displayed for sale. Moreover, there were distributions of money. Respectable people were compelled to spend it; disreputable people did so gladly'.[24]

Nero also aspired to poetic taste and to listening after his dinner as philosophers debated, like Trimalchio aping the customs of the more serious Romans. Suetonius reported that his 'feasts lasted from noon to midnight, with an occasional break for diving into a warm bath, or if it were summer, into snow-cooled water'.[25] That Nero's banquets reflected the stratified and public nature of dining of the time can be verified by the account of one in which he arranged for the murder of his half-brother Britannicus by poisoning his drink – a second attempt according to Suetonius. As Tacitus relates: 'It was the custom for young imperial princes to eat with other noblemen's children of the same age at a special, less luxurious, table before the eyes of their relations: that is where Britannicus dined'.[26] It can be no surprise that when a disastrous fire engulfed Rome, suspicion persisted that it had been instigated by the emperor himself (Tacitus was uncertain). But Nero used the Christians as scapegoats; they were torn to death by dogs, crucified as in the case of St Peter, and made into human torches to light up his gardens.

Christians in the first and second century Roman world

Yet the 'notoriously depraved Christians',[27] as Tacitus calls them, continued to 'come together', as St Paul had put it, for prayer, for baptism and for the Lord's Supper, as is evident from Paul's letters. In the concluding chapter sixteen of the Letter to the Romans (which may have been a circular letter, and not one sent to the church at Rome), he sent greetings to named leaders of churches in many different places, some described as meeting in households. There has been much study devoted to establishing what can be learned about the social status of these people, but only probable conclusions reached, based on, for example, the fact that some had Greek names or that an individual was owner of a home sufficiently large to accommodate the community.[28] Overall, there is a lack of information about the church of the first generation in Rome or elsewhere. In the judgement of Peter Brown, '(f)ar less than we might wish can be said with certainty about the pre-Constantinian church. Its members and rate of expansion are likely to remain forever obscure'.[29]

The leadership of the Christian communities in Rome in the first century was traditionally expressed in terms of a list of successive, named popes first given by Irenaeus of Lyons in 180. But evidence from various writings of the first and second centuries indicates that there were unnamed leaders of the church there and the question of a succession in authority over the Christians of the various communities is much less certain.

> If we ask ... whether the primitive Church was aware, after Peter's death, that his authority had passed to the next bishop of Rome, or in other words that the head of the community at Rome was now the successor of Peter, the church's rock and hence the subject of the promise in Matthew 16:18-19, the question, put in those terms, must certainly be given a negative answer.[30]

However, in the mid-second century a named bishop of Rome, Anicetus, was recognised as the acknowledged leader by Polycarp of Smyrna, who had known the apostle John in his old age. He visited Anicetus and discussed the date of Easter with him. The occasion was the controversy over the date of Easter, whether it was to be dated on the Sunday after the Jewish Passover or on the Passover itself – those who observed the latter also fasted the day before, influenced by the Jewish Feast of Unleavened Bread. In the course of time, the Sunday celebration of Easter became universal and adopted an eve of the feast fast, even though early Christianity, because of its Jewish roots, considered Saturday unsuitable for a fast out of continuing regard for the Jewish Sabbath. There was already the Christian practice of fasting on Wednesday and Friday, as noted earlier, and this led to the introduction of a two-day fast, Friday and Saturday, before Easter Sunday.

Initiation

Initiation into the community in the first and second century followed the pattern described in the Acts of the Apostles, but according to the *Didache*, [31] an early-second century document, in addition to the twice a week fast for all Christians, a fast of 'one or two days' should be required of those to be baptised before the ceremony, and the minister of the baptism should also fast. The *Didache* envisages baptism in 'living water' where possible, implying an outdoor celebration. A generation or so later in Rome, Justin[32] spoke also of the community praying and fasting with those who are to be baptised before they are 'led to a place where there is water', for the baptism. They are then led back to where the community is assembled, where the kiss of peace is exchanged at the end of the prayers. Then bread and a cup of wine mixed with water are brought to the president of the assembly for a celebration of the Eucharist. Various early accounts of baptism, such that as that found in Tertullian's *De baptismo,* (with references also in others of his works), add elements such as anointing and imposition of hands and the giving of a cup of milk and honey to the newly baptised. The ceremony has precise ritual elements, though prayers after the baptism were presumably spontaneous as Tertullian speaks of the newly baptised spreading their hands in prayer for the first time in their mother's house. There is a festive atmosphere, but the Eucharist in these cases is celebrated as a simple final ritual – there is no suggestion of a banquet in which it is incorporated.

The celebration of the Eucharist

How often these Christians prayed or these communities met cannot be known and what days they met cannot be ascertained but a preference for the first day of the week, the day of the Resurrection, emerged early; the earliest account of a celebration of the Eucharist after apostolic times was given by Justin in the mid second-century and refers to the assembly in one place of all who live in town or country 'on the day called Sunday'.[33]

There is evidence already for this basic pattern in a letter from Pliny the Younger to the Emperor Trajan about 111 A.D. He got his infor-

63

mation from former Christians, who were 'under examination', that is, being tortured. He refers to a 'stated day' for the gathering and indicates two phases of the worship:

> (O)n a stated day they had been accustomed to meet before daybreak and to recite a hymn among themselves to Christ, as though he were a god, and that so far from binding themselves by oath to commit any crime, their oath was to abstain from theft, robbery, adultery, and from breach of faith, and not to deny trust money placed in their keeping when called upon to deliver it. When this ceremony was concluded, it had been their custom to depart and meet again to take food, but it was of no special character and quite harmless.[34]

His reference to 'no special food' in the Christian assembly hints at a development which will become typical of the celebration of the Eucharist and lead to an understanding of it where the meal element becomes less significant than its significance as a memorial of Christ as the sacrificial Paschal lamb.

In itself, the comment seems an indication of Pliny's view that the banquets held in his own social circles were extravagant and very class conscious. In a letter to a young friend, Avitus, he explained how he avoided the excesses which were so common. He reports a conversation he had with a fellow guest at a banquet where the host was both lavish and mean; he set the best dishes before himself and a few others and treated the rest to cheap and scrappy food. Pliny told his fellow guest: 'I set the same before all,... for I invite my friends to dine not to grade them one above the other, and those whom I have set at equal places at my board and on my couches I treat as equals in every respect'. To the guest's question whether that included freedmen and if it cost him a lot, he replied: 'Yes, for then I regard them as my guests at table, not as freedmen... It's easily done; because my freedmen do not drink the same wine as I do, but I drink the same as they do'.[35]

If Pliny's assessment of the Christians was true fifty years after Paul's complaint about conduct in Corinth, then the Christians in some places at least – he was writing from Bithynia – must have retained high standards, a cohesiveness that could be expected from people who were being persecuted for their faith, as they would be, intermittently at least, for almost another two hundred years. A hostile commentator, the pagan philosopher Celsus writing about 170, was unflattering in his description of them as a community that excluded the educated: 'they desire and are able to gain over only the silly, and the mean, and the stupid, with women and children.'[36] According to him, this was true from the beginning; Jesus had only been able to gather around him 'ten or eleven persons of notorious character, the very wickedest of tax-gatherers and sailors'[37] These quotations are taken from Origen's *Contra Celsum*, his tract devoted to repudiating Celsus' arguments.

The Eucharist as meal

The understanding of the Eucharist as a meal, an action, in memory of Jesus' offering of himself to create a new covenant in his blood, enabled the participants to see the action – as the early prayers indicated – as a sacrifice of praise and of petition in succession to the sacrifices of the old covenant. The early descriptions, that by Justin, for example, also included an emphasis on the Eucharist as food 'over which thanks have been given by a word of prayer which is from him; (the food) from which our flesh and blood are fed by transformation is both the flesh and blood of that incarnate Jesus'.[38] The fact that some portions were taken to those who could not be present, as Justin says, and the practice mentioned by Basil of Caesarea in the fourth Century of taking the Eucharistic elements home for communion during the week, bring this understanding of shared food to the fore, and will lead to concentration on how the elements are changed into the body and blood of Jesus. As will be discussed later, this focus on consecration of the elements will by the Middle Ages have led to the largescale suppression of the awareness of the Eucharist as a meal. The table for the meal will be seen and architecturally realised as the altar of sacrifice.

Tertullian on fasting

Early documentation on fasting relates to the asceticism required in the Christian life rather than to its festive liturgical dimension. In fact an element of negativity manifests itself rather clearly in relation to bodily life in the third century, especially in the writings of Tertullian, who in his *Apologia* described himself and fellow Christians as 'lean with fastings and emaciated from all forms of self-restraint'.[39] He showed leanings towards, and eventually joined, the heretical Montanist movement with its negative attitude towards the physical world. His tract, *De jejunio adversus psychicos*, was written against the Roman church after he had seceded to the Montanists. His initial assertion was that lust was accompanied by voraciousness in the life of his opponents - the mainstream church in his native Carthage and elsewhere. He responded to the charges of novelty made against the practices of his new community, namely, prolonged fasting and in particular eating dry food and 'abstinence from the bath, congruent with our dry diet'.[40] The reference to dry food indicates a special motive for fasting among the Montanists and other ascetics of the time: preoccupation with keeping the body light and thus a fit container for the soul, keeping it free from earthly, heavy elements. Avoiding water on the skin made the body crisp and light.[41] It was obviously the kind of fasting that excluded all festive activity.

But Tertullian's vision was not wholly negative. Among his innovative and positive teachings was one that receiving Communion on a fast day did not break the fast,[42] that there should be no fasting or kneeling on the Lord's Day and between Easter and Pentecost. He also held that an offering should be made for masses for the dead on their anniversaries. This idea of special, commemorative masses accords with a slightly later development: the *Liber Pontificalis* records a significant liturgical innovation in the decree by the third century pope, Felix, that mass be celebrated 'over the memorials of the martyrs'.[43] The practice may well have been inspired by the pagan tradition of commemorating the dead in a set of rituals beginning with a meal celebrated on the day of the death of a family member, followed by another at the tomb to mark the end of a period of mourning. Anniversaries of the date of birth were celebrated at tombs which lined the roads out of Rome; there were both family and public ceremonies, called *Parentalia* and *Lemuria* respectively. The funerals of members of the aristocracy were occasions for sacrifices of food offered to the gods and followed by public feasting. Felix's decree drew attention to the martyrs of the various persecutions, who were to be considered family members by the whole Christian community and in some cases may have had no remaining family to remember them.

It was a practice that became widespread, especially when Pope Damasus in the fourth century, at the prompting of Jerome, used the resources he had to have 'the suburban tombs of the martyrs refurbished, with magnificently carved inscriptions in verse added'.[44] It had been important for maintaining the morale of the community in earlier more difficult times.

Conclusion

The evidence regarding the breaking of bread in the *Acts of the Apostles* is significant and is amplified by the information supplied by St Paul in *I Corinthians* 11. Here there is a hint of what will emerge more clearly with time, that there were two forms of community meeting, one which was certainly the Eucharist and another which took the form of a love feast or *agapé*. Paul may have had this type of encounter in mind when he expounded the importance of charity in *I Corinthians* 13. The meetings of the dispersed communities took place initially in houses, necessarily so in times of persecution, and in that case the format was obviously that of a meal. Such a setting favoured the practice of the *agapé*, and it is not known when this practice ceased. As buildings for the celebration of the Eucharist began to be constructed for larger gatherings, the less intimate atmosphere favoured the interpretation of the rite as a commemoration of Jesus' Passion and the table used to be seen as an altar, though both terms were used, as Augustine would do later.

The Roman world in which Christians lived, the society in which they inevitably mixed, presented a contrast and a challenge in the hedonism which was endemic, and the pagan worship as well as the cult of the divinised emperors were both a source of persecution and a stimulus to Christians to follow their distinctive way of living and of worship, causing puzzlement to people like Pliny the Younger. Ascetical trends grew in such an atmosphere, as the writings of Tertullian testified.

ENDNOTES

1   Roy Strong, *Feast. A History of Grand Eating* (London: Jonathan Cape, 2002) 6

2   Ibid. 53

3   Wayne Meeks, *The First Urban Christians* (New Haven: Yale University Press, 1983) 52

4   Gustav Deissmann, *Paulus: Eine Culture und religionsgeschtliche Skizze* (Tübingen: Mohr, 1911) 51, cited by Meeks, op. cit. 52

5   Justin, *First Apology 67.3*. Text in R.C.D. Jasper and G.J. Cuming, eds., *Prayers of the Eucharist: Early and Reformed* (New York: Oxford University Press, 1980²) 19

6   Dennis E. Smith, *From Symposium to Eucharist. The Banquet in the Early Christian World* (Minneapolis: Fortress Press, 2003) 285

7   Clement of Alexandria, *Paedagogus* 2.1 trans. Simon Wood (Washington: Catholic University of America, 1951) 96

8   Wayne Meeks, *The First Urban Christians*, 31, quoting A. H. M. Jones, 'The Economic Life of the towns of the Roman Empire' in Jean Virenne, ed., *La Ville*, (Brussels: Libraire Encyclopédique, 1955)172 ,

9   Michael Mullins, *Called to be Saints. Christian Living in the First Century* (Dublin: Veritas, 1991) 40-1

10 Ibid., 42.

11 Justin Martyr, *Second Apology*. VIII, 1.

12 Justin Martyr, *First Apology*, LVI

13 Cf. Roy Strong, *Feast* 19

14 John Edwards, *The Roman Cookery of Apicius, Translated and Adapted for the Modern Kitchen* (London: Random House, 1984) ix

15 Ibid. 6

16 Ibid. 4

17 Madeleine Pelner Cosman, *Medieval Holidays and Festivals* (London: Piatkus, 1984) 13

18 Stephen Mennell, *All Manners of Food. Eating and Taste in England and France from the Middle Ages to the Present* (Oxford: Basil Blackwell, 1985) 22

19 Augustus Hare, *Walks in Rome*, Vol, I (London: George Allen, 1903¹⁶) 203

20 Suetonius, *The Twelve Caesars*, Robert Graves trans. (London: Guild Publishing,1990) 273

21 Ibid. 206

22 Cicero, *De senectute*,13.45, Andrew Peabody trans. (Boston: Brown and Company, 1884) 36

23 'Cicero' in Plutarch, The Fall of the Roman Republic, Rex Walker trans. (London: Penguin, 1958) 314

24 Tacitus, *The Annals of Imperial Rome*, Michael Grant trans. (London: Penguin Classics, 1989²) 321

25 Suetonius, *The Twelve Caesars* 227

26 Ibid. 291

27   Ibid 365

28   Cf. Wayne Meeks, *The First Urban Christians,* 56-60

29   Peter Brown, *The Making of Late Antiquity* (Cambridge, Mass: Harvard University Press, 1978) 57

30   Klaus Schatz, S.J., *Papal Primacy. From its Origins to the Present* (Collegeville: Liturgical Press, 1996) 2

31   *Didache* 7

32   *I Apologia* 61,65

33   Justin Martyr, *I Apol.* 67.3

34   Pliny the Younger, *Letters* 10. 96. 9 (http://www.attalus.org/old/pliny10b.html)

35   Pliny, *Letters* 2.6 (http://www.attalus.org/old/pliny2.html)

36   Origen, *Contra Celsum* 3.44 (http://www.ccel.org/ccel/schaff/anf04.vi.ix.iii.xliv.html)

37   Ibid. 1.62.

38   Justin, *I Apol.* 66, 1-2.

39   Tertullian, 'Apology' in *The Fathers of the Church* Vol. 10 (Washington: Catholic University of America, 1950) 104

40   Tertullian, 'On Fasting' in *The Writings of Tertullian* Vol.III, Ante-Nicene Christian Library Vol. XVIII (Edinburgh: T & T Clark: 1871) 124

41   Cf. Peter Brown, *The Making of Late Antiquity,* 44

42   *De oratione* XIX, Edited and Translated by Ernest Evans (London: S.P.C.K., 1953) 24

43   *The Book of Pontiffs (Liber Pontificalis),* Translated with an Introduction by Raymond Davis (Liverpool: Liverpool University Press, 1989) 11

44   Bertrand Lançon, *Rome in Late Antiquity* (Edinburgh: University Press, 1995) 30

CHAPTER FOUR

The toleration of Christianity and consolidation of its position

Jerome's version of the promises to Peter used familiar Roman legal words for binding and loosing – *ligare* and *solvere* – which underlined the legal character of the Pope's unique claims.[1]

The situation of the Christian communities in the empire changed fundamentally at the beginning of the fourth century. After a period of fierce persecution beginning in 298, the co-emperor Galerius issued an edict of toleration on his deathbed in 311. The circumstances made it inevitable: the church was an efficiently organised body which had established a coherent intellectual and moral system and a visible presence by building a number of churches during previous periods of peaceful co-existence with the empire and its pagan rites. In contrast, the empire was prone to increasing instability because of civil wars, a rapid succession of short-lived emperors and confusion between differing religious philosophies.[2]

Emperor Constantine and St Peter's Basilica

As is well known, the church's status increased manifold with the accession of the Emperor Constantine (272-337), who ruled as a co-emperor with Licinius until he defeated him in 324. Together they had issued the Edict of Milan in 313, giving official tolerance to Christianity (and to any other religion). 'As Emperor, Constantine still fulfilled the role of a pagan *pontifex maximus* and allowed pagan cults to continue.'[3] But, because of the Edict, the church gained both by the acquisition and provision of buildings, the funds needed to maintain them and the privileged status granted to the clergy, who were exempted from taxation. In becoming an institution in society, respected, even favoured, by the secular authorities, the church's lifestyle inevitably changed. What had

Marble portrait head of the Emperor Constantine I. Year ca. A.D. 325-370.

been clandestine services – ritual meals - in houses, or in about 25 small church buildings called *tituli*,[4] gradually became elaborate rites in splendid architectural surroundings. Constantine provided both a residence and a church for Pope Sylvester I and made a very significant contribution to the church's establishment by the building of a church over the reputed site of Peter's grave, a project that was made extremely difficult by the sloping site containing a working-class cemetery on the Vatican hill outside the city boundary. Though smaller than the current building, St Peter's was an impressive structure modelled on the *basilica*, the state's tribunal building, and became a magnet for pilgrims. It was ever afterwards referred to as St Peter's Basilica. The resulting flow of donations facilitated development of elaborate ceremonies as well as the socially superior lifestyle of pope and bishops, putting everything to do with the church on an imperial footing.[5]

The *Liber Pontificalis*

What is known about the life of Pope Sylvester I who reigned from 314 to 335 in this initial period of consolidation, has to do with the building and equipping of churches. The *Liber Pontificalis* (*The Book of the Popes*), which gives an account of his actions, presents itself as a history of the popes from the beginning, compiled by Pope Damasus up to his own time in the fourth century. Scholarly research has shown that its first edition must have been about the middle of the sixth century and may be held to contain reliable statistics about such things as ordinations, but earlier material must have been based on snippets of information and apocryphal sources. Nevertheless, the endowments of churches made by Sylvester are very detailed and seem a record of the changed status of the church under Constantine. If, as the *Liber Pontificalis* says, Sylvester built a church on the estate of one of his priests named Equitius and endowed it with many sacred vessels of silver and gold along with the revenue from five farms, two houses and a garden in the city, he must himself have been the recipient of various revenues. The record also indicates that he made many administrative decisions and issued judicial decrees of the kind that would indicate a superior status in society and undoubtedly a corresponding lifestyle. This is borne out by the text's account of Constantine's similar and even more extensive activities in building and endowing of churches.

What cannot be established is the detail of Sylvester's lifestyle, but the fact that Constantine built the Lateran Palace for him along with a cathedral and a baptistery certainly shows that his standard of accommodation, at least, was on the level of the Roman aristocracy of the time. The basilica's walls were clad in yellow marble, causing it to be called the *basilica aurea* (golden basilica) and, significantly, it rivalled in size the state basilica of Maxentius, the previous co-emperor.[6] It is not known, however, how much he may have practised personal austerity. In a decision which offers some insight into the Christians of the time, his predecessor, Miltiades 'decreed that none of the faithful should on any account fast on Sunday or Thursday, because the pagans kept those days as a holy fast'.[7]

73

Lifestyles and fasting rules

The early second century document the *Didache* had required that Christians should fast, and the *Liber Pontificalis* says, however reliably, that a second century pope, Telesphorus, introduced a fast of seven weeks before Easter, and therefore liturgical in origin, linking fast with feast. A third century pope, Callistus, decreed that on Saturdays three times a year, in the fourth, seventh and tenth months, 'there should be a fast from corn, wine and oil'.[8] Given the nature of the items of the fast, there is some connection with the harvests, as in the case of Jewish feasts, but whether they were Christianised versions of agricultural feasts of pagan Rome is not certain. A century or so later, a new kind of seasonal fast was superimposed on this pattern, extending the fast to Wednesdays, Fridays and Saturdays between the third and fourth Sundays of Advent, the first and second Sundays of Lent, between Pentecost and Trinity Sunday and the week containing the Wednesday after the Feast of the Holy Cross, September 14th. These days were called Ember Days, the English term being derived from the German version, Quatember, of the Latin *Quatuor Tempora,* Four Times.

In the new political and religious situation that obtained, Sylvester and at least some of his fellow Christians would in all likelihood have had the resources to enjoy the delights of the table, like other Romans, as well as the challenge to observe the fasts of earlier and less privileged times. According to one researcher, 'it appears that the bishop of Rome in the fourth century had an annual income of some 30,000 *solidi* and possessed about half a tonne of gold in the form of liturgical vessels'.[9] Depending on how the value of gold related to its present day value, the assets may have been the equivalent of over half a million Euro. Clearly, the bishop and higher clergy had a social status on a level with the nobility. 'In 318, Constantine conferred on bishops civil jurisdiction over court litigations that involved Christians.' This led to them having 'the titles and insignia that state dignitaries enjoyed'.[10] The pope's participation in ceremonies evoked the atmosphere of imperial rituals: the cape with a long train, the imperial *cappa magna,* being greeted by a choir on entering a church, the use of a throne, these were the trappings of imperial ceremonies. The sacred vessels of gold and silver likewise reflected this approach to the liturgy, but in essence the celebration of the Eucharist in this grand environment, which had over a couple of centuries assumed a fixed form consisting of readings and prayers, had long since ceased to have the character of a festive meal, or any kind of meal.

New buildings and the liturgy

During the third century, there had been periods when Christians were not being persecuted and as the number of Christians increased domestic settings for meetings of the community were no longer sufficient. This led to the construction of what Porphyry (233-305) described in 268 as 'large halls where they gathered to pray'.[11] According to the historian Eusebius these were to be found throughout Italy before the great persecution begun by the Emperor Diocletian in 303. But the newly built basilicas of the Constantinian era 'were of such magnitude and magnificence that they almost compelled a similar embellishment of the services'.[12] The services in these buildings, in addition to the Sunday Eucharist, consisted of daily prayer. Little is known about how that prayer was organised in Rome in the fourth century or who participated, but there are references to it being a feature of the church's life everywhere. Cassian (360-435), who influenced the development of monasticism in Europe at the end of the fourth century, spoke of Psalm 50 being sung at the Morning Office celebrated 'throughout Italy in all the churches'.[13] The monk, Jerome, wrote a letter to Laeta, about the early training of her daughter whom she wished to prepare for a life of consecrated virginity. He referred to the celebration of the liturgical hours, saying that if the young girl (*virguncula*) wished to take part in solemn evening prayers or all-night vigils, her mother was to be at her side.[14] These would be celebrations in church, but she was also to recite prayers and sing hymns at the third sixth and ninth hours, probably at home.

Information about the celebration of these offices in Rome is scarce, but it is clear from the writings of Saint Ambrose (c339-397) that by his time, towards the end of the fourth century, there were daily services of prayer in the cathedral in Milan (with celebrations of the Eucharist on some days at noon). An initiative of his proved very important: when local Arian Christians (opponents of the orthodox teaching of the Council of Nicaea) endeavoured to take possession of one of the churches in 386, the faithful occupied it. To sustain them in their vigil, Ambrose wrote attractive Latin hymns to be sung by them rather than by a choir as had been customary.[15] Apart from that particularly exigent situation, these hymns proved to be an enduring resource in the offices attended by the faithful. This helps to show that the church's liturgical life at that time depended for the creation of an atmosphere of celebration not so much on the celebrations of the Eucharist but a mutually supportive community meeting regularly, even daily, for hymns and prayers – in fact not so much for Scripture readings, study of Scripture being a more domestic activity.

The liturgy in the Eastern Empire

In the later part of the fourth century, when Constantinople had become the seat of Constantine's new Eastern empire, the setting and performance of the liturgy of the Greek Church benefited from imperial donation as the West had done. While Eastern emperors were arrayed magnificently, the special character of the liturgy was not borrowed from the secular realm in the way that happened in the West. There was – and is - a difference of approach to liturgy between East and West in that the East more than the West emphasised the nearness of the *eschaton*, the end-time, when the liturgy was celebrated; this will be discussed in detail in Chapter 15. This fact alone tended to favour elaborate vestments, art and music to a greater extent than obtained in the West.

Chrysostom on fasting

In that context, a homily by John Chrysostom (347- 407) towards the end of the century is of particular interest. In a homily on Matthew's gospel on the last judgment (Mt 25), he made it clear that the festal approach to the liturgy must not be isolated from the harsh reality of life experienced by the poor:

> Do you wish to honor the Body of the Saviour? Do not despise it when it is naked. Do not honor it in church with silk vestments while outside it is naked and numb with cold. He who said, "This is my body," and made it so by his word, is the same who said, 'You saw me hungry and you gave me no food. As you did it not to the least of these, you did it not to me.' Honour him then by sharing your property with the poor. For what God needs are not golden chalices but golden souls. [16]

He drove home the point in his inimitable way: 'For not having adorned the church no one was ever blamed, but for not having helped the poor, hell is threatened'. It is worth noting that even with an eschatological emphasis in the liturgy - a sense of anticipation of the return of the Lord - the prophecy of Jesus that then they would fast did not lead Chrysostom to speak of fasting but of almsgiving instead, and as a matter not simply of charity but of justice. Fasting for ascetical motives was not relevant to his argument.

This was the case even though the ascetical movement in Christianity came earlier in the East than in the West with the rise of monasticism, originally in the form of solitary life in the Egyptian desert and in Syria. The wise comments on the demands of the Christian life of the desert fathers (and mothers) have been gathered into various collections, the best known being *The Sayings of the Desert Fathers*.[17] This literature 'points backwards to a milieu where the tensions of living in the "world" had proved unbearable'.[18] These ascetics were known originally for a solitary life of prayer and fasting – fasting in the sense of extreme simplicity and meagreness of diet, though not prolonged fasting without nourishment. Mortification of the senses was a central part of the defence against the temptations of the devil. The ascetical movement did find an echo in the Roman world from the time of Tertullian (155-240) in North Africa at the latest, though there was serious competition from the Roman lifestyle.

The Roman lifestyle

After the death of Sylvester in December 335, he was followed by Mark who lived only ten months. The three popes following him were all affected – persecuted or exiled – by the heretical son of Constantine, Constantius. The conflict with an Arian party continued during the reign of Damasus (366-384), who overcame the opposition in a bloody conflict to become the undisputed holder of the see and a capable exponent of the primacy of the Roman See. He is of special interest, however, for his reputed lifestyle. Various authors[19], perhaps depending too much on each other, have described his tendency to extract money from wealthy ladies; they report his nick-name, 'the ladies' ear-tickler'. 'A contemporary remarked that the episcopal table put a royal banquet in the shade.'[20] All are agreed that he paid a mob to use violence against his opponent for the papacy, Ursinus, leaving 137 dead.

In fourth century Rome, the nobility were both rich and powerful and from their ranks the administrative posts such as senator were drawn. The members of these families were surrounded by a crowd of followers and dependents, known as *clientes*, in effect courtiers, who even escorted them through the streets of Rome and depended on their patronage, their *liberalitas*. There was an upper-middleclass, the *equites,* and at the bottom of the social order the *plebs*, numbering tens of thousands, who lived in *insulae,* multi-storey tenements, and supported themselves in labouring jobs or were unemployed. The *plebs* did not benefit directly from the largesse of the nobles but were able to avail of the food distributed free on the authority of successive emperors. For example, in the third century, the emperor Severus Alexander decreed that ready-baked bread rather than grain should be distributed to the people. Some decades later, Aurelian 'increased the daily ration to almost one and a half pounds, added pork fat to the list and, anxious to use up the wine paid as tax by the growers, threw that in too'. [21] The ordinary people were also given the leftovers from the public banquets held after the funerals of their betters.[22] The noble families owned villas and estates in the country and throughout the empire, which were populated by tenants and slaves, and artisans to supply products other than food needed by the estates' inhabitants. The rich were very rich; it has been estimated that a great Roman family's annual revenue from landed property combined with the value of goods in kind amounted to the equivalent of seventy million Euro, 'a staggering sum'.[23] A fourth century Roman pagan historian, Ammianus Marcellinus (330-400), in *Res Gestae,* described some of the Roman nobility as disorderly and irresponsible, 'turning the traditional values of the senatorial rank upside down and marginalising the cultured men of their rank'.[24] According to him:

> A few great houses, formerly with a serious and dignified reputation, resounded with entertainments when interminable and indigestible banquets were held. The sound of voices mingles with that of wind instruments, lyres, hydraulic organs and flutes – the bigger the better.[25]

The reference to indigestible banquets recalls that of Trimalchio three centuries previously, with its many bizarre courses. It is unlikely that there were Christians among these reprobates, as Christianity, in addition to establishing itself among the lower classes in earlier centuries, was in the fourth gradually gaining a following among the upper, even senatorial classes, because its values were more in accord with those of the more traditional and serious nobility, and this despite the fact that the conservative upper class was the great defender of the pagan rites. Ammianus, the pagan historian, saw Christianity as a just and gentle religion.[26] The progress of Christianity was gradual, however. 'It was at the close of the fourth century that Christians had a majority in the Senate.'[27]

St Jerome

The monk, Saint Jerome, played an important part in the life of the church at this time. Born on the Adriatic coast about 347, he studied in Rome and was baptised at eighteen. Ten years later he went to Syria where he shared the extremely ascetic life of monks in the desert, while

Saint Jerome in His Study. Caravaggio. 1605–1606.

studying Greek and Hebrew along with their Syriac language. He then went to Constantinople for the Council that took place there in 381 and from there accompanied a Greek-speaking bishop to Rome. By then, there were members of prominent noble families who were Christian. Among them was Marcella, whose palace or *domus* was on the Aventine – most of those residences were on the hills. It was there that Jerome gathered women of her rank and taught them Greek and Hebrew as well as instructing them in the Scriptures. Whether he gained financially from them is unlikely, as he lived an austere monastic life and preached it to his followers. He was not averse to giving very detailed advice to his disciples: in a letter to Furia, a young widow, he dissuaded her from contemplating a second marriage and did so in 'language that at times offends our modern sense of delicacy and propriety'.[28] He gave detailed advice on diet; she was to drink water and avoid all hot food and eat vegetables in moderation. Frugality and a state of constant hunger were better than three days of fasting. The crux of his advice was that undigested food and belching (*ructus*) inflame the passions and should be considered poison![29]

Clearly a forceful personality, he was quite influential in promoting an ascetic way of life among his followers and in criticising the attitudes and way of life of others, especially the clergy, using his mastery of satire. Among his targets were ecclesiastics who made a fuss when the food and wine at their tables fell below standard.[30] Pope Damasus favoured him because of his scholarship and commissioned him to translate the bible into Latin; his version, known in English as the *Vulgate*, became the officially approved version for many centuries - his undoubted scholarship would lead to his being declared a Doctor of the Church in 1298.

But people noticed how quickly this monk had worked his way into favour with Damasus, whose lifestyle was in strong contrast with that of the ascetic Jerome. Opposition to him soon grew, and hardened when he wrote a tract against a layman named Helvidius, who had produced a tract claiming that, after the birth of Jesus, Mary and Joseph had lived a normal family life, becoming parents of several children. Helvidius' aim was to assert the dignity of marriage against what he considered the over exaltation of virginity. Damasus died in December 384 and in August 385 Jerome decided to leave Rome for Jerusalem. As his ship was preparing to sail he wrote a long letter to a woman who lived as a solitary, Asella, in which he poured out his anger against his enemies. It contained an account of how he believed he was perceived by the opposition, a spirited defence of himself and also an extraordinary tribute to one of his closest friends, Paula, a young widow who would in fact leave her young children behind to join him on the pilgrimage to Jerusalem.

He said he had been described as an infamous rascal, a liar who used Satan's arts to deceive, but he had never accepted money from anyone or shown a lustful attitude, despite hints that his relationship with Paula was improper. His rhetoric in describing Paula can certainly cause raised eyebrows about his attitude towards asceticism, but it is impossible to say that this was the actual way of life of a mother of small children, as the Latin of Jerome's rhetoric can be translated so as to create an extreme impression:

> No other matron in Rome could dominate (*edomare*) my mind but one who mourned and fasted, who was squalid with dirt (*squalens sordibus*), almost blinded by weeping, who every night besought the Lord and seldom saw the sun. The psalms were her music, the gospels her conversation, continence her luxury, her life a fast. No other could give me pleasure but one whom I never saw eating food.[31]

It is true that Paula did leave her young children behind, except for her daughter Eustochium, when she embarked for Jerusalem, but it is difficult to establish how much a mother of her social class would be involved with the rearing of children. It is clear from one of Jerome's letters that Christian parents at that time did have the practice of offering their young daughters (but not sons) for a life of consecrated virginity, though usually at home under parental supervision. Independently of Jerome, the rich among the Christians were experiencing the challenge of the gospels and undergoing conversion to a more radical way of expressing their faith. Pammachus, a senator in the late fourth and early fifth century, was a Christian who embraced the ascetic life - dramatically demonstrating his decision by entering the Senate on one occasion wearing a monk's garb - and later founded a hostel for pilgrim. The asceticism of Jerome needs to be put in the context of the monasticism of the time as well as that of Roman society

Monastic asceticism. Simeon Stylites

Among ascetics of the East, he was no more extraordinary than, for example, Simeon Stylites, his contemporary when he was in Syria. Simeon went from being a monk among others to being a hermit who lived on top of a succession of high pillars at Telanissus from 423 until his death in 459. His fasting was extreme, in particular, his going without food for all of Lent, in imitation of Jesus' fast. How he gradually achieved this was described by his biographer in 440, bishop Theodoret of Cyrrhus (393-457), in what appears to be a personal witness of 'his contests that beggar description. It could appear to posterity as a myth totally devoid of truth', Theodoret agreed, 'for the facts surpass human nature'.[32]

Simeon, after an earlier period of three years as a recluse, wished to emulate men like Moses and Elijah by fasting for forty days, and arranged that bread rolls and water would be left in his cell, with the door sealed. After forty days the door was opened and he was found lying, unable to move or speak, with the rolls and water untouched. He was revived by being administered the Eucharist and then took a little food, lettuce and chicory. He took to observing Lent by praying standing as many days as he could and then performing the liturgy seated and during the final days lying down. Because of the crowds that came to ask his blessing, he had a pillar constructed – successively higher ones - on which he remained until his death, and there he stood to pray until weakness made him resort to having a beam in place to which he tied himself.

> Subsequently, enjoying henceforward still more grace from above, he has not needed even this support, but stands throughout the forty days, but strengthened by zeal and divine grace.[33]

His spiritual stature came not only from his rigorous fasting but also from the long hours he spent in prayer. Theodoret attests to his reputation for holiness and to the miracles he worked for the crowds who came to ask his blessing or seek healing for themselves or others.

It would not be surprising if such an extraordinary individual, as Simeon undoubtedly was, had engaged in Delphic utterances in response to those who consulted him. But, Theodoret said:

> (He) is as modest in spirit as if he were the last of all men in worth. In addition to his modest spirit, he is extremely approachable, sweet and charming, and makes answer to everyone who addresses him, whether he be artisan, beggar or peasant. [34]

The Egyptian monks

The recorded sayings of the monks of the Egyptian desert tend to be rather different. As theirs were very often in the form of a response to a question, a request for guidance, they were generally somewhat mono-syllabic. But their asceticism did not go to the extremes of Simeon in terms of physical hardship and fasting, though fasting was part of their ascetical programme. One of the most famous of the Egyptian monks, Abba Poemon (there may have been more than one of that name, because it means 'shepherd'), in reply to a question said: 'How can we acquire the fear of God when our belly is full of cheese and preserved foods?' When Abba Isaac visited him and found him washing his feet, he pointed out that others treated their bodies hardly. Abba Poemon replied: 'We have not been taught to kill our bodies, but to kill our passions'.[35] He also said: 'there are three things I am not able to do without: food, clothing and sleep, but I can restrict them to some extent'.[36] The best known of the Desert Fathers, Anthony (250-356), in response to a question, 'What should I do?', replied 'Do not trust in your own righteousness, do not worry about the past, but control your tongue and your stomach'.[37] From his sayings it seems his custom was to take a 'little food at the ninth hour'[38] on the days when he did eat, but, according to his biographer, St Athanasius, he sometimes fasted two or even four days in a row.[39] What-ever their frequency, his meals consisted only of bread, salt and water, raising for people today the unresolvable issue of the lack of protein, calcium and other necessary components of the human diet.

According to Peter Brown, in his study, *The Body and Society,* the des-ert at the time of St Anthony and the other Egyptian monks was thought of as the zone deprived of human food, a zone of the non-human.

> For this reason, the most bitter struggle of the desert ascetic was not so much a struggle with his sexuality as with his belly. It was his triumph in the struggle with hunger that released, in the popular imagina-tion, the most majestic and most haunting image of a new humanity. Nothing less than the hope of Paradise regained flickered, spasmod-

ically but recognisably, around the figures who had dared to create a human 'city' in a landscape void of human food.[40]

Skellig Michael

The Irish monastic tradition, which flourished several hundred years after the period of the Desert Fathers, differed significantly from that of the desert for climatic and geographical reasons and yet shared the strongly ascetical outlook. One notable example of the difference in respect of the dietary regime is the case of the monastic community on Skellig Michael, a crag in the sea some eleven kilometres off the coast of County Kerry.[41] Established, it is believed, in the sixth century, it was remarkably different from a desert community in that to create it the monks engaged in a spectacular work of creating three sets of stone steps from sea-level rising about 180 metres. One set consists of 618 steps, all of them having required both skilled workmanship and herculean labour as some of the stones penetrate deeply into the side of the crag. The building of beehive stone huts to house the members also required both great skill and labour.

The community lived there several hundred years and archaeological evidence indicates that despite being exposed to the extremes of Atlantic weather, they were able to engage in horticulture by ingenious arrangement of walls to create an enclosure which was sheltered and a sun-trap. They must inevitably have required substantial amounts of food in order to carry out this work and to survive in very harsh weather conditions. They could catch sea birds such as the puffin and razorbill of the auk family, and take the single egg laid by each bird. Both are present in great flocks on the rock from March to August. They could also engage in fishing, but cereals would have been imported from the nearby coast. They were thus very different from desert monks, but the surviving structures are evidence of monastic living both in community form and in hermitages.[42] The island has two peaks, the area between the two providing access to the site of the community. There are six beehive-shaped cells and a larger and a smaller oratory on the site in different states of preservation. The southernmost peak is much more difficult to reach. Here there are

Skellig Michael, beehive cells and Small Skellig.

remains of a hermitage consisting of two terraces created by retaining walls, one to provide a garden and possibly a cell, the other an oratory, and with connecting passages. Two stone basins were carved out of the rock to store rain water.[43] The hermitage must have been created with the help of the monks of the monastery as a later development. Clearly, both hermits and a community chose this isolated place (as did communities in Europe in similar island foundations, such as Mont Saint-Michel in Normandy) in order to live away from the world in prayer and meditation. That would not have been possible without substantial physical nourishment.

In physical contrast with that lifestyle, in Egypt Saint Anthony lived for twenty years in a cell at the bottom of a ruined fort and when he emerged from it in 305, the bystanders were amazed to see that his body had maintained its former condition, neither fat for lack of exercise, nor emaciated from fasting and combat with demons, but just as it was when they had known him previous to his withdrawal.[44]

It was as if he had already received the embodiment of the spirit predicted by Paul for the just at the resurrection of the dead (I Cor 15:44). This condition, which could be described as belonging to the 'end-time' or *eschaton,* was apparently reached through solitude, prayer and fasting and without the transformative influence of the liturgy.

Conclusion

The status granted to Christianity by Emperor Constantine began a period of privilege for it among the ranks of Roman society and enrichment to match, with mixed results for the health of the church. Having its own legal jurisdiction could protect the church from malicious forces but it could also lead to tolerance of abuses. A patrician lifestyle had its consequences for the liturgy as imperial deportment and dress interpolated itself into the ceremonies and bishops vested as if they were of imperial dignity. The endowing of churches with great numbers of gold and silver vessels must have helped, however, to impress upon the laity the sacred character of the proceedings. It is difficult to say to what extent the liturgy suffered at its core as the Roman rite over those centuries produced a dignified and theologically rich Eucharistic text.

Higher social status for bishops and clergy meant higher standards of living also, on a par with the nobility, and little inclination to frugality when invitations to fine dining events meant reciprocal invitations would be expected. The church enjoyed a similar status in the Eastern Empire, but the liturgy had a character more redolent of mystery than any imperial ceremony and was able to resist secular incursion until the iconoclastic controversy several centuries later. In the West it was inevitable that there would be an ascetical reaction to worldliness, and records of a 'flight from the world' exist in areas as diverse as the Egyptian desert and islands off the coast of Europe as far west as southern Ireland.

ENDNOTES

1   Eamon Duffy, *Saints and Sinners. A History of the Popes* (Newhaven: Yale University Press, 2001) 39

2   Ibid. 24-5

3   Robin Lane Fox, *Pagans and Christians* (London: Penguin Books, 1988) 666

4   Bertrand Lançon, *Rome in Late Antiquity*, Antonia Nevill trans. (Edinburgh: Edinburgh University Press, 2000) 104

5   Friedrich Gontard, *The Popes,* A. J. and E.J. Peeler trans. (London: Barrie & Rockliff, 1959) 104

6   Bertrand Lançon, *Rome in Late Antiquity*, 27

7   *The Book of Pontiffs. (Liber Pontificalis)* Translated with an Introduction by Raymond Davis (Liverpool: Liverpool University Press, 1989) 14

8   Ibid. 7

9   C. Petri, *Roma Christiana: Recherches sur l'Église de Rome, son organisation, sa politique, son idéologie de Miltiade a Sixte III(311-40)*, 84, cited in Bertrand Lançon, *Rome in Late Antiquity,* 100

10 Ansgar Chupungco, 'History of the Liturgy until the Fourth Century' in *Introduction to the Liturgy. Handbook for Liturgical Studies,*Vol. I, (Collegeville: Liturgical Press, 1997) 108

11 *Liturgia,* a cura di D. Sartore et al. (Cinisello: Edizioni Paoline, 2001) 1111

12 Josef Jungmann, *The Early Liturgy. To the Time of Gregory the Great* (London: Darton, Longman and Todd, 1960) 197

13 John Cassian, *The Institutes,* Ancient Christian Writers 58, Boniface Ramsey O.P. trans. (New York: The Newman Press, 2000) 64

14 *The Letters of Saint Jerome. The Latin Text.* Edited with Introduction and Commentary by James Duff (Dublin: Browne and Nolan, 1942) Letter 107, 294

15 Robert Wilken, *The Spirit of Early Christian Thought* (Newhaven: Yale University Press, 2003) 218

16 Chrysostom, *Homily 50* in *Homilies on the Gospel of Matthew*, in *Nicene and Post-Nicene Fathers*, Vol. X, P. Schaff, H. Wace eds. (Buffalo, NY: Christian Literature Publishing Co.,1896.)

17 Benedicta Ward, trans. (Oxford:O.U.P., 1975)

18 Peter Brown, *The Making of Late Antiquity* (Cambridge, Mass.; Harvard University Press, 1975) 82

19 Richard McBrien, *Lives of the Popes. The Pontiffs from St Peter to John Paul II* (San Francisco: Harper,1997) 63: 'His grand lifestyle and lavish hospitality endeared him to upper-class pagan families'; J.N.D. Kelly, *The Oxford Dictionary of the Popes* (Oxford: O.U.P., 1986) 33: 'He enjoyed the favour of court and aristocracy, not least of wealthy ladies.'

20 Bertrand Lançon, *Rome in Late Antiquity* 101

21 Reay Tannahill, *Food in History* (London: Headine Publishing, 1998²) 71

22   Veronika Grimm, *From Feasting to Fasting. The Evolution of a Sin* (London: Routledge, 1996) 39

23   Bertrand Lançon, *Rome in Late Antiquity* 63

24   Ibid. 67

25   Ibid. 67-8

26   Robin Lane Fox, *Pagans and Christians* (London: Penguin, 1986) 669

27   Bertrand Lançon, *Rome in Late Antiquity* 71

28   *The Letters of Saint Jerome. The Latin Text,* Letter 54, 207.

29   Ibid. 212-3

30   J. N. D. Kelly, *Jerome. His Life, Writings and Controversies* (London: Duckworth: 1975) 109

31   *The Letters of Saint Jerome. The Latin Text*, Letter 45.2, Translation in F.A. Wright, *Select Letters of Saint Jerome* (Harvard : Loeb Classical Library, 1989) 193

32   Theodoret of Cyrrhus, *A History of the Monks of Syria,* R. M. Price trans. (Kalamazoo: Cistercian Publications, 1985) 160

33   Ibid. 164

34   Ibid. 171

35   *The Sayings of the Desert Fathers,* Benedicta Ward trans.(Oxford: Mowbray, 1975) 193

36   Idem

37   Ibid. 2

38   Ibid. 8

39   Athanasius, *Life of Anthony* 7, Cistercian Studies 45 (Kalamazoo: Cistercian Publications, 1980) 301

40   Peter Brown, *The Body and Society. Men, Women and Sexual Renunciation in Early Christianity* (New York: Columbia University Press, 1998) 218

41   Des Lavelle, *The Skellig Story. Ancient Monastic Outpost* (Dublin: The O'Brien Press, 1976) 12-3

42   Des Lavelle, *Skellig. Island Outpost of Europe* (Dublin: The O'Brien Press, 1977^2) 74-6

43   Walter Horn, Jenny White Marshall, Grellan D. Rourke, *The Forgotten Hermitage of Skellig Michael* (Berkeley, University of California Press, 1990) 32-50

44   Athanasius, *Life of Anthony* 14

CHAPTER FIVE

The demands of Christian living.
From Augustine to Benedict

Whoever needs less should thank God and not be discontented; but whoever needs more should feel humble because of his weakness, not self- important because of the kindness shown him.[1]

Augustine (354-430) and the ascetical life

Those who embraced the ascetical life were inevitably a minority among Christians as in society generally and banqueting continued to be important in the Roman lifestyle, including banquets in memory of the dead, pagan and Christian. These appear to have led to abuses when celebrations got out of hand, as Saint Augustine testified about the practice in North Africa, some two centuries after Pope Felix had called for masses to be said over the memorials of the martyrs. People now had freedom to celebrate as they wished. Augustine, not yet a bishop in 392, was quite scathing in his comments in a letter to the archbishop of Carthage, Aurelius:

> (R)ioting and drunkenness are so tolerated and allowed by public opinion, that even in services designed to honour the memory of the blessed martyrs - not only on the annual festivals, but every day - they are openly practised.

He was prepared to share communion in convivial meetings within the walls of private houses, in the disorder and even luxury of family life,

> but at least let outrageous insult be kept far away from the tombs of the sainted dead, from the scenes of sacramental privilege, and from the houses of prayer. For who may venture to forbid in pri-

vate life excesses which, when they are practised by crowds in holy places, are called an honouring of the martyrs? [2]

He suggested that Aurelius should encourage people to provide meals at the church for poor persons, instead of holding a 'fiesta to the martyrs' for their friends in the cemetery.

Augustine was concerned that Christians were turning the celebration of the memory of the martyrs – a celebration of the Eucharist, the context makes clear – into a bacchanalian carnival. A generation later, Pope Gregory (r590-604) wrote to Abbot Mellitus on his departure for Britain advising him about how he was to treat the people whose temples he was purifying for Christian worship (rather than destroying them). The people were accustomed to 'sacrificing oxen to devils', so now he could replace this practice by celebrating the festival of the martyrs, whose relics were enshrined in the temple, and have the people participate 'with devout feasting'. 'If the people are allowed some worldly pleasures in this way, they will more readily come to desire the joys of the Spirit.' [3] This represented a change of policy on Gregory's part as he had already written to King Ethelbert urging him to be

> eager to spread the Christian faith among the people under your rule; in all uprightness increase your zeal for their conversion; suppress the worship of idols; overthrow the structures of the temples; establish the manners of your subjects by much cleanness of life, exhorting, terrifying, winning, correcting, and showing forth an example of good works.[4]

It would be a case of celebrating the Eucharist but whether the 'people' were by now Christians, or perhaps catechumens, is not clear. It would take the form which would be well established by the seventh century, but presumably the practice more familiar to the people of slaughtering and eating oxen – once it was made clear it was not a case of pagan sacrifice – could be absorbed into the celebration. The example illustrates how difficult it could be to change the habits of new converts, so that they could appreciate and adapt to the simple Christian ritual.

Augustine on food and fasting

The candour Augustine showed throughout his *Confessions* caused him, not surprisingly, to comment on his need to control his participation in feasting in his own life. He recognised that food and drink were necessary to repair the 'daily deterioration of the body' and looked forward to the day when God will clothe corruptible nature with incorruptible life.

> But for the present time the necessity is sweet to me, and I fight against that sweetness lest I be taken captive by it. I wage daily war upon it by fasting, bringing my body again and again into subjection; but the pain this gives me is driven away by the pleasure (of eating and drinking). For hunger and thirst really are painful; they burn and kill, like fever, unless food comes as medicine for their healing. ... This you taught me, that I should learn to take my food as a kind of medicine.[5]

Considering food as medicine rather than as nature's way of maintaining life is highly significant in relation to the understanding of human life which Augustine had, as did other proponents of asceticism already mentioned. From his Neoplatonist understanding of the relationship between soul and body, he was less aware of food's natural role of nourishing than of the therapeutic needs of the soul. Whether 'greed was a far more acute and revealing source of disquiet for him than sexual temptation', as one historian observed,[6] and therefore to be combatted rigorously by fasting, is of importance as far as his approach to the body is concerned. He did believe that sexual temptation could be repudiated once and for all, but the appetite for food had to be constantly kept in check; 'the reins of the throat are to held somewhere between too tightly and too lightly'.[7] Though drunkenness was not a problem for him, Augustine considered over-eating a temptation. In his *Confessions,* he felt the need to quote Lk 21:34: 'Do not let your hearts grow dull with revelry and drunkenness'.[8]

In his later years, as bishop, banquets could of course cause problems. His attempt to keep up his regime of fasting, or at least abstaining from meat, may have been involved when he adopted a novel approach to a situation that occurred at a banquet. While it was ostensibly an experiment on the antiseptic properties of peacock flesh, that may not have been the real explanation for his attitude to a slice of roasted peacock served to him:

> It happened in Carthage that a bird of this kind was cooked and served up to me, and, taking a suitable slice from its breast, I ordered it to be kept, and when it had been kept as many days as make any other flesh stinking, it was produced and set before me, and emitted no offensive smell. [9]

The experiment was repeated and after a year it was a 'little more shrivelled and dried'!

His sermons on fasting

Given the importance of Augustine's thought for the church in subsequent centuries, it is worth noting how he dealt with fasting in his sermons. There are seven Lenten Season sermons recorded along with a treatise, *On the usefulness of fasting*, which may also have been in fact a sermon. In this text, he makes a distinction between two kinds of food, earthly and heavenly. 'On the former, the life of men depends; on the latter, the life of angels'.[10] Faithful men are not to be compared with the infidels who consider that happiness is nothing else but the enjoyment of earthly pleasures, but neither are they like the inhabitants of heaven whose sole delight is the heavenly bread by whom they were created. Being in the middle, between being heavenly and being earthly, they are torn by conflicting desires. They are on the way, but not yet rejoicing. Augustine could here have relied on our Lord's saying that in his absence his disciples will fast, but he does not quote it and instead emphasises a Neoplatonist dualism; the flesh draws to the earth, the mind tends upwards. The flesh is below and God is above. A modern author, Veronika Grimm, a former professor of psychology, holds that:

> In this view, in which the Platonic distinction is drawn to its extreme conclusion, the human personality is split, the body is made into an object or at best a slave, it becomes divorced from and external to the person, who is to work upon it, shape it, restrain it and mortify it, until it becomes like a piece of inanimate clay.[11]

The author does at the same time acknowledge:

> To be fair, Augustine was more charitable than many of the famous athletes of asceticism, and did caution his monks against a too severe mortification of their bodies by extreme fasting.[12]

Augustine, in Chapter 5 of the treatise, adopts the pastoral and dynamic view that 'fasting is for our journey' and proposes to consider its nature, but gets caught up in criticism of pagans and Jews, who also sometimes fast but have not discovered the way on which Christians walk. In a series of sermons 'For the Lenten Season', *Sermon 205* uses that pilgrim concept by exhorting the hearer not to sink into the mire of the earth by coming down from the cross. This should be the case especially during the forty days, which should also be days of fast and abstinence from conjugal relations. 'What you deprive yourself of by fasting add to your almsgiving; ... the body which engaged in carnal love prostrate in earnest prayer; the hands which were entwined in embraces extend in supplication.'[13] In a later sermon he repeats the call for special restraint to be practised even by married people. [14]

Rome in the early fifth century

While Augustine in Africa dealt with the ascetical demands of the Christian life in his own case and instructed others in his sermons, the earlier ascetical tradition in Rome continued in a new generation. During the pontificate of Innocent I (r401- 417), an aristocratic couple, Pinianus and Melania, became the first couple of senatorial rank to 'trample underfoot the vanities of worldly glory', according to their biographer, Gerontios.[15] Melania, inspired by her grandmother, also named Melania, wished to live a life of virginity but 'the demands of her patrician family required that she provide heirs'.[16] Two children were born, the first, a daughter, was dedicated by the couple to a life of virginity, the second died shortly after birth. Between the two, they had an enormous fortune, in estates throughout the empire and in palaces; but wished to live a life of great simplicity, abandoning all the outward show of their rank. Melania put aside the silken garments and wore coarse wool, while Pinianus adopted the goat's hair dress which originated in Cilicia and was typical of soldiers and sailors. Despite opposition from family and Roman nobles, they were intent on disposing of their assets - though no one could be found who possessed sufficient means to purchase Pinianus' sumptuous mansion on the Caelian Hill. The intermittent siege of Rome from December 408 to August 410 by the Gothic leader Alaric caused the couple to flee to Africa where on the advice of Augustine they made a gift of premises and revenues to the monasteries in the area. After her husband's death, Melania moved to Jerusalem, where she founded a monastery for women on the Mount of Olives and one for men near the Church of the Ascension.[17] The case of Melania and Pinianus was the most notable example of the ascetic trend and was a considerable shock to the nobility for whom wealth provided the underpinning of senatorial power.

For those in power, a great change of fortune occurred at the beginning of the fifth century because of the invasion of Italy and the long-running siege of Rome by Alaric. During that time food stocks in Rome became depleted and daily allowance of bread increasingly reduced so that alternatives such as flour made from acorns were tried. The Goths eventually entered and sacked Rome, but Alaric decreed that St Peter's should be untouched and be a refuge for people and their possessions. Rome recovered quickly from the disaster. Pope Innocent, who was active in negotiations with the Goths, consolidated the church's position both

before and after the sack of the city, by such pastoral moves as establishing rules for monasteries and draconian measures against the Montanist
heretics by sending them into exile. In a departure from tradition, he
decreed that the faithful should fast on Saturdays because it was on a Saturday that the Lord had lain in the tomb. Evidently he had wide ranging
authority, in effect on a level with secular authorities.

A lady named Vestina, from the very upper ranks of the nobility, the
illustres, died during his pontificate and in her will gave instructions for
the building of a basilica, to be paid for by the sale of her jewellery, or
as much as was needed for the project! Pope Innocent seems to have had
the resources to make a matching gesture. Along with some forty silver
vessels and thirty-six bronze chandeliers, he presented the basilica with
various sources of revenue: various houses, two baths, a bakery and five
properties within and outside Rome, with their revenues - presumably all
of these had already been willed to the church.

His successor, who lasted little over a year (417-8), a Greek named
Zozimus, made liturgical rules and 'ordered that no cleric should drink
in a public tavern but only in cellars owned by the faithful, particularly
by clerics'.[18] Between the death of Zozimus and the pontificate of the
great Pope Leo I from 440, three popes had made rules about how mass
was to be celebrated and that no woman should wash or even touch the
cloth used to purify sacred vessels. The third, Xystus, built a monastery -
evidence that there was need to gather ascetics who lived independently
in the city into communities.

Pope Leo the Great (r440-461)
Leo is known in history as the Great, principally for his decisive contribution to the theological issue of the time, the Christological debate. He
sent a letter outlining his position to Flavian of Constantinople in 449
and it was recognised as articulating the orthodox position at the Council
of Chalcedon in 451. His documentary output included also pastoral
guidelines for church life and in a sermon preached in December ('the
tenth month') he declared:

The solemn fast of the tenth month, is now to be kept by us according to yearly custom, because it is altogether just and godly to give thanks to the Divine bounty for the crops which the earth has produced for the use of men under the guiding hand of supreme Providence. And to show that we do this with ready mind, we must exercise not only the self-restraint of fasting, but also diligence in almsgiving, that from the ground of our heart also may spring the germ of righteousness and the fruit of love, and that we may deserve God's mercy by showing mercy to His poor. [19]

In his Fourth Sermon on Lent, he said:

Our fast does not consist chiefly of mere abstinence from food, nor are dainties withdrawn from our bodily appetites with profit, unless the mind is recalled from wrong-doing and the tongue restrained from slandering. This is a time of gentleness and long-suffering, of peace and tranquillity: when all the pollutions of vice are to be eradicated and continuance of virtue is to be attained by us.[20]

There is a note of prosperity and piety in his writings. It establishes a sound foundation on which to begin to consider fasting as a balancing force in living the Christian life. The December sermon is the first mention of a seasonal fast and there are no detailed rules. It is related to the harvest and is connected with thanksgiving, with feasting, though there is no mention of a 'harvest festival' – something which would be undesirably evocative of the Jewish inheritance, though in Judaism it would not involve fasting. Still, festival in the sense of thanksgiving and fast, are linked. It is couched in positive terms: motivation should be well thought out – involve 'ready minds' – and lead to positive action. In addition to self-restraint mercy should be shown to the poor.

There is even a hint of peaceful times, even though Leo's ministry took place during a time not only of theological dispute but also political upheaval as the Huns ravaged Italy. In 452 he travelled to Mantua to negotiate with Attila and persuaded him to turn back his armies from attacking Rome. In 455, however, the city was looted by the armies of Gaiseric and Leo could only persuade him to refrain from torching the city. Subsequently, he melted down the six silver water jars at the Lateran Basilica, two at St Peter's and two at St Paul's to replace all the consecrated vessels that had been looted. [21]

The church after Leo

The popes who followed Leo up to the end of the fifth century had to deal, according to the *Liber Pontificalis*, with doctrinal deviations in Alexandria and subsequently in Constantinople, while having to cope also with the discovery of a group of adherents to the Manichean heresy in Rome itself during the time of Gelasius (492-496). Nonetheless, Hilarus (461-468) managed to build two monasteries, a bath, 'and another in the open air', and two libraries, while Gelasius was 'a lover of the clergy and of the poor...and delivered the city of Rome from danger of famine'.[22] Evidently the papacy was strong, but the empire before its actual collapse was weak because of 'the impact of barbarian tribal confederacies on the economic infrastructure, which drastically reduced military numbers and overall capability'[23].

King Theodoric (454-526)

In fact the Western Empire is considered to have come to an end in 476 with the deposition of Romulus Augustus by Odoacer (434-493), a man of uncertain ethnic origin, but apparently a member of the Roman army and in practice King of Italy from then on. Though an Arian Christian, he did not intervene in the affairs of the church. In his last years, he was opposed by the Ostrogothic king, Theodoric the Great, who at first agreed to rule Italy with him. It was a sign of the new order of things that a guest visiting Theodoric noted with surprise that his host sat rather than reclined at the table.[24] To recline on couches, leaning on the left elbow and taking food with the right was always the custom at Roman banquets in the heyday of the empire. At the end of the sixth century a survivor of the Roman culture, Bishop Venantius Fortunatus visited his friend Bishop Leontius and found him reclining to eat in what was a crumbling Roman villa, but that was a reminder of old times.

The new seating arrangement facilitated Theodoric's treachery. In 493 he invited Odoacer to a banquet in Ravenna and there rose suddenly from his chair and slew him with his sword. The menu for that sinister occasion is not known but it would have reflected the custom of the time to include a large amount of meat; these warrior chieftains spent much time fighting and believed that meat was fundamental to keeping up their strength. They were dedicated to hunting to find the wild boar and fowl for the table, while honing their riding skills in preparation for battle. Appetites were voracious and meals were without ceremony; both hands were employed to hold large portions. The old traditions of luxury were more or less remodelled by Germanic barbarism.[25] The elaborate spices of earlier times were no longer available because of the decline of the empire, and the menus reflected instead the agrarian economy of the tribal territories. '(The) culinary tradition was inevitably breaking down as the social context gave way to that of the new barbarian courts and classical education crumbled.'[26] A new culture and a new approach to meals were soon to come with the establishment of monasticism.

St Benedict (480-543)

Some years before the ending of the empire, monasticism had established a foothold in Monteluco in the Umbrian province of Italy with the arrival of a Syrian monk named Julian. It spread into the uplands surrounding Norcia, an ancient town, and there Benedict, who would come to be regarded as the patriarch of Western monasticism, was born a few years after the deposition of Romulus. The basic facts of Benedict's life are known from the biography of him written towards the end of the sixth century by Pope Gregory the Great, himself a monk who followed the *Rule* written by Benedict. While Benedict is of major importance for the story of monasticism in Europe, and for the monastic tradition credited with preserving Christian culture throughout what are called the dark

St Benedict of Nursia. Jean de Court II. 1st quarter, 17th century

ages, in the present context he is of interest for his teaching in his *Rule of Benedict* (hereafter *RB*) on how food and fasting are related in the Christian life.

The *Rule* is a unique source of information on food and fasting in monasteries at that time and for many centuries afterwards. The progress of civilisation has altered many details but a core of values has remained and can be recognised in contemporary monastic practice. What the *Rule* says about meals, their content, their timing, their community dimension, the restrictions and the relaxations surrounding them, displays a view of life which brings food into the spiritual realm, what has been called 'a kind of universal mysticism of things and nature that sees in them the very hand of the creator'.[27] That comment was made in relation to a verse of the *Rule* (*RB* 31.10-11): 'He should consider the pots of the monastery and all its goods as if they were the holy bowls of the altar'. In monastic history, this verse has been considered a basis for attributing a sacred character to the ritual of monastic dining, relating it to the liturgy itself, even if that goes further than what is implied by the inclusion of 'all its goods'.

Meals are events in the monastery; they are integral to its spiritual ethos and discipline, they require monks to be there in time and to be sensitive to the needs of others at table. The monks are given consideration regarding their dietary needs, but can be excluded from the common meals because of faults. The choreography of meals is very similar to that regulating behaviour during the liturgy. It will be noted later that in subsequent ages there was also a choreography governing the banquets of the aristocracy in what seemed an echo of a lost awareness of the 'mysticism of things' – practices such as ceremonial washing of hands, rituals surrounding the carving of meat, the serving of drink.

Given that the text of the *Rule* incorporates various comments on fasting into discussion of the meal regime, there does seem to be here a view of life in which there is a tension of the spiritual order between feasting and fasting, but they are not the polar opposites which previous history and the centuries following have made them. The two are nicely linked in the chapter on Lent: '(L)et each one deny himself some food, drink, sleep, needless talking and idle jesting, and look forward to holy Easter with joy and spiritual longing' (*RB* 49.7). This perhaps explains why in Chapter 4, 'On the Tools of Good Works', the strong expression, 'To love fasting' is used. To love fasting is very different from disdain for the body, or accepting a regulation, or working for a reward. 'What is loved is internalised and made one's own.'[28] It could of course be an expression of an excessively ascetical mind-set, but in the spirituality of the *Rule* it is not. The references to fasting all have the mark of the moderation which is one of its famous characteristics. In fact more attention is paid to providing food than to withholding it, so that two kinds of cooked food are to be provided at meals, because of individual weaknesses of digestion: 'In this way, the person who may not be able to eat one kind of food may partake of the other' (*RB* 39.2). If work is heavier than usual, extra food may be provided. But overindulgence is to be avoided as something inconsistent with the life of the Christian (*RB* 39.8), a prophetic utterance in light of the excesses which characterised the way of life of monasteries, as well as of the nobility, in the late medieval period - not to mention the binge drinking of today.

Conclusion

Augustine was one of the most respected and quoted of the early teachers or Fathers in the church and what he says about food and fasting is only a small part of his writings. His debt to Neoplatonist philosophy is seen throughout his works but is perhaps more evident here than elsewhere. He teaching on fasting comes towards the end of a tradition which began with the New Testament and early commentaries such as that found in the *Didache*. Saint Irenaeus (c.130 – c. 202) in his day referred to a controversy not merely as regards the day, but also as regards the form itself of the Christians' fast, yet there seems to have been consensus regarding fasting. Tertullian, as noted previously, was happy with emaciation. The desert Fathers typically thought it was better not to fast than to be inflated with pride. While Basil the Great (330-79) taught the importance of fasting, he stressed its interior character in his *Homily on Fasting,*10: 'True fast is the estrangement from evil, temperance of tongue, abstinence from anger, separation from desires, slander, falsehood and perjury'. Chrysostom (347-407), spoke about almsgiving rather than fasting in connection with the liturgy and as a matter not simply of charity but of justice. By the time of St Leo, the balance between exterior practice and inner purity of intention was well established, with less emphasis on extreme asceticism, mainly through linking it with the liturgy, as Leo did.

While the church was a dominant influence in society, fasting had an appropriate place, but with the collapse of the Roman Empire and the emergence of tribal chieftains not noted for their restraint in relation to food or anything else, the church's witness was obscured. The era of St Benedict was one of recovery from a chaotic past and it is noticeable that with him there was a move towards moderation in everything, including food and fasting. His legacy would prove important in the recovery of civilised living which was part of the Carolingian regime, to be considered in the next chapter.

ENDNOTES

1   *Rule of Benedict* 34.3-4, Timothy Fry ed. (Collegeville: Liturgical Press, 1982) 57

2   Augustine *Letter* 22.1.3, J. G. Cunningham trans., *Nicene and Post-Nicene Fathers, First Series*, Vol. 1, Edited by Philip Schaff (Buffalo, N.Y: Christian Literature Publishing Co., 1887)

3   Bede, *A History of the English Church and People*, Translated with an Introduction by Leo Sherley-Price (Harmondsworth: Penguin Books, 1965²) 87

4   Pope Gregory to King Ethelbert, in *Bede's Ecclesiastical History of England. Also The Anglo-Saxon Chronicle*, Chapter XXXII, J.A. Giles ed. (London: Henry Bohn, 1849²) 54-5

5   Augustine, *Confessions*, X. 31, Frank Sheed trans. (London: Sheed and Ward, 1954) 191

6   Peter Brown, *Augustine of Hippo. A Biography* (London: Faber and Faber, 1967) 179

7   Augustine, *Confessions*, X.31, 193

8   ibid. 192

9   Augustine, *The City of God*, XXXI, Marcus Dodds trans. (New York: the Modern Library, 1950) 766-7

10 Augustine, *On the Usefulness of Fasting. Treatises on Various Subjects*. The Fathers of the Church, Vol.14 (Washington: Catholic University Press, 1952) 405

11 Veronika Grimm, *From Feasting to Fasting, The Evolution of a Sin. Attitudes to Food in Late Antiquity* (London: Routledge, 1996) 188

12 Ibid. 189

13 Augustine, *Sermon 205, Sermons on the Liturgical Seasons*, Vol. 38 (New York: The Fathers of the Church, 1959) 85

14 Ibid. *Sermon 207*

15 Cited in Bertrand Lançon, *Rome in Late Antiquity* 73

16 Joyce E. Salisbury, *Church Fathers. Independent Virgins* (London: Verso, 1991) 89

17 Annelise Freisenbruch, *The First Ladies of Rome. The Women Behind the Caesars* (London: Jonathan Cape, 2010) 306

18 *Liber Pontificalis* 33

19 Pope Leo the Great, *Sermon 17, Nicene and Post-Nicene Fathers, Second Series*, Vol. 12. P. Schaff and H. Wace eds. (Buffalo, NY: Christian Literature Publishing Co., 1895.) 236

20 Ibid. *Sermon XLII, Sermon IV on Lent* 262

21 *Liber Pontificalis* 38

22 Ibid. 38-42

23 Mark Merrony, *The Plight of Rome in the Fifth Century* (Abingdon, Oxon: Routledge, 2017) 2

24 Roy Strong, *Feast. A History of Grand Eating* (London: Jonathan Cape, 2002) 40

25 P. Boissonnade, *Life and Work in Medieval Europe*, Eileen Power trans. (New York: Dorset Press, 1927) 87

26 Roy Strong, *Feast* 40

27 Terrence Kardong, *Benedict's Rule. A Translation and Commentary* (Collegeville, MN: The Liturgical Press, 1996) 272

28 Ibid. 84

CHAPTER SIX

The Carolingian Era. Civilising a tribal world

The motives for the remarkable liturgical activity in the ninth century are quite clear and they are those of the Carolingian reform generally: the extirpation of paganism, promotion of unity, the proclamation of Christianity, and above all, the instruction of the people.[1]

Charlemagne and the influence of monasticism

The monastic tradition established by St Benedict contributed for some centuries to the renewal of the church and of society. Its influence was important in the consolidation of the Frankish kingdom with its Christian values in the mid-eighth century, as Pepin (714-768), the first king, had been educated by the monks of Saint-Denis in Paris. Charlemagne (742-814), his son, established a close relation with Pope Hadrian I, was crowned Emperor in 800 by Pope Leo III, and thus claimed to revive the defunct empire of the West and its universal scope (to the chagrin of the eastern Emperor). He inherited the religious convictions of Pepin. To assist in his programme of religious and educational renewal he recruited the Englishman, Alcuin (735-804), a priest-scholar who subsequently became Abbot of Tour. Charlemagne's cousin, Adalhard (751-827), was abbot of the monastery of Corbie and an adviser to the emperor. Later, Benedict of Aniane (747-821), who had been educated at the court of Pepin, joined the court of Charlemagne, before leaving to enter a monastery and subsequently returning to his own estate to become a monastic founder. With many of these being contemporaries, the monastic institution and imperial regime became much intertwined, especially when the monastic reform established by Benedict of Aniane was promoted by Louis the Pious (778-840), the son of Charlemagne, and co-Emperor with him from 813.

Charles I, Holy Roman Emperor. Cropped from the painting Kaiser
Karl der Große. Albrecht Dürer, 1512.

Charlemagne brought about the Romanisation of the Frankish culture, which not long previously had been pagan and violent. But he retained some of its characteristics in the violence of his campaigns against other tribes, the Saxons, for example. He continued to wear tribal dress and had five wives in succession, but as a devotee of Roman culture he spoke and wrote in several languages. He made Latin the diplomatic *lingua franca* of his empire.[2] He is an interesting figure in relation to the theme of food, feast and fast, as there is a considerable amount of personal information available about him and his lifestyle in annals of the Frankish kingdom, in records of correspondence, in biographies of his contemporaries and especially in two lives, one by the ninth-century Einhard and another slightly later, by Notker, a monk of Sankt Gallen. From these, information on court life can be gathered. Einhard's biography had a political purpose; it was 'to celebrate Charlemagne and, in its final paragraphs, to underscore Louis the Pious's legitimacy, the imperial rule and the legitimacy of the succession'.[3] It is of interest here, however, for the detail it supplies regarding the food culture and the liturgical renewal promoted by Charlemagne.

Imperial lifestyle and celebration

It becomes clear that the revival of the empire meant also the revival of courtly ceremonial, and of course feasting, though Charlemagne himself appears to have been a man of moderate habits and an enthusiastic participant in *liturgical* feasts - even though his marriages and other liaisons might seem to offer counter evidence. Einhard states plainly: 'Charlemagne practised the Christian religion with great devotion and piety, for he had been brought up in this faith since earliest childhood'.[4] He gives details of Charlemagne's religious observance, his attendance at the early morning mass, morning and evening prayer and late-night vigils, where he sang with the rest of the congregation in a low voice. He took great pains to ensure that the liturgy, which included the various liturgical hours during the day, was performed 'with the utmost dignity'.[5] It may be that attendance at daily mass regularly included reception of the sacrament, as the liturgical books used in his kingdom were, with some local variations, those in use in Rome, where the procedure to be followed included the reception of the sacrament – both host and chalice - by the faithful at masses celebrated by the pope. Within a century or so, communion for the laity would become a rare event. Charlemagne had a deep appreciation of liturgical feasts and provided the best of sacred vessels and vestments – so that even the doorkeepers were specially vested.

> On feast days he walked in procession in a suit of cloth of gold, with jewelled shoes, his cloak fastened with a golden brooch and with a crown of gold and precious stones on his head. On ordinary days his dress differed hardly at all from that of the common people.[6]

According to Einhard,

> He was moderate in his eating and drinking, and especially in his drinking.... All the same he could not go long without food, and he often used to complain that fasting made him feel ill.[7]

Significantly, he rarely gave banquets for his household but did so on high feast days. On those occasions he would invite many guests in order to prolong the sense of celebration of the liturgical feast. Einhard remarks that so many foreigners visited him and were given lavish hospitality that this was 'rightly held to be a burden not only to the palace, but also to the whole realm'.[8]

> Exotic wares of distant countries are named with precision by writers of this time; Asiatic spices – pepper, cloves, cinnamon and the like – are used freely to disguise the flavours of food and wine, or to act as aids to digestion. But the needs of the Imperial household are mainly satisfied by the produce of the enormous royal estates; fish, game, cheese, butter, mustard, vinegar, honey, wax, soap and wine are all provided from this source, while cucumbers, melons,

artichokes, peas, carrots and onions, leeks and radishes are also mentioned in the *Capitulare de villis,* which contains regulations for the ordering of the royal manors.[9]

The Lenten fast

Charlemagne observed the Lenten fast faithfully, eating his one meal alone in the evening, but at a time which allowed all the members of his court, who according to protocol dined after him in order of importance, to have eaten by midnight, when the fast resumed.

In Roman times, the one daily meal had been gradually moved forward from evening towards earlier parts of the day, but Charlemagne, at least in Lent, did not follow this practice. Shortly after his death, a decree allowed monks, who had dined earlier in the day, a drink (probably barley gruel) as they listened to the reading of the *Conferences of Cassian* which the *Rule of Benedict* prescribed for the interval before Compline, the final prayer of the day. This was the basis for the subsequent development in the Lenten regulations for the whole church of the concession that a light meal could be taken at some time in the day in addition to the main meal. This took the name Collation from the Latin title of the *Conferences of Cassian*, even though it had nothing to do with the original monastic practice of listening to a reading.[10]

Charlemagne was a man conscious of his responsibility for the affairs of church and state. He felt his support for Pope Hadrian in relation to the creation of Papal States in Italy gave him reciprocal rights in relation to affairs of the church in his realm, and even over pilgrimages to Rome and to the shrine of St Martin at Tours. At the Council of Chalon-sur-Saone in 813 he expressed grave concern about the motivations of pilgrims and suggested that paupers travelled to these places from no loftier a motive than the better prospects for begging to be found there.[11]

Raising standards

He also oversaw the appointment and dismissal of bishops. He gave orders on one occasion that all the bishops were to preach on a certain day in their cathedrals and this frightened one man, as 'fine living and arrogant behaviour were really the sum total of his knowledge'.[12] This story by the second biographer, Notker, shows how in this case at least there was a mismatch between the liturgical and material idea of a feast. The bishop preached a farcical sermon and then gave 'at least an imitation' of the ceremonies of the mass. The banquet which followed in the bishop's palace 'was served so lavishly, on gold plate and silver, and in vessels studded with jewels, that it was capable of tickling the palate of even the most dainty of eaters'.[13] Choristers were accompanied by musical instruments and there was every imaginable variety of drink. There may be satirical intent on Notker's part, but there is enough evidence from elsewhere that Charlemagne had a problem in trying to raise the standard of religious observance on the part of his Frankish bishops.

Presumably he was able to impose the rule of fasting in Lent, but abstinence from meat was clearly not part of the spiritual outlook of at least one bishop. Charlemagne observed the rule of abstinence from meat on Fridays and Einhard reports how the emperor visited a bishop unexpectedly one Friday, to the embarrassment of the latter, as he had no fish to serve him and had to serve cheese instead. It does seem that Friday abstinence from meat was generally observed as there are records of fish ponds on his estates and of fish being supplied to various monasteries – though the amount of fish supplied to some monasteries indicates that if meat was not on the menu the lack was made up by ample quantities of fish. Evidence for this will be seen in records from a somewhat later period than the Carolingian empire.

Monastic lifestyle

Records of the time exist for life in the monastery of Corbie where Charlemagne's cousin, Adalhard was abbot. The *Consuetudines Corbienses* have detailed instructions regarding the supply of pig meat for a year. As there were three hundred monks and one hundred and fifty 'auxiliaries' (workers on the lands and probably boys in a school in the monastery) to be fed every day, the 370 killed every year indicates that most of the meat of one pig in the form of salted bacon (*baccones*) would on average be used every day, though no meat was eaten during the forty days of Lent and the Ember days and fifty were set aside for the abbot, who at that time dined in his own quarters with guests.[14] In contrast, The *Rule of Benedict*, on which monastic life in Corbie and elsewhere was based, had ruled out the meat of four legged animals, except in cases of illness. A letter of that same time from the Abbot of Monte Cassino in Italy, indicates that in accord with this rule only fowl was consumed there.[15] But in Carolingian territory, the close relationship between the monasteries and the empire, the fact too that the palaces and the monasteries incorporated large estates with many dependents and that most monks came from court families, meant that the lifestyle of the two often differed little.

Benedict of Aniane and asceticism

After the death of Charlemagne, his successor, Louis the Pious, officially encouraged the monastic reform instituted by Benedict of Aniane, who wished monastic life to follow closely the norms laid down by St Benedict centuries previously. At an early stage in his monastic career he lived a very austere life with a few companions, not eating meat and without vines or sheep or cattle – they lived mostly on bread and water[16] - but he subsequently built a great monastery with grants from Frankish counts and, despite continuing personal austerity, included a church of great splendour and liturgical services to match. While Charlemagne still ruled he gave the title of this monastery to him – basically its property rights - and so the emphasis on liturgical feasts continued, even if in the case of Benedict of Aniane a corresponding sense of the appropriateness of table feasting was lacking.

Benedict's approach was not shared by Adalhard and other monastic superiors who were content with a more mixed tradition of monastic observance. Their custom allowed, as has been noted, the use of meat and in particular a more lordly way of life for the abbot, who had his own establishment with a kitchen providing fare suited to hospitality for guests of similar social status. This did not preclude, however, catering also for poor travellers; in the part of the *Constitutiones* dealing with the hostel for the poor it was laid down that each man was to receive a three-pound loaf for the evening, a half loaf in the morning and two glasses of beer.[17] This combination of care for the poor and attachment to higher ranks of society – with varying levels of lifestyle for the monks themselves in between - will continue at least up to the time of the crisis brought on by the Reformation, and new moves to reform the monasteries that continued to exist.

Monks and priests

Though care for the life of the church which was so obvious in the life of Charlemagne was continued by his successor, Louis, changes began to affect how liturgy and life were related. These arose from internal and extraneous causes; how life developed in monasteries was an internal factor, while the external one was principally the campaigns against the surrounding pagan tribes to conquer and Christianise them through pastoral care. In the era of St Benedict and his early successors, the monastery was basically a lay community, but by the eighth century there were numbers of priests in various monasteries; for example, there were twenty-two among the ninety-seven monks in St Peter's, Salzburg. This led to the practice of monks celebrating - or better, reading - mass daily in private at side altars in the main church, though with one non-ordained monk to minister during it. Inevitably, the ceremonial or festal aspect was minimised and there was even less sense of food shared – the celebrant received but the server may not have.

Outside of the monasteries, as the Saxons, for example, became part of the Frankish kingdom, the programme of catechising them raised questions which up to then had not needed to be faced. In particular, how could the Eucharist, a ritual involving bread and wine which made Christ present, be explained? In response to questions received from some 'young' churches, a monk of Corbie, Paschasius Radbertus (785-865), relied on texts by Irenaeus and Hilary from the early centuries to set out as plainly as he could the teaching of the church on the Eucharist. This had gone unquestioned and not been written about for many centuries.

There are reasons why this unenquiring attitude obtained. Since the early centuries, when both Eastern and Western fathers of the church had reflected on the Eucharist in a way inspired by experience of the liturgy, experience predominated rather than speculation, and there were later centuries when the breakdown of civilisation left little opportunity for scholarly work. This would change noticeably shortly after Paschasius' time when the period of the eleventh to the thirteenth century would see a new flourishing of creative thinking. Paschasius' intervention would not go unquestioned in his own time, but in later centuries theological reflection on the Eucharist would become a dominant feature of the church's life.

Paschasius and Ratramnus

It appears that Louis' successor, the emperor Charles the Bald (823-877), to whom Paschasius sent his text, was not happy with what he considered an overly realistic or physical presentation of the presence of Christ in the Eucharist. Perhaps a little undiplomatically, as Paschasius was the abbot, Charles asked another monk of Corbie, Ratramnus (800-868), to give him his view. Paschasius had said in a devout but rather simplistic way that the Eucharistic body of Christ was the same as the body which was now in heaven, God's omnipotence making possible a multiplication of this body on altars throughout the world - a position Luther would adopt seven centuries later. He was clearer than Luther would be in his day that the body was the glorified body of Christ and therefore a 'spiritual body'.

To an opponent, Paschasius' explanation could seem to involve a miracle when he called on God's power to bring about the presence of Christ in the Eucharist in many places at the same time, but this for him was not a case of breaking a law of nature because it was the body of the risen Christ. For Ratramnus, however, this position seemed to be asserting that Christ was 'physically' present in a *historical* sense in the Eucharist and therefore a miracle rather than a sacrament, the external sign of invisible grace. Following Augustine, he used the concepts of sign and reality; the physical sign (bread) participated in the spiritual reality (the body of

Christ), so that the reality received in the Eucharist is a reality in 'sign' or 'figure', and that 'it is one thing which appears to the bodily senses but another which faith believes'.[18] For him 'if mystery is performed under no figure, then it is not rightly called mystery'.[19]

In fact, Augustine had left a somewhat confused legacy to the sacramental theology of the future, as he used both the figurative and the realist approach in different parts of his works.[20] In a critical comment Ratramnus maintained: 'we confess that in the sacrament of the body and blood of the Lord, whatever exterior thing is consumed is adapted to refection by the body. The Word of God, the invisible bread existing in the sacrament, through their participation invisibly nourishes the minds of the faithful.'[21] More explicitly he maintained further on in the same text:

> From all that has been said up to now, it has been shown that the body and blood of Christ which the faithful receive are figures in the visible realm, but according to the invisible substance, that is, according to the power of the divine Word, truly exist as the body and blood of Christ. Therefore, in the realm of the visible creature they nourish the body, in that of the more powerful strength of substance they nourish and sanctify the minds of the faithful. [22]

He did hold that the elements received contributed to the nourishment of the body, but not for eternal life as Irenaeus had held. (See below.)

The basis for Ratramnus' position was his denial that the Eucharistic body was identical with the body that was born of Mary.

> The concept of the changes in Christ's resurrected body, despite its continued corporality, helped him to affirm that even without containing the historical entities the Eucharist was still correctly believed to hold the true body and blood of Christ.[23]

The difference between him and Paschasius is that Paschasius insisted on actual contact between the recipient's body and the body of Christ for the ritual to be a saving one. But the difference between the two should not be one of contradiction and both were assuming that Christ's risen body was beyond the concentric spheres of Ptolemy's (c. 140 A.D.) geocentric model of the universe, present with God in the void which that Aristotelian model predicated as being 'beyond the spheres'. Paschasius spoke of the 'spiritual' body of Christ, and he was not proposing a grossly materialistic idea of eating with his view of the 'real' body of Christ. In fact the two men lived peaceably together in Corbie and for long afterwards the two views co-existed even though Paschasius' 'realistic' view was the most commonly held.

Eucharist as food

From the point of view of the Eucharist as food, Paschasius' view gives greater significance to the physical nature of the Eucharist and to the nourishment, not simply physically but in a saving way, of the body through being real food; it evokes a text of Irenaeus (130-202) who used the language of eating in speaking of the Eucharist. He opposed the Gnostics of his time who claimed that in the Eucharist the bread and wine became the body and blood of Christ, but this had no saving effect on the communicant's body; they subscribed to a dualistic view of reality which left the body something evil. Irenaeus responded:

> So then, if the mixed cup and the manufactured bread receive the Word of God and become the Eucharist, that is to say, the Blood and Body of Christ, which fortify and build up the substance of our flesh, how can these people claim that the flesh is incapable of receiving God's gift of eternal life, when it is nourished by Christ's Blood and Body and is His member? As the blessed apostle says in his letter to the Ephesians, 'For we are members of His Body, of His flesh and of His bones' (Eph. 5:30). He is not talking about some kind of 'spiritual' and 'invisible' man, 'for a spirit does not have flesh and bones' (Lk. 24:39). No, he is talking of the organism possessed by a real human being, composed of flesh and

117

nerves and bones. It is this which is nourished by the cup which is His Blood, and is fortified by the bread which is His Body.[24]

Ratramnus was closer to the Gnostic position by his implication that the 'external thing consumed is adapted (only) to the nourishment of the body' while the saving effect is at the level of the soul.

The positions were debated in monastic circles throughout the tenth century, neither controversially or polemically, but with a tendency to favour Paschasius' view. Unfortunately, the issue was revived and became controversial in the eleventh century when Berengarius (998-1059), following the same Augustinian line of argument as Ratramnus, but with a new emphasis on logic and grammar, could not accept what seemed to him a miraculous operation in the sacrament and sought to find a link between that which stood to reason and that which scripture taught and faith accepted.[25] Lanfranc of Bec (1005-1089), who was also a grammarian, opposed Berengarius and followed the emerging trend to accept that substance and accidents (or appearances) could exist separately – the body of Christ substantially present under the appearance of bread. However, he could not justify his position in the Aristotelian terms which Thomas Aquinas would use two centuries later. Lanfranc's thesis made its way into the collection of laws concerning the Eucharist, being used in the twelfth-century by Gratian in his collection of laws known as the *Decretum*.[26] Berengarius on the other hand held that in the statement '*Hoc est corpus meum*' the pronoun, '*Hoc*', precisely because it was a pronoun, must refer to the bread on the altar and the predicate '*corpus meum*' could not be allowed to destroy its subject, but must have a figurative sense.

Emergence of 'Real Presence' terminology
Others in Bec as well as Lanfranc wrote tracts against Berengarius, quoting extensively from Paschasius. Their thesis was that 'the physical (or as they preferred to put it the "natural") body of the risen Lord must be present in the sacrament, for it is the natural contact with this glorified

body which saves us'.[27] Berengarius was forced to renounce his position at a Synod in Rome in 1059 and subscribe to an oath which contained the words 'Christ's body and blood are truly physically and not merely sacramentally …crushed by the teeth of the faithful'[28] in describing the reception of the sacrament – a formula which he repudiated soon afterwards. It was soon clear to theologians of the time that this grossly stated formula was an error and efforts were made to find a new approach. Berengarius was required to take a new oath at a Synod in Rome in 1079, where the distinction between substance and accidents was employed to defend the 'realist' position.

In a rather speculative tract, Abbot Rupert of Deutz (1075-1129) took the argument based on the presence of the 'natural' body of the Lord to extreme lengths, reckoning that all who had died before the time of Christ would have had to receive Communion before entering heaven, so that their bodies would be prepared for eternal life.[29] Carried to such extremes, it would make nonsense of the argument of Paschasius – and of Irenaeus. It ignores the fact that the economy of salvation for us who live in the time after the Resurrection is expressed in terms of sacraments; what preceded the Incarnation remains a mystery. There was more positive teaching, however, in the publications of Rupert; Pope Benedict XVI in a homily for his feast day in 2009 praised him for his fidelity to the doctrine of the Eucharist, which the pope neatly summed up as:

> The Risen Christ is really present in the Eucharist with his Risen Body which is placed in our hands to draw us out of ourselves, to incorporate us into his immortal body and thereby lead us to new life.[30]

Conclusion

Charlemagne was a dominant figure in the civilisation of the late first millennium. He seems to have overcome his native tribal limitations and to have had more than a superficial grasp of the riches and requirements of a Christian society. His formation in the Christian faith in a monastic milieu was undoubtedly influential in his lifestyle and even in his governing policy, however rough his treatment of political contemporaries may have been. Einhard's famous biography did have political motivation, but the detailed description of the emperor's participation in the liturgy could hardly have been without a basis in fact. It shows how the Roman liturgy could have crossed cultural barriers and geographical boundaries to become a formative influence in the emergence of a new civilisation. The details of Charlemagne's eating habits, and especially of his observance of Lent, show that his faith had a day-to-day influence on his life, and this was some centuries before the juridically strong institution of the church, with its detailed code of laws concerning fasting and everything else, had recovered the original ability to play a fundamental role in the life of the its members.

The story indicates that Charlemagne's reforming zeal had to contend with bishops who knew how to celebrate at the table in their palaces if not always at the table of the Lord; for some, the Eucharist could be a less than festive ritual and one not greatly understood, while a lordly lifestyle involved little dietary restraint. How much the lifestyle of monks helped in this reforming process is not clear. The diet of monks like those of Corbie did not exclude or perhaps even restrict the eating of meat, unlike that of some at least of their Italian contemporaries, but they would certainly have been sensitive to the chapter of the *Rule of Benedict* in relation to the ascetical demands of Lent.

Monasticism was exhibiting a new feature, perhaps even as part of the Carolingian reform, in the tendency for monks to be ordained as priests, and this had the effect of reducing the sense of a shared event to an individual one in which the sacrificial dimension was dominant. It was a perception of the mass to which Luther in his day would react and very likely influence him towards his denial of the mass as sacrifice. To the tribes of the ninth century, the ritual of the mass, especially when there was little or no participation by a community, must have seemed puzzling and even 'magical' in some sense and there was a pastoral need for catechetical instruction. Thus began a period of speculation and controversy which in the following centuries would exercise the minds of such people as Thomas Aquinas.

ENDNOTES

1   Rosamond McKitterick, *The Frankish Church and the Carolingian Reform 789-895* (London: Royal Historical Society, 1977) 154

2   Steven Ozment, *A Mighty Fortress. A New History of the German People* (New York: Harper Perennial, 2005) 40

3   Rosamond McKitterick, *Charlemagne. The Formation of a European Identity* (Cambridge: C.U.P., 2008) 11

4   Einhard and Notker the Stammerer, *Two Lives of Charlemagne* , Lewis Thorpe trans., Part I, Einhard, *The Life of Charlemagne* (Harmondsworth: Penguin Books, 1969) Bk III, 26, 79

5   Ibid., 80

6   Ibid., 23,78

7   Ibid., 24,78

8   Ibid., 76

9   H. St. L. B. Moss, *The Birth of the Middle Ages 395-814* (Oxford: O.U.P., 1963) 238

10   Herbert Thurston, *Lent and Holy Week* (London: Forgottten Books, 2018) 41

11   James Obelkevich, *Religion and the People, 800 -1700* (Chapel NC: University of North Carolina Press, 1979)11-2

12   Einhard and Notker the Stammerer, *Two Lives of Charlemagne* , Part II, Notker, *The Life of Charlemagne,* 111.

13   Ibid.,112

14   *Corpus Consuetudinum Monasticarum,* Tome 1, *A cura* Cassius Hallinger (Siegburg: Franciscum Schmitt, 1963) 403-6

15   *Corpus Consuetudinum,* 133

16   Eleanor Shipley Duckett, *Alcuin, Friend of Charlemagne* (New York, Macmillan, 1951) 148

17   *Corpus Consuetudinum,* 372

18   Ratramnus, *De Corpore et Sanguine Domini,* 2. English translation in *Of the Body and Blood of Christ* (Oxford: J.H. Parker, 1838) 2

19   Ibid 5

20   Pamela Jackson, 'Eucharist' in Allan D. Fitzgerald O.S.A. ed. *Augustine Through the Ages. An Encyclopedia* (Grand Rapids: William B. Eerdmans, 1992) 332-3

21   *Ratramni Opera Omnia,* (Paris: J.P. Migne, 1852) 121. 146. XLIV

22   Ibid. 121.147. XLIX Vol. 47 (1992), pp. 1-36 (36 pages

23   Celia Chazelle, 'Figure, Character and the Glorified Body in the Carolingian Eucharistic Controversy', *Traditio,* Vol. 47, (1992) 4

24   S. Irenaei, *Libri quinque adversus Haereses,* Tom. II, W. W. Harvey ed. (Cantabrigiae: Typis academicis, 1857) 204-5

25   Miri Rubin, *Corpus Christi. The Eucharist in Late Medieval Culture* (Cambridge: C.U.P., 1991) 17

26 Thomas Izbicki, *The Eucharist in Medieval Canon Law* (Cambridge: C.U.P., 2015) 26, n.28

27 Gary Macy, *The Banquet's Wisdom. A Short History of the Theologies of the Lord's Supper* (Mahwah N.J.: Paulist Press, 1992) 78

28 *Enchiridion Symbolorum, Definitionum et Declarationum*, 690, H. Denzinger et A. Schoenmetetzer edd. (Freiburg: Herder,1965[23])

29 Gary Macy, *The Banquet's Wisdom* 79

30 Pope Benedict XVI, *General Audience*, Wednesday, 9 December 2009

CHAPTER SEVEN

The social effects of Eucharistic theology

By the thirteenth century the Eucharist, once a communal meal that bound Christians together and fed them with the comfort of heaven, had become an object of adoration.[1]

A new millennium

In the years after Charlemagne, the Carolingian dynasty, which had been so important in church renewal, was weakened by internal conflicts, disputes and even wars between his descendants, and effectively came to an end with the ninth century. There followed a number of short-lived dynasties until the role of Roman Emperor was re-established by the Ottonian dynasty as an elected position (though this was not always the case). In an important development, the marriage of the first Emperor, Otto I (912-973), brought most of Italy into the empire and laid the ground for disputes between the papacy and the empire. By the thirteenth century, the empire was styled the Holy Roman Empire and the relationship between the church and the secular authority would prove crucial during successive centuries. With the rise of the universities in the thirteenth century, a third player would enter into the balancing of power, and by the sixteenth century turmoil would emerge because of conflicting ideas as to the nature of the Christian life, its feasts and its fasts.

The period from the eleventh to the fourteenth century was, despite reversals, a time of economic and cultural development; this aspect of the period will be discussed in the next chapter. Theologically, much attention would be given to the doctrine of the Eucharist, with emphasis placed on the need to underpin the 'realist' position of Paschasius and Lanfranc. As stated in the last chapter, at a Synod in Rome in 1079, the distinction between substance and accidents was employed to defend the 'realist' position. The understanding of the term 'substance' was still vague at that time for the doctrine of the Eucharist; it would be used to formulate that doctrine at the Fourth Lateran Council in 1215 and formulated in the language of Aristotle's philosophy by Thomas Aquinas soon afterwards.

In the first centuries of the new millennium, however, the speculation about the Eucharist, which had begun in the monasteries, remained within the ambit of the church's life, with pastoral issues to the fore. It is not surprising that there were two contrasting outcomes: the rise of the practice of 'spiritual communion' by the laity and exhortations from church officials and writers to receive the sacrament rather than feast the eyes on it whenever opportunity arose. The Fourth Lateran Council's decision that the faithful should confess their sins and receive the Eucharist at least once a year was pastorally prudent yet minimalist; the attitude of the faithful was mostly one of caution and excessive abstention. Religious women set the pace in creating the devotional atmosphere and in their case contemplative adoration was practically if not logically predominant. Religious men, especially Franciscans and Dominicans, were pastorally engaged and endeavoured by preaching and the ministry of the sacrament of Penance to bring people to the reception of the Eucharist with more than minimum frequency.

There was in all this, however, a clear move away not only from the gross error of seeing the Eucharist as flesh to be crushed by the teeth, but also from seeing it as food to be ingested. The elements, seen as accidents with no substantial form, could hardly be presented as food in such a way that the rite could be regarded as a community meal, even though Thomas Aquinas (1225-74), in the liturgy he composed for the Feast of Corpus Christi about 1260, referred to the Eucharist as a *sacrum convivium* or Sacred Banquet. In the Hymn for Lauds of the Feast, one verse read:

> Under a twofold appearance, he gave them his flesh and blood, that he might wholly feed us made of a twofold substance.

The Latin text, *ut duplicis substantiae totum cibaret hominem,* makes it clear that he considered the Eucharist nourished the body – for eternal life as Irenaeus had said, though in Aquinas' scheme it is difficult to see what nourishment of the body meant when only the accidents of the bread and wine remained.

The concentration on the way Christ was present in the Eucharist led to simplistic views on the part of an uneducated faithful, namely that it meant God's suspension of the laws of nature – a localised presence of Christ, whereas for theologians from Paschasius onwards the attempt had been to present a theological explanation of the sacramental system.

The Real Presence

During the crucial centuries up to the time of Aquinas there were frequent reports of the visions of Christ in the Eucharistic bread, especially because this had for some centuries previously taken the form of a white circular disc, the Host, and begun to be shown to the people both during the mass and afterwards in a receptacle which came to be called a monstrance - from the Latin word 'to show'. Some of these private visions were of a bizarre nature – a bleeding host, for example – while others were of a sentimental kind – the child Jesus appearing in the host, reputedly to King Edward the Confessor in eleventh century England.[2] Some of them found a permanent place in history, for example, the event in Bolsena in Italy, where in 1263 a priest who had difficulty in accepting the doctrine of what came to be called the Real Presence was reported as having seen blood seeping from the host and on to the cloth corporal after he pronounced the words of consecration. The corporal is still preserved in a shrine in the nearby Cathedral of Orvieto. Pope Paul VI visited there in 1964 and sent a televised message to The International Eucharistic Congress being held in Philadelphia, U.S.A.

The Social Miracle

By the Middle Ages, every Sunday was a feast day in a civic as well as liturgical sense, in that it was a day of rest and recreation, and there were many feasts, both local and for the whole church, to honour the saints. These were all public holidays. The confraternities and trade guilds were active in such celebrations, putting their enthusiasm for ritual to good use in verse plays staged during processions. The fundamental principle underlying all such activity was the conviction that social integration was a fundamental end of the Christian life, even if the state of charity, of communion, could only be achieved on occasion. This social integration came to the fore when the confraternities or guilds engaged in their rituals of induction and at annual meetings. 'The rituals of participation were meeting, greeting and eating'.[3] At such times, a festive meal was the central act of fraternity and was in places described as the *prandium caritatis,* the love feast, evoking the memory of the *agapé* of the early church.

The religious culture pervaded civic life and the church building was prominently situated in the town, causing the liturgical celebration to extend out on occasion into the street, on the feasts of patronal saints and especially on the Feast of Corpus Christi. The involvement of these organisations in public celebrations brought that principle of fraternal love into play in a remarkable demonstration of what has been called the social miracle,[4] when enmities between groups were put aside for the day and all went in procession together leading the Blessed Sacrament of the Eucharist under its canopy on Corpus Christi and concluding with 'the neighbourhood conviviality of the evening'.[5] As the celebration of the Passion of the Lord in Holy Week had been given more emphasis than the institution of the Eucharist at the Last Supper, the introduction of the Feast of Corpus Christi as a separate feast at the end of the Easter season highlighted the Eucharist as the sacrament of unity, duly honoured in the procession and fraternal meals. Even the poorest would endeavour to have something special on such feast days.

Beginning around 1300, there was a remarkable development in devotion to the Host exposed for adoration, when peasants brought their horses into visual contact with it by riding through specially placed doors in churches and exiting at doors on the opposite side. They would ride their specially decorated animals through the door into the middle of the church, to have them look either at the exposed Eucharist or at the windows of the container housing it. The priests also prepared the horses for their meeting with the Host by blessing them with holy water.[6] Strange as this practice sounds, it was in fact a variation of the custom called the *Umritt* (Ride around), the practice whereby peasants came with decorated wagons on the feast days of patron saints and rode three times around the church where the feast was celebrated.

Another effect of the emphasis on the Real Presence was the focusing on the priest as the one who had received the power of bringing it about, thereby creating a gap between him and the faithful within what should be a community celebration; the faithful were simply in attendance at this mysterious rite. From the earliest days of the church when celebration of the Eucharist could only be envisaged in terms of participation by all present, there had been a decline over the centuries in the reception of the sacrament by the faithful, though not at the same rate over time or the same everywhere. It has been suggested that over the period from the beginning to the tenth century the communion of the faithful varied from the early daily practice, to communion on Sundays and ultimately three times a year.[7] Certainly, from the tenth century the discipline connected with communion required sacramental confession on each occasion. By the time of the Fourth Lateran Council of 1215, the norm was that the faithful were required to receive both sacraments once a year, during Paschal time.

Anti-social movements

In thirteenth and fourteenth century Germany, an emerging class of lesser nobles was noted for a crusading mentality inherited from the earlier crusades and was particularly hostile to Jews. They were responsible for destruction of whole communities and for establishing shrines on sites where they had been. It has been noted that whereas many medieval shrines to Our Lady were already established, this movement resulted in shrines dedicated to Christ in the Eucharist. This was in part due to the increasing devotion to the Real Presence, especially with the gradual spread of the Feast of Corpus Christi to Germany after its introduction in Liège in 1246. But it was also a reaction to the widespread belief that Jews had engaged in acts of desecration of the Host. A document written in lower Bavaria in 1338 included:

> The Jews, who deny the Christian faith, have ... stolen the consecrated Host, throwing it into a fiery oven, striking it with hammers, and afflicting it with other indignities. Upon notice of these events, Sir Hartmann of Degenberg, together with his neighbours from Deggendorf, captured the Jews, burned them, and offered up their possessions for plunder.[8]

From communion to contemplation

Religious life for women became a prominent feature of these centuries and in new forms rather than that observed by the traditional orders such as the Benedictines and the Cistercians. The new groups, not all of which were orthodox in belief, included the Beguines, who probably began in the twelfth century but by the thirteenth were well organised in small communities in the towns of the Low Countries. They were women who lived a semi-monastic life, though without vows, and owned their own houses. They have been described as having 'a concern for affective religious experience, an extreme form of penitential asceticism, an emphasis both on Christ's humanity and on the inspiration of the Spirit, and a bypassing of clerical authority'.[9] All of these characteristics, except to an extent the last, were evident in the devotion of these women to Christ in the Eucharist, especially in the Host, which was seen at the elevation in the mass, and even more in the visions they reported to their spiritual guides, men belonging to the religious orders. The experiences of some prominent women seem to have been accurately but uncritically recorded by these authors in their biographical accounts. While tradition always held that the Eucharist was food for the soul, for these women this was a much more powerful metaphor in that the reality behind the symbol of food was taken to a new level of seriousness. They sometimes fasted for prolonged periods from ordinary food (as did St Catherine of Siena in Italy) while reception of the Eucharist could lead to days of ecstasy. They used food imagery not only for their experience of the Eucharist but for other mystical experiences as well.

The short-lived but very influential Mary of Oignies (1177-1213) was one of the most prominent of the Beguines, particularly because of her biography by James of Vitry, an auxiliary bishop of Liège, which was widely circulated and came to influence Francis of Assisi. According to the author, in her reception of the Eucharist

> she felt all delectation and savour of sweetness ... not just in her soul but even in her mouth.... Sometimes she happily accepted her Lord under the appearance of a child, sometimes as a taste of honey, sometimes as a sweet smell.[10]

Psychology today would classify this as a psycho-somatic phenomenon, irrespective of its spiritual authenticity, and this would be even more the assessment of what her spiritual director described as the experience of a thirteenth Cistercian nun, Ida of Louvain:

> It frequently happened that when the priest received the holy communion at the altar... she in the intensity of her desire received with her mouth at the selfsame moment the most sacred pledge of the host of the Saviour (brought we believe by a ministering angel) and discerned with the sense of taste and even chewed with her teeth.[11]

Blessed Ida had to overcome strong opposition from her wealthy parents and was chained up by them at one stage and considered insane.

Mary of Oignies was one of many women of the time for whom seeing or receiving the Eucharist was a substitute for ordinary food and caused them to engage in long fasts, even to the extent of being incapable of eating ordinary food.

The mystique surrounding the elements of the Eucharist, particularly the bread, caused it to be seen as belonging to a totally different category from ordinary food, especially since unleavened bread had become the norm in various places during the ninth century, though it did not become a universal practice until the middle of the eleventh, This was the time when the Eucharist had become the object of contemplation and unleavened bread made in the form of a white disc lent itself more easily to this devotional development.

The bread of the Eucharist

By the end of the first millennium, the faithful no longer brought bread offerings for the Eucharist, largely because of the convenience that money offerings provided, and by then bread made specially for the Eucharist differed only from ordinary bread in that only the best flour was used and the bread was baked in a special shape, typically as a *corona,* or crown, the dough having been braided and then made into a circle, while there was also a simpler form: a round loaf divided by a cross. This was normal yeast bread. By the eleventh century, when devotion to the Eucharistic species had become so marked, the making of the bread in some places took on a liturgical format. According to the customs of the Abbey of Hirsau in Germany, the wheat had to be selected kernel by kernel and there were ceremonies surrounding the milling with a machine that had been cleaned and hung about with curtains. The four monks who baked the bread had to wear liturgical vestments and three of them had to be deacons or priests.[12]

In medieval Europe the availability of grain varied during the centuries because of outbreaks of diseases such as the deadly ergot fungus (affecting rye particularly) and black stem rust which could ravage whole harvests. In the thirteenth-century, the Hanseatic League of guilds and north German towns brought stability to the distribution and price of grain supplies, especially when grain became available from the plains of Eastern Europe. The plentiful supply made it possible to provide flour of the finest quality. The Eucharistic bread made from the finest flour was very different from the bread which the poor consumed, if they had any at all, and this must have had an effect on how the Eucharist was perceived, the extent to which it was seen as food. Certainly, it had little to do with people's daily bread, which for the poor would lie on the lower end the scale of bread of different degrees of fineness. Bread could be made from wheat, or a mixture of wheat and rye (originally rye was simply a weed which grew through the wheat), from barley, rye on its own, oats or even bran mixed with beans.

The round white Host

As already mentioned, there had also been a development in relation to the bread of the Eucharist which began in late eighth-century, the time of Alcuin of York (whom Charlemagne had invited to become a teacher in his Court) and would take several centuries to become standard: the introduction of the small white wafer of unleavened bread. Why this occurred seems to be linked with the theology of the Real Presence which had generated the controversy in Carolingian circles involving Paschasius and Ratramnus and ultimately Berengarius and led to the practice of the adoration of the Eucharist in a monstrance. Clearly, a white wafer, less liable to fragmentation because unleavened, made this more feasible, but the fact that it was now called the 'Host' was indicative of the emphasis on the sacrificial nature of the Eucharistic celebration, as the word in its Latin version, *hostia*, meant 'victim'. The use of unleavened bread would, of course, serve to bring into relief the origin of the Eucharist in the Paschal meal, which the gospel witness indicated to be the form taken by the Last Supper, when the Lord celebrated with his disciples using unleavened bread as the rite required. But this departure from the appearance of bread had the effect of lessening the sense of a meal as medieval people who were accustomed to coarse bread would have understood it.

The celebratory wafer

Another factor also came into play. With the development of commerce and industry, to be discussed in the next chapter, flour became a commodity, with bread the stuff of commerce rather than the staff of life, and this could well have made the perception of bread less immediate and tangible, opening up the possibility, despite appearances, of regarding even the small, round and white wafer as bread, especially since at the upper levels of society, each guest at a banquet was given a wafer of fine white bread as part of the celebration. This was much larger than the Eucharistic wafer but the practice may hint at a desire to link the banquet with the Eucharist, especially as the wafer was commonly referred to as 'angel's bread'. There is evidence in illustrations found in various publications of the period for the popularity of these delicacies in the later Middle Ages. The end product and the equipment needed for making them, two flat irons held together in the fire, are often shown.

> Of all delicacies, perhaps the most universally adored was the wafer, made of batter and cooked between two greased, heated iron moulds to fragile, crisp perfection. ... A wafer could be savoury, with a cheese filling, or spicy with ginger, but the classic one was sweetened with sugar or honey.[13]

Communion 'under one kind'
By the thirteenth century, the faithful, when they did communicate, received only the Host, as veneration of the Real Presence created fears that reception from the chalice might lead to some of the precious blood being spilled.[14] There had been an intervening period when the 'lay chalice' was used, a chalice containing un-consecrated wine to which a drop of the precious blood had been added, a practice which gave way to the use simply of a chalice of wine from which the faithful drank to cleanse the mouth after communion.[15]

The withdrawal of the chalice also arose from the development of the theory of concomitance, according to which Christ was present body and blood in each of the elements. Development of this idea went back to discussions in the Sorbonne University in Paris at the end of the twelfth century as to whether Christ was already present after the words of consecration were pronounced over the bread or only after this had been done over the chalice also. The theologians decided in favour of the first view and it is one of the quirks of liturgical history that it was this decision which led to the official introduction of the emotionally charged practice of the Elevation of the Host and of the chalice to the mass - though it was already in the Cistercian statutes of 1152.[16]

The Elevation

The practice of elevating the Host was sanctioned by a Synod of Paris in 1204 after its introduction at mass in Notre Dame Cathedral at a time when Paris was under interdict by Pope Innocent III (because of a charge of adultery against King Philip II). When an obliging priest elevated them, the faithful deprived of the sacrament could get a glimpse of the elements through holes in the walls of the building, which was under construction since 1163. So important was this action that it had to be strictly in accordance with rubrics lest the people be misled into adoring what was merely bread: a statute from Liège in 1287 instructed the priest not to elevate the host before he had said the words of consecration, while Parisian statutes warned the priest that he must hold the Host close to his breast until after he had said them.[17]

The restriction of reception to the Host, with the Eucharist now becoming food without drink, accelerated the distancing of the celebration from its perception as physical nourishment or a meal, a situation which was already evident from the fact that only the priest received on most occasions. In addition, restriction of reception of both elements to the priest celebrant was defended by Thomas Aquinas[18] and others on the basis that the priest received on behalf of the people.

The Eucharistic fast

Fasting rules were also involved because of the increasing emphasis on the presence of Christ in the Eucharist, and how it came about. This led to greater fears of unworthy reception and the need for intense preparation in every case, a preparation that invariably included fasting as well as other ascetical practices, some of them evocative of Old Testament purification laws, such as abstention from communion on the part of menstruating women. The Eucharistic fast was an addition therefore to the recurring fasts associated with days such as Fridays, and seasons such as Lent, and to the fast which in earlier centuries had been associated with the process of public reconciliation of sinners.

By the end of the first millennium, the custom of reconciliation through a private rite had established itself, largely through the pastoral approach of Celtic monks in their missionary work in some continental countries, and involved performing a penance before absolution from the guilt of sin was granted. It did spread into the Frankish kingdom, but here there was a conflict with the rite of public penance inspired by Roman practice. The two forms of reconciliation co-existed, with various local synods accepting private penance for sins of a more private nature and public penance for public sins and breaches of ecclesiastical discipline.[19]

The Eucharistic fast would only be relevant after a sinner had been reconciled, a process which itself could include fasting. In the case of private reconciliation, there were manuals known as *Penitentials*, which contained lists of penances to be imposed on the penitent person before absolution would be granted. The penances were related to the kinds of sins committed and accordingly fasting would be imposed for sins of gluttony; this was fasting simply focused on action contrary to abuse of the natural appetite and did not require the ancient tradition of diversion of resources to the needy. Perhaps as a way of improving its essentially inward looking nature, or more likely as a way of mitigating punishment, penitents favoured the practice of substituting for the fast a fine payable to the church. In principle at least, the money was used for the relief of the poor. As some *Penitentials* imposed draconian penances requiring fasting - for example, ten years of a fast as penance for homicide according to an eighth century *Penitential* - the relief the system offered was extensively exploited. It came to be called the *tariffs* system, and the priest's manual contained also a list of the appropriate tariffs.

The Eucharistic fast itself concerned the length and conditions of preparation for communion and varied from place to place. Generally, a six days' abstinence from flesh meat was required, while in one case, a Synod of Coventry in 1237 in England, a fast of half a week from food was required.[20] The need for great purity in accessing the sacrament caused widespread uncertainty as to the appropriateness of sexual intercourse before communion.[21]

A continuous fast for some, but not for others

If the fast before receiving became a dominant feature of the Christian life, the regime of fasting as part of daily life and of the seasons was a regular heavy burden which could be legitimately mitigated or even avoided by various stratagems. Evidence for how this was achieved comes largely from the meals of the upper classes of medieval and later times and of the monasteries under their patronage; the poor majority, serfs and peasants, were on a continuous fast in the sense of a monotonous and sometimes sparse diet, as poems such as the tale of the Nun's Priest in Chaucer's *Canterbury Tales* or Langland's *The Vision of Piers Plowman* indicate. For Langland, writing towards the end of the fourteenth century, the poor are starving and hungry, yet keep up a respectable appearance and have at best cold flesh and fish instead of venison, while on Fridays and days of fast a farthing-worth of mussels or as many cockles would be a feast.[22]

How accurate the picture presented by the poem actually was is questionable; presumably there were differences in economic status from place to place among the peasants throughout Europe, as will be discussed in the next chapter, though it is true also that there was quite a gulf between the upper classes and the labouring class, whose way of life was very basic as regards accommodation, clothing and diet

An indication of how the upper classes dealt with the demands of the seasonal fasts can be found in the fourteenth century poem, Sir Gawain and the Green Knight. The noble Sir Gawain, a knight of King Arthur's Round Table, arrives unexpectedly at the castle of an unnamed lord on Christmas Eve and is graciously welcomed by servants who set up a table with a white cloth and set with silver spoons and salt-cellars. Emphasis on white cloths will be found in accounts of medieval banquets and seems, with 'angel's bread', to be evidence of medieval Christian culture's acknowledgment of the connection between festal dining and the Eucharist. The hand washing seems to have been more a ritual than a necessity, and evocative too of the Eucharist, though perhaps not without its usefulness in an age when people did not bathe frequently.

The servants brought him

> Several fine soups, seasoned lavishly, twice-fold, as is fitting, and fish of all kinds – some baked in bread, some browned on coals, some seethed, some stewed and savoured with spice, but always subtly sauced, and so the man liked it. The gentle knight generously judged it a feast, and often said so, while the servants spurred him on thus (as he ate): 'This present penance do. It soon shall be offset'.[23]

It is worth noting here that while abstinence from meat was observed on this Christmas Eve fast day, there was no reduction of the amount of food, but rather an attempt to compensate for hardship by elaborately prepared fish dishes. This approach will be found in monasteries as well, as an example from the autobiography of the cleric-historian, Gerald of Wales (1146-1204) illustrates, though it must be noted that he was prone to exaggeration in his descriptions of events. He visited the monastery of Canterbury on Trinity Sunday 1180 and under the heading, The Gluttony of the Monks of Canterbury, recorded his impressions of life there, in particular a meal in silence in the refectory. He sat with the Prior, who sent many dishes to the lower tables where the monks gesticulated their thanks with their fingers and whistled to one another in lieu of speaking. Sixteen very costly dishes or even more were placed on the table.

> For you might see so many kinds of fish, roast and boiled, stuffed and fried, so many dishes contrived with eggs and pepper by dextrous cooks, so many flavourings and condiments, compounded with like dexterity to tickle gluttony and awaken appetite. More-

136

over you might see in the midst of such abundance wine and strong drink, metheglin and claret, must, mead and mulberry juice and all that can intoxicate.[24]

This is speculation about the kinds of dishes 'you might see', but there is presumably some factual basis for it, as records from other monasteries of the same and later centuries will show.

Conclusion

It is clear that this was an age of faith, reverent and unquestioning and at times superstitious on the part of the laity, while what would soon seem to authorities to be a threatening cloud of theological speculation was growing. A philosophical movement, Nominalism, sought to replace the theology of people like Thomas Aquinas and lay the foundations for serious revision of how food and feast could come together in the sacrament of the Eucharist. Would it be a sacrifice without a meal as seemed to be the case in the tradition or a meal without a sacrifice? It was a slow process and in the meantime medieval society continued to reflect the progress characteristic of the Middle Ages. The survey of food, feast and fast in medieval times will be continued in the next chapter, when more attention will be devoted to economic and population trends, and the development of commerce and industry. Restricted access to the Eucharist continued to be the norm, but faith and popular imagination at a time when the social miracle still had influence led to a new kind of celebration in the form of mystery or miracle plays.

ENDNOTES

1   Caroline Bynum, *Holy Feast and Holy Fast. The Religious Significance of Food to Medieval Women* (Berkeley: University of California Press, 1987) 53

2   Miri Rubin, *Corpus Christi. The Eucharist in Late Medieval Culture* (Cambridge: C.U.P., 1991) 117

3   John Bossy, *in the West 1400-1700* (Oxford: O.U.P.,1982) 59

4   Ibid., 57

5   Ibid., 72

6   Ibid. 30

7   Miri Rubin, *Corpus Christi* 64.

8   Cited in James Obelkevich, *Religion and the People, 800 -1700* (Chapel NC: University of North Carolina Press, 1979) 29

9   Caroline Bynum, *Holy Feast and Holy Fast* 17

10 Ibid. 59

11 Ibid. 117

12 Joseph Jungmann, *The Mass of the Roman Rite. Its Origins and Development*, F.A. Brunner trans. (London: Burns & Oates, 1959³) 330-1

13 Bridget Ann Henisch, *Food in Medieval Society. Food in Medieval Society* (University Park PA: Pennsylvania State University Press, 1976) 77

14 Miri Rubin, *Corpus Christi* 70

15 Caroline Bynum, *Holy Feast and Holy Fast* 56

16 Thomas Izbicki, *The Eucharist in Medieval Canon Law* (Cambridge: C.U.P., 2015) 102, n.115

17 Ibid. 114-5

18 *Summa Theologiae*, III, q. 80, a. 12

19 Frank Senn, *Christian Liturgy. Catholic and Evangelical* (Minneapolis: Fortress Press, 1997) 197

20 Joseph Jungmann S.J., *The Mass of the Roman Rite. Its Origins and Development* 500

21 Miri Rubin, *Corpus Christi* 149

22 *both afyngred and afurste, to turne the fayre outward… a feste with such folke, or so fele cockes* : William Langland, *Piers Plowman*. A New Annotated of the C-text by Derek Pearsall, Passus IX, 85 (Exeter: Exeter University Press, 2008) 174-5

23 *Sir Gawain and the Green Knight*, Translated with an Introduction by Brian Stone (Harmondsworth: Penguin Books: 1974²) 54-5

24 *The Autobiography of Gerald of Wales*, Translated and edited by H. E. Butler (Woodbridge: Boydell & Brewer, 2005) 71

138

CHAPTER EIGHT

An urban culture and its way of celebrating

Three gold pears on a silver shield made up the arms of the Cistercian Abbey of Wardon in Bedfordshire, and it has been suggested that the pear was first developed there, but no more than a heraldic pun may have been intended.[1]

Medieval social structures

Life in Europe at the beginning of the second millennium was structured according to what was later called the feudal system, one which gave rise to the manorial class, that category of dwellers in castles or large residences, with large domains where dependents belonging to various categories lived and served their lords in many capacities from military to agricultural to craft work. In the eleventh century, for example,

> the governing classes, lords and men of religion, obtained for themselves goods manufactured by the labour of various groups (*familiae*) of servile workers, traditionally attached to the work – millers, bakers, brewers, weavers, tailors, tanners, shoemakers, masons, carpenters, smiths, potters, armourers, and even goldsmiths.[2]

From the eleventh to the fourteenth century in Europe, there was, however, a transformation of the feudal agrarian economy, described even as a revolution, because of the colonising movement of land reclamation, the introduction of an improved form of crop rotation and the advent of a money economy from which the growing towns benefited. Crop rotation changed from the Roman system of using half the land for a crop and leaving the other half fallow to a two-thirds, one-third one, that allowed for the growing of oats as feed for horses. This radical development led to increasing numbers of horses and two particular benefits. While villages and towns continued to follow the old pattern of being within a day's walk of each other, the peasant could now save time and energy by using this new form of transport. In addition, the development of heavy nailed horseshoes made horses suitable also for ploughing. Overall, the increase and improvement in horse-breeding brought about an increase of the equestrian knights and in fact made the Crusades a feasible project.

All of this was part of a social revolution which had negative consequences for the feudal lords. They were not usually well versed in business matters and did not know how to exploit the reclamation process which introduced these changes. From expediency, many allowed the emancipation of the serfs, who then for a rent became tenant farmers, generally at a subsistence level. After initial financial gains, the former seigniorial class sometimes descended into poverty, though some among them consolidated their position by creating, in conjunction with royal authorities, princely estates which brought an end to the anarchical and warlike environment of the older feudal society.

Developments in farming

The peasant farmers, on the other hand, had considerable scope for development, especially by sheep farming. Sheep farming had been extensive in Europe since Roman times, with Spain and England being the major centres in the Middle Ages. The colonisation of the previously unused land by the Cistercian monks led to them becoming major sheep farmers. The Cistercians had a system of granges or outlying farms efficiently worked by so-called *conversi*, lay brothers, whose day was dedicated more to manual work than would be possible for the monks who spent long hours celebrating the liturgy in the monastery. 'A Cistercian abbey, Las Huelgas, near Burgos in Spain, had the lands of sixty four townships in its possession.'[3] The two major Cistercian Abbeys in England had great flocks; Rievaulx had about nineteen thousand and Fountains fourteen thousand. Such holdings made these large communities self-sufficient, as they also had horticultural holdings around the Abbey buildings to supply them with the vegetables and fruit needed for a meat-free diet, as well as herbs for their herbal remedies.

The peasants in their small holdings near the towns experienced an improvement above all in their food. It became at least abundant and substantial, if not very varied nor as healthy as the Cistercian diet.

> (Sheep) supplied milk and meat, fat for cooking and tallow for lighting, wool to clothe the people of the north and skins that were much in demand by the parchment makers, whose business had begun to boom as literacy spread outside the walls of the monasteries and into the realms of business and everyday life.[4]

The growth of towns

Major agents of change came with the progress of the money economy generated by financial transactions in the developing commerce of the towns. 'By 1200 one could sell one's surplus production and buy what one could not produce.'[5] Commerce supplied the incentive for industrial activity, giving rise to an economy which was often more vibrant than that obtaining in what has been called the 'sleepy' atmosphere of the domains. Italy and France were great centres of progress in this industrial revolution, with artisans working at home and sometimes hiring extra labour, having gained their freedom from the restrictions of the landed proprietors on payment of certain dues. Powered by windmills and water wheels, industries used various metals to produce not only articles of war such as swords and shields but also cutlery for domestic use while weaving produced fabrics for clothing and fine material for things like table cloths, especially in the towns of Italy.

But the towns also showed the characteristics of settlements of people of peasant origin who brought the practices of the countryside with them. Streets were no more than passages between houses and there many patches of muddy pasture where sheep grazed and there are many references in chronicles and decrees of medieval town to pigs rooting in the refuse littering the streets and obstructing people passing by. 'In Frank-

141

furt in 1481 an edict was passed against the pigsties cluttering the streets in front of the houses but ... little attention seems to have been paid.'[6]

In the towns of the North of France at that time, the daily wage would have allowed for the purchase of 1.9 kg of beef, or 1.7 kg of bacon, of 2.8 to 6 litres of wine, but the other expenses of daily living would mean that only a fraction of the wage could be spent on meat, and families were large. In northern Europe generally, 'dark bread, cabbage, beans or salt pork from the stockpot, with curds to round off the meal'[7] constituted the menu.

> These, however, were only the basics, and because they sound dull it is too easy to assume that they *were* dull. Yet there must have been good cooks in the fourteenth century, ... cooks who knew how to make good use of the seasonal bounty of the countryside. Some peasants in some places may have eaten consistently well.[8]

The more prosperous among the town dwellers – closer to the peasantry than to the feudal nobility – butchers, bakers, pastry-makers, cookshop-keepers, could give dinners for their equals, but not yet of the standards of sophistication of their betters. This was particularly true of dessert, which since the days of the Roman Empire had graced the tables of aristocratic banquets - extravagant concoctions known as 'sotelties' (jellies or pastries moulded into elaborate representations of lions , eagles, crowns or coats of arms).

A feature of town life which was relevant both to ordinary and better-off residents, and also in fact went back to Roman days was the cookshop. It was a significant product of the money economy and allowed people to avail of ready cooked meals, basically meat and fish dishes. In London in 1183 there was already one famous example. Their popularity stemmed from the cheaper price that this larger scale production made possible, but they were also ways of avoiding the hazards of cooking in the fire-prone simple thatched dwellings, just as in Roman times the dwellers in the large tenements, the insulae, would have been at risk if they cooked in those crowded small apartments.

Butchers, bakers and others organised themselves into corporations or guilds in the twelfth and thirteenth centuries and there was even an export trade in sea biscuits from Italy, at a time when spices and silks were being imported from the Far East through Egypt. From this background there emerged a new class of burgesses, men of business, organisers of transport, shipowners, money-changers and bankers, and these allied themselves with the traditional aristocracy, the patrician class, who had palaces in the towns as well as manors in the country. Between them they took control of municipal government and

> were able to regulate hours of labour, the level of wages, the price of food, to submit trade and the crafts to a rigid discipline, and to promulgate or revise the statutes of the corporations.[9]

Urban lifestyle
With this status went a lavish lifestyle, such as sumptuous attire for ladies and abundance of food, expensive wines and silver plate on their tables. The burgesses aped the traditional nobility, but in doing so provoked the masses of the common people. In reaction, the small traders and workmen, with the support of the church, formed associations for piety and mutual assistance, distinct from the guilds and called fraternities or sodalities, and these grew in number as the labour of the masses in the period from the twelfth to the fourteenth century became the preponderant element in the economy of the towns of France, Germany and Italy. Even earlier, professions where brainwork rather than manual work was dominant, such as notaries, apothecaries, physicians and goldsmiths, formed themselves into corporations.

As a result, from the thirteenth century a democratic movement which often assumed a revolutionary character grew in Europe and by the fourteenth century had achieved the emancipation of the commercial and industrial classes, giving the urban worker freedom and security of labour, though there were still wage-earners subjected to control by entrepreneurs and paid only famine wages.[10] A rising economic tide does not necessarily lift all boats, and a large class of poorly paid workers was to be found in all the increasingly prosperous cities. For all, however, work was hard and the working day varied.

> (In) practice, deducting intervals for meals, it was usually from eight to thirteen hours; night work was in general forbidden and paid extra when it was allowed; and numerous feast days provided the artisan with intervals of rest, which together amounted to at least a quarter of the year.[11]

Population change, the Black Death
Until about 1300 the population of Europe grew steadily, but levelled off about then and reduced because of a number of factors including a widespread famine and with it epidemics of plague from 1315-17, the result, it appears, of a climate change, a reduction of about one degree over a long period, but enough to alter the length of the growing season and bring extra rainfall.

The effects that were felt then were small compared with what marked the years 1347-1350, the plague known as the Black Death, which caused the death – it is generally agreed – of nearly a third of the population of Europe. The remaining half of the century saw a further decline as outbreaks of plague continued, so that by 1400 the population was reduced almost to half of what it had been before the mid-century. It began to increase again in the fifteenth century.[12]

Effects on religion
The calamity that had struck Europe had a serious effect on religion, as people struggled to understand its cause, some believing it was an attack of the devil, others punishment by God. This resulted in a distortion of religious practice, the thanksgiving, festal, dimension of worship giving way to pleas for pardon and for help. A vindictive attitude towards Jews, who were considered responsible by poisoning of wells, led to barbaric massacres of innocent people. The church's ministry suffered as clergy died, leaving their flocks

without leadership, pastoral care in their illness or burial rites when they died. A new morbidity crept into people's approach to life and even into art; so that early in the fifteenth century the *danse macabre* or 'Dance of Death' began to be represented on the walls of churches. Art chosen for the decoration of churches does say something about the religious culture obtaining at the time – this will become very evident in the use of didactic art in Protestant churches after the Reformation. The Dance of Death theme had gone by the late sixteenth-century.

As Europe moved from times of progress to decline and back again, the church, because of its efficient administration and promotion of rec-lamation, gained territorially and financially, often through the finan-cial gifts and land bequests of the faithful. Independently of the church authorities, the newer religious orders such as the Cistercians and the Premonstratensians, made similar gains. The bishops also increased the territory and resources of their dioceses. At a time of weakness in the Holy Roman Empire, the Archbishops of Mainz and Trier, because of the wealth accruing to the church through the commercial success of their cities, became Electors of the Empire and as a result territorial princes, with an aristocratic way of life.

Worship and society

The church did provide respite from the hardships of daily life by way of feast days, in places fifty of them in a year after Sundays are taken into account.[13] These were celebrated in a festive atmosphere and with all classes participating, so that divisions were lessened at least for the day, though there is evidence from medieval England of discrimination: 'nobody might sit in the chancel but lords and "patrons", who were gen-erally in earlier days, the local squires'.[14] As already described, the 'social miracle' of the Eucharist was effective during the early centuries of the second millennium, binding communities together through its power. But sometime in these centuries, new physical structures began to a have a disruptive effect: pews began to be placed in the naves of churches. Evidence from art history is indecisive as images of the interiors of great cathedrals could have such furniture 'photo-shopped' out, so to speak. It may be that liturgical reform (following on Gregory VII's eleventh-century moves against lay investiture) meant that lay personages of note were displaced from the chancel, but had to have seating provided for them in the nave and that this practice spread, leading in England to the introduction of the box-pew after the Reformation. The pew in the Anglican churches 'represented, more or less, the distribution of households or families in the parish and erected appropriate barriers between them'.[15] The history of the furnishing of Catholic churches is more obscure, and after the Council of Trent in the latter half of the sixteenth-century may have had to do with the segregation of the sexes. Cardinal Charles Borromeo's 'device of a wooden barrier for this purpose down the middle of churches does not seem to have caught on'.[16]

The early centuries of the second millennium, were a period of great activity in church building and creativity in church architecture, from the great Romanesque abbey church of La Madeleine at Vézelay in France in the early twelfth century to the soaring Gothic Cologne Cathedral in the mid-thirteenth and the mighty façades such as that of Notre Dame in Paris. The Romanesque embraced the faithful, the Gothic made the spirit soar and the sculptures on the entrance portal, the Last Judgement as portrayed at Notre Dame, for example, stimulated reflection. The faithful contributed to the building of these churches over centuries – even by their own voluntary manual work in the case of Chartres cathedral – and felt at home in them, even though the liturgy was little understood. The Elevation of the Host continued to fascinate and create among the faithful (who may have been walking up and down in the side isles) at least a momentary sense of being one – an additional expression of the social miracle of the Eucharist.

Buildings as aids to celebration

In these buildings of vast scale and height the liturgy was celebrated in the sanctuary by priests and clerics of diverse ranks, often quite a number, but with some roles reduced by the general lack of reception of the Eucharist by the laity. But since the time of Charlemagne, who had promoted the enhancement of liturgical ceremonies, there had been a growth of artistic activity to embellish the performance of the rites and give new roles to the clergy, especially the introduction of the *trope,* an extension to the liturgical Latin musical text to enhance poetic quality and emphasise its meaning. It is not surprising that given the number of participants in the sanctuary, these tropes developed into dramas to explicate the text, as in the case of a trope based on the Introit of Easter morning, *Quem quaeritis,* which developed into a liturgical drama, though with the passage of time the basic musical performance seems to have been reduced as a result of this new art form. The first version seems to have been by Tutilo, a monk of St Gallen in Switzerland.[17] A later version was given fixed form by a Bishop Ethelwold of Winchester, England, a monk-bishop who in the late tenth century replaced the Canons of his cathedral with ordained monks and had three of them represent the three Marys who came to Jesus' tomb, while a fourth sang the part of the angel who asked them whom they were seeking. There was singing and movement – in the sanctuary – and the ringing of bells. All of this took place at a distance from the people who stood in the nave or even walked up and down in the side-aisles and it was meant to attract their attention.

For several centuries these dramas were enacted in church and one in particular was very popular, The Harrowing of Hell, based on the apocryphal gospel of Nicodemus, which describes Christ descending into the underworld on Holy Saturday to liberate Adam and Eve and the patriarchal figures of the Old Testament. A version created by a fourteenth century abbess had the nuns of the community locked in a chapel until the priest stood outside and sang the liturgical text *Tollite portas* (Lift up the gates) and the nuns processed out singing and waving palms of victory.

Mystery plays and the faithful

This drama is an example of those mystery or miracle plays which by the thirteenth century were taken over by the laity and brought out on to the streets, especially in English towns, where they were performed by the guilds and gradually developed into pageants through the streets

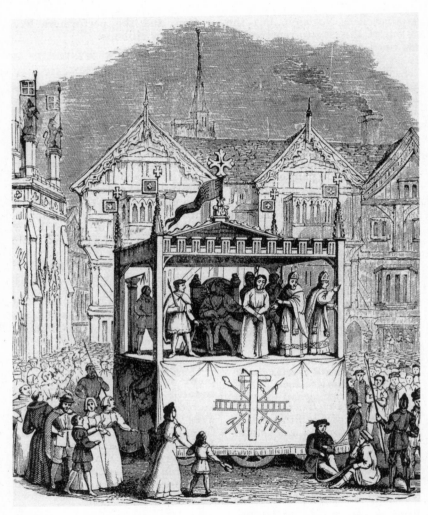

Representation of a Pageant Vehicle at the time of Performance.

lasting several hours. The pageants were so arranged that each guild could advertise the skills of its trade, by having a guild enact its part in the area or street where its members had their shops. The municipal authorities were in charge overall, and the guilds paid for the stages, props and costumes needed, which in some cases were very elaborate, as in the case of a Coventry Passion play. It included hell's mouth with its fire, a barrel used somehow to produce an earthquake and three painted worlds.[18] There are records of its performance up to the sixteenth century in England but Reformation radicalism appears to have been the main reason why it came to an end.

> It is a far cry from a tenth-century Latin trope for Easter, which was the beginning of the liturgical drama, to the vernacular *Resurrection* pageant of the fifteenth-century York cycle or from a simple Christmas trope to the sophisticated *Second Shepherds' Pageant of Wakefield*. But during the four or five centuries ... all the dramatic traditions, religious and secular, of the Middle Ages had had time to converge and so enrich the parent stock of the liturgical drama.[19]

Festa della Palombella

A spectacular event still continues in Orvieto, Italy, on Pentecost Sunday, to mark the descent of the Holy Spirit. The *Festa della Palombella* (the word *palombella* basically means a wood-pigeon) dramatises the arrival of the Spirit by arranging for a basket containing a pigeon to slide a hundred metres or more from an adjoining building down a wire to an elaborate wooden tower in front of the cathedral, where fireworks - presumably intended to represent the tongues of fire of the biblical story - produce a great explosion of light and noise, and much cheering. If the hapless bird survives, the cage with its possibly stunned occupant is given to a newly married couple.

That is the central moment in a celebration which involves marching bands and processions of people in medieval costumes. Food obviously becomes a significant part of the revelry on the Sunday afternoon. To what extent this is a religious event could be questioned by an outside observer, but in a way this would be an irrelevant question. It has its origins in the liturgy, it arose as part of the popular expression of faith in the mystery celebrated and became embedded in the culture. Today it presumably has diverse levels of meaning for the people who throng the piazza, but overall the culture of which it is part has openness to the transcendent or even to the faith, which may not be present in the culture of many parts of Europe. This was true also of the medieval miracle-plays of England when they were a standard part of the culture.

Conclusion

The expansion of Europe's population in the Middle Ages, the traumatic effects of plagues and of the Black Death, the recovery and the growth of an urban civilisation all had their effects on how people lived and how they celebrated. Despite social disparities, a common culture made itself evident in the town dwellers' love of the miracle or mystery plays – two somewhat different dramatisations of the Christian mystery. These were examples of the liturgical feast becoming a feast with a broader meaning, because of the contribution of the faithful expressed in popular culture. It is hardly a surprise that the broader meaning included food and drink, street parties which had their remote origin in celebrations marking the induction of a new Roman emperor, and therefore drawing on a deep seated pagan inheritance – though also in the case of England more re-cent druidic festivals. There were complaints from church leaders as tra-ditions tolerant of excess were gradually created, beyond the control of church or municipal authorities. In fourteenth-century France, a Bishop Guillaume of Angers complained to the pope that

> on those holy-days, on which God should more especially be wor-shipped, the Devil is worshipped; the churches are left empty, the lawcourts and taverns and workshops resound with quarrels, tu-mults, blasphemies and perjuries, and almost all sorts of crimes are there committed.[20]

150

But the Corpus Christi procession, which became popular in the thirteenth-century not long after the feast itself was established, is an example of a celebration where the depth of reverence for the mystery of the Real Presence placed restrictions on what popular culture might contribute, or through undisciplined enthusiasm distort. It was a procession of the victorious Lord through the streets and required that the people in their various guilds march before him and that the way be prepared decorously for his approach. The heart of the liturgical event with its ministers in ceremonial apparel came out into the streets. But the feast did inspire dramatic celebrations of various size and frequency in towns and villages.

> By the second quarter of the fourteenth century we witness in England and on the Continent the beginning of the formation of dramatic sections in the procession. In some places these were *tableaux vivants*, scenes arranged and moved on pageant wagons along the processional route. Such scenes could be elaborated with a number of spoken lines by the actors, or with music.[21]

An incident from the beginnings of the Reformation in Germany shows the power and the challenge of this ceremony for those who were establishing a new religious culture destined to become an expression of the Protestant faith. The Emperor Charles V convoked the Diet (Imperial Parliament) of Augsburg in 1530 to bring the religious controversy to an end, in effect, to suppress or at least greatly restrict the Protestant movement. To test the waters, he required all who were attending to take part in the Corpus Christi procession the day before proceedings were to open. The Protestant princes stayed away – their leader, Philip of Hesse, having refused to kneel the previous day when Charles and the delegates entered the cathedral to pray.

ENDNOTES

1 Bridget Ann Henisch, *Fast and Feast* (University Park PA: Pennsylvania State University, 1976) 114. Pears could be spelt 'perez' or 'peres', echoing the French for 'fathers'. The Cistercians were of French origin.

2 P. Boissannade, *Life and Work in Medieval Europe* (New York: Dorset Press, 1927) 179

3 Ibid., 243.

4 Reay Tannahill, *Food in History* (London: Headline Book Publishing, 2003³) 170

5 Brian Tierney and Sidney Painter, *Western Europe in the Middle Ages: 300-1475* (Boston: McGraw-Hill College, 1999⁶) 271

6 Reay Tannahill, *Food in History* 159

7 Ibid., 184

8 Idem.

9 P. Boissannade, *Life and Work in Medieval Europe*, 209

10 Ibid., 220

11 Ibid., 221

12 Brian Tierney and Sidney Painter, *Western Europe in the Middle Ages*, 470-1

13 Ibid. 288

14 G.G. Coulton, *The Medieval Village* (New York: Dover Publications, 1989) 281.

15 John Bossy, *Christianity in the West 1400-1700* (Oxford: O.U.P.,1983) 143

16 Ibid. 142

17 Martha Kirk, 'Liturgical drama', in *The New Dictionary of Sacramental Worship*, Peter Fink, ed. (Dublin: Gill and Macmillan, 1990) 371

18 'Introduction' in *Everyman and Medieval Miracle Plays*, A.C. Cawley ed. (London: Dent, 1957²) xiii

19 Ibid., vii

20 G.G. Coulton, *The Medieval Village*, 273

21 Miri Rubin, *Corpus Christi. The Eucharist in Late medieval Culture* (Cambridge: C.U.P., 1991) 272

CHAPTER NINE

—————

The Protestant Reformation: a new epoch

The ignorant wretches (the papists) are not able to distinguish between the cup, which pertains to the substance of the sacrament, and fasting, which is an accidental, carnal thing, of no weight at all. The one has God's express word and command, the other consists in our will and choice.[1]

Festival in a changing religious culture

The Protestant Reformation is considered to have begun with the protest against Indulgences by Martin Luther (1483-1546) in 1517, though there were already protest movements in the previous two centuries at least. It was a watershed event in the life of the Christian community. Streams of religious, social, intellectual and political life met and merged to produce new and diversified and often conflictual cultures, with different emphases on liberty, conformity, social norms, religious faith and public life. A transition was emerging from medieval to modern society.

Hitherto, medieval people did not regard religion as something private, as having no impact on life in the public square – to use a modern expression. Liturgical feasts led to public festivities and brought the natural follow-up of feasting. But feasting could get out of hand. This was an aspect of life that authorities condemned and sometimes managed to control, but was not considered to put a question mark against how society was structured. Luther's protest against abuses did, however, give rise to fundamental questions about religious faith and its public manifestations and about the freedom of the Christian in face of the conformity required by church regulations, including the rules of fasting. With its conviction about freedom, the Reformation would prove to be the beginning of a radically new approach to fasting.

As mentioned at the end of the last chapter, the reform movement had already by 1530 questioned how the faith was to be practised publicly. In effect the nature of the Christian faith itself was in question, though at a superficial level concern was with externals, the religious culture. The princes who had embraced the reform had a difficulty with - among other aspects of religious practice - how the Sacrament should be treated. They complained about the number of feast days in the Church's calendar and with the excesses which followed from their observance by the faithful. Already, in a submission to a Diet at Nuremberg in 1522-3, they listed a hundred 'grievances', of which no. 37 included:

> The great multitude of the laity is inordinately burdened by such a profusion of holydays and festivals. And no wonder, when so many days are reserved for religious purposes that scarcely time enough is left to the husbandmen for gathering into their barns the produce of the earth, so painfully elicited by the sweat of the brow, sometimes endangered by floods or rain or excessive heat... In addition, on the festival days, which no doubt were originally consecrated with good intentions, and in honour of the Supreme Being, innumerable offences, sins and iniquities are perpetrated, rather than the Almighty worshipped and honoured.[2]

That there were many abuses in the life of the church at the level of administration and in the lifestyle of the people in the centuries leading to the Reformation is well known, and Luther and the other reformers were not the first to draw attention to them.

Desiderius Erasmus: a proponent of change

Desiderius Erasmus (1466-1536) was the best known critic of the Christian community of his day, because of his credentials as a humanist scholar. In origin an ill-defined movement to promote rhetorical eloquence, humanism soon developed a fashion for writing in classical Latin style and re-discovering Greek literature in its original texts. A great attraction of the classics was that they seemed to show an attitude to life which anticipated that of the humanists. Being 'concerned with ethics and morality on the one hand, and source texts on the other, (the humanists) at some point expressed opinions on religious questions'.[3] Erasmus' early work, *The Handbook of the Militant Christian* (1503) began with a chapter heading: 'We must watch and look about us evermore while we be in this life'[4] and went on to suggest that prayer, self-knowledge and an understanding of the Scriptures – aided by familiarity with classical literature - were the means to avoid the snares of evil and live a good Christian life.

Satirical works

His satirical work, *In Praise of Folly* (1511) did not spare clergy or religious. In another of his works, the *Colloquy*, 'Concerning the eating of fish', the laity are castigated. The fishmonger tells the butcher:

> In the centre of the cities and in the alehouses next to the churches on the most solemn holidays there was drinking, singing, dancing, fighting, and such noise and tumult that divine services could not be performed, nor could one word the priest said be heard.

The fishmonger continues, turning now to the prohibitions imposed by the church on the people. He appears to suggest a reason why people were in a rebellious mood:

> But if the same men had sown a stitch in a shoe, or eaten pork on a Friday, they would have been handled severely. ... But is this not a strange perversion of judgement?[5]

The stitch in a shoe refers obviously to Sundays and major feasts while pork refers to abstinence from meat on Fridays.

Meat or fish?

Throughout the colloquy, the prohibition of meat seems to be accompanied, in Erasmus' mind, with a *requirement* to eat fish - he has the fishmonger and butcher discuss it as if it were compulsory. He had said in a letter to a bishop friend: 'To require the eating of fish where fish is scarce is to decree a famine'.[6] This was a problem for him as he had a strong dislike for fish, which he claimed made him ill, so the standard practice of eating fish on Fridays was repulsive to him. In the various anecdotes involving named characters in the colloquy, the character Eros represents himself, and he tells of a misadventure which befell Eros when he visited a friend, 'a great man and one of the pillars of the church'.

> When the eating of fish started, so did his old condition. A whole troop of disorders came upon him, fever, severe headache, vomiting and the stone. His landlord, though he saw his friend in this danger, did not dare give him a bit of fresh meat. But why didn't he? He saw a great many reasons why he might do it and likewise saw the papal dispensation, but he was afraid of public censure.[7]

This was just one of the aspects of church life which Erasmus critiqued and sometimes caricatured and he was echoing a writer whom he admired, the fourteenth-century Chancellor of Paris University, Jean Gerson, who had said that the rules of the church covering every aspect of public and private life made 'the light yoke of Christ and the laws of liberty an iron yoke and a heavy burden pressing on the necks of Christians'.[8]

Martin Luther (1483-1546)

Erasmus published his criticisms both before and during the years of the Reformation begun by Martin Luther, but he always maintained his distance from Luther's campaign and was criticised by Luther for not siding with his movement. Luther in his *Tabletalk,* sayings of his recorded by students as they sat at table with him, called him the 'King of Amphibians' (*rex amphibiolorum*), by which he seems to have meant the king of ambivalence. He would challenge Erasmus and if by God's grace he overcame him, then he would purify the church.[9] Erasmus had no desire to debate with Luther; he never met him and never had time to read his books 'beyond glancing over a few pages'[10] though he would finally engage with him by way of a theological tract on the freedom of the will.

Christian Freedom

For Luther, the human person rather than being free was by nature enslaved to sin. Human effort could not make the person acceptable to God and so all the traditional devotional practices were to no avail. The person who through faith in Christ becomes acceptable to God is then capable and free to engage in good works such as acts of love for the neighbour. In 1520 he set out his views in what was to prove one of his most successful tracts, *On the Freedom of a Christian,* which includes a summary statement: 'A Christian is a perfectly free lord of all, subject to none. A Christian is a perfectly dutiful servant of all, subject to all'.[11] He held that these two propositions were not contradictory, and on this basis asserted that while the justified person

> has all that he needs, except insofar as this faith and these riches must grow from day to day even to the future life; yet he remains in this mortal body on earth. In this life he must control his own body and have dealings with men. Here the works begin; here a man cannot enjoy leisure; here he must indeed take care to discipline his body by fastings, watchings, labours, and other reasonable discipline and to subject it to the Spirit...[12]

The free Christian will encounter both those people who 'boast of, prescribe and insist upon their ceremonies as means of justification' and 'the simple-minded, ignorant men, weak in faith'. The first he 'must resist, do the very opposite'. 'In the presence of such men it is good to eat meat, break the fasts, and for the sake of the liberty of faith do other things which they regard as the greatest of sins'. The others, 'he must take care not to offend'.[13] This was what Luther felt was the appropriate approach to the situation which existed in Germany at that time and by 1530 the official Lutheran position set out in the *Confession of Augsburg* (see below) reflected his views. Article XXVI, 1- 40, applied the Lutheran doctrine of justification by grace and not by works to the practice of fasting, condemning the traditional teaching that by fasting people could merit grace. It also repeated the charge that it was in any case impossible to keep all the laws prescribed by the church and ended by claiming the support of both Irenaeus and Pope Gregory that 'diversity concerning fasting does not destroy the harmony of faith'.[14]

A frugal but enjoyable life
To what extent Luther himself lived in accordance with these principles is not clear, but circumstances forced him to live frugally. After his marriage to Catherine von Bora in 1525 - he married mostly to please his father, who wanted grandchildren - he and Katie lived in the rambling Augustinian Friary in Wittenberg, the now empty building presented to him as a wedding gift by his overlord, Friedrich, Elector of Saxony. They had six children and took in four orphans. They also took in students as lodgers and Luther wasn't good at managing money, so they relied very much on what they grew themselves.

> He took care of the garden, which produced lettuce, cabbage, peas, beans, melons and cucumbers. Katie looked after an orchard beyond the village, which supplied them with apples, grapes, pears, nuts and peaches. She also had a fish pond from which she netted trout, carp, pike and perch. She looked after the barnyard with hens, ducks, pigs and cows, and did the slaughtering herself.[15]

For a woman who was reared in a minor noble family and then entered a convent for girls of her social status, this was quite an achievement, especially as on her arrival in Wittenberg she had the problem of not being suited to the work of a servant, which seemed the only work available to a refugee. Her relationship with Luther was a happy one and he showed his affection for her in letters when circumstances took him away from home. Luther liked wine, which they couldn't afford (though Duke Frederick sometimes sent them some), and Katie brewed beer for him herself, believing it was better for him. The meals with his large household, often including visiting lectures to Wittenberg University, appear from the *Tabletalk* to have been jolly occasions, while giving him opportunity to expand on his teaching before a receptive audience of students who came to Wittenberg because of its reputation as a centre of the reform movement. In accordance with the customs of the time, Katie did not dine with him, but served instead. She outlived him by six years, dying in 1552.

The pamphlet campaign

Others throughout Germany had absorbed his message after the publication of his *Ninety Five Theses on Indulgences* in 1517-8, and this was especially true after he had defended his position at the Diet of Worms in 1521. Various popular writers, especially satirists and humourists, produced pamphlets and tracts setting out the new understanding of religion. The effort was aided by the exciting new medium of the printed word, both sides in the controversy making good use of it.

One who became a pamphleteer of note was Johann Eberlin (+1533), who had been a Franciscan friar and well-known preacher in Basel, Freiburg, Tübingen and Ulm. He went over to the Reformation after reading Luther's earliest tracts and himself wrote a series of fifteen pamphlets, the first after Luther had taken his famous stand at Worms. In this first pamphlet, Eberlin produced for Emperor Charles V a list of reformers, humanists (among them Erasmus) and schoolmasters, who, he said, were working for 'pure and evangelical teaching in the schools and pulpits' of the empire, and went on to excoriate the mendicant orders for money-grabbing, a theme familiar from Erasmus' writings. He examined religious life in a series of four further pamphlets, charging the male religious with laying intolerable burdens on women religious, which they did not observe themselves: 'Nuns must fast often, while monks eat boiled or fried meat, which the nuns must prepare but cannot enjoy'.[16] In a subsequent pamphlet, Eberlin, in his protest against mandatory lay fasting rejected the modelling of lay piety on monastic piety.

The fasting rules

He was writing in the context of the severe fasting regime that existed in Germany at the time. 'In pre-Reformation Germany, there were as many as 161 days of penance: fasting (65) or abstinence (96) – over one-third of the year when Christians were expected to abstain from one or more types of food, basically cheese, fat, eggs, meat, milk, and/or flour.'[17] Because of this imposition, Eberlin calculated that 100,000 mortal sins were committed each year. An intolerable burden was being placed on ordinary people. Mandatory fasting was against both the letter and the spirit of the New Testament. New Testament Christians are free to fast or not.

This word 'mandatory' appears frequently in the early Reformation literature; mandatory fasting is always included in the list of things for which an end is called: the cult of saints, relics and images; indulgences, religious festivals, pilgrimages and shrines; votive masses for the dead; belief in purgatory; clerical celibacy and clerical immunity from civil taxation and criminal prosecution. What was to be excluded was *mandatory* fasting; the same Scriptures that confer freedom on the Christian also quote Christ himself saying that when the bridegroom would be absent, then the disciples would fast.

It has to be asked just how rigorous was the Lenten regime in the medieval church, which all the Reformers no longer regarded as binding? Eberlin had said in one of his pamphlets that 'no layman, young or old, rich or poor, healthy or sick, is bound on pain of mortal sin to fast during Lent'.[18] But it has been observed that the popularity of Laetare Sunday, which marked the half-way point in the season of Lent, is enough to show the dismal character of the season it alleviated.[19] (For that Sunday, flowers were allowed on the altar and the organ was used.) Some amelio-

The Fight Between Carnival and Lent. Pieter Bruegel the Elder, 1559.

ration of Lenten rigour does seem to have developed over the centuries before the Reformation, but the absolute ban from Ash Wednesday to Holy Saturday, including Sundays, on the eating of meat persisted. There was a further ban on *lacticinia*, foods derived from animals or poultry (milk, butter, cheese and eggs) – hence the origin of Pancake Tuesday, to use up the eggs.

Peter Brueghel's painting *The Fight between Carnival and Lent* of 1559 purports to show how people at the time perceived the arrival of Lent (in some parts of the Netherlands at least). It depicts a rotund man carried on a barrel while brandishing a lance on which a fowl and meat are skewered. He is confronting a nun-like figure carrying a staff to which a platter with fish is attached. Behind the barrel come figures singing and dancing, while on the other side there are well-behaved children. In the background, on the right there is a church from which nuns are emerging, while on the left clients are enjoying themselves at an inn. The paint-

161

ing does show the contrast between people's enjoyment of life and what the church expected of them as the penitential season began. But it is true too that some of the hardship could be avoided. In the fifteenth-century dispensations could be got, by paying a fee, and by the end of the century these were being bought on a sufficient scale to pay for the 'Butter Tower' of Rouen Cathedral, to the great annoyance of Martin Luther.[20]

The results of liberation

In practice, the lifting of the burdens of the 'old religion' left people with little taste for voluntary mortification. In Strasbourg, where the Reformation, under the strong leadership of the ex-Dominican, Martin Bucer, had taken hold, a preacher was complaining as early as 1534 about standards of behaviour. 'One no longer prays, fasts or gives alms as was done under the papacy', a new way of life of which he has to approve. However, he adds: 'But one also does not do as one should in a true Christendom'. All that the priests, monks and nuns did in the past was to eat drink and frolic about in the most offensive ways. 'But now it is the workers and youth who run wild and many have no respect for God, worship, good works or any honourable thing.'[21] It is interesting that in some of the cities that stayed Catholic, there was a move on the part of the civil authorities to lessen the repressive elements of the Church regime. The magistrates of Regensburg issued a decree in 1524, introducing many reforms, including the prohibition of the customary enforcement by excommunication of the fasting laws. That early move by Regensburg is considered to be one of the reasons why the city remained Catholic.

Luther on the mass

Luther had cut his teeth, theologically speaking, on dispensations and indulgences and the theological issues underlying them. His stance at the Diet of Worms in April 1521, where he refused to retract his teaching on justification by faith alone, and remained adamant in his dismissal of the Papal church as the Antichrist, resulted in him put under the ban of the Empire by Charles V. He had been excommunicated by Pope Leo

X some months earlier. For Luther, the issue of dispensations no longer arose after his return to Wittenberg to a new way of life in 1522, having spent ten months in Wartburg Castle for his own protection. During that time he had written a treatise against what he called the 'private mass' (*De abroganda missa privata*), mass celebrated by a priest without a congregation. He chose not do so himself, [22] a logical move considering he had already declared in a tract of 1520 that the mass was not a sacrifice. It was 'Christ's testament which he left behind him at his death, to be distributed among his believers'.[23] In that case the celebration of the Eucharist should only take place when there was a congregation present to hear what Christ gave in his testament, the forgiveness of their sins.

He seems to have been unaware of the powerful testimony of his theological mentor, St Augustine, who in a comment on Romans 12:1 ('Offer your bodies as a living sacrifice.') in his *City of God,* concluded:

> This is the sacrifice of Christians, who are many, making up one body in Christ. This is the sacrifice which the church continually celebrates in the sacrament of the altar, a sacrament well-known to the faithful, where it is shown to the church that she herself is offered in the offering which she presents to God. [24]

He was now committed to the reform programme, which manifested itself in an obvious way by the changes in the liturgy. He was of a conservative mind in matters liturgical, quite apart from the fact that he believed strongly in the Real Presence in the Eucharist; he was in fact shocked at the changes introduced into the mass by his own followers, including the introduction of the vernacular, during his absence from the town since 1521. This regard for tradition had an important bearing on the form taken by the liturgical changes he introduced, including the musical elements of the liturgy. Compared with the changes introduced by the other major Reformers, Luther's liturgy retained more of the elements, both recited and sung, of the medieval mass.

Nevertheless, his theological position led him to make significant changes. As he denied the mass was a propitiatory sacrifice, the offertory (and the music provided for it), which appeared to have strongly sacrificial language, was suppressed in his first edition of the new liturgy, the Formula Missae of 1523. The Canon of the mass was greatly reduced and communion administered in both kinds. His conservatism prevented him from making some changes at this stage which his theological principles would have called for. For example, he considered that all liturgy was in essence a celebration of the Word, the mass being in essence the recitation of Christ's last will and testament, contained in the Narrative of Institution ('Take this all of you ...') and should therefore be in the vernacular so that people could hear it. But in 1523 the mass remained in Latin, apart from the reading of the Epistle and Gospel. This meant, however, that much of the old Latin music could be retained. By 1526, Luther accepted the need for further revision and produced the text of his *Deutsche Messe*, most of which was in German. In the introduction, he expressed the wish that his previous Latin mass should still be used, but in the German mass simplicity should prevail, in the chants and in the ritual.

Taken with what he said about the freedom to retain vestments, candles etc., the somewhat mixed message given by Luther in these liturgical innovations had in the long run the effect of creating a Lutheran liturgy into which much of the former liturgical music fitted. When the contribution of J. S. Bach nearly two centuries later is taken into account, the Lutheran liturgy, with its practice of communion under both kinds, became in principle a significant expression of the festal nature of the Eucharist.

There was, however, the fundamental omission of its sacrificial dimension in contradiction of official teaching and age-old tradition. Luther's dismissal of the sacrifice of the mass became in practice the fault-line between all of the subsequent Reformation tradition and the Roman Church, despite the efforts of Philip Melanchthon to gloss over the differences, when he deputised for Luther at the Diet of Augsburg in 1530, Luther being unable to attend as he was under the ban of the Empire.

In the *Confession of Augsburg* Melanchthon formulated the Lutheran position on the mass:

Falsely are our churches accused of abolishing the Mass; for the Mass is retained among us, and celebrated with the highest reverence. Nearly all the usual ceremonies are also preserved, save that the parts sung in Latin are interspersed here and there with German hymns, which have been added to teach the people.[25]

The irenic Melanchthon did wish to find a common position with Rome, but his efforts were concentrated on showing the need to eliminate the financial abuses connected with 'private' masses and the stipends which went with them, and he devoted much attention to the benefits the sacrament conferred, making only a passing reference to the mass not being a 'work', that is, a rite in which the people made an offering.

The festal nature of the Lutheran liturgy

The Lutheran tradition did then promote a celebration of the Eucharist 'with the highest reverence', and the addition of German hymns significantly enhanced it. It also included the polyphonic mass, which 'was all sacrament and no sacrifice'[26]. This could be regarded as a pure embodiment of the sacred by Lutherans and it continued its appeal, so that it is not a surprise that Bach was inspired to compose his B Minor mass (though it was for the Catholic liturgy of the king of Poland). But in this way an important transition took place. Such masses, freed from their attachment to a liturgical theology, could have the character of a spiritual concert and seem to have done so in the churches of Lutheran Germany. Those who listened no longer did so quite as they did when polyphonic settings of the mass were used in pre-Reformation days as accompaniment to the sacrifice; as one writer put it, now they were 'no longer exactly a congregation, but more than an audience'.[27] 'Thus, it would seem, the quasi-sacred institution of the classical music concert was born.'[28] Compared with what developed in Zürich at the same time and subsequently in Geneva, the Lutheran liturgy for a number of centuries at least had an attractive festal character, which modern Lutheran liturgical reform endeavours to replicate.

Conclusion

Luther's important publication, *The Freedom of the Christian,* echoed the theme of Erasmus' publications and would be the leitmotiv of Zwingli's preaching (to be considered in the next chapter), though all three would wish to be considered independent of each other in their thinking. It is difficult to say whether the fasting regime of Luther's day could have continued for long without his protest, or would have broken down under its own weight. It is interesting that some of the cities which moved to mitigate its demands in light of people's experience avoided the radical theological changes and remained Catholic.

Luther's new theology had far reaching consequence for Christian worship in subsequent centuries, not least the polarised approaches of Catholics and Protestants. But Luther's own personality, with his enthusiasm for music, had a positive effect not only on the Lutheran worship tradition but was the origin also of a now treasured musical tradition typified by Bach's music for concert hall as well as church.

166

ENDNOTES

1   Martin Luther, *Table Talk*, William Hazlitt trans. (London: Fount, Harper Collins, 1995) 183

2   *One Hundred Grievances. A Chapter from the History of Pre-Reformation Days*, C.H. Collette, ed. (London:Partridge,1869) 231-3

3   Euan Cameron, *The European Reformation* (Oxford: Clarendon Press, 1991) 64

4   Desiderius Erasmus, *A Book called in Latin Enchiridion Militis Christiani and in English the Manual of the Christian Knight* (London: Methuen & Co. 1905) 43

5   *The Essential Erasmus*, With Introduction and Commentary by John P. Dolan (New York: The New American Library, 1964) 314

6   Cited in Roland H. Bainton, *Erasmus of Christendom* (London: Collins, 1970) 218-9

7   Ibid. 318-9

8   Cited in *The Essential Erasmus*, 273

9   Martin Luther, *Tischreden 1531-46*, 3392b in *D Martin Luthers Werke* (Weimar, 1883-1929)

10 Cited in *The Reformation in its Own Words*, Hans Hillerbrand ed. (London: S.C.M. Press, 1964) 424

11 Martin Luther, *On the Freedom of a Christian* in *Martin Luther's Basic Theological Works*, Timothy Lull, ed. (Minneapolis: Fortress Press, 1989) 596

12 Ibid., 610

13 Ibid., 625

14 *The Confession of Augsburg* XXVI, 1- 40 in *Concordia. The Lutheran Book of Confessions* (St Louis MO: Concordia Publishing, 2007)

15 Roland H. Bainton, *Here I Stand. Martin Luther* (Oxford: Lion Books, 1978) 292

16 Steven Ozment, *The Reformation in the Cities* (New Haven: Yale University Press, 1975) 92-3

17 Ibid., 94

18 Ibid., 95

19 John Bossy, *Christianity in the West. 1400-1700* (Oxford: O.U.P., 1985) 50

20 Ibid. 51

21 Steven Ozment, *The Reformation in the Cities* 154

22 See my *Martin Luther. His Challenge Then and Now* (Dublin: Columba Press, 2017) 117f

23 *The Babylonian Captivity of the Church* in *Martin Luther's Basic Theological Works*, Timothy Lull ed., 293

24 Augustine, *City of God* X.6 (New York: Image Books, 1958) 194

25 *The Confession of Augsburg* XXIV, 1-3 in *Concordia. The Lutheran Book of Confessions*

26 John Bossy, *Christianity in the West* 165

27 Idem

28 Fintan Lyons O.S.B., 'Church Music and the Reformation' in Helen Phelan ed., *Anáil Dé. The Breath of God* (Dublin: Veritas, 2001) 167

CHAPTER TEN

Christian freedom and enforcing virtue. The Swiss Reformation

The most formidable of the 'false brethren', as Luther preferred to call anti-Romanists who disagreed with him, were to his south, in Switzerland. [1]

1. HULDRYCH ZWINGLI

Humanism's pervasive influence

The Reformation took hold in Switzerland at about the same time as in Germany, becoming the established church in various cities because of the control the municipal authorities could exert. One after another of the cities, Zürich, Bern, Lausanne went over to the reform, with Zürich leading the way. Huldrych Zwingli (1484-1531), the leader of the Reformation in Zürich was born about 60 km from there a few weeks after Luther's birth, The relationship between the two Reformers began with initial enthusiasm on Zwingli's part for Luther's writings – he ordered several hundred copies of a volume containing five of Luther's works for circulation in Switzerland at the beginning of his own career. He did not meet Luther until 1529 (at a Colloquy at Marburg) and by that time he was more ambivalent in his attitude, while Luther was dismissive of him, saying in his *Confession Concerning Christ's Supper* of 1528: 'I regard Zwingli as un-Christian, with all his teaching, for he holds and teaches no part of the Christian faith rightly'.[2]

The Zürich reform programme

Unlike Luther, Zwingli had not studied theology formally, though he was familiar with one aspect of Thomas Aquinas' teaching at least, that on predestination. He had undertaken humanist studies in Basel, Bern and Vienna and during those years he immersed himself in the writings of Erasmus, making use especially of Erasmus' translation of the Greek New Testament. He was ordained a priest in 1506 to serve in the town of Glarus and subsequently in Einsiedeln in the Canton of Schwyz. His biographical details are of particular interest because of the information it provides about the underlying cultural factors in the emergence of the Reformation in Switzerland.

In late 1518 he was appointed the 'people's priest' (*Leutpriester*) in the principal church in Zürich, the *Grossmünster,* and began immediately to preach directly from the Scriptures rather than following the standard official programme. Initially, there was nothing unorthodox about his preaching, but his emphasis was on the freedom of the Christian, on the contrast between Law and Gospel as taught by St Paul. However, his preaching generated in some at least the wish and determination to decide for themselves the extent to which they were bound by the laws of the church. A simple incident which occurred on Ash Wednesday morning, 1522, brought the whole question into the open. The printer, Froschauer, had his maid cook sausages for himself and a few others. Zwingli was present but did not partake, so it seems this was an agreed testing of the waters in relation to a campaign in favour of a new Christian freedom.

When Froschauer was hauled before the town council because of the breach of the Lenten regulations, he defended himself in a statement which has been preserved:

> Prudent, gracious, pious and dear Lords, as it has come to your knowledge that I have eaten flesh in my house, I plead guilty, and in the following manner: I have so much work on hand, and it is costing me so much in body, goods and work, that I have to get on and work at it day and night, holy day and work-a-day, so that I may get it ready for the Frankfurt Fair.[3]

The work in hand was the Epistles of St Paul, presumably in the interests of the new reform movement, or it could simply reflect the demand for such works on the part of the humanists of the day. It is worth noting that the defence the printer gave provides a very early glimpse of the culture which has come to be called Modernity. The scientific revolution that formed that culture fully had yet to come, but the relationship between man and the world is already altering here, barely seventy years after the invention of printing. The machine is beginning to impose its rhythms on human life and Froschauer feels its pressure.[4]

The following Sunday Zwingli drew on this incident to develop his theme of the defence of Christian freedom, referring now to liturgically mandated fasting and any other kind, though he supported fasting until after hearing the Word of God and partaking of the Lord's Supper on Sunday. In general, as there was no prohibition of fasting in the scriptures, he believed, and people were free to undertake it if they wished.[5] But the importance of the issue of freedom from fasting regulations was that it was in the wider context of the movement for change, for reform of traditional ways, including worship.

His dedication to evangelical preaching sprang from the same belief in the primacy of the Word underpinning both Luther's and Calvin's ministry. Theologically, he had admired and accepted Luther's doctrine of justification by faith in the life of the individual as he began to think of reform, but he was more concerned with the outward signs of reform in church and society. Reform of society in the direction of freedom for citizens in a situation where the Bishop of Constance was the temporal as well as the ecclesiastical overlord was bound to lead to conflict, especially as Zwingli got the town council over to his side very quickly, having got a seat on it in 1521.

In the ecclesiastical sphere he had a problem in that he contracted a secret marriage with a widow, Anna Reinhart, a woman of higher social standing than himself.[6] This could not remain hidden for long so he wrote a very long letter in July 1522 on behalf of himself and ten other priests to the Bishop asking for his acceptance of the legitimacy of clerical marriage - not just permission for this group to marry their concubines. The bishop's refusal was not unexpected. As support for his programme built up, a public debate between himself and a representative of the bishop, a Vicar General, took place in January 1523. Zwingli was adjudged the winner.

Zwingli's social and liturgical theology

He then drew up his Sixty Seven Articles, summarising the new theology.

One of the articles stated:

> XXIV. That no Christian is bound to do those things which God has not decreed, therefore one may eat at all times all food, wherefrom one learns that the decree about cheese and butter is a Roman swindle.

Another was:

> XXIX. That all who are called clericals sin when they do not protect themselves by marriage after they have become conscious that God has not enabled them to remain chaste.[7]

With this concentration on the social aspects of religion, his theology of church and Eucharist could be expected to be less concerned with the individual's devotional life centred on faith and more concerned with the charity binding the community into one. He defended infant baptism against some of his own friends, who subsequently left him to form a group which accepted baptism of believers only, a second baptism therefore for the majority of people and the origin of what came to be called the Radical Reformation. For him, baptism was the corresponding rite in Christianity to circumcision in the Old Testament, a mark of belonging not only to the church but to civil society as well; baptism was to contribute to the reshaping of society along godly lines. The relationship between church and state was very close: 'the kingdom of Christ is also external'.[8]

The Lord's Supper, a memorial meal

Zwingli's theology of the Eucharist might then be expected to highlight the social bond created by its celebration and this did prove to be the case. But there was another factor affecting his approach to the liturgy, a reductionist one which made him regard the Eucharist simply a commemorative meal. For him, Christ's flesh profited enormously, but as put to death, not as eaten. Christ's flesh was now with the Father in heaven. Various reasons can be given for Zwingli's iconoclastic attitude - to all of liturgical ceremonial, including music. The most fundamental one is perhaps indicated by his preference for the scripture text, John 6:63: 'It is the spirit that gives life, the flesh is of no avail'. This text he saw as support for direct unmediated conferring of grace by the Holy Spirit and for his disparagement of all mediation by external rites. His was a dualistic approach that involved a distrust of material things where the relationship with God was concerned. Images in churches were idols, organs a distraction, singing made it more difficult to attend to the word of God itself.

His first reform of the liturgy might therefore be expected to be very radical but in fact he feared a reaction from those who were 'weaker in the faith'[9] and the rite described in his *De Canone Missae Epicheiresis* (1523), while theologically a fundamental departure from the tradition, was not much changed in externals. Vestments were retained, the language (except for the lessons) was Latin but four new prayers took the place of the official Canon of the mass. As a trained humanist, he considered the Latin of the Roman Missal barbarous, but he also wanted to remove all reference to sacrificial language. The Kyrie, Gloria, Sanctus, Agnus Dei were retained, sung by a choir, who still had the use of the organ for some time after the great clearing out of the churches of all images, altars, and ornaments had been undertaken by a team of craftsmen under the supervision of the city architect in June 1524.[10]

As Luther was finding in the same period in Germany, Zwingli's reform of the mass satisfied neither conservatives nor radicals, and by the following Easter the Council of Zürich decided to abolish the traditional mass and replace it with a communion service in accordance with the theology of the Eucharist Zwingli had been promoting. Zwingli was ready with his new order of service, *Action oder Brauch des Nachtmahls*, and this came into use on Holy Thursday, 1525. Ceremonies were reduced to the barest minimum; it was no longer the mass but the 'Lord's Supper', a fellowship meal with the participants sitting around a table placed in the nave. As it was Holy Thursday, the ceremony was intended to be evocative of the Last Supper. 'The ministers, dressed in simple dark gowns rather than clerical vestments, distributed the loaf of bread and the jug of wine among the worshipers.'11

In the new rite the principal elements were introductory prayers and a sermon, an epistle and gospel, an exhortation to devout communion, the Lord's Prayer, a prayer of 'humble access' and the Narrative of the Institution. As first published, the Gloria was included, to be said antiphonally, but this was omitted from 1529, so that none of the traditional sung elements remained. The organ was removed from the principal church, the *Grossmünster*, in 1527,[12] other smaller instruments having being removed from various churches in the previous three years.[13] (The organ was restored there only in 1874.)

A worthy but dull Christian polity
This rejection of music is in contrast with the attitude of Luther, who introduced hymns sung by the congregation in his German mass of 1526. The history of Protestant hymnals begins in fact with the *Achtliederbuch* of the Nuremberg printer Jobst Gutknecht in 1523-4, containing four hymns by Luther himself. Luther and Zwingli both had a good singing voice and each played several instruments.[14] But Zwingli frequently made pejorative remarks about church music.[15] He did approve of simple, monotone, chanting but he made no effort to encourage congregational singing (of the psalms, for example) while Luther wanted 'to see all the arts, especially music, used in the service of him who gave and made them'.[16].

It is obvious that Zwingli's reform was a very radical one – the vandalism of the removal of the organs is a good symbol of it. What remained by way of festival approach to the quotidian, either in worship or social life, seems ambiguous. The Eucharist had become a love feast - as he once apparently described it - in external form, but deprived of the aids to rejoicing as most people would have understood them. Daily life certainly had some of the traditional restrictions removed from it; people could fast if they wished, clergy could marry, all could eat meat any time they liked. But Zwingli's reference to not eating until after the Lord's Supper (actually a morning celebration) hardly amounted to a fast before a feast, as the Eucharistic feast itself seems to have been somewhat meagre. Overall, the godly society which Zwingli promoted may have been one which was worthy but dull.

2. JOHN CALVIN

The Genevan reform programme

John Calvin was a native of Noyon in France, born there in 1509. He came to subscribe to the reform movement during his university studies in Paris, was a refugee from the crackdown by King Francis I on this new movement and in the course of his travels arrived by chance in Geneva in 1536, where the reform had taken hold and was being led by Guillaume Farel. Farel persuaded him to stay, even threatening him with God's condemnation if he refused. Together they implemented a reform programme of a demanding kind in the city, to such a degree of detail that they encountered mounting opposition and were ejected from the city in 1538. Calvin went to Strasbourg where the reform was in train under the leadership of Martin Bucer, a former Dominican, and was soon leader of a French speaking congregation there. Discipline in Geneva deteriorated so much that the city authorities recalled Calvin in 1541 and he remained there until his death in 1564, having become over the years its dominant figure, though (as a Frenchman) he was only given citizen status in 1558.

Geneva under his leadership from 1541 was the most prominent of the reformed cities of Switzerland, because of his oversight of its progress and his clear setting out of the Swiss version of the new theology. It became a more thoroughly theocratic state than Zwingli's Zürich, and always had problems enforcing the reformed regime. While the reform was meant to be about freeing people from what was considered the repressive papal regime, the people of Geneva found themselves under greater control than before. Geneva differed in significant ways from what developed under Luther's leadership in Germany, while retaining the basic theology of justification by faith.

German and Swiss cultural differences

In the first place, the Germans differed as a people from the Swiss. Authority in Germany was in the hands of princes of various standards of theological awareness, religious practice and cultural refinement, along with differing degrees of administrative ability. The cities of Switzerland had a tradition of commerce that required consistent attention to detail as well as the avoidance of the kind of conflicts that nobles and knights in Germany engaged in for the enriching or expanding of their territories – the Swiss hired mercenary armies when their interests required it.

The two leaders are usually perceived as rather contrasting personalities, with Luther regarded as one who delighted in the good things of life, food, music, laughter, family life, while Calvin is pictured as one who succeeded in foisting his austere view of life on a whole city. An early and hostile biographer, Jerome Bolsec, created that enduring picture of him, based, however on unsubstantiated oral reports. 'Nevertheless, it is probably fair to suggest that Calvin was not a particularly attractive person, lacking the wit, humour and warmth which made Luther so entertaining at dinner parties', according to a present-day Reformation scholar.[17]

The perceived contrast, however, is due in great part to the fact that Luther made a great deal known about himself in his writings and correspondence and because his family life in Wittenberg was chronicled by others, while Calvin was a much more private person. While he was in exile in Strasbourg, he married Idelette de Bure, a widow, in 1540. They had one child, a boy who died in infancy. On returning to Geneva in 1541 he began to consolidate his position with a council of ministers to back him. Idelette died in 1549, leaving him with little to concern him except his task as leader of the reform movement in Geneva. The sad fact seems to be that by nature, as he said himself, he was more inclined to a quiet life of scholarship than to public ministry, and in a way typical of such a personality he compensated for his feelings of inadequacy by excessive activity. 'Calvin was ...a driven man, driven by external demands, but above all by powerful impulses within himself.'[18]

Austerity and the Christian life

Asceticism is understood as self-chosen, austerity not necessarily so. By the late 1540s, Calvin and his ministers along with a reform minded municipal council, the *Petit Conseil,* controlled, or tried to, all aspects of life in the city. There was an attempt by the council in 1546 to deal with carousing and brawling by closing the hostelries and replacing them with five 'abbayes',

> each under the supervision of a senior magistrate, where strict regulations governing drunkenness, licentious singing, blasphemy, and (of course) treasonous talk were intended to ensure a godliness of conversation. Bibles were to be provided (at the expense of mine host, for the Genevan authorities had little money to disburse on godly ventures) in case pious conversation should flag. The experiment lasted two months.[19]

Though public dancing was forbidden, it appears that music and dancing went on in private in some homes.[20]

It can be a surprise, then, to read how positive a view Calvin took of the good things of creation: God has given human beings 'a superabundance of good things, in our drinking, and in our eating and in everything'. That comment was in the course of a sermon on I Cor 10, referencing v.26 that the earth and everything in it belongs to the Lord.[21] In his *Institutes of the Christian Religion* (Book III, Chapter X), he gave detailed consideration to how the good things of this life are to be enjoyed, basing it on the principle that the use of God's gifts is not wrongly directed when it is referred to that end to which the Author himself created and destined them for us, since he created them for our good, not for our ruin. ... Now if we ponder to what end God created food, we will find that he meant not only to provide for necessity but also for delight and good cheer.[22]

In addition to food, he considered also other aspects of the good things of life in a succinct articulation of his aesthetics:

Has the Lord clothed the flowers with the great beauty that greets our eyes, the sweetness of smell that is wafted upon our nostrils, and yet will it be unlawful for our eyes to be affected by the beauty, or our sense of smell by the sweetness of that odour? ... Did he not, in short, render many things attractive to us, apart from their necessary use? [23]

He also entered a caveat: 'But, no less diligently, we must resist the lust of the flesh, which, unless it is kept in order, overflows without measure',[24] and he quoted I Cor 7:29-31 in support of his assertion that those who use this world should be so affected, as if they did not use it. He believed, also, that Protestants fasted too little.[25]

In another part of the Institutes (Book III, Chapter XIX) he discussed Christian freedom, as Luther had done. It is perversely interpreted by those who use it as an excuse for extravagant living, for ostentatious banquets.

We have never been forbidden to laugh, or to be filled, or to join new possessions to old ancestral ones, or to delight in musical harmony, or to drink wine. True indeed, but where there is plenty, to wallow in delights, to gorge oneself, to intoxicate mind and heart with present pleasures and be always panting after new ones – such are very far removed from a lawful use of God's gifts.[26]

178

Here he differs little from what St Benedict said a thousand years earlier in his Rule: 'the monk should never be overtaken by surfeiting' (RB 39).

Given the well-argued but rather qualified approach Calvin had to aesthetics and celebration, it is no surprise that his ideas on worship and the liturgical regime he introduced in 1541are likewise hedged around with restrictive comments. As pastor of the French speaking church in Strasbourg during his exile, he had experienced the singing of psalms by the congregation in metrical form. This led him in 1539 to publish a collection of French translations of psalms made by a French poet, Marot, and by himself, and set to tunes in use by the German speaking church in the city. This was the first step towards what was to become the well-known Genevan Psalter which was published in Paris, because Calvin objected to the harmonisations Louis Bourgeois wanted to include in it.[27] Calvin wished the people to sing only an unadorned melody line.

Communion by the power of the Spirit

With this accent on psalmody as a principal form of worship, Calvin then had the task of incorporating sacramental worship, which he dealt with in his *La forme des prières et chants ecclésiastiques* [28] (1542). Unlike Luther, he did not adapt the existing rite of the mass to take account of his theology, which in fact differed from Luther's on the crucial issue of how the believer came into contact with the body and blood of Christ. For Calvin, as for Luther, the Word was the central reality in the celebration of the liturgy. He did not use the concept of the Eucharist as the expression of Christ's last will and testament, as Luther had, but concentrated on the action of the Holy Spirit, which correlated Word and sacrament to produce the union of the believer with Christ. And he emphasised that this work of the Spirit was a great mystery:

> Now if anyone should ask me how this (presence and union) takes place, I shall not be ashamed to confess that it is a secret too lofty for my mind to comprehend or my words to declare. And, to speak more clearly, I rather experience than understand it.[29]

His teaching on the Eucharist was articulated in the context of a double controversy, one with the Lutherans (after Luther's death) and another with Zwingli's followers (after his death). For him, the Lutheran position – the presence of Christ, body and blood in the Eucharist with the bread and wine - was grossly physical or 'carnal', and did not reflect the reality that Christ's body was spatially distant, in heaven. He argued steadfastly against the Lutherans, that since Christ's human flesh was real, it must conform to the condition of flesh: 'it must subsist in one definite place, with its own size and form'.[30]

On the other hand, he was sharply critical of the Zwinglian position that since Christ was bodily in heaven, the Eucharist was simply a memorial meal, the 'body of Christ' being therefore simply the body of believers. The subtleties of Calvin's theology of the Eucharist are considerable, and often puzzling, but it is important to note not only that he considered the union with Christ a mystery but, following John Chrysostom, held from early in his career that 'the efficacy of his Spirit is limited by no bounds, but is able really to unite and bring together into one things that are disjointed in local space'[31]

The celebration of the Eucharist began with penitential prayer, followed by the singing of 'a psalm', unaccompanied. Prayers and readings, a sermon, intercessions, an exhortation, followed and then the recitation of the Institution Narrative, as the fundamental proclamation of the Word. Then came the distribution of the bread and wine, while again a psalm was sung. A prayer of thanksgiving and a blessing concluded the service. The rites for baptism and for ordination made no mention of singing and are notable for a stated wish to avoid all superfluous ceremony, so that even the imposition of hands in ordination could be omitted because of the danger of superstition.

Even more than Luther's rite, Calvin's Eucharist took a very simple form. As much as in Luther's case, bread and wine were signs that had to be consumed by the communicant in order that union (substantial union, as he put it) with the body and blood Christ should take place. 'The mystery perishes... unless true bread represents the true body of

180

Christ.'[32] But his insistence on true bread and on Christ being bodily in heaven along with his solution to union with him being through the power of the Spirit to unite things separated in space, raise the question of how can people gathered around a table really satisfy the conditions for a true Eucharist.

In his arguments against transubstantiation and Luther's position of ubiquitous presence (usually called consubstantiation) he says simply: 'they do not understand the manner of descent by which he lifts us up to himself'.[33] He could have added that this descent-ascent indicates the transcendence of space-time involved in the encounter. It is of interest that a twentieth-century theologian, Thomas Torrance, in his *Space, Time and Incarnation*, presented Luther's position on the Eucharist as implying a container notion of space, derived from Aristotle, and Calvin's (now the Calvinist one) as relational, following Plato and the early Fathers.[34]

Calvin regulated church life in detail and did find a place for music in it, in accordance with his well thought out views expressed in the *Institutes*. For him, public prayer and singing, unless they sprang from deep feeling of the heart, had no value or profit with God.

> We do not here condemn speaking and singing but rather strongly commend them, provided they are associated with the heart's affection. ... Moreover, since the glory of God ought, in a measure, to shine in the several parts of our bodies, it is especially fitting that the tongue has been assigned and destined for this task, both through singing and through speaking. For it was peculiarly created to tell and proclaim the praise of God.[35]

On the other hand, 'such songs as have been composed only for sweetness and delight of the ear are unbecoming to the majesty of the church and cannot but displease God in the highest degree.'[36] It could be said that there is here as much a distrust of beauty as there is a defence of sobriety, but the effect of Calvin's attitude and strict regulation of music in the Genevan liturgy was the creation of a unique 'sacred style' and the relegation to the secular sphere of all art music. The dominant feature of Geneva's life of worship, however, was the daily sermon in the early morning, lasting 'the best part of an hour' and with no congregational singing.[37]

Conclusion

Given the complexity, or even ambiguities, of Calvin's thinking on aesthetics and the doctrinal issue of the Eucharist, the issue of how his liturgy in general could have a festive quality and how the celebration of the Eucharist – certainly not to be considered a sacrifice – could be regarded as a meal needs careful consideration. He excluded harmony, but nonetheless created a sacred style of chant and the point of it all was that he wanted worship to be purified of what he considered unworthy elements, something Luther had never bothered about as he composed Christmas songs for children. Those who were likeminded could and did find his way of worshipping attractive and it did give rise to a whole tradition which those who belonged to it must have found in some sense festive, but it could hardly have had the appeal that has been associated with Lutheran worship.

As indicated above, the Eucharist did have the form of a meal and was marked by Calvin's insistence that its purpose was to be an expression of the unity of the community. Hence the careful examination of people who proposed to attend the monthly communion, to ensure that they were worthy. (He had failed to convince the *Petit Conseil* of the appropriateness of a weekly celebration.) There was no mention of fasting beforehand but the event was characterised by sobriety. It was liable to give rise to tensions in the city as some were excluded despite their protests. It could not have been an 'ostentatious banquet', but whether the participants shared Calvin's sense of what was appropriate for a celebration and were always happy with it in a city where life was strictly supervised, cannot be known. There was, in fact, an official occasion for banqueting, ironically perhaps, after the annual meeting of the council of ministers for the purpose of confession of faults. There was one such event as Calvin was in his last illness, and he insisted on it being held in his house, though he was too ill to attend.

Calvin devoted five sections of Book IV, Chapter xii of the *Institutes* to the subject of fasting, describing its purpose, its links with prayer and with the practice of penance. Luther had never dealt with the issue in detail in the first generation of the reform movement, but Calvin, who began his reforming career in the last decade of Luther's life, was by nature a methodical thinker. He dealt with fasting in the context of the need which arose when issues had to be decided or difficulties faced. Pastors were 'to urge the people to fasting and public prayers'. Many, he felt, did not understand how useful fasting was, or thought it unnecessary or rejected it. It was, however, both holy and lawful:

> Holy and lawful fasting has three objectives We use it either to weaken and subdue the flesh that it may not act wantonly, or that we may be better prepared for prayers and holy meditations, or that it may be a testimony of our self-abasement before God when we wish to confess our guilt before him.[38]

The final section defines what fasting is:

> Throughout its course, the life of the godly indeed ought to be tempered with sobriety and frugality, so that as far as possible it bears some resemblance to a fast. But, in addition, there is another sort of fasting, temporary in character, when we withdraw something from the normal regimen of living, either for one day or for a definite time, and pledge ourselves to a tighter and more severe restraint in diet than ordinarily. This consists in three things: in time, in quality of foods, and in smallness of quantity. …. Quality consists in that all elegance be absent, and that, content with common or baser foods, we should not whet our palate with delicacies. The rule of quantity in this is that we should eat more sparingly and lightly than is our custom; only for need, not for pleasure.[39]

183

In the following sections of the chapter, he discusses the history of fasting, referring to 'the superstitious observance of Lent (which) had prevailed everywhere'. It would be much more satisfactory if fasting were not observed at all, than diligently observed and at the same time corrupted with false and pernicious opinions. He picks out for particular condemnation the rules concerning meat, noting the tendency to substitute other dainties for it. For such people, 'the ultimate impiety, scarcely to be expiated by death, is for anyone to taste the slightest bit of bacon fat or rancid meat with dark bread'.[40]

It is interesting that much of what he says echoes the dialogue between the fishmonger and butcher in Erasmus' *On the Eating of Fish,* but it is not known if he ever read it. He had been a student in the Collège de Montaigu in Paris a generation after Erasmus and absorbed much of the humanist tradition, but after his conversion to the reform movement he had condemned humanists in general. He has been described as 'the heir of Erasmus, far more than is generally admitted',[41] or than he himself would admit.

ENDNOTES

1   Carlos Eire, *Reformations. The Early Modern World, 1450-1650* (New Haven: Yale University Press, 2016) 217

2   *Martin Luther's Basic Theological Writings,* Timothy Lull ed. (Minneapolis: Fortress Press, 1989) 400; *Weimar Ausgabe* XXVI, 342

3   *Documents Illustrative of the Continental Reformation,* B. J. Kidd, ed. (Oxford: Clarendon Press, 1911) 391

4   Cf. Fintan Lyons O.S.B., *Martin Luther. His Challenge Then and Now* (Dublin: Columba Press, 2017) 21

5   W. P. Stephens, *Zwingli: An Introduction to his Thought* (Oxford: Clarendon Press, 1992) 24

6   Bernard Reardon, *Religious Thought in the Reformation* (London: Longman 1981) 94

7   *Selected Works of Huldreich Zwingli (1484-1531. The Reformer of Switzerland,* Edited and Introduction by S. M. Jackson (Philadelphia: University of Pennsylvania, 1901) 113-4

8   Cited in Timothy George, *The Theology of the Reformers* (Nashville: Broadman and Holman, 1988) 111

9   R. C. D. Jasper, and Cuming, G. J., *Prayers of the Eucharist: Early and Reformed* (Collegeville: Liturgical Press 1987) 181

10 Bernard Reardon, *Religious Thought in the Reformation,* 95

11 Timothy George, *The Theology of the Reformers,* 158

12 Ulrich Gäbler, *Huldrych Zwingli. His Life and Work,* Ruth Gritsch trans. (Edinburgh: T.&T. Clark 1986) 107

13 Timothy George, *The Theology of the Reformers,*131

14 Roland Bainton, *Here I Stand. Martin Luther* (Oxford: Lion Books 1978) 340; Jean Rilliet, *Zwingli. Third Man of the Reformation,* H. Knight trans. (London: Lutterworth Press 1964) 25.

15 In the Second Dispute (about reform) at Zürich, 27 October 1523, he said: 'Since chant and vestments both distract us from true prayer, that is, the raising of the mind to God, they are to be removed, in the right way and at the right time'. B. J. Kidd, *op. cit.,* 436 (my translation)

16 Luther in his 'Preface to the Wittenberg Hymnal' in *Luther's Works,* Vol. 53, Ulrich Leupold ed. (Philadelphia: Fortress Press 1965) 316

17 Alister McGrath, *A Life of John Calvin. A Study in the Shaping of Western Culture* (Oxford: Blackwell, 1990) 17

18 William J. Bouwsma, *John Calvin. A Sixteenth Century Portrait* (New York: O.U.P., 1988) 29

19 Harro Höpfl, *The Christian Polity of John Calvin* (Cambridge: C.U.P., 1982) 201

20 Robert M. Kingdon, *Adultery and Divorce in Calvin's Geneva* (Cambridge, Mass.: Harvard University Press, 1995) 100-1

21 *Sermon on I Cor 10,* in *Joannis Calvini opera quae supersunt omnia,* Vol. XLIX (Brunsvigae: C.A. Schwetschke, 1892) 478

22 John Calvin. *Institutes of the Christian Religion,* Vol. 2, Ford L. Battles trans. (Philadelphia: Westminster Press, 1960) III.x.2

23 Idem.

24 Ibid., IV.xii.3

25 John Calvin, *Commentary on Matthew 4:1* in *A Harmony of the Gospels. Matthew, Mark and Luke,* Vol. I, A. W. Morrison trans. (Edinburgh: St Andrew's Press,1972) 133

26 *Institutes,* III.xix.9

27 Frank Senn, *Christian Liturgy. Catholic and Evangelical* (Minneapolis: Fortress Press 1997) 368.

28 The full title was: *Forme des prières et chants ecclésiastiques., avec la manière d'administrer les sacrements et consacrer le mariage selon la coutume de l'Église ancienne.*

29 *Institutes,* IV.xvii.32

30 Ibid., IV.xvii.24

31 John Calvin, *Confession of Faith Concerning the Eucharist (1537),* in *Calvin Theological Treatises,* J.K.L. Reid ed. (Philadelphia: Westminster Press, 1964) 168

32 *Institutes,* IV.xvii.14

33 Ibid., IV.xvii.16

34 Thomas F. Torrance. *Space, Time and Incarnation* (Edinburgh: T & T Clark, 1969) 31ff

35 *Institutes*, III.xx.31

36 Ibid., III.xx.32

37 T.H.L. Parker, *John Calvin* (Berkhamsted: Lion Publishing 1975) 109

38 *Institutes,* IV.xii.15

39 Ibid., IV.xii.18

40 Ibid., IV.xii.21

41 Hugh Trevor-Roper, *Religion, Reformation and Social Change* (London: Macmillan, 1967) 26, cited in William J. Bouwsma, *John Calvin. A Sixteenth Century Portrait,* 239

CHAPTER ELEVEN

Leo X and the Italian *Rinascimento*

Rome possessed in the unique court of Leo X a society to which the history of the world offers no parallel.[1]

Italy's unique situation

To include Italy in a survey of the connections between daily life, religious and other festivities and the intrinsically ascetic demands of the Christian faith, is to consider a unique scenario. This is true of any historical period but especially of the sixteenth-century. Elsewhere, there were cities and city-states where the Reformation had introduced new religious freedom, though it was restricted in practice by their theocratic constitutions. In comparison, the Italian situation was complicated by a unique entanglement of church and state. In other countries abuses were identified and reformers set about remedying them. In Italy, abuses were well known and reformers of one kind or another, such as popes and religious, addressed them, but there were always complications. A pope wanted to put an end to trading in benefices, but had to confer a cardinal's hat on family members, because this was the only way he could function; the power that cardinals from other noble families had could be used against him if he lacked support from those of his own. 'In such circumstances, the promotion of a kinsman to the cardinalate might be the only way to ensure colleagues and collaborators who could be relied on.'[2]

However ill-matched, but tenuously held together the daily and the festive and the ascetic aspects of life might be in Papal Italy, the place of religion at the centre could not be questioned. If imperial Rome had been the *umbilicus mundi,* Rome was now the centre of the Christian faith. Because of this, it has to be realised how great a threat the reform movements in Germany and Switzerland constituted for the culture of Italy and for the popes who were protégés of Renaissance families. It was in Italy that Renaissance humanism began – and so the name should properly be *Rinascimento* – and the form it took was such that a distinction has to be made between southern humanism and the northern more monochrome variety of which the literary, satirical Erasmus was the father figure. The 'human' was somehow more full of life in the Italian sunshine. The art of Luther's friend Cranach lacked the vibrant colour of Raphael's rooms in the papal palace, though the contrast between south and north would grow less in succeeding centuries. In so many expressions of their culture, Italians could embrace tragedy and entertainment, splendid liturgy and rumbustious processions, feasting and fasting, with apparent aplomb. Italian cuisine was a real life expression of the psalmist's reference to 'wine to cheer man's heart; oil, to make his face shine and bread to strengthen man's heart'. (Ps104:15)

Italy in general, and Rome, Florence, Milan and Venice in particular, promoted artistic liberty in art and music in a way that fitted in rather easily with long established and perhaps questionable Catholic traditions, ones which northern humanism considered abuses. The patronage of the arts by ecclesiastics and popes saw a flowering of artistic treasures and depended very much on the money which the sale of benefices provided. This could be in the form of granting bishoprics on payment of considerable sums, a one-off gain for the pope, but when it was in the form of selling curial offices, it was in effect taking out a mortgage because the income from that office (the granting of dispensations) went to the office holder and not to the papal treasury. When, therefore, the calls for reform began to reach the church at Rome, much compromise had to be found. The popes who could be considered Renaissance men - most of those in the sixteenth-century - had to live with the tensions that such a programme would entail. The love of the finer things in life, especially in the case of Leo X (r1513-1521), could lead to a chronic shortage of money and a scrambling around for ways to replenish a fast diminishing treasury.

Popes Alexander VI and Julius II

Leo's recent predecessors included two notorious popes, one more so than the other, Alexander VI, Rodrigo Borgia, elected in 1492 and Julius II in 1503. Being Spanish, Borgia was opposed as much as possible by the great Roman families. To protect his position he devoted his attention to the aggrandisement of his family, especially his even more notorious son, Caesare, by conferring lordship of the Papal States on them. Most of his reign was taken up with intermittent campaigns against, and conciliatory agreements with, Charles VIII of France, whom the reform minded believed to be a true Christian who could rid them of a pope they considered a non-believer. In one of the periods of peace between the two rulers, the pope said mass in St Peter's in January 1495 and Charles handed him the holy water.

It seems that whatever conflicts, conspiracies and treacheries were rending the fabric of the Christian community, liturgical practice remained untouched; the anniversary of Alexander's election was duly commemorated annually by mass and festive celebrations throughout the city. Unfortunately, no information survives about how Lent was observed, but it has been claimed that there was a contrast between his generally debauched lifestyle and the diet 'spartan and coarse (a good many sardines) which he himself preferred and imposed on his household'.[3] He was of course Spanish and his preference for fish was at odds with the Roman more sophisticated love of food.

Poisoning was in fashion against enemies at the time and Alexander, who used the technique when appropriate, himself succumbed to it in 1503. He and his son, Caesare, had been invited for a meal by Cardinal Castelli and this presented an opportunity for them to rid themselves of a Roman opponent. However, something went wrong; the guests accidentally tasted a sweetmeat to which their poisonous powder had been added, but did not suffer any immediate aftereffects,[4] while Castelli suffered a violent but passing stomach disorder. After a few days, however, they both suffered a fever which was wrongly diagnosed as the not uncommon quartan fever, but in fact was the result of arsenic poisoning.

The younger man survived, but Alexander's condition deteriorated; he was given a drink of powdered and roasted emeralds and treated by regular bleeding over a few days. This in addition to the arsenic was more than enough to finish him off. The usual proprieties were observed: he made his confession, mass was said and he received Communion. Thus ended the life of a man whose career had begun with his receiving the abbacy of the ancient Benedictine monastery of Subiaco from Sixtus IV,[5] but who seems to have been untouched by the most basic moral demands of the faith. The extraordinary thing about his life and that of many of his contemporaries is that the rites of the church were an unquestioned part of their inheritance. By this time, the Sistine choir was employed to add beauty to the liturgy. He may even have had a sense of satisfaction at the beauty they added to the liturgy, but whether this meant a sense of belonging to the church and in a way that accepted its discipline is more than doubtful.

It was a time when the canonical requirements for membership were faith, the sacraments and acceptance of the hierarchical authority. Faith, however, was thought of in terms of intellectual adscription to the creed, the sacraments were conferred in rites which were considered objectively effective, even in the case of defective faith on the part of the recipients, and Alexander was himself the supreme hierarchical authority. He was not the only one whose belonging to the church meant little more than being part of the culture of the time. The threat to the continuance of this situation would soon appear in Germany and Switzerland.

He was followed by Julius II (1503-13), who had benefited from the largesse of his uncle Sixtus IV in the form of multiples benefices and had fathered three children by the time of his election. Nonetheless, he could be regarded as a saviour of the papacy as it was understood at the time, because he set out to regain by military means the territories his predecessors had bestowed on their relatives or simply frittered away in reckless financial gambles. Erasmus described him as 'warlike' [6] and his contemporaries used the term *papa terribile*. It is thought that he took the name Julius in memory of Julius Caesar.

There are more references to money spent on a suit of armour of silver for his military campaigns than to expenditure on silver plate for his table or sacred vessels for the altar. He was, however, in the true Renaissance tradition a patron of the arts, though dismissive in his assessment of his own cultural attainment. When Michelangelo asked whether he wanted a book or a sword in the left hand of a statue marking his re-capture of Bologna – the right hand was raised either in blessing or threat – Julius said: 'Give me a sword. I don't hold with all this scribbling. I'm no scholastic'.[7] His patronage of the arts did show itself in his choice of Raphael to decorate his apartments when he moved upstairs in the papal palace to get away from the lavishly decorated apartment of his hated predecessor, Alexander VI.

He did feel the pressure of the religious reform movement coming from the north, and convoked the Fifth Lateran Council in 1512, the year before he died, but he tended to identify reform as coming also from politically motivated French cardinals and saw it therefore as including a threat to his own position. The Council continued to sit until 1517 and issued decrees meant to reform the religious orders and even the cardinals' lifestyle, but they were ignored by his successor, Leo X (r1513-21), and by everyone else.

Pope Leo X

As will be seen, Pope Leo X, Giovanni de' Medici, could not claim to contribute much to a religious revival in Rome. He was born in 1475, the middle son of the *de facto* ruler of the Republic of Florence Lorenzo the Magnificent (1449-1492), a despot and yet a devout Christian by the norms of the time. Lorenzo considered him clever and set out to create an ecclesiastical career for him, utilising the banking empire's branch in Lyons, France to acquire various benefices for him while still a boy.

> Having received the tonsure at the age of eight, he was presented with the Abbey of Fontdouce by the king of France, who would also have made him archbishop of Aix in Provence had it not been discovered just in time that the present Archbishop was still alive.

To compensate him for this disappointment, Giovanni was given the priory of Saint-Gemme near Chartres, made a canon of every cathedral in Tuscany and presented with the abbeys of Passignano and Monte Cassino…[8]

Lorenzo persuaded Pope Innocent VIII to make him a cardinal at the age of sixteen – this was achieved by arranging the marriage of his daughter to the pope's son. Lorenzo worried about what might befall Giovanni on going to Rome and wrote him a letter saying he had been much comforted by seeing that of his own accord Giovanni had often gone to confession and to Holy Communion, but that in going to live in Rome, 'which is a sink of iniquity, you will find it hard to follow this advice'. He also advised that his food should be plain, that he take sufficient exercise and, most importantly, that he should rise early.[9] Things took an unfortunate turn after Lorenzo's death in 1492; his son Piero (whom Lorenzo had considered foolish) came to power in Florence. He entered into unwise political alliances, which alienated the people of Florence and led to the banishing of the family, including Cardinal Giovanni who was still residing in Florence, from the city in 1494. It was a time when Savonarola was preaching in Florence against Alexander VI.

Girolamo Savonarola (1452-98), the Dominican Prior in Florence and scourge of the popes in his preaching, railed against the abuses of the regime of Alexander, whom he regarded as 'no pope',[10] but papal power both religious and temporal could be used against him and he failed to realise that his appeal to another secular power, France, only complicated relations with his fellow citizens. Excommunication and threats against Florentine merchants in Rome were enough to turn Florence against him and bring about his torture and execution in 1498 after an obliging ecclesiastical court had declared him a heretic.[11]

Giovanni went to Rome and became part of Alexander's court. Hearing that Florence had put a price on his head, he got permission from Alexander to travel abroad but within a year was back in Rome – feeling safe as Alexander had quarrelled with Florence. He now had meagre re-

Portrait of Pope Leo X and his cousins, cardinals Giulio de' Medici and
Luigi de' Rossi. Raphael. Between 1518 and 1519.

sources but did not follow his father's advice. Instead he played the part
of lavish host and was frequently in debt, a sign of things to come.

> His guests became used to the constant disappearance and reap-
> pearance of his most valuable piece of silver, which made their way
> between his dining-room and the shops of the Roman pawnbro-
> kers…. He spent long evenings at the dining-table, long mornings
> discussing the several arts in which he took a lively interest and
> long afternoons hunting and hawking in the Campagna – explain-
> ing that such exercise, incongruous though it might be for a cardi-
> nal, was a necessary duty for one so corpulent…[12]

This, in remarkable detail, was to be the pattern of his papacy also. But before that, he would be involved in the final military campaign of Pope Julius II in 1512, be captured, but escape in time to be put in charge of the pope's plan to re-instate the Medici in Florence. He was in Florence when Julius died and had to make his way to Rome with haste for the Consistory to elect a successor. He arrived in Rome in early March 1513, too late for the opening of the Consistory. Exhausted from the journey, he was too weak to get out of bed for several days. Meanwhile the cardinals deliberated, but could reach no conclusion, so the Camerlengo, who managed affairs during the interregnum, reduced the daily meal to a single unappetising dish to encourage their collaboration for a decision. To forestall any financial bargaining among them, the meal was served on earthenware dishes, as mysterious numbers had been found scratched into the silverware ones.[13] Surprisingly, as he was only thirty-eight, Giovanni was chosen, but this was in part due to the support of the younger cardinals. 'He had held a prominent position under Julius II ...to say nothing of his personal qualities, his love of peace, his generosity, and his blameless morals.'[14] The fact that his health was not good was something of an advantage, as if his regime proved unpopular it might in any case be of short duration, as turned out to be the case. Before he could be crowned with the triple tiara, he had to be ordained a priest, as he had been a deacon up to that point. He was consecrated a bishop (as the theology of the time would have it) two days later and formally crowned and enthroned on March 19th, 1513. The diary of the Master of Ceremonies recorded how he lit a bunch of tow attached to a rod and addressed the pope: 'Thus passes the glory of the world'.[15] How Leo reacted he did not say, but the response may have been one of amusement on the part of a man who revelled in theatricality.

The *Sacro Possesso*
A detailed account exists in a letter [16] to Leo's sister, the Contessa Ridolfi, of the proceedings on April 11th, the feast of Pope St Leo the Great, as he took possession of the basilica and palace of St John Lateran, the pope's

official seat, though the popes had long ago deserted those buildings in favour of St Peter's. Called the *Sacro Possesso,* it took the form of a procession from one to the other, and between going there and the return in the evening it took the whole day. Preparations took weeks and the cost was enormous; Leo's own expenditure was 100,000 scudi, a quarter of the resources Julius had left after him. But the wealthy merchants and cardinals of the city also spent lavishly.

> Triumphal arches, many of them real works of art in themselves and the invention of the leading painters and architects in Rome, had been erected to span the streets at various points, for the wealthy merchants, headed by the famous Sienese banker, Agostino Chigi, were all vying to attract the notice and win the praise of their new ruler.[17]

In addition to these expensive structures, the streets were strewn with sprigs of box and myrtle, the doorways festooned with wreaths, and the populace was in festal attire. Some of the public fountains were made to run with wine instead of water. In the procession itself, there were men-at-arms - households of prelates of the court and cardinals, all richly clad in scarlet. These were followed in ascending order of importance by standard bearers of the various zones of Rome, then horsemen with papal ensigns, milk-white mules from the papal stables, one hundred equerries of the court, all of noble birth and clad in gala robes of red fringed with ermine, the rearmost bearing papal crowns and jewelled mitres. These were succeeded by a hundred Roman barons, each followed by an armed escort of servants dressed in their master's livery. Then there were representatives from Florence, ambassadors of foreign countries and the retinue of the late pope's nephew, the Duke of Urbino, these latter decorously apparelled in sable fur of deep mourning. (The Duke would have additional reason to mourn within a short time, as will be seen.) The turn of the clergy then came, escorted by sacristans and pages in crimson velvet, to lead the docile palfrey bearing the Blessed Sacrament, above which was held a canopy of cloth of gold; it was accompanied by twenty-five torchbearers. Bishops and abbots came next and after them the cardinals, each astride a steed with trailing white covering and each surrounded by eight chamberlains. They were followed by two hundred members of Julius' Swiss Guards and lastly the pontiff himself, mounted on his white Arab stallion. Above him was held a canopy of embroidered silk to shield him from the sun. His appearance did not make a good impression.

> As he rode in procession sitting side-saddle on a white Arab horse, it was noticed how his face, almost purple with the heat, ran with sweat despite the canopy of embroidered silk which was held over his head by eight Romans of distinguished birth. It was noticed too how corpulent he was, how vast his paunch, how fleshy his short neck, how fat the rolls beneath his chin, how bulging his weak eyes.[18]

In fact, his sight was quite poor and he regularly used a small telescopic device, a 'spy-glass', with which he viewed the inscriptions on the triumphal arches and surveyed the crowds on either side, while taking delight in seeing his officials throwing large amounts of coins to them. There was good reason for his riding side-saddle, as he suffered from an anal fistula which had been operated upon just before he had entered the conclave some weeks previously. The *Sacro Possesso* was a physical trial for him, but relief came when it reached St John Lateran, where he was helped to dismount and enter to take possession of his episcopal seat.

> After the due performance of the rites incidental to *Sacro Possesso*, there followed a banquet in the great hall of the palace, served with all the ostentatious luxury of which the Italian renaissance was capable. The meal ended, the glittering train prepared to start homewards in the glowing atmosphere of an April sunset.[19]

The letter to Leo's sister does not give details of the banquet – her correspondent probably did not have access to it – but, more importantly, says nothing about how the Blessed Sacrament was treated during the intermission. At that point it was probably retained in the Basilica of St John Lateran, rather than being included in the return journey, but its inclusion in the procession at all, in some kind of shrine – admittedly canopied - set on a horse's back and going ahead of the principal participant, gives the impression of it being something of a talisman included to bring good fortune.

Medici ambitions

Leo's personal appearance (recorded for posterity by Raphael's celebrated portrait) was not attractive, but in daily life his amiable expression, his obvious contentment, his pleasant tone of voice and elegant manner of speaking, all endeared him to the members of his court, concealing from them his determined ambition to make the House of Medici once more dominant in Italian politics and his own family in key positions. His plans for the family were progressing. In September of that first year, he suggested to the compliant authorities of the city of Rome that his younger brother, Giuliano, might be made a Roman Patrician, and this was done in a lavish ceremony on the Capitol, with endless addresses of welcome to this Medici prince from every public body in Rome and concluding with a banquet which lasted six hours.

He met and made an agreement with the new king of France, Francis I, at Bologna in December, 1515, giving Francis the right to appoint bishops in France, but in return there would be no French opposition to his plan to remove Francesco, Duke of the della Rovere family, from the lordship of Urbino, which he had held on behalf of the papacy. This was now conferred on Lorenzo, the pope's nephew, in August 1516, the first definite step towards creating a Central Italian state to form the nucleus of a Medici empire.[20] It would have unfortunate consequences for his papacy. Cardinal Riario never forgave him for driving his della Rovere kinsman from Urbino, nor did Cardinal Petrucci forget how Leo had helped to remove his brother from the government of Siena, all of this as part of the promotion of Medici interests.

Though he had emerged as the favourite in 1513 at the Conclave, by 1517 opposition began to coalesce among members of the court. Cardinal Petrucci, 'the handsome, arrogant, dissolute twenty-two year old',[21] spoke openly against him. Plans to dispose of Leo were discussed; at first the easiest way seemed to be for an assassin to stab him while he was out hunting, but then a more subtle plan was devised. Petrucci had access to a quack doctor who could be introduced to Leo as someone able to relieve his painful fistula. He would then apply a poisoned bandage, while Petrucci departed to discuss the hoped for consequences with the deposed Duke of Urbino. Through the indiscretion of a page, the plot was discovered, and the quack, Petrucci's secretary and a Sienese friend who had also conspired were handed over to the papal rack-master. Within three days, Leo laid a trap by calling a consistory of the cardinals with some of the Swiss Guard in attendance - an unusual arrangement. As soon as Cardinal Riario entered, Leo left the chamber and the door was locked. Riario was kept under guard in the Vatican. Another Consistory was held a few days later at which two cardinals confessed to conspiracy under pressure from Leo and were fined twenty-five thousand ducats - which helped to pay some of his debts. Riario was relieved of an even greater sum. Petrucci was given a safe conduct to return to Rome to discuss certain matters with the pope and took the risk, only to be arrested and executed by the pope's Muslim hangman. His secretary and the quack doctor suffered a worse fate, being dragged by horses through the streets, mutilated and hanged on the parapet of the bridge at Castel Sant'Angelo. For some time Leo stayed within the palace confines, until the eve of the feast of Saints Peter and Paul, when he went to Vespers accompanied by a cohort of soldiers and with the surrounding streets closed off.[22] The affair ended with his appointing in a single day, July 1st, 1517, thirty-one new cardinals whom he thought he could trust. He also had a bodyguard of soldiers every time he said mass in public.

For the four short years of his life that remained he continued the lifestyle of a Renaissance prince, promoting the arts, entertaining and being entertained and enjoying the hunt. He was determined to make Rome the most cultured city in Europe and 'offered numerous inducements to attract the most accomplished artists, writers and scholars to live there, making freely available to them his extensive library to which he was constantly adding valuable manuscripts'.[23] His patronage of the arts led him to invite Raphael to continue the decoration of the papal apartments he had begun for Julius II. Now, however, in the *Stanza della Segnatura*, the figure of Leo himself appears instead of Julius as had been planned; the confrontation of Attila by Leo the Great becomes an allegory of Leo X confronting the French forces of Louis XII at Ravenna, with Leo mounted on his favourite white steed. (In fact, as Cardinal Medici, he had been captured by the French in that battle in 1512!)

Leo and the arts

The courteous and modest Raphael became part of the court and went on, with his assistants, to decorate the Loggia which bears his name. But during Leo's pontificate, the great Michelangelo and Leonardo da Vinci were noticeably absent from the court. Leo and Michelangelo were almost contemporaries when growing up in Florence, but their personalities were very different and the cheerful Pope Leo found it difficult to cope with the melancholic and abrasive artist who, unlike the gentle Raphael, could hardly accept that an artist was reckoned simply a decorator and held on a lower level of esteem than the scholars and poets in a court where 'Latin epigrams were daily bread'.[24] Leo encouraged him to return to Florence and gave him the commission to design and create a new façade for Brunelleschi's San Lorenzo, the Medici family church, a project in which he was at least nominally engaged until Leo's death.

Leo's love of the theatre was not limited to the classic plays; the first comedy in the Italian language was performed in his court and he also promoted performances of a vulgar kind, thus showing a basically Florentine love for the burlesque. 'Dwarfs, buffoons and jesters were nearly always to be found at his table where guests were encouraged to laugh at their antics and at the cruel jokes which were played upon them.' It seems a perverted sense of humour to find great amusement, as Leo did, in seeing one of his fools devour a pie consisting of carrion, cooked complete with beak and feathers.[25]

Leo and banqueting

In contrast, his dinners were noted for their rare delicacies such as peacocks' tongues - in this he was simply keeping up a tradition that went back to the banquets of imperial Rome.[26] There are ambassadors' reports of dinners given by the rich in Rome, including the cardinals; for example, the Venetian ambassador sent an account of a dinner given by Cardinal Cornaro where there were sixty-five courses, each consisting of three different dishes, all served on the finest of silver plate.[27]

Leo himself was often at these banquets, but health considerations constrained his partaking of the many courses. His hosts, however, could impress him in other ways. Two banquets given by the banker Chigi, the first in the loggia of his Villa Farnesina above the banks of the Tiber, illustrate the point. In 1520, he entertained Leo and some cardinals to dinner there, 'grandly showing off his wealth by having the silver plate from each completed course tossed into the river. (He did not let on that nets were concealed underwater to catch it.)'[28] On another occasion, he gave a banquet for the pope in a new building, a beautifully proportioned hall hung with the finest tapestries. The pope and the distinguished guests were astonished at the splendid hangings and the luxury of the meal, and were amazed to find that every piece of plate in use had already been engraved with the armorial bearings of those invited. (Some of the silverware vanished during the feast – a piece engraved with one's own name could have been a source of temptation – but Chigi gave orders that this was not to be mentioned.)[29]

> At the conclusion of so sumptuous a feast, the Pontiff himself began to congratulate his host on his magnificent chamber, regretting that even the Vatican could show no room equally spacious or richly furnished; whereupon Chigi, who was evidently expecting the expression of some such sentiment, gave the signal to his ser-

vants to unfasten the cords supporting the arras, which immediately fell in a mass to the floor, exhibiting to the astounded pope the empty racks and mangers of the steeds that were shortly to be installed in the vast apartment which had so excited the envious admiration of the splendour-loving Medici – 'Your Holiness, this is not my banqueting hall; it is merely my stable'.[30]

This occurred during the last year of Leo's life, the final year of a pontificate in which his political concerns and his promotion of the Renaissance culture had – along with the good life and hunting – been most prominent. There was little evidence of theological concerns except for his issuing of a Bull, *Pastor aeternus*, in 1516, declaring the supremacy of the papacy over church councils. As early as 1518, his attention had been drawn to the nascent theological challenge represented by the Augustinian friar, Martin Luther from Saxony. How seriously he took it initially is uncertain – the response to Luther was left to the papal theologian, Prierias. Being a Dominican, he might be considered somewhat partisan in his approach to an Augustinian.

Leo and Luther

There is the oft repeated story that Leo on being informed of Luther's *Ninety Five Theses* and their widespread circulation in Germany thought light of it and made two comments: 'It is a drunken German who wrote the Theses; when sober he will change his mind', but subsequently altered his view to: 'Brother Martin is a man of fine genius and this is a mere squabble of envious monks'. The authoritative biographer of Luther, Roland Bainton,[31] considered it unlikely that these were genuine, but they were nevertheless included by the Protestant historian, Philip Schaff in his history of the German Reformation.[32]

For Leo to have described Luther as a fine genius at one point is not beyond the bounds of possibility as in the course of the political manoeuvring in relation to the election of the successor to the Holy Roman Emperor, Maximilian, it suited Leo to try to influence Luther's overlord and protector, the Elector Friedrich, and part of the strategy was to make it known that in return for his vote a cardinal's hat would be on offer to one of his friends. This was in 1519, a year before Leo was forced to take action against Luther.

> In Rome at that time Luther was considered to be the friend of the elector. Out of concern for the papal State and the position of the Medici in Italy, then, the pope behaved as though Luther and his protectors had not been declared heretics.[33] .

Leo's approach would be governed by the need to suppress challenges to his own supreme authority, for religious reasons certainly, but also because on that authority, both religious and secular, depended his ability to protect the interests of the Medici family and by now Luther was describing the institution of the papacy as the Antichrist. It was at the urgings of his own cousin, Cardinal Giulio de' Medici, that he took the challenge of Luther's writings in hand by setting up a commission in February 1520. It sat for months and as the summer heat came on Leo left for his hunting lodge at Magliana,[34] a village now just off the motorway from Rome to Fiumicino Airport, where its findings were presented to him. This led him to issue the Bull of condemnation of Luther's teachings, *Exsurge Domine,* on June 24th 1520. The opening words reflect the environment in which it was produced: 'Arise O Lord, and judge your cause. A wild boar has invaded your vineyard'.

Forty-one of Luther's teachings were condemned. Only one, No. 15, referred to the Eucharist. It was Luther's assertion that only faith makes a person worthy to receive it, not reliance on having confessed and not being conscious of any mortal sin. Such people eat and drink judgement on themselves. This assertion was a consequence of Luther's main doctrine of justification by faith alone and was a judgement on the faith and practice of people like Leo who did in fact remain faithful to the rites of the church, including his personal duties to recite the Divine Office and attend, if not celebrate, daily mass. One of Luther's chief tenets, that the mass was not a sacrifice, was not mentioned, an indication that the commission had not gone about its work competently – to the chagrin of its most qualified theologian, Cardinal Cajetan. This could be a reason why Leo never fully appreciated the threat the religious reform coming from the north would have for the church of which he was the supreme ruler. Nevertheless, he did excommunicate Luther the following January, but it took twenty-five years for the Council of Trent to begin to defend Catholic teaching.

Leo and the hunt

Hunting played a big part in Leo's life, as a cardinal and as pope. His first biographer, Bishop Giovio of Nocera (in 1549), told how he would live in a palace near Ostia for months, neglecting his duties, becoming frustrated when the hunt went badly and showing munificence to all suitors when it went well – a comment which was repeated and embellished by a hostile biographer a century later.[35] The hunt was always a well organised affair, the ground to be hunted sealed off and guarded by gamekeepers and soldiers of the Swiss Guard, trapping the animals within. When Leo had been helped to mount his horse and gave the signal, men entered the area and with trumpets and exploding charges of gunpowder drove the game towards a gap in the sealed off area – stags, boars, hares and rabbits, even wolves and goats. The members of the hunt would then fall upon them with spears or swords or halberds – muskets were not allowed - and gallop after any that escaped, until the area was covered with blood from dead or dying animals. The kill could amount to fifty stags and twenty wild boar as well as the smaller game. 'If an animal became entangled in a net or rope, the pope would proceed closer and, holding his glass to his left eye and taking up a spear, he would kill the struggling creature, cheerfully acknowledging the congratulations of his attendants.[36] At the Villa Magliana, Leo also had a well-stocked netted enclosure where hundreds of birds were kept for hawking, as well as housing for hawks ranging from the merlin to the goshawk. There was a structure for ferrets and a large sandy area for rabbits, which were regularly fed with meal, as entries in the papal accounts of the period testify.[37]

Leo and religious observance

In spite of this worldly lifestyle, his contemporaries, especially the ever-watchful Venetian ambassadors, all testified to his conscientious fulfilment of 'his religious duties – such as saying his Office, attending at divine worship, and observing the fasts – and that he manifested his piety on many occasions'[38]. 'It was this piety which led the busy Pope to hear Mass daily in the Chapel of San Lorenzo… Whenever the Pope said Mass, he went first to confession.'[39] It was not unusual for him to attend mass but not receive Communion.

Leo died after a short and mysterious illness on December 1st, 1521. By then, the treasury was so depleted that the candles around his catafalque were not new but had already been used for a cardinal's funeral some time previously. There were suspicious black patches on the body and the master of ceremonies remembered that the pope had grumbled to his cupbearer at supper the night before he became ill that the wine tasted bad and bitter. [40]

Conclusion

The Renaissance in sixteenth-century Italy was a period in which a uniquely cultured and luxurious lifestyle was enjoyed by noble families and especially by those who were ecclesiastics, Leo X being the outstanding example. Never before or since would a humanist inspired culture reach such heights of literary and artistic activity, combined with excessive banquets and entertainment ranging from classical theatre to vulgar comedy. That world was underpinned by a religious culture largely oblivious of the need to examine its foundations in face of the threat from another culture, partly humanist, partly religious and populist and undoubtedly political, coming from non-Mediterranean countries. Rome was the centre of the universal church and however corrupt, even violent, the ecclesiastics might be, from popes and cardinals in their courts to the curial functionaries attending upon them, they still somehow symbolised by their status and daily life the practical reality of a church both spiritual and temporal. The rites of the church were celebrated in a way which befitted this situation, that is with external decorum, and there could be signs of genuine belief and piety, as in the case of Leo X, but such considerations were secondary, except in the case of some like Giovanni Caraffa, Paul IV (r1554-1559), who was entirely focused on reform and eschewed the refinements as well as the excesses of Renaissance culture.

Attention has been drawn here to an aspect of the culture which would hardly be considered central or very significant at a time when bloodshed was so common, namely the hunt. It is true of course that this sport was necessarily a much bloodier business in the centuries before hunting guns were available, but there seems to have been a satisfaction involved in inflicting pain on animals such as to indicate a superficial understanding of humanity's place in creation, and which later centuries would find repulsive. At banquets, a whole boar was displayed on the table; large birds eviscerated and filled with live small birds could be carried in to the accompaniment of music and the birds released suddenly. Elaborate desserts made from sugar often took the form of an animal. A very large pie could have a small child burst up through its crust and lisp the praises of the host. The coarseness attendant on feasting, the cruelty inflicted on animals, the mutilation of prisoners, the strategic use of poison to assassinate enemies, all of this gives the impression that something of the truly human was lacking in a culture which exalted humanism. In feasts and even in the quotidian partaking of food, to make a connection between life as it was lived and a liturgy centred on bread and wine could hardly be possible. The fundamentals of the Christian life require that transition from a festive domestic table to the table of the Lord or vice versa should be a harmonious process; such a transition cannot be envisaged in that culture. It seems clear that the failure was not only in the excesses of banqueting but also in traditional liturgical life. Gilded chalices and patens, elaborate vestments, superb choral music, could indeed evoke the image of a banquet (if only for one), but there was a more powerful imagery at work. The understanding of the mass was based more on an allegorical representation of Christ's Passion; such details as the steps the priest climbed wearing a chasuble with a large cross, the cincture he wore, other details throughout the mass, all of these, together with a strong devotion to the Five Wounds of Christ, evoked the memory of Calvary, making the mass a sacrificial offering in an un-bloody manner of a bloody sacrifice This, rather than the gift of nourishment from above, as Luther would have it, was the *leitmotiv* of the ritual centred on food and drink.

ENDNOTES

1   Jacob Burckhardt, *The Civilization of Renaissance Italy* (London: Phaidon Press, 1995³) 249

2   Eamon Duffy, *Saints and Sinners. A History of the Popes* (New Haven: Yale Nota Bene, 2001²) 191

3   Ibid. 189

4   Jacob Burckhardt, *The Civilization of Renaissance Italy* 79

5   Friedrich Gontard, *The Popes*, trans. A. J. and E.J. Peeler (London: Barrie & Rockliff, 1959) 346

6   Desiderius Erasmus, *In Praise of Folly*, in *The Essential Erasmus*, John P. Dolan ed. (New York: Mentor Omega, 1964) 25

7   Friedrich Gontard, *The Popes* 365

8   Christopher Hibbert, *The Rise and Fall of the House of Medici* (Harmondsworth: Penguin Books, 1979) 202

9   Herbert M. Vaughan, *The Medici Popes, Leo X and Clement VII* (London: Methuen & Co., 1908) 23-6

10 Friedrich Gontard, *The Popes* 355

11 *History of the Church* Vol. IV, Hubert Jedin ed. (London: Burns and Oates, 1980) 554

12 Christopher Hibbert, *The Rise and Fall of the House of Medici* 206

13 Ludwig Pastor, *The History of the Popes,* Vol. VII (London: Kegan Paul) 25

14 Ibid. 23

15 Herbert M. Vaughan, *The Medici Popes* 113

16 Reproduced in William Roscoe and Luigi Bossi, *Vita e pontificato di Leone X., di Guglielmo Roscoe. Tradotta e corredata di annotazioni é di alcuni documenti inediti dal conte cav. Luigi Bossi,* Vol. 5 (Lexington: Ulan Press, 2012) 189-231

17 Herbert M. Vaughan, *The Medici Popes* 120

18 Christopher Hibbert, *The Rise and Fall of the House of Medici.* 218

19 Herbert M. Vaughan, *The Medici Popes* 126

20 Ibid. 159

21 Christopher Hibbert, *The Rise and Fall of the House of Medici* 233

22 Ludwig Pastor, *The History of the Popes,* Vol. VII. 184

23 Ibid. 228

24 Jacob Burckhardt, *The Civilization of Renaissance Italy* 172

25 Ibid. 225-6

26 Stephen Mennell, *All Manners of Food. Eating and Taste in England and France from the Middle Ages to the Present* (Oxford: Basil Blackwell,1985) 52

27 Herbert M. Vaughan, *The Medici Popes* 187

28 Roy Strong, *Feast. A History of Grand Eating* (Jonathan Cape: London, 2002) 152

29 Idem.

30 Herbert M. Vaughan, *The Medici Popes* 188

31 Roland Bainton, *Here I Stand. Martin Luther* (Oxford: Lion Publishing, 1978) 85

32 Philip Schaff, *History of the Christian Church, Vol. VII, Modern Christianity. The German Reformation.* (Oak Harbor WA: Logos Research Systems, 1997) C3. No. 34

33 Hubert Jedin, ed., *History of the Church,* Vol. V (London: Burns & Oates, 1980) 62

34 The buildings, which were decorated by Raphael and his school, fell into decay in the following century and the frescoes were eventually detached and given to various museums. The complex got a new lease of life in 1959 when taken over by the Order of Malta to serve as an administration block for their nearby Hospital of San Giovanni.

35 Robert Burton, *The Anatomy of Melancholy* (1621) cited in Herbert M. Vaughan, *The Medici Popes* 192

36 Christopher Hibbert, *The Rise and Fall of the House of Medici* 231

37 Herbert M. Vaughan, *The Medici Popes* 196

38 Ludwig Pastor, *The History of the Popes,* Vol. VIII. 78

39 Ibid. 79

40 Friedrich Gontard, *The Popes* 393

CHAPTER TWELVE

Tudor England and the effects of the Reformation

Cranmer put as much distance as possible between himself and London, making his escape for August down to the delights of hunting and his study at Ford.[1]

English banqueting

The celebrated and well documented banquets of Renaissance Italy can create a misleading impression of what the typical eating pattern was in that period. Not only were these the prerogative of the upper classes, but it is also difficult to establish how much any of the participants ate. It was also the custom for the leftovers from the principal table to be given to various suppliants, who are usually depicted in the margins of the paintings that record these events, especially royal ones. These marginal figures did belong generally to the household of the principal diners; in the case of a cardinal, not to mention the court of a pope like Leo X, their number could be quite considerable and their rights unquestioned, even if they had to wait till their turn to partake came. More importantly, the Christian duty to come to the aid of the needy could be conveniently fulfilled and extravagance exercised by sending servants laden with food to those too poor even to come near the scene of celebration. The accounts of events such as those recorded in the last chapter need therefore to be understood in that context. In earlier centuries, the contents of meals were often reckoned in terms of households which included the whole demesne of a medieval lord.

In the ecclesiastical realm in England, large scale events such as the enthronement of an archbishop called for banqueting on a corresponding scale. At the enthronement of Archbishop Nevill in York, England's second most prestigious see, in 1465,

1000 sheep, 2000 pigs, 2000 geese, 4000 rabbits, fish and game by the hundred, numerous kinds of bird, and twelve porpoises and seals were eaten.[2]

It is not known how many guests there were or how long the celebration lasted, or how much food was wasted, but there is little doubt that guests could eat as much as they liked and probably over several days.

In the sixteenth-century, the banqueting tradition continued in England among the leaders of society, in both the secular realm and the church, though not perhaps with the same degree of flamboyance as in Renaissance Rome. Cardinal Thomas Wolsey (1473-1530) had a foot in both camps, as he was for a period both Archbishop of York and Lord Chancellor of England. He also had what might be called another distinction in that he is generally considered of humble origin, the son of a butcher. He became a priest and academic, as Dean of Divinity at Magdalen College, Oxford, and was appointed a royal chaplain by King Henry VII. He rose rapidly in favour with the accession of Henry VIII in 1509, becoming Archbishop of York in 1514, created a Cardinal by Pope Leo X in 1515 and appointed Lord Chancellor by Henry VIII the same year. But he fell from favour with Henry when he failed to negotiate an annulment of Henry's marriage to Catherine of Aragon and died in 1530 before he could be brought to trial for treason. There were some glory years in between, however, as he engaged in international diplomacy, one of his triumphs being the meeting in 1520 between Henry VIII and Francis I of France, known as 'The Field of the Cloth of God', because of the splendour of the arrangements. The layout was a perfect example of the hierarchical motivation governing such events – in that a very complicated structure emerged because of the presence of two sovereigns.

Henry VIII went to the castle of Ardres, where he was seated with the French queen, the queen mother, the king's sister... In a second room, the princes of England were feasted by the Duke of Alençon, while in another far larger one, where music and dancing were to take place later, there was a public banquet. Meanwhile, Francis I was dining in the temporary palace erected by the English at Guisnes. He sat opposite the English queen while Cardinal Wolsey and Henry VIII's sister, Mary, duchess of Suffolk, sat at the ends of the table. In the hall, twenty gentlemen waited on a hundred and thirty ladies. ... In all of these arrangements, the principal concern was the visual enactment of hierarchy through acts of separation.[3]

The menus for this occasion have not been recorded; they would also have had a hierarchical order. Part of that for a banquet given by Wolsey seven years later for the French ambassador at Hampton Court has been preserved. It described what would now be called dessert, and listed the various shapes, called subtleties into which sugar was moulded - earlier, the term was sotelties, and *trionfi* in Italian.

> Anon came up the second course, with so many dishes, subtleties and curious devices, which were about a hundred in number, of so goodly proportion and costly, that I suppose the Frenchman never saw the like. ... There were beasts, birds, fowls of divers kinds, and personages, most lively made and counterfeit in dishes.[4]

The subtleties were important in making clear the distinctions between the ranks of society. At a banquet given by Henry V of England in 1416 at which Emperor Sigismund was the honoured guest, three subtleties decorated with pictures were served only to the king and the emperor, and subtleties served to the other lords after their rank and degree.

In addition to accounts of the menus and amounts involved in these banquets, there are also many records of the foodstuffs supplied to these households, including detailed registers of the quantity of each item supplied to medieval English monasteries. In the case of the monasteries, where the rules for the exercise of Christian charity could be expected to apply in exemplary fashion, it can be difficult to establish how many belonged to the 'household' in that guests were often quite numerous and were provided for in accordance with the monastic rule as guests at the abbot's table, served from a separate kitchen. In addition, various retainers, who were not monks but were closely associated with the community because of domestic tasks they carried out, had the right to be fed. The records of medieval monasteries were generally well kept, though many studies of them may still be only approximate in their conclusions as to how much monks actually ate. A previous chapter gave an account of such calculations in the case of the monastery of Corbie in France towards the end of the first millennium.

English monasticism

A study of the eating habits of the monks of the English monastery of Westminster at the end of the fifteenth-century assumed that these would reflect the pattern obtaining in the genteel households outside the cloister, so that they are of more general interest. The liturgy had of course a greater impact on the life of monks than could be expected to be the case in secular households. As a result, there were many feast days honouring the saints, especially the patron or patrons of the monastery and the diet took account of this by way of extra or special dishes on these occasions. Records showed that on ordinary days more than six types of fish were included in the diet and that meat was also very much part of it, though a distinction was made between flesh meat cut from the carcass and dishes prepared from offal.[5]

A division was created between places where food was taken; the normal restricted diet applied in the main eating space, the refectory, but there was also a place cut off from it where meals could be eaten and a third, the misericord, which was developed as a successor to the infirmary of earlier times, as the name implied, and where the meat of 'four footed animals' was allowed in accordance with Benedict's Rule. Elaborate rules were created to establish how many monks would have to remain in the refectory in order that some might avail of the less restricted diet which applied in the misericord. There, the practice which had existed from the time of St Benedict of granting the use of the flesh of quadrupeds to those who were ill now obtained for all who dined there. It was a simple way of getting around the old rule against the eating of meat. Even in the refectory, meat was supplied but only in the form of 'meaty' dishes made from offal.

This distinction obviously did not apply in the upper class households. Another way in which monasteries and secular households differed was in the level of comfort available to the residents. Monasteries had very limited heating, partly because of their architectural layout, with cloisters open to the outside air and a high ceilinged church, while families could ensure that their actual living space was well heated. This can be advanced as an explanation of the large amount of food which the records show was consumed in a monastery like Westminster; it could simply have been to keep warm.[6]

When the Reformation began in England, Westminster was among the many religious houses in which the new religious authorities took an interest, as a first step towards their dissolution and the incorporation in some cases of their buildings into the structure of the national church as diocesan cathedrals. This would be the fate of Westminster Abbey.

Thomas Cromwell and Thomas Cranmer

Thomas Cromwell (1485-1540), Henry VIII's chief minister, would take the lead against the religious communities, but Thomas Cranmer (1489-1556), Archbishop of Canterbury since 1533, was the main promoter of the theology and religious culture of the Reformation. Cranmer became archbishop twelve years after Pope Leo X's death and was, like him, a very public and powerful figure, but, unlike Leo, he was apparently a rather private person. According to an early biographer,

> being the storms never so terrible or odious, nor the prosperous estate of the time never so pleasant, joyous or acceptable, to the face of (the) world his countenance, diet or sleep commonly never altered or changed...[7].

Cranmer enjoyed hunting - like Leo X - at his country home in Kent. Nevertheless, as a former Fellow of Jesus College, Cambridge, 'he continued to devote to study the same amount of time as at Cambridge, three quarters of the day; and part of the remainder was allotted to shooting, walking, chess or riding, for he was a fine rider'.[8]

213

Though chief bishop of the Church of England he was in a subservient position to the volatile Henry VIII, who declared himself the supreme authority in the church by the Act of Supremacy in 1534 after the refusal of his application to have his marriage with Catherine of Aragon annulled. It looked for a time that the king would be successful, but when Pope Clement VII (the nephew of Leo X) became in effect a prisoner of the Emperor Charles V after the sack of Rome in 1527, it was no longer possible – the emperor was Catherine's favourite nephew. Cranmer was not politically astute – 'not a force in politics', as one historian put it [9], and during the tempestuous years of Henry's marital affairs which followed, Cranmer's efforts on behalf of the monarch, his abandonment in the end of Anne Boleyn, left 'a stain on his reputation'.[10] He had his own marital difficulty: before he became Archbishop he was sent by Henry as an emissary to the court of the emperor, Charles V, with an instruction to seek Lutheran leaders' support for Henry's marriage problem and during a stay in Nuremberg in 1532 he secretly married the niece of the wife of the prominent Lutheran leader, Andreas Osiander. He was therefore forced to conceal the fact when Henry ensured he should become Archbishop of Canterbury on his return in 1533. He never conceded that this showed a lack of integrity on his part; in reformed Nuremberg he had been impressed by the smooth transition to a married clergy.

While he had taken an oath of loyalty to the pope at his consecration, he had also 'promised not to obstruct the reformation of the Christian religion'; in effect he could claim he was being true to his new but concealed convictions.[11] His attitude towards the papacy certainly became hostile when he began to act for Henry in relation to Catherine of Aragon, but he had to move carefully in introducing the ideas of the Reformation, because he could not be sure to what extent the king would want changes in the church, as he had written a defence of the sacraments in 1521 after the publication of Luther's *Babylonian Captivity of the Church* and been granted the title *Defender of the Faith* by Pope Leo X, shortly before Leo died. While asserting his control of the church in England, Henry continued to regard himself orthodox, so that Cranmer had to move cautiously in promoting theological changes in a church which Henry now considered his to guard as well as govern.

Liturgical reform

Even though the rites of the church continued to be celebrated as before, a party favouring theological reform according to Lutheran principles was allowed to develop and included some bishops – it is usually labelled the evangelical party. This group produced documents questioning the number of sacraments, while a conservative opposition re-asserted traditional teaching. Cranmer began to look for opportunities to give the evangelicals a platform and in 1534 pushed two leading evangelical preachers, Hugh Latimer and Nicholas Shaxton, into the Lent cycle of preaching at Court before the King and Queen. In doing so he went over the head of the Dean of the Chapel Royal, who was far from pleased. His first open description of the pope as Antichrist came in a sermon in 1536, when he was now actively campaigning for the reform of the church in accordance with Lutheran theology. During Henry's lifetime there were several setbacks for Cranmer and the others seeking theological change.

A sharp re-assertion of the traditional position occurred in 1539 with the passage through Parliament of the Act of the Six Articles, which rigidly insisted on such doctrines as transubstantiation, private masses, auricular confession and clerical celibacy, with drastic penalties for non-compliance; denial of transubstantiation meant death by burning, though this law was not in practice enforced. The non-celibate Cranmer vigorously opposed its passage in the House of Lords, but yielded when the traditionally minded Henry appeared in the House.[12] With the publication of the King's Book in 1543, it was made clear that Henry supported the traditional theology, with, however, the important exclusion of papal supremacy, Rome's claims being described as a 'usurpation'. Cranmer's own theology of the Eucharist was undergoing change during those years; by 1546, he had rejected transubstantiation and in later years would depart from the 'realist' approach of Luther, under the influence of the German Reformer, Martin Bucer. The discovery of the writings of the ninth-cen-

215

tury monk Ratramnus may also 'have alerted Cranmer's acute theological antennae'.[13] As recounted in Chapter Six, Ratramnus had opposed the 'realist' position of his fellow monk of Corbie, Paschasius, by appealing to what he believed to be the sacramental theology of Augustine.

Cranmer's reform of the liturgy of the church after Henry's death in 1547 led him to produce in his lifetime two versions of the *Book of Common Prayer*, in 1549 and 1552, both in English. His programme of theological and pastoral changes continued until his downfall and execution in 1556, during the reign of the Catholic Queen Mary (1553-58)

One of his early practical successes was the introduction of the English language Bible, with Henry's approval in 1537; now all doctrine could be assessed in terms of its conformity with the text of the Bible. This allowed him to watch for any indications of conservative opposition to the changes he wished to introduce. The celebration of saints' days quickly became an issue. Their abolition had been decided and backed up by royal proclamation at a Convocation of bishops and clergy in 1536, but Cranmer discovered that the monks of Canterbury Priory had staged an exhibition of relics on a prohibited holy day. To Cranmer's annoyance it was in his own diocese, but the incident showed the sensitivities of the ordinary people and the resentment aroused by the authorities' interference in the popular celebration of feast days. He found that there was still widespread observance of holy days and was irritated by the fact that they were being observed in the court of King Henry.

Fasting law reform

In 1536 the king promulgated an injunction that no one could 'alter or change the order and manner of any fasting-day that is commanded and indicted by the church' until the king would so order.[14]

> At some point ... in late 1536 or 1537, Cranmer tried to give a practical example of what the change entailed by ostentatiously ignoring the fast for the eve of one of the feasts of St Thomas Becket: he ate meat in his parlour with his 'family' (that is, his household) and thereby caused a sensation in Canterbury.[15]

In 1538, he gave the monks of Canterbury a further practical demonstration of how evangelicals should observe a holy season by giving a series of public lectures on the Letter to the Hebrews in the Cathedral precincts during the first half of Lent. Underlying this programme to promote the reading and study of scripture was an attempt to turn people away from Lenten devotional practices traditionally considered to merit God' grace, whereas the basic Lutheran principle Cranmer wanted to assert was that justification of the Christian before God could only come from faith not 'works', such as Lenten penances. He was encouraged by the fact that the king had that year for the first time suspended the traditional ban on eating eggs and dairy produce during Lent.[16]

Henry's assertion of supremacy allowed Cromwell to turn his attention to the affairs of the religious houses. The stated aim of Royal Injunctions of 1535 and 1536 was to bring needed reform to them in the sense of correcting abuses, but there was a further hidden plan to empty them of their members and confiscate their assets. Cranmer agreed, perhaps unwittingly, with this ulterior motive by saying in a sermon during a parliamentary session in 1536 that people should not be concerned at the suppression of the monasteries because it would mean that the king would not have to turn to them to finance the realm's affairs.[17] The Injunctions required that in each monastery the monks should eat together in the same room, thus ending the tradition of meals of a different type being served in the misericord. Various office-holders were also prohibited from eating in their own quarters. As much as reforming an abuse, this could be understood as a move towards greater economy, thereby increasing the assets of the community in preparation for a takeover. When the king appointed Cromwell Steward of Westminster in 1533, the corrodies, or benefits, which went with the post were free bread and ale and the right to occupy the gatehouse, though he was allowed to appoint a deputy to live there. Here, the aim was to control the movement of the monks, including their spending. He was appointed Visitor of the religious houses in 1535 and this led to their dissolution, which was complete with the closure of Westminster and establishment of the cathedral in January 1540.

When the Reformation was firmly established in England with the accession in 1558 of the daughter of Anne Boleyn, Queen Elizabeth, the established church could now formulate its doctrinal standards, and this resulted in the Thirty Nine Articles of Religion in 1562, setting out its beliefs. Article 28 declared that transubstantiation could not be proved from Scripture and had given rise to many superstitions. The sacrament should not be 'reserved, carried about, lifted up or worshipped'. 'The body of Christ is given, taken and eaten in the Supper, only after a heavenly and spiritual manner.'

With the Articles were included two books of Homilies, written by Bishop Jewel. In the second book, The Third Homily expounded the teaching on fasting, relying, it appears, on what Calvin included in his *Institutes*. The *Articles* and the list of Homilies were included in all subsequent editions of the *Book of Common Prayer*, as a guide for members of the Church of England. Though not obligatory, fasting was recommended as something acceptable to God and profitable for the Christian. Three motives were proposed. 'The first is to chastise the flesh that it be not too wanton, but tamed and brought into subjection to the spirit. ... The second, that the spirit be more earnest and fervent in prayer. ... The third, that our fast be a testimony and witness with us before God, of our humble submission to his high majesty, when we confess and acknowledge our sins unto him and are inwardly touched with sorrowfulness of heart, bewailing the same in the afflictions of our bodies.' The Fourth Homily warned lest people's hearts be overcome with surfeiting and drunkenness and the cares of this world. The Fifth Homily admonished people about the 'detestable abuse' of the 'gorgeous' apparel they wore, which 'godly and necessary laws' made by their princes, and often repeated, were unable to prevent, 'to the great peril of the Realm'.

This Fifth Homily referred to a long standing practice – going back even to the reign of Nero [18] - of creating sumptuary edicts not only to regulate clothing but even the food which might be consumed. Regulations about clothing were explicitly aimed at preventing conspicuous displays of wealth; for example, the king of France in 1284 forbade 'bourgeois man or woman' to wear garments of luxury materials or ornaments of gold or precious stones. Even the number of garments a person could own was restricted by social rank. The same law limited the number of dishes that could be served at any one meal.[19]

Sumptuary laws

During the sixteenth-century there was an upsurge in these sumptuary laws, enacted by Protestant and Catholic authorities for somewhat different reasons and concerned to an increasing degree with food. Catholic legislators, following old traditions, tended to be concerned with what was eaten, Protestants with how much. In the latter case, this could lead to restrictions on the number attending a function; in 1529, the city council in Zürich was concerned that wedding banquets were becoming too extravagant and limited the banquet guests to twenty-four or, if there were many relations, to forty. From similar concerns, a law in Basel in 1629 included a suggested menu, limited to three courses, and ruled that the dinner should begin at twelve o'clock, stop at four and that everyone must be gone by five.[20] In Catholic France, a royal edict of 1533 'forbade the eating of lamb and beef, and was repeated in a series of laws in the mid sixteenth century against luxury apparel and the eating of certain meats'.[21] Motivations for such laws also included the intention to prevent the importing of expensive food and other items and one of the main purposes was to ensure that the wealthy would donate surplus income to charity, echoing the rationale of the great Renaissance banquets and the retention for the poor of food left over. The sumptuary decrees were not always successful, as the practice of repeating enactments showed.

While laws relating to food were not mentioned in Bishop Jewel's Fifth Homily, they had been enacted in England centuries before the Reformation. In fourteenth-century England, for example, King Edward III ruled that servants of gentlemen, merchants and artificers should have only one meal of flesh or fish per day. In 1513, before his quarrel with Rome, 'Henry VIII allowed his subjects all of the varieties of meats and games that were forbidden to the French and Italians, ... however he limited them to one dish'.[22]

These laws existed in Cranmer's day; by that time banquets in England had become excessive, as the example of Wolsey's banquet indicates. He seems to have been exempt from the provisions of a law passed ten years previously, which 'decreed that the number of courses be regulated according to the rank of the highest person present: nine courses for a cardinal, six for a lord of Parliament and three for a citizen with a yearly income of £500'.[23]

In 1541, Cranmer and the bishops agreed on very detailed rules in this regard, carefully grading the number of courses and number of dishes which the archbishops, bishops, deans, archdeacons and junior clergy might eat; but Cranmer appends a sad little memorandum 'that this order was kept for two or three months, till, by the disusing of certain wilful persons, it came again to the old excess.'[24]

As the Fifth Homily decried 'gorgeous apparel', it is clear that the sumptuary laws were concerned not only with excessive displays of wealth but also and perhaps above all with maintaining class structures; if there were to be restrictions on banqueting they were aimed at maintaining distinctions within the upper classes, The monotonous diet of the poor needed no regulation; they could only indulge occasionally in excessive drinking of cheap beer and that abuse was targeted in the Fourth Homily. Ever since St Paul had condemned drunkenness in the Letter to the Galatians (5:20) on the grounds of loss of self-control, it had been denounced in preaching and church teaching, while over-eating usually escaped stricture.

The proclamations throughout Elizabeth's reign continue to reiterate the hierarchical nature of legislation passed under the earlier Tudors. For example one of the statutes frequently invoked was issued under Henry VIII. In 1533, *An Acte for Reformacyon of Excesse in Apparayle* distinguishes between the various social ranks, and what they could wear. None but the King and the royal family were allowed to wear purple silk, or cloth made of gold tissue, however, Dukes and Marquises were allowed to "use in their Dublettes and Slevelesse Cootes, Clothe of Gold of Tissue and in none other their garments."[25]

The Anglican Church was meant to be the church of all the people, but it became particularly aligned with the upper classes because of Henry's involvement in its direction, his appointment of bishops from noble families and the influence of Court ceremonial on its worship. While Wolsey had been of humble origins, the way to preferment was, with inevitable exceptions, now narrowed down to members of those families who belonged to the right circles. Ordinary clergy now needed levels of literacy appropriate to conducting services in English and particularly for preaching.

An upper and middle class clergy had also of course to minister to the poor, but the shortcomings of the ministry provided by the established church during the reign of Queen Elizabeth (r1558-1603) began to be apparent, making the poorer classes open to the influence of the more radical Protestant groups who from the beginning were at odds with the worship pattern of the established church. These will be discussed in Chapter Fourteen.

The Anglican Eucharist

The Reformation in England occurred in a situation where church and state were very closely linked. With the repudiation of papal supremacy this relationship became a tight bond, for which the term 'established church' can hardly do full justice. Once this had occurred, a layman like Thomas Cromwell could initiate moves in Parliament to define what church teaching was on any subject, while Archbishop Cranmer and his supporters, most of them bishops, could introduce new liturgical books in which the Eucharistic rite was formulated according to the reformed theology introduced from continental Europe. The influence of court ceremonial meant, however, that the rite had a solemnity which saved it from being reduced to the infrequency and simplified form to which the new theology could have led. The title of the 1549 Prayer Book, *'The supper of the Lord and holy communion, commonly called the mass'*, indicated that a change of theology had been introduced. But the search for a formula of administration of the sacrament actually emphasised Eucharistic nourishment of body and soul: 'The Body of our Lord Jesus Christ, which was given for thee, preserve thy body and soul unto everlasting life.

Take and eat this in remembrance that Christ died for thee, and feed on him in thy heart by faith with thanksgiving'. The Eucharist was received kneeling, but the bread used was leavened and placed in the hand of the communicant. Communion was received under both kinds. Ironically, Cranmer's conservative opponents – those who held with the traditional understanding of the Eucharist, while accepting Royal Supremacy – asserted that the formula used did not indicate a departure from traditional orthodoxy, and this led Cranmer to make his position clear in 1550 in his *Defence of the Sacrament*.[26] He declared that the great errors which needed to be corrected were 'the popish doctrine of transubstantiation, of the real presence of Christ's flesh and blood in the sacrament of the altar (as they call it) and of the sacrifice and oblation of Christ made by the priest for the salvation of the quick and the dead'.[27] Clergy were in some cases coerced to accept the new Prayer Book, while the laity were often confused by the change or simply noticed that the mass was now in English.

As in the case of Luther's reform of the mass in 1523, there were rumblings of discontent concerning the 1549 book, the complaint, for example of John Knox, the Scottish reformer, that Communion should be received sitting. This, along with the critical observation of the German reformer, Martin Bucer, who was by then a professor in Cambridge, led to reformulation in 1552 of the words of administration of the sacrament to one that implied a 'remembrance' of Christ rather than a real presence and this version was reproduced in later editions after Cranmer's death.

His version of the liturgy in 1549 included services for morning and evening prayer, a reform of the liturgy of the hours which had been celebrated daily in the early centuries in cathedrals, but for several hundred years privately by the clergy and not in parish churches. The new Book introduced in 1552 laid down that these hours were to be celebrated by the clergy daily and added that the laity were to be encouraged to attend: 'parish priests are to toll a bell before the services, "that such as be disposed may come to hear God's word and to pray…" and the services are to be said "in such place of the church… as the people may best hear", rather than "in the quire"'.[28] Because the liturgy of the hours had long ceased to be part of regular services in any but cathedral churches, this was an innovation as much as being a reform. In the Preface to the 1549 Book, the thrust of Cranmer's argument in favour of reform was the need to return to the original plan of the 'ancient Fathers' that the 'whole Bible (or the greatest part thereof)' should be read to the people in daily services. But so many stories and legends had been introduced, and the Latin language used, that people heard 'with their ears only and heart, spirit and mind were not edified'.[29] Cranmer's interest was clearly centred on the liturgy of the Word as the daily service of the church, and the detailed instructions as to how Morning Prayer was to be conducted also made arrangements for the changes to be made if the 'Holy Communion' service were to follow. In practice, the standard Sunday service consisted of Morning Prayer, the Litany and what was called the Ante-Communion, this last being prayers which would be part of the Communion Service, if it were held, and closing with a blessing. Holy Communion was, however, celebrated regularly, though not necessarily weekly, and a list of feasts of the Lord was created, though not of the saints.

At first no hymns were included and both services were starkly simple, but a Royal Injunction was issued by Queen Elizabeth in 1559 encouraging more use of music in the parishes. A hymn or song of praise 'in the best sort of melody and music that may conveniently be devised' should be sung before or after Morning Prayer and Evensong, provided that the words were understandable.[30] This decree led to a gradual transformation of evening prayer with the introduction of settings, called Services, of the *Magnificat* and *Nunc Dimittis* Canticles, as well as choral Anthems by prominent composers, musical compositions of great beauty and complexity, giving opportunity for very skilled performance while not excluding hymns for the people. *Evensong*, when celebrated in cathedrals or university colleges became one of the great treasures of Anglican worship, making liturgy truly festal. The formality with which this liturgy was celebrated, the vested choir, the solemnity with which prayers were intoned, all reflected Court ceremonial and created the atmosphere characteristic of Anglican worship.

Conclusion

Several versions of the *Book of Common Prayer* have appeared in the centuries since Cranmer's introduction of the Reformation into the church in England, culminating in the publication of *Common Worship* in 2000, This is in fact a collection of books which include the liturgy of the Eucharist in various formulations, one being very similar to that produced for the Catholic Church in the liturgical renewal mandated by the Second Vatican Council. In general, a corresponding liturgical renewal in the Anglican Church has taken account of ecumenical consensus arising from contemporary scholarship

An innovation can be seen in the introduction of *Common Worship: Daily Prayer* in 2005, based on an Anglican Franciscan book of the same name and a resource providing a modern substitute for the original form found in Cranmer's and later versions of the *Book of Common Prayer*. It was described by the then Archbishop of Canterbury as 'a simple and more celebratory form of common prayer for our time'.

However, the original worship pattern for evening prayer continues in the sung *Evensong* in various places, especially in Anglican Cathedrals and university colleges which are officially Anglican, and situations arise where a formal meal follows in a university college dining hall which was designed in the style of a monastic refectory - or was originally a monastic refectory. If the formalities of the occasion demonstrate awareness of the tradition enshrined in monastic dining, then the transition from worship to feast will be a grace-filled occasion as a symbiosis occurs between the two aspects of festal living.

Such a happy outcome depends obviously on both events being informed by Christian faith and an instinctive appreciation of the monastic ethos which the architectural environment evokes. This would require a re-discovery in some sense of monastic tradition or religious community life in the larger sense in England. Attempts to revive such a life within Anglicanism have never had noticeable success, but a felt need for its spirituality is manifesting itself at the present time through such experiments as the Community of St Anselm, founded by the Archbishop

224

of Canterbury, Justin Welby, and based in his residence, Lambeth Palace, and the Chemin Neuf Community which at his invitation resides in Lambeth. These initiatives are supported by books such as Reforming the Monastery, Protestant Theologies of the Religious Life, [31] in the series New Monastic Library, which publishes books recording the reviving interest in monasticism among Evangelical Christians. The focus of such books is on the growing awareness that there is need to turn to monastic history to learn that a fully Christian life is one suffused with values both celebratory and ascetic.

Anglicanism is found throughout the world wherever English is spoken, and especially in countries once part of the English Empire. Inculturation in widely diverse cultures has its effects but Anglicanism retains its basic ethos wherever the church is found. The church has never in recent centuries claimed the authority to impose a regime of fasting and has never appealed to the sumptuary rules which were laid down by Cranmer. Doctrinal issues do on occasion lead to appeals to the *Thirty Nine Articles*, but the Homilies attached to them, with their rules about fasting, seem to be of no more than of historical interest. Anglicanism has had the inherent characteristic that authority could never be strong enough to bring about a significant observance of a penitential regime, and for this and other reasons has suffered from the inroads of secularism. But as will be seen later it is not alone in the resulting shift in the relationship between food, feasting and fasting.

ENDNOTES

1   Diarmaid MacCulloch, *Thomas Cranmer. A Life* (New Haven: Yale University Press, 1996) 196

2   Stephen Mennell, *All Manners of Food. Eating and Taste in England and France from the Middle Ages to the Present* (Oxford: Basil Blackwell,1985) 22

3   Roy Strong, *Feast. A History of Grand Eating* (London: Jonathan Cape, 2002) 95

4   Ibid. 87

5   Barbara Harvey, *Living and Dying in England 1100-1540. The Monastic Experience* (Oxford: Clarendon Press, 1993) 34-71

6   Ibid. 71

7   Diarmaid MacCulloch, *Thomas Cranmer. A Life* 1

8   Owen Chadwick, *The Reformation* (Harmondsworth: Penguin Books, 1964) 115

9   Idem

10   Diarmaid MacCulloch, *Thomas Cranmer. A Life* 158

11   Ibid. 88

12   Bernard M. G. Reardon, *Religious Thought in the Reformation* (London: Longman, 1981) 245

13   Diarmaid MacCulloch, *Thomas Cranmer. A Life* 181

14   David Grumett and Rachel Muers, *Theology on the Menu. Asceticism, meat and the Christian diet* (London: Routledge, 2010) 28

15   Ibid. 198

16   Idem

17   Ibid. 151

18   Suetonius, *The Twelve Caesars,* Robert Graves trans. (London: Guild Publishing,1990) 221

19   Johanna B. Moyer, 'The Food Police. Sumptuary Prohibitions on Food in the Reformation', in *Food and Faith in Christian Culture,* Ken Albala and Trudy Eden eds. (New York: Columbia University Press, 2011) 60

20   Ibid. 62-3

21   Ibid. 62

22   Ibid. 63

23   Roy Strong, *Feast* 104

24   Stephen Mennell, *All Manners of Food. Eating and Taste in England and France from the Middle Ages to the Present* 30

25   Leah Kirtio, 'The inordinate excess in apparel': Sumptuary Legislation in Tudor England', in *University of Alberta* Student *Journal* 3 (1) (2012) 18 https://journals.library.ualberta. ca/constellations/index.php/constellations/.../13071

26   The full title was: *A defence of the true and Catholic doctrine of the sacrament of the body and blood of our saviour Christ.* It was Cranmer's first printed book.

27   Cited in Diarmaid MacCulloch, *Thomas Cranmer. A Life* 469

28   G. J. Cuming, 'The Office in the Anglican Communion' in Cheslyn Jones *et al.*, *The Study of the Liturgy* (London: S.P.C.K., 1992²) 444-5

29   *The Book of Common Prayer and the Administration of the Sacraments of the Church of England* (Oxford: O.U.P., 1910) vii

30   Hugh Benham, *Latin Church Music in England 1460-1575* (London: Da Capo Press 1977) 165

31   Greg Peters (Eugene OR: Cascade Books, 2014)

CHAPTER THIRTEEN

Food, Feast and Fast in a time of transition. Italy and France

Enquiring of his (an Italian cook's) charge and particular qualities, he told me a long, formall and eloquent discourse of the science or skill of epicurisme and gluttonie with such an Oratorie-gravitie and Magistrale countenance as if he had discoursed of some high mysterious point of divinitie.[1]

Reacting against the Renaissance: Pope Paul IV

In the sixteenth and seventeenth centuries, the combined results of the Reformation and the counter movement of Catholic renewal, often called the Counter-Reformation, affected the lives of the popes in significant ways and frequently complicated their relations with the monarchies of Europe. The Council which began in 1545 in a belated response to the Reformation and finally moved to Trent, was held over three separate periods until 1563, being prorogued on one occasion because of an invasion by a Protestant prince, Maurice of Saxony. Its programme of reform and renewal, which reasserted traditional teaching about all major areas of the Christian life, including the Eucharist and fasting, depended for its implementation very much on the papacy. Over a period of more than a century around that time the See of Peter was occupied by men as different from one another in what can simply be called worldliness or unworldliness as was true of the lives of their pre-Reformation rather colourful predecessors.

Bishop Giovanni Caraffa of Chieti, born in Naples in 1476, was a man who devoted himself to reform in his diocese of Theate and for that purpose co-founded the Theatine Order. Made a Cardinal, he remained a supporter of the order and persuaded the pope, Paul III, to set up the Inquisition for the suppression of heresy. Elected pope himself in 1555

227

as Paul IV and at the age of 79, he became a remarkably energetic and formidable figure, generating both awe and terror in all who had to deal with him. He despised the humanist values of the Renaissance, and the memory therefore of some of his predecessors.

> He did not like to be disturbed in the morning, as he wished to say mass and recite his office slowly and with great devotion. He would not be tied down to any fixed hours for his meals, though he wished his table to be served very generously, in accordance with his high position. He himself ate very little, and in spite of his advanced age, kept the rules of fasting and abstinence in the strictest manner.[2]

Over the four years of his pontificate, Paul devoted his energy to a root and branch elimination of whatever he considered heresy and for this purpose he always attended the weekly meetings of the Inquisition, which was strengthened in its powers and numbers. In 1557, 'it was decreed that the members of the Inquisition ... upon whose judgement and sentence the shedding of blood under torture or death should ensue, were liable to no censure or irregularity'.[3] The judgments of the Inquisition brought about the death of two thousand people in Calabria, while six hundred more were in prison, an observer reported to the Duke of Urbino.[4]

The other principal cause for the pope was the removal of the Spanish presence from his native Naples and from Milan, and to achieve his aim he was prepared to enter an alliance with France, though his ultimate aim was to free Italy from every foreign influence. 'They are all barbarians, and it would be a good thing if they remained at home, and nothing but Italian were spoken in our country', he once said to the Venetian ambassador.[5] In pursuance of this policy, he conferred power in all temporal matters on his nephew, Giovanni, in an act of nepotism which he had always condemned in his earlier days. In doing so he made the tragic mistake of trusting a man who proved totally unscrupulous and immoral. He also made his other equally unsuitable nephew, Carlo, a cardinal. The military campaigns of Giovanni Caraffa proved unsuccessful and Paul was forced to make peace with Spain in 1557. Giovanni continued to have his uncle's confidence and it was only in January 1559 that the truth concerning his dissolute life and abuse of power became known to the astonished Paul, who then banished the two nephews, without however inflicting the punishment that he meted out to others for less serious misdemeanours.

He had come to realise that because of his own tendency to confine himself to his rooms it had been possible to isolate him from the cardinals and from envoys and ambassadors, and therefore from decision making in all matters affecting church and the Papal States. After the dismissal of his nephews he endeavoured to be more amenable to visitors and continued his programme of reform. He was astonished to learn about taxes that had been levied without his knowledge and he reduced some of them.

As the year 1559 progressed he became more ill with dropsy, but still attended a weekly meeting of the Inquisition. His end was hastened by his insistence on continuing to fast and abstain and this finally brought about his death on August 18th. Rioting and looting broke out in Rome straight away as the people took revenge for the hardship the war against Spain had caused and the taxes imposed by his nephews. The buildings of the Inquisition were raided, documents destroyed, officials mistreated and the buildings set on fire. A decree of the city of Rome ordered the removal of all Caraffa coats of arms and inscriptions. 'Yet the next day the Romans poured into the Vatican to kiss the feet of the pontiff as he lay in state.'[6]

The judgement of historians on Paul has had to take account of great contrasts in his personality and in the nature of the reforms he instituted, as well as in the consequences not only for the people of Rome and the Papal States but also for the entire church. The positive judgment of the Venetian ambassador of the time is open to question: he felt that Rome had been turned into a well-ordered monastery! The twentieth-century historian, Ludwig Von Pastor, pointed to a fundamental ambiguity: 'Even if the unbounded violence of the character of Paul IV awakened fear and hatred in wide circles, his otherwise pious and exemplary life called forth the greatest admiration'. It is true, in any case, that Paul achieved the elimination of abuses which previous popes such as Alexander VI and Leo X tolerated and even availed of for the aggrandisement of their own families.[7] Because of Paul and the Council of Trent (even though he did not approve of its 'foreign' makeup), later popes were able to continue a policy of renewal for the church's ministry in the world.

The Banquet or the Liturgical Feast: Pius V

While Paul IV grimly fasted and abstained and tried to turn Rome into a 'well-ordered monastery', a culture was developing which drew on Renaissance learning and applied it to the art of cooking. 'For the first time in more than a millennium, food was worthy of a learned pen.'[8] The Renaissance had looked back to classical authors like Socrates, who had considered gastronomic interests a form of gluttony, but the literary establishment could not prevent the appearance of books in which a new set of insights was devoted to more mundane interests than philosophy. There was in any case the precedence of the oldest recipe book, the *De re coquinaria*, attributed to one Apicius at the time of the Emperor Augustus, and reproduced in a ninth century Latin transcription, so that it was known during the Renaissance. But sixteenth-century Italy saw the publication of new books of recipes and cooking techniques. Cristoforo da Messibugo's evocatively titled *Banchetti* appeared in 1549 and the famous *Opera* of Bartolomeo Scappi in 1570, dedicated rather oddly, as will be seen, to Pope Pius V (r1566-1572). Scappi's book demonstrated considerable advances in technique – methods such as marinating, braising and poaching were prominent.[9] To what extent Pius availed of this cooking is not known, but Scappi, who had begun his career in the service of a cardinal, subsequently worked for Pius, managed his coronation banquet and was described as his 'personal cook', though this was probably a sinecure.[10]

Pius V was born Michele Ghislieri to impoverished parents in 1504 in Northern Italy. He became a Dominican friar, was an extraordinarily hard worker, yet travelled everywhere on foot, and rose to prominence in the order. Recruited into the papal service, he soon played a very large role in

Les Grandes Chroniques de France de Charles V. between circa 1370 and circa 1379. Illumination on parchment. Bibliothèque nationale de France.

Paul IV's Inquisition, but showed more moderation in implementing its decrees, to Paul's displeasure. Elected pope himself in 1566 he continued to wear his white and rough Dominican habit as part of his papal attire. For many years he suffered the typical medieval malady of the 'stone', presumably a reference to kidney stones or bladder stones, from which he claimed asses' milk gave him relief. He thought that the best way to deal with oppressive heat was to eat and drink very little. His diet was simple:

> At noon he took some bread-soup with two eggs and half a cup of wine, and his supper in the evening generally consisted of some vegetable broth, salad, shell-fish and cooked fruit. Only twice a week did meat appear at his table.[11]

231

Present-day understanding would see this as a healthy diet, especially as he continued his former practice of taking a great deal of exercise, but the amount consumed would have needed to be greater than it seems to have been in his case. According to one of his biographers, Girolamo Catena, in 1567 he 'still further reduced his table, on which he only spends three and a half scudi a day'.[12]

For Pius, the true feast was the liturgical one and he devoted himself to liturgical reform with considerable success. The liturgy of the mass, which had existed with many variations throughout Europe, became the object of thorough research and the result was a new rite which was based on the early liturgy of Rome and imposed, with some exceptions, on the whole church. That there should be one universally observed rite was a cause dear to Pius and perceived as a factor in uniting the church in face of the threat from Turkish invasion.

Scappi's book was overtaken in importance by new books of recipes which went into great detail about the formalities of banqueting, in particular the role of three officials: the supervisor, or *scalco*, who had control over everything from the overall effect to the smallest detail, the meat carver, or *trinciante*, and the *credenziere*, who was in charge of the drinks. For several centuries, eating in public on the part of the aristocracy had become a choreographed event which brought to the fore an atmosphere of sociability as much as social structure - a significant advance on feudal times. However, the rituals preserved order while giving the appearance of free exchange among the participants. The shape of the tables and order of seating were designed to promote both purposes. The meal was about to become part of an overall experience, while the food was about to take on a symbolic role.

Messisbugo's book, *Banchetti*, which is still available as a print on demand book,[13] had its source in the author's role as *scalco* in the household of Ercole II d'Este, Duke of Ferrara, a position he held until his death in 1548. In addition to that role, he produced his book detailing the items served at the ducal banquets. It gives details of the Renaissance obsession with figurative food, which came to be called *trionfi* after the large-scale

Figurative *trionfi* for the feast on Holy Thursday at the Vatican, drawing by
Pierre Paul Sevin, 1668.

and equally artificial triumphal arches used for public processions. 'Here
are pastry castles and coats of arms as well as descriptions of wooden
and iron moulds capable of turning out eagles and *fleur-de-lys* (in sugar)
of Este family arms.'[14] The book also makes plain that the meal itself
is only one aspect of what should be 'a whole sequence of experiences,
usually opening with a play, a poetry reading, a concert or games and, in
most cases, winding up with the removal of the tables and dancing'.[15] By
the start of the seventeenth century, the excellence of the food produced
from Scappi's recipes was subordinated to the visual effects that could be
achieved by manipulation of food items to produce *trionfi*. This was true
even for a dinner for clergy - as distinct from a banquet for the aristocracy
- held each year in Rome on Holy Thursday after the ceremony in which
the pope washed the feet of twelve poor priests. A set of drawings of the
trionfi for the dinner held in 1668 survives.

What to modern eyes is so bizarre is to see dining tables exhibiting
food sculptures in the form of Christ carrying the Cross, the Ag-

ony in the Garden of Gethsemane and angels clasping the instruments of the Passion. Interwoven among these are vases of flowers, trees bearing fruit and such features as a *tempietto* supporting the family arms of the reigning pope.[16]

On a visit of the new King, Henry III of France, to Venice in 1574 the display of *trionfi* included a maritime theme:

> (T)wo tables were covered with entire armadas, colourful flags, horses, lions, tigers, and a host of characters paying tribute to the sovereign, as well as the candied heads of Pontiffs, Kings, Cardinals and Doges, amounting in all to about two hundred figures.[17]

How and when this understanding of the banquet in all its intricate details spread from Renaissance Italy to France or England is not clear, but 'of the prestige of all things Italian in the countries to the north in the sixteenth century there can be no doubt'.[18] The great example of this type of banquet will be that held in the Palace of Versailles in the reign of Louis XIV.

The Banquet as Statement
The absolute monarchy of Louis XIV (1638-1715) ensured the continuity of a class structured society and its lifestyle in a country which had gone through a religious upheaval in the previous century. Conflict followed the spread of the Reformation from Switzerland into France and resulted in the St Bartholomew's Day massacre of 1572, when Catholic reaction led by the Guise family to the growing number of Calvinist communities led to the massacre of their leader, Admiral de Coligny (a convert from Catholicism) and a large number of Calvinists.[19] Dissenters from the official religion who subscribed to Calvinist beliefs were called Huguenots and had left France in large numbers during subsequent periods of violence, many taking refuge in Reformation England. (There they would again become a dissenting minority in seventeenth-century England after the restoration of the English monarchy.) In France religious tolerance

was granted in the Edict of Nantes in 1598, but Louis XIV revoked it in 1685 for motives of less than religious fervour; he was determined to unite France, but as a Catholic country under his own authority, and with a view to sequestering ecclesiastical income. The strength of his position came in many ways from the Concordat which Leo X had made with Francis I in 1516 when, as part of his manoeuvring to influence the election of a new Holy Roman Emperor, he had made many concessions to Francis. Louis demanded of the Curia in Rome toleration of the Gallican Articles, four claims made by an assembly of the clergy in 1682,[20] which included a declaration of the superiority of a General Council over the pope, and limited papal authority in such a way that appointments of bishops and certain revenues would be under control of the king. There followed a period of conflict with Pope Innocent XI (r1675-1689), in which the lifestyles of the two men were in remarkable contrast.

Louis, known as the Sun King, held court in the Palace of Versailles, where 'between three and five thousand were fed daily by means of a hierarchy of tables'.[21] During the decade 1664-74 he held three major festivals in the magnificent gardens, in each case celebrating a military victory, and each of them the subject of a handsome tome recording the proceedings in elaborate detail. A festival in May 1664 extended over two weeks and included tournaments, ballets, fireworks displays and food in abundance. By the time the dinner took place, night had fallen but a small forest of chandeliers painted silver and green, together with two hundred masked men clasping torches, resulted in a clarity almost as bright as day. A newspaper of the time summed up the aim of the fête as one of transforming the setting in such a way that no one knew where reality ended and fantasy began. The feast itself was of a 'sumptuosity which surpassed anything one could describe, as much for its abundance as for the delicacy of the things which were served'.[22] 'Sumptuosity' probably indicates extravagance as well as luxury and could have resulted also in considerable waste. How much the poor, far from the Versailles gardens, may have benefited from the banquet cannot be known. Another festival, in 1668, held from evening until the following morning in spe-

Portrait of Louis XIV. Painted by Hyacinthe Riguard in 1701.

cially erected enclosures in the gardens, included a supper which 'consist-ed of five courses, each one of fifty-six dishes, carried in by members of the Swiss Guard. The dessert included sixteen vast pyramids of preserved fruit'.[23] There were large numbers of guests present and invitations for these events were eagerly sought by those who were not entitled to be there as members of the Court.

The custom of the king to dine in public on other occasions than these festivals was an expression of a tradition which had developed as a means of maintaining a rigid class structure and to ensure that all knew their place. This situation had obtained in the Roman Empire of old, but with the greater upward mobility of the modern era, such control was less easily achieved and a monarch like Louis had to have recourse to daz-zling displays of wealth in the elaborate architectural structures created for the festivals, theatrical diversions, and choreographed meals above all, to maintain his position, all of which required that income be continually increased by whatever means possible and particularly by encroaching on the finances of the church.

Early in his reign, Louis ate both dinner and supper in public but in the 1690s dinner at midday became a private event except on the great feast days, such as Easter and Pentecost and New Year's Day. Not that private meant just that, as though he dined alone in his state bedroom or elsewhere, in addition to the servants a group of nobles and state officials always stood at a respectful distance looking on. Fifteen persons were required to carry the meal to the table. There was a ceremony attached to his having a glass of wine; it involved a gentleman receiving a gold tray with two decanters and a glass covered with a napkin from the chief cupbearer and presenting it to the king, bowing at the appropriate times.

Supper was always held in public and for the members of court in-volved processing from one state chamber to another and a ceremonial setting of the tables before the king finally entered. An item for the table famous since the Middle Ages, the *nef*, was no longer placed in front of the king, but was kept in a glass case and people passing by were expected to genuflect. It was a boat shaped silver dish which in earlier times held a small knife, a spoon and a napkin (and in the case of the Emperor Charles V a serpent's tongue used for detecting poison). The king sat alone on one side of a table, with six other members of the royal family facing each other to his right and to his left. Behind the king stood the first Gentleman of the Chamber along with the Captain of the Guard, a doctor and a surgeon. The meal began with the Almoner saying grace and this was followed by a hand washing ceremony. Each course of the meal was served by five or six gentlemen. Many formalities accompanied the end of the meal and the king's retirement. 'It is extraordinary that this crippling performance went on virtually unchanged until 1789.'[24]

Fasting as Counter-Statement: Innocent XI

The pope who had to deal with this display of power, Innocent XI (r1676-89), lived in another world from that of Louis, materially and spiritually. At the height of the conflict between the two, the extremely austere Innocent was in his seventies, and when persuaded to live in the Quirinal Palace, 'chose for himself the worst rooms, from which there was no view'.[25]

> In his study, there was only a wooden table with a simple ivory crucifix, a few religious books, three old pictures of saints, a wooden chair and an old silk-covered chair for visitors of mark.[26]

This was consistent with his previous life, as though he had come from a reasonably prosperous family in Como, as a papal official he had been distinguished by his care for the poor, being described even as 'father of the poor'. In contrast with Pope Leo X in the previous century, when he took possession – the *Sacro Possesso* - of the Lateran Basilica in 1676, he insisted on the avoidance of all display and expressly forbade the erection of the customary triumphal arches. He would have liked to carry out the ceremony without the College of Cardinals, but gave in to their wishes to be involved in this cherished ritual. But again unlike Leo, he changed the custom of throwing coins to the crowd and instead had wheat money distributed to the parishes. His humility made the acclamations of the people painful to him and he showed himself very little in public – something for which he was criticised. He never walked in the gardens of the Vatican or the Quirinal but lived a rather eremitical life. Endeavouring to live in poverty, he ruled that his daily meal must cost no more than a Roman florin.[27] Not surprisingly, his health was poor and this, along with extreme conscientiousness, accounts for the fact that he only said Mass on Sunday, and never without first receiving the sacrament of Penance.[28]

Such a man could seem an unequal combatant in a conflict with Louis XIV. Louis was in excellent health, was well nourished and had the backing of most of the bishops of France. He effectively controlled the church in France with its thirty-five million members, compared with eight million in Italy, ten in Germany, seven in Spain and five in Poland.[29] Remarkably, rather than giving all his attention to France, Innocent maintained a policy of concern for the common good of the church against the Turkish inroads into Europe – they would not be not forced out of Hungary until 1687. He even held the personal qualities of Louis XIV in high regard and hoped he would mobilise his forces against the Turks.[30] This allowed Louis to assert his power by such moves as the occupation of the papal territories of Avignon and the Venaisson in France. Diplomatic relations were maintained, however, and Innocent did make counter-moves of a limited sort, such as abolishing the customary extension of extraterritoriality surrounding ambassadors' residences, which was used to harbour spies and even armed hostile militias. Support for him built up through the denunciation of the Four Articles by prelates and theologians in other parts of Europe. But the situation remained unresolved at Innocence's death in 1689. 'It would take the efforts of another two popes to heal the breach between Paris and Rome.'[31]

The conflict between the two men sheds light on the fundamental issue of the preparedness of the ascetic Christian to deal with the world. Innocent's almost eremitical way of life deprived him of experience of the world and of the ability to judge people and situations realistically. Yet his detachment did allow him to mediate successfully between European powers in the all-important issue of the Turkish threat. The worldly wise

Louis had a focused but more blinkered view. The result was a stalemate while Innocent was alive and after his death there was a gradual erosion of Louis' position during his remaining years; he ceded, for example, the occupied territories. He came to find the Versailles routine oppressive and sought escape from it in the privacy of a small château, where he could invite a select number of guests.

Grand couvert or *souper intime*

Thus began a new era of intimate dining. The dress code was less formal, but some of the rituals of the meal itself were retained: the king never sat at the table with a man except a member of his own family, he was served on silver gilt plate, the princesses on silver and the rest on the house plate. The suppers could become boisterous affairs: the king threw bread at the ladies, who in turn threw theirs back at him.[32] The baroque celebrations at Versailles became infrequent during the successive reigns; Louis XV (1710-1774) enacted the ceremony of public dining, the *grand couvert*, only twice a week, on Tuesdays and Sundays, Louis XVI (1754-1793) and Marie Antoinette only on Sundays and feast days. The spectacle, for that is what it was, had become less effective as a unifying force for a nation which was now less impressed by aristocracy – as the end of the eighteenth-century would abundantly demonstrate. For another reason too, the *grand couvert* was less attractive to the participants; they had discovered the delights of the *souper intime*. These intimate suppers enjoyed by Louis XV and his circle took place in specially built apartments at Versailles and also in the smaller chateaux of La Muette and Choisy where he could dine after a day's hunting with a select group of guests including ladies.

The determination to shun public display in favour of privacy gradually brought about a new style of dining: ritual was banished; round tables liberated guests from problems of precedence; there could be uninhibited flow of conversation and, with few servants or none present after a certain stage of the meal, opportunities for flirtation were readily grasped.

The demise of fasting: a new role for food

At the death of Louis XIV, France could be described as a Catholic country, despite the opposition to Rome aroused by the Jansenist movement and its heretical tendencies, which led to a condemnatory Bull, *Unigenitus,* on the part of Pope Clement XI in 1715. Later in the century pastoral care on the part of many bishops proved much below reasonable standards, as many were absent from their dioceses. Their large incomes were more readily spent at Court and in Parisian aristocratic circles, and many were themselves of that class. The church as an institution was also very rich, as much of the land of France was owned by it. As the financial position of the kingdom deteriorated through the century, there was much resentment at the church's immunity from taxation.

> On the eve of the Revolution, when the situation was manifestly dangerous, Cardinal Loménie de Brienne, then first minister, suggested to his fellow churchmen a sum he regarded as their rightful contribution to a crying need; in response they offered a quarter of what he asked. [33]

As regards religious thought, the church suffered setbacks because of the advance of the Enlightenment movement, which subjected all religious doctrine to the scrutiny of reason. The reaction of religious authorities to the series of volumes of the *Encyclopédie* was to assume that new discoveries in science should be subject to the test of religious orthodoxy. This led to the conclusion on the part of the new thinkers, the *philosophes*, that religion must be the enemy of progress. [34]

In such a climate, ecclesiastical disciplines such as fasting could find little conviction and acceptance among the educated and the well-off upper classes. The French lawyer and commentator on society, Jean Brillat-Savarin (1755-1826), was the pioneer of a new genre of literature, the gastronomic essay, with his *The Physiology of Taste: Or Meditations on Transcendental Gastronomy.* The book which was published in 1825 and has never gone out of print, was in the form of a leisurely discussion of themes indicated by the title; it included Meditation XIV, On the Pleasures of the Table, but also Meditation XXI, On Obesity, and Meditation XXIV, On Fasting. He agreed that 'though contrary to our tastes and habits', fasting was of the greatest antiquity. Authors had explained that people of old felt they should 'macerate' their body when their soul was oppressed by public calamities or private ones. 'This idea seized on all nations and filled them with the thought of mourning, prayers, sacrifice, abstinence, mortification, etc.' [35] He noted that 'the practice of fasting, I am sorry to say, has become very rare' and listed the three meals customary in his day, adding that 'in Paris there are always more magnificent suppers, which begin after the play'. He described how fasting used to be, remarking that after dining on fish and vegetables

> at five o'clock all were furiously hungry, looked at their watches and became enraged, though they were securing their soul's salvation... I have seen two of my grand uncles, very excellent men, too, almost faint with pleasure when at Easter they saw a ham or a *paté* brought to the table. A degenerate race like the present experiences no such sensation'. [36]

He concluded by describing the origin of the removal of fasting, which had 'advanced by almost insensible degrees', echoing Erasmus two centuries previously:

> People began to find out that fasting disagreed with them and kept them awake. All the little accidents that man is subject to were then attributed to it, so that people did not fast because they thought themselves sick, or that they would be so. ... This was not all; some winters were so severe that people began to fear a scarcity of vegetables, and the ecclesiastical power relaxed its rigour. The duty, however, was recognised and permission was always asked.[37]

He noted that with the Revolution everything changed; no one thought of priests, who were looked on as enemies of the state. The hours for meals had changed and 'a totally different arrangement would be required for fasting.... I have not seen a Lenten table or a collation ten times in twenty-five years'.

Brillat-Savarin, the gourmand, was pleasantly surprised when he visited the Cistercian monastery of Saint-Sulpice 'about 1782' at the invitation of the abbot. He was in his twenties and the leader of a group of amateur musicians who had been invited to play during mass and during vespers. They arrived in the early hours of the morning and were met by the cellarer, who led them to the refectory where a meal awaited them.

> Amid the display of the table arose a *paté* like a cathedral; on one side was a quarter of cold veal, artichokes etc. ... There were various kinds of fruits, napkins, knives and plate; at the foot of the table were many attentive servants.[38]

There were more than a hundred bottles of wine and they could 'snuff' the aroma of coffee. There was too much food, but they did their best and then went to sleep until awakened by 'a great fat friar' and brought to the church for mass, where they played a symphony at the offertory, sang a motet at the elevation and at the end a piece for four wind instruments. The dinner that day was 'such as people used to eat in the fifteenth century'.

> There were few superfluities, but the choice of dishes was admirable. We had plain, honest and substantial stews, good meats and dishes of vegetables, which made one regret they were not more general. The dessert was the more remarkable, as it was composed of fruits not produced at that altitude. ... There was no want of liqueurs, but coffee needs a particular reference. It was clear, perfumed and strong, ... served in huge bowls, into which the monks dipped their lips and smacked them with delight.[39]

There was more to come, as after vespers, at which the group sang antiphons composed by Brillat-Savarin, there was 'a glorious supper' at

243

about nine. Three servants came with fresh buttered toast and a sweet-ened preparation of brandy punch. This was enjoyed by all until the ab-bey clock struck twelve and all retired to their cells.

There is no mention of fish in this account, but it may be that the monks had a meat-less dinner in their own refectory, as accounts of life in other French Cistercian monasteries of the time would imply. Towards the end of the century, the son of a duke recorded enjoying 'excellent fish' at one of them; Chateaubriand remembered a dinner of 'eggs, carp and an enormous pike'.[40]

The account of the stay at the Abbey of Saint-Sulpice mentions 'many attentive servants' and this draws attention to a social phenomenon of pre-Revolution France. Until 1782, when the French Assembly declared the property of the church to be at the disposal of the nation, the mon-asteries as well as the dioceses possessed significant resources in land and money. Whatever shortcomings there were in ecclesiastical administra-tion, the monasteries did provide a service to the state by giving employ-ment in both agriculture and craft work and very often in construction. The charitable work of a monastery embraced distribution of food to the needy – admittedly mainly the surplus from the monks' own table, but monastic charity also included the care of workers after their retirement through providing accommodation and meals.

> The number of permanent servants, if funds allowed, was sure to be excessive. The eight monks of the Cistercian monastery of Per-eigne in 1789 had two cooks, a baker, two porters, a brazier, a gardener, two cowherds, a boy to look after the guest-house, three women (housekeeper, sewing maid, and dairy maid) and an archi-vist with legal qualifications. At this time, the Grande Chartreuse had 100 monks and 300 servants.[41]

Revolutionary France

After the 1789 Revolution, there were enormous changes in society. A few days after the storming of the Bastille prison, the Marquis Charles de

Villette, who had renounced his title and written pamphlets supporting the Revolution, proposed a new form of public banqueting, a people's *grand couvert*, expressing equality and fraternity rather than class division. It was to take the form of rich and poor alike as one great family throughout Paris dining together in the streets (it was July!) at a single table, symbolically speaking. Such events were staged from time to time during the early, more extreme stages of the Revolution.

On 14 July 1790, the first anniversary of the fall of the Bastille, a Festival of Federation was staged, prefaced the previous day by two thousand spectators watching members of the National Assembly share an open-air 'patriotic meal' in the Circus of the Palais Royal. On the day itself General Lafayette invited provincial participants in the festival to feast at one of the 'endless tables' which had been set up beneath the trees of the Parc de la Muette. The left-overs from this fraternal repast were distributed afterwards to the poor.[42]

This way of dining served the cause of the state just as much as the banquets of Versailles had served the cause of the monarchy, but in the end its contrived nature could not bear repetition and the meal returned to its more fundamental function of expressing a family or friendship role. This did lead to a change in the status of women even before the Revolution.

> In France, since about 1770 there had been restaurants where respectable ladies might go with a family party, but the first London restaurants, serving mainly French food, were not established until about 1830, and for the next forty years or more it continued to be thought improper for a lady to be seen in a public dining-room.[43]

Gradually, dining facilities emerged in the hotels of London where people were becoming accustomed to dining-rooms shared with other parties and, paradoxically, privacy could be maintained by simply ignoring others dining at other well separated tables. In the late nineteenth-century, this became the norm throughout Europe for many shared meals, though the emergence of the formal dinner party held at home would become a feature of English Victorian life and introduce a diminished form of the ritual of earlier times – there were no hand-washings or ceremonies surrounding the serving of a glass of wine, rituals which for believers could suggest a spiritual dimension in a shared meal. The heritage and the myth of the Roman Empire and Renaissance banqueting tradition were fast fading. What replaced them was the cult of intimate dining and, it has been remarked, 'a body displaying a pot belly and a waistcoat'.[44] Such an environment was probably even less conducive to seeing the shared meal as intrinsically connected with the Eucharist.

Conclusion

The three centuries, the sixteenth to the eighteenth, mark a transition from the Renaissance to the modern world. They saw profound religious and social changes in which popes and kings sought to model society in accordance with their world views. For Paul IV, defending orthodox faith, rather than celebrating the achievements of Renaissance culture, was the priority. It resulted in an austere and ruthless regime, while his own family, without his knowing it, tasted all the pleasures of the table and other kinds as well. A more benign successor than he, Pius V, eschewed the dietary delights which his own official cook, Bartolomeo Scappi, brought to the attention of the nobility who thronged the papal court. They felt that religion and the finer things of material existence could be happily combined. Not all of his successors replicated his austere lifestyle and the election of popes tended to follow a pattern of reaction and new direction.

As the sixteenth-century gave way to its successor there were changes which created a new level of conflict, as popes undertook reform programmes in response to the worldliness of their predecessors and the challenge of the Reformation, while kings asserted what they believed were their divine rights and saw opportunity to assert and increment their status by taking control of the church. Food, feasting and fasting would be used in pursuit of their contrasting visions. Age-old philosophies lay behind their visions. The religious understanding had its roots

in an asceticism which was not found in the ministry of Jesus or mani-
festly evident in the New Testament, but was influenced by the reaction
of Christians like Jerome in the early centuries against the hedonism of
secular society, and against the ways in which popes over many centuries
had adopted the standards of the world. With the demise of the old feudal order and the emergence of centralised power in the hands of kings,
the temptation was to identify, as Louis XIV was reputed to have done,
the state with the person of the king. As popes tended to assert their
universal rule in the church and defend their secular rule at least as far as
Italy was concerned, conflicts were inevitable. Each side wished to present their particular identity in high profile, the pope in his cell and with
meagre diet, the king with the great public banquet.

Some popes of the eighteenth-century had greater skills in dealing
with the world than others, but in general 'found their room for manoeu-
vre more and more restricted as the monarchs of Europe increasingly
flexed their muscles and sought to bring the structures of the church under state control'.[45] Popes who lived lives of impressive humility continued to be elected, but generally lacked the wisdom to counter the moves
of the monarchs, and repeated the mistakes of some of their predecessors.
Benedict XIII (1724-1730) of the Orsini family was, like Pius V, a Dominican. He renounced his rights to the dukedom in favour of his brother, who subsequently used his wife's connection with Pope Clement X to
have his modest, ascetic brother raised to the cardinalate. This eventually
led to his election to the papacy and his insistence on living – as Pius V
had done – the life of a religious, refusing to reside in the papal apartments and – like Innocent XI – doing with the minimum of furniture.
Unlike many of his predecessors he took on much pastoral work, in the
course of which he made unannounced visits and dined without ceremony in ordinary convents. He was as unfortunate as Paul IV had been in
his choice of confidants. Not nephews this time but a Niccolo Coscia, a
Neapolitan of obscure origin, who as a member of his staff while he was
Archbishop of Benevento, gradually became his all-powerful minister in
all matters relating to the Papal States, as Benedict wished to engage sole-

ly in ecclesiastical affairs. But Coscia also took over much of the Curia's function and enriched himself by corrupt practices. Benedict could not be persuaded of his total venality and trusted him up to his own death.[46]

Benedict did assume responsibility for such problems as the opposition in France to the Bull of his predecessor, Clement XI, *Unigenitus,* condemning Jansenism and re-asserted its findings despite the objections of some of his fellow Dominicans in France. But his focus was more local and pastoral. In 1725, his commitment to his spiritual duties resulted in this seventy-six old celebrating all the liturgical functions of Holy Week. On Holy Saturday, these lasted for nine hours, while he observed the fast from midnight required for mass. On that day, after a drink of chocolate, he spent the remaining hours in the confessional.[47] As the historian of the papacy, Von Pastor commented: 'Thanks to ceaseless work, extreme moderation in food and drink, and regular exercise, Benedict XIII … preserved an enviable robustness up to the threshold of his eightieth year'. But in the end it was fasting and overwork that brought about his end in 1730, ironically, during the Carnival celebrations in the city.[48] The judgment of Von Pastor on this former friar evokes the memory of quite a number of popes over the centuries: 'to be an able Pope, it is not enough to be an excellent religious'. This was a rather polarised view but it was true that it was not enough to ignore the modern world and the changing perception of the many sided nature of a truly human life. The Renaissance and the Enlightenment made their contributions to the emergence of the modern person; to keep up, religious thought would need to have done more than combat Jansenism. The structures and worship of the church remained unchanged during those centuries, with the hierarchical character of both reflecting class division rather than community. As will be seen later, a deeper understanding of liturgical tradition would have been the key to renewing both worship and the church's authority structure, and would have provided a foundation for the Christian form of humanism needed to meet the challenge of the age.

ENDNOTES

1 Michel de Montaigne, *The Essayes of Michael Lord of Montaigne,* Vol. I, John Florio trans. (London: Grant Richards, 1904) 399

2 Ludwig Von Pastor, *History of the Popes,* Vol. XIV (London: Kegan Paul, 1924) 66

3 Ibid. 264

4 Friedrich Gontard, *The Popes* A. J. and E. F. Peeler trans. (London: Barrie and Rockliff, 1964) 429

5 Ludwig Von Pastor, *History of the Popes,* Vol. XIV 78

6 Friedrich Gontard, *The Popes* 430

7 Ludwig Von Pastor, *History of the Popes,* Vol. XIV 422

8 Roy Strong, *Feast. A History of Grand Eating* (London: Jonathan Cape, 2002) 139

9 Stephen Mennell, *All Manners of Food* (Oxford: Blackwell, 1985) 69

10 Roy Strong, *Feast* 144

11 Ludwig Von Pastor, *History of the Popes,* Vol. XVII (London: Kegan Paul, 1929) 55

12 Ibid. 55 n.2

13 Cristoforo Messisbugo, *Banchetti compositioni di vivande et apparecchio generale 1549* (Delhi: Gyan Books Pvt. Ltd., 2016)

14 Roy Strong, *Feast* 135∑

15 Idem

16 Ibid. 218

17 Alberto Capatti and Massimo Montanari, *Italian Cuisine. A Cultural History* (New York: Columbia University Press, 1999) 137

18 Stephen Mennell, *All Manners of Food* 70

19 Euan Cameron, *The European Reformation* (Oxford: Clarendon Press, 1991) 376

20 Roy Strong, Feast 238

21 Ibid. 249

22 Ibid. 259

23 Ibid. 260

24 Ibid. 255

25 Ludwig Von Pastor, *History of the Popes,* Vol. XXXII (London: Kegan Paul, 1940) 15

26 Ibid. 14

27 Friedrich Gontard, *The Popes* 459

28 Ludwig Von Pastor, *History of the Popes,* Vol. XXXII, 17

29 Friedrich Gontard, *The Popes* 460

30 Ludwig Von Pastor, *History of the Popes,* Vol. XXXII 234

31 Eamon Duffy, *Saints and Sinners, A History of the Popes* (New Haven: Yale University Press, 2001) 238

32 Roy Strong, *Feast* 263

33 Gerald R. Cragg, *The Church in the Age of Reason* (Harmondsworth: Penguin Books, 1966) 201

34 James Byrne, *Glory, Jest and Riddle. Religious Thought in the Enlightenment* (London: S.C.M. Press, 1996) 142

35 Jean Brillat-Savarin, *The Physiology of Taste: Or Meditations on Transcendental Gastronomy* (Scotts Valley CA: Create Space Independent Publishing Platform, 2017) 93

36 Ibid. 94

37 Idem

38 Ibid. 114

39 Idem

40 John McManners, *Church and Society in Eighteenth Century France*. Vol. 1: *The Clerical Establishment and its Social Ramifications* (Oxford: Clarendon Press, 1998) 507

41 Ibid 506

42 Ibid. 275

43 Reay Tannahill, *Food in History* (London: Headline Book Publishing, 2002³) 327

44 Alberto Capatti and Massimo Montanari, *Italian Cuisine. A Cultural History,* Aine O'Healy trans. (New York: Columbia University Press, 2003) 288

45 Eamon Duffy, *Saints and Sinners* 241-2

46 Ludwig Von Pastor, *History of the Popes,* Vol. XXXIV (London: Kegan Paul, 1941) 131, 297

47 Ibid. 121

48 Ibid. 292-3

CHAPTER FOURTEEN

Puritan belief and devotion

If we can never have any certainty of our being in a state of salvation, good reason is that every moment should be spent, not in joy, but in fear.[1]

Civil religion is the attemp to empower religion not for the good of religion but for the creation of the citizen.[2]

The English Puritans

The political turmoil in eighteenth-century France and its tragic outcome in the Revolution had been preceded in a similar set of events in seventeenth-century England. In that case the religious context was different. In the England of Henry VIII and his successor, Elizabeth I, monarchy and church had been closely allied; this would be the case at the beginning of the seventeenth-century and would again be before the end, but there would be much upheaval in between. Under the influence of the Calvinism which had flourished in European cities or states of anti-royalist views, a dissident movement emerged in England among people who had become alienated from a church with close royal connections. They came to be called Puritans and would have a prominent role in the civil war of the mid-century. The term Puritan is a label rather than a formal name given to these more radical Protestants who sought a new Reformation to complete the 'half-Reformation of 1517' and were dissatisfied with the extent to which the Church of England in its efforts to follow what it called a middle way had 'purified' itself from Catholic beliefs and practices. It is estimated that these dissidents amounted to 'something like half the population of the religiously alert members of the population (though not half of the population as a whole)'.[3] Nevertheless, the Church of England was officially the church of the whole population, and the king was its head. As it happened, King Charles I (r1625-

251

1649), together with Archbishop Laud (1573-1645), favoured ritual in the church's worship to such an extent that the opponents of ritual, who were divided among themselves, became a cohesive dissenting party.[4]

Charles' high-handed treatment of Parliament, in which there were many of that party, led to opposing forces that became collectively known as the Roundheads because of their preference for short haircuts – a stern rejection of the high fashion favoured by their opponents. In subsequent centuries, this rejection of the lifestyle of the royalists in favour of a more austere way of life has sometimes been considered evidence that the Puritans favoured not only simplicity but also meagreness of diet. But there is no strong evidence that this was the case. They condemned church feasts in principle while observing the Sabbath as a day of rest, and were concerned about abuses such as drunkenness associated with feasts, abuses which the official church in the Homilies also condemned – as did the Catholic Church. Before civil war broke out, the Parliament abolished the complex pattern of fasting which had persisted in the established church, inaugurating in its place a single fast on the final Wednesday of the month. This was a way of responding to the political crisis, but it was abolished in 1649 on grounds of neglect.[5]

Charles I lost the civil war and was executed in 1649. The Parliament was divided into different factions, but Oliver Cromwell, who had led the campaign against the king, ejected all who disagreed with him and formed a republic, which he called a Commonwealth, to take the place of the monarchy. With Cromwell's death in 1658 confusion reigned, as there was no one with his ability to succeed him, and it became possible for the son of the executed monarch to return from exile as King Charles II and head of the Church of England, now restored to its position as official church in place of the loose grouping of the former dissenters of various Puritan proclivities. The restored church proved non-accommodating to such people and a deadline for acceptance of the confessional standards led to the departure of three thousand clergy and the laity who supported them.[6] The former fasting regulations were re-introduced by King Charles II in 1664, but with limited success and the last prosecution for infringement was made shortly afterwards.

The dissenting Christians became a minority who were considered an irritant by the established church and were discriminated against, while a certain tolerance was practised towards the upper-class Catholics who had suffered persecution during Elizabeth's reign a century earlier

The Puritans belonged to a growing industrious class of farmers, merchants and artisans who recognised the importance of regular work and rest patterns, though this was truer of the town dwellers than of the farming community, where the changing seasons imposed their own rhythm. Their outlook was that of the mobile small craftsman, accustomed to working for survival.[7] Their diet may have been plain in reaction to the excesses of the higher social classes, but their work would require it to be substantial rather than meagre. All were imbued with Calvinist principles which stressed the importance of serious engagement with the affairs of the world as a way of acknowledging God's sovereignty.

The essential qualities of Puritan spirituality were listed in a work by an Anglican Bishop, Lewis Bayly, who was an ardent Puritan in his devotional life and a minimalist in ceremonies. It was published about 1610, was translated into many languages and had a significant influence on John Bunyan (1628-188), who became the best known Puritan writer with his *Pilgrim's Progress*. The essence of piety, according to Bayly, was

> to joyne together, in watching, fasting, praying, reading the Scriptures, keeping his Sabbaths, hearing Sermons, receiving the holy Communion, relieving the Poore, exercising in all humilitie the works of Pietie to God, and walking conscionably in the duties of our calling towards men.[8]

A story from the life of John Bunyan showed the devotional environment which was characteristic of these families.

> 'Child', says Elizabeth Bunyan to one of her children, 'eat not with thy fingers. Hath not thy father made us forks with which to take up our food from the platter? 'But, mother-Elizabeth', pleads the child,

'was it not the custom to use fingers even in good Queen Bess's time?' 'Ay, ay', interposes John Bunyan, 'but hearken, my child, as Rome does, so do ye!' 'We aren't in Rome, John, and God grant we may never be!' rejoins Elizabeth. 'Ay, for certain, wife if our faith might thereby be jeopardised; but, nevertheless, from Rome we get the fork and that not long since, as our bairn hath said'.[9]

Bunyan was not accurate in his account of the origins of the fork, but the story shows that within a century Puritans had begun to see the early days of the English Reformation as the beginning of religious liberation, though by this time they were distancing themselves from the mainstream - while sharing abhorrence of 'Rome'.

New England

When in the course of the seventeenth-century some of these dissenters moved to New England, they had great difficulty at first in feeding themselves, because they tried to maintain the diet to which they were accustomed in England. But they learned gradually from the Indian tribes what to grow and recipes for making it palatable, the foundations of the American diet of later centuries.[10] They brought with them their Puritan values and tried to maintain them. The Mayflower pilgrims of 1620, for example, of whom only fifty of the hundred and two survived an illness on arrival, made a compact promising 'all due submission and obedience to all just and equal laws' which the government they set up might pass.[11] There were two different calendars in use initially, the Julian, adhered to by immigrants from England, and the Gregorian by those from continental Europe, and this led to some confusion about traditional feasts. But these, including Christmas, were generally ignored in any case. Sunday, identified as the Sabbath, was observed, but with diverse approaches to how the day was spent. 'The Dutch openly practised a Continental Sunday, one of conviviality after church.'[12]

The influence of immigrants like them would prove foundational for the civic and religious ethos of Protestant America in subsequent centuries. The emphasis on the priesthood of believers in the original Lutheran Reformation had reduced the authority of the clergy, but the established church in England remained quite a clerical institution because of its royal patronage, while recognising also, as both Henry VIII and Queen Elizabeth had done, the importance of the head of the household. In Puritan families, this authority became even more marked with bible reading led by the father who also instructed the children. The biblical story of the Fall caused women to be seen as inherently weak morally, though maternal influence inevitably was strong in families, which typically were large.

Paradoxically, for people whose religious life was lived in a family context and who repudiated the Catholic tradition of religious life under vows, they relied on traditional techniques from the ascetic and contemplative tradition. Meditative reading of Scripture, poring over the text, or 'porismatic' reading, was the daily routine. Bishop Bayly directed the devout to read a chapter morning, noon and night, so as to read the entire Bible in a year. Compunction, the deep sense of sorrow for sin cultivated in the monastic tradition and often leading to tears, was a commonplace experience.

> (A practice which) figured prominently in the Puritan regimen, both publicly and privately, was fasting or 'humiliation'. In both Old and New England officials called for fasts during times of crisis, convinced that the public welfare depended on the piety of the faithful. The General Court of Massachusetts, for instance, set July 7, 1681 as 'a day of public Humiliation' on the grounds that the time required 'greater fervency and frequency in the most solemn seekings of God in the face of Jesus Christ than wee have ordinarily had experience of ... '.[13]

Cotton Mather (1681-1724), a Congregationalist minister in the Boston colony, was one of the most prominent Puritan pastors of the late seventeenth-century and the first to describe a European colonist as an American.[14] He had the custom of a 'secret fast' on Saturdays, many of which were recorded in his diary. The motive often came from his awareness of his great sinfulness, but also on one recorded occasion it was the adultery of a woman in his congregation.

> I therefore sett apart this Day, for prayer with fasting in my study, that I might obtain the pardon of all my own vile sinfulness, which the sins of others led me to reflect upon: and I obtained it.[15]

It might appear surprising that he referred to 'horrible crimes' among some members of his congregation but by the early eighteenth-century in the American colonies,

> the once raging fires of Puritanism were banked. People in general attended 'meetings', listened to sermons or slept during them, kept (outwardly, at least) the Sabbath, and attempted to keep the other commandments; but they were falling away from the antique faith.[16]

An aspect of the 'antique faith' which became neglected in Puritanism was the emphasis on sacramental rites Anglicanism adhered to as part of the mainstream Reformation tradition. The Puritan tradition of worship was initially closely linked to Anglican usage as people like Lewis Bayly and Edward Reynolds (1599-1676) were Anglican bishops who were also members of the Puritan movement. But when Parliament appealed for help to Scotland in the Civil War, the price it had to pay was to accept the dominance of Scottish Presbyterian divines and the setting up of the Westminster Assembly which drew up a *Directory of Publick Worship* (1645) reflecting Scottish Calvinist theology. The *Directory* modified the way in which the Eucharist was to be celebrated; following the principle of adhering strictly to Scripture, the rite would no longer be called Holy Communion but 'The Lord's Supper'.

The ceremony was reduced to a form reflecting its description in Scripture. Its theology hardly differed, however, from that of Anglicanism in that both were fundamentally based on rejection of the Roman doctrine of transubstantiation and instead on Calvin's doctrine of the Eucharist, the subtleties of which had not, however, survived migration to Knox's Scotland (or indeed to Cranmer's England). Both the Anglican and the Presbyterian traditions did however regard the rite as a saving ordinance, not a simple kind of remembrance of Christ's saving work, as had been held by Ulrich Zwingli in sixteenth-century Zürich. (The *Directory* used the same terms, 'receiving by faith' and 'feeding on Christ' as in the *Book of Common Prayer*.) The various dissenting groups based themselves on the *Directory*, but celebrated the Lord's Supper with their own chosen frequency, ranging from weekly to quarterly to even less frequently. Basically this was because worship was focused on sermons designed to bring about conversion, thereby creating an individualistic, internalised religious sensibility where a Communion rite assumed a secondary place.

The 'Great Awakening'

If the once 'raging fires of Puritanism' had become banked in America by the early eighteenth-century, that situation changed famously with the advent of the First Great Awakening in 1734 among colonists of diverse congregations and denominations, especially Presbyterians and Congregationalists. A similar phenomenon occurred in Britain. In America, it had its beginning in the revivalist preaching of the Congregationalist minister, Jonathan Edwards (1703-1758), at Northampton, Massachusetts. Things may have slipped somewhat in Mather's congregation, but people who attended Edwards' sermons were not likely to have slept, though he always remained calm and unemotional while he preached. It is no surprise that his listeners shrieked and moaned in exquisite agony, especially those who heard his most famous sermon, 'Sinners in the hands of an angry God' of 1741:

> The God that holds you over the pit of hell, much as one holds a spider or some loathsome creature over the fire, abhors you, and is dreadfully provoked; his wrath towards you burns like fire; he looks upon you as worthy of nothing else but to be cast into the fire; he is of purer eyes than to bear to have you in his sight; you are

ten thousand times so abominable in his eyes as the most hateful and venomous is in ours.[17]

The Great Awakening movement was, however, resisted by the majority of the clergy as a vulgar travesty of religion, with the result that members of their congregations seceded and set up churches of their own. But the American equivalent of the European Enlightenment was taking hold and people like Benjamin Franklin (1706-1790), scientist, philosopher, one of the Founding Fathers of the United States, had not, in his youth, been impressed by the clerical establishment of his native Boston headed by Cotton Mather - what he described as 'the governing party' [18] - nor later by his own contemporary, Jonathan Edwards. Edwards had in his youth been an avid student of the natural world and had studied and written about the spiders he was later to mention in his sermon. But he was ordained a minister and went through a personal conversion to a rigid way of thinking based on God's absolute sovereignty. His pamphlet, *A Faithful Narrative of the Surprising Work of God in the Conversion of Many Hundreds of Souls in Northampton*, published in 1736 proved a great support for the Revival. But the movement passed its peak and Edwards was affected by the backlash against it. He retired to a small frontier town and became a missionary to an Indian reservation. Being a former college tutor, he was invited to become President of the College of New Jersey at Princeton in 1757 and died there soon afterwards.[19] A second Awakening, mostly among Methodists, occurred in the early nineteenth-century as a reaction to the rationalism of the Enlightenment. It centred on camp meetings, where an atmosphere of excitement was create by the large crowds and led to dancing, singing and shouting, and in contrast with the earlier phenomenon, an atmosphere of celebratory meals rather than of fasting.

Methodism

Among those who read the *Faithful Narrative* was an Anglican priest, John Wesley (1703-1791), while he walked from London to Oxford. He had begun an apostolate to the virtually unchurched lower classes and

258

been gradually excluded from involvement in his own church. His ministry in Britain and that of the ministers he sent to America was in fact influenced by the First Great Awakening. In his youth, he was presumably influenced by his mother's understanding of dietary abstinence. She saw the principal aim of abstinence as being 'to bring all the sensual appetites into a due subjection to the superior powers of the mind'.[20]

As an Oxford student, he had begun to deepen his life of prayer and with his brother, Charles, gathered some friends of like mind for regular meetings, at one of which a new member, John Clayton, 'urged them to keep the fasts of the primitive church which were enjoined in the *Book of Common Prayer* but yet had lapsed from general use'.[21]

> (The Wesley brothers) began to fast every Wednesday and Friday. On the next visit to Epworth they refused to breakfast with their parents on a Wednesday or a Friday, to the rector's dudgeon, and on their way home they walked on empty stomachs until evening.[22]

As a rule, they fasted on those days until three in the afternoon.[23] But, as John said in his *Journal (18 January to 24 May 1738)*, 'I knew not how to go any further'.[24] This was in 1731. He had been ordained and was a Fellow of Lincoln College, Oxford, where he lived an austere life, doing without a fire in his rooms, praying at intervals during the day and visiting prisoners in the local jail. He and his friends stood out among their contemporaries and because of the regularity of their meeting and their religious practice they had received the nickname 'Methodists' in the university community.

His life changed when he accepted an invitation to go as a missionary to Georgia in America and while on the voyage met members of the Moravian Church engaged in a similar mission. Disappointed by the results of his preaching in Georgia, he returned to England in 1738 and through attendance at a Moravian meeting suddenly had a deeper conversion experience. This led him to engage in preaching on Sundays in the early morning outside closed Anglican churches to servants who were not free to attend official services. Gradually his followers were organised into Societies and found premises for services, so that eventually all these groups came to be regarded as the Methodist Church, though Wesley himself remained an Anglican priest until his death. From being a devout Oxford Fellow with a limited ministry he was now a missionary whose aim was to bring about the conversion to living faith of the large numbers who flocked to hear him preach. Inevitably, his relationship with the authorities of the church became strained. He was careful not to preach in the parishes at the time of statutory services and consistently urged his followers to attend those services, especially Holy Communion, but the presence in a parish of these newly converted Methodists, who often showed signs of an undesirable 'enthusiasm', created a problem even for the pastorally minded clergy.

Those who opposed his movement could appeal to the Act of Toleration of 1689, which had regulated the activities of the dissenting Christians. By this Act, building and attending chapels for non-Anglican worship was allowed, provided the teaching given there was not Roman Catholic or Anti-Trinitarian and the place was registered as a Dissenting Chapel. Wesley considered that his movement was Anglican in nature and resisted the requirement to register both the building and the preachers themselves and it was only in 1787, four years before his death, that he advised compliance with the law.[25]

Love feasts
By that time the Methodist Church was well established in England and in America (established there by Methodist immigrants from Ireland). Because of its origin in revivalist type preaching and the early recommendation to attend Holy Communion services in parish churches, the celebration of Holy Communion emerged only gradually, with its place being taken initially by Love Feasts. These were first held by small groups of more intensely committed believers known as 'bands', but spread to all members of the community. The rite was borrowed from the Moravians, but also inspired by the *agapé* of the early church.

John and Charles Wesley took part in a Love Feast with four other clergy and sixty members of the Fetter Lane (London) Society on the evening of January 1ˢᵗ, 1739, sharing bread and water with them.

> 'About three in the morning' records Wesley, 'as we were continuing instant in prayer, the power of God came mightily upon us, insofar that many cried out for exceeding joy, and many fell to the ground. As soon as we were recovered a little from that awe and amazement at the presence of his majesty we broke out with one voice: 'We praise thee, O God, we acknowledge Thee to be the Lord'.[26]

It is interesting that the subjective and emotional aspect of the experience transitioned immediately to the church's objective worship in the hymn, the *Te Deum* evocative of the relationship that had obtained in the early church. At other times, the Love Feast had more of a 'stand alone' character and became a healing service. Wesley reported how this occurred in his own case when he had been feeling ill at a service in 1741:

> I called on Jesus aloud, to 'increase my faith' and to 'confirm the word of his grace.' While I was speaking, my pain vanished away; the fever left me; my bodily strength returned, and for many weeks I felt neither weakness nor pain.[27]

The first explicit reference to Love Feasts in America was in 1770 at Philadelphia, but its use became widespread there and it was considered a means of grace. One account from such a gathering in July 1776 alleged that people experienced new birth and 'entire sanctification', though John Wesley himself was cautious about accepting such claims; he had no timetable for the emergence of this gift.[28] A participant testified:

> We held our general love-feast. It began between eight and nine on Wednesday morning, and continued till noon. Many testified that they had 'redemption in the blood of Jesus, even the forgiveness of sins.' And many were enabled to declare that it had 'cleansed

them from all sin'. So clear, so full, so strong was their testimony
that while some were speaking of their experience hundreds were in
tears, and others vehemently crying to God for pardon or holiness.[29]

The Love Feast was important among the frontier people of eighteenth-century America, but when it became acceptable for Methodists
to hold their own Holy Communion services and ordained ministers
were available in sufficient numbers, it was less used,[30] though its atmosphere of spiritual sharing still has an effect on how Holy Communion is
celebrated in some congregations.

It seems that in Wesley's mind there was a close connection between
Holy Communion and the Love Feast because of an apparent appreciation of the 'sacral' nature of eating and drinking.

> In the lived realty of eating and drinking, in the ritualized versions
> of that in church and preaching house, in his 'families' and among
> the schoolboys of Kingswood, he reminded early Methodists of
> the sacral nature of their daily eating and drinking.[31]

As regards official Anglican worship, John Wesley and his brother
Charles subscribed to belief in the Eucharist insofar as it was articulated
in the 1662 *Book of Common Prayer*. They believed the Eucharist was a
divinely appointed means of grace. According to the English Methodist
Conference Report of 2003:

> The undefined but real presence of Christ was proclaimed in their
> sermons and hymns. The Wesleys taught an understanding of the
> Eucharistic sacrifice as one in which the offering of the obedient
> hearts and lives of the communicants was united by grace to the
> perfect, complete, ever-present and all-atoning sacrifice of Christ.[32]

It would be difficult to establish to what extent their position was
shared in the congregations which were established in the course of time,

as Non-Wesleyan Methodist denominations emerged in Britain, and American Methodists developed their own Orders of Service.[33]

Wesley's ministry was originally confined to London but on the urging of one of his clerical associates, George Whitefield, who was himself preaching to large crowds, he travelled by horseback to Bristol in 1739 to join Whitefield there. In this way he began to extend the scope of a ministry which would take him throughout the country and over to Ireland; he travelled unceasingly for the remainder of his days.

The ascetical practices of his former austere way of life seem to have been mitigated by the demands of his ministry, for in his *Journal* in 1744 he expressed astonishment at a letter he received from a fellow clergyman. This man had been surprised when Wesley told him that he carried things too far 'in denying the lawful pleasures of eating'. The letter had included advice the writer had given to another: 'if there are two dishes set before you, by the rule of self-denial, you ought to eat of that which you like the least'. It was a rule he desired to observe himself, 'always to choose what is less pleasing and cheapest'.[34]

This astonished Wesley, who advised moderation in the consumption of both wine and food but also felt they were to be enjoyed: 'It is usually innocent, mixed with a little mirth, which is said to help digestion'.[35] But he was at other times harshly critical of what he called the dissipation so widespread in England. By it he meant not only being 'violently attached to women, gaming, drinking, to dances, balls, races…, but (dissipation) equally belongs to a serious fool who forgets God by a close attention to any worldly employment'.[36] In a sermon on riches from his later years, he explained that

'The desire of the flesh' is generally understood in far too narrow a meaning. It does not, as is commonly supposed, refer to one of the senses only, but takes in all the pleasures of sense, the gratification of any of the outward senses. It has reference to the taste in particular. How many thousands do we find at this day, in whom the ruling principle is the desire to enlarge the pleasure of tasteing (*sic*). Perhaps they do not gratify this desire in a gross manner, so as to incur the imputation of intemperance; much less so as to violate health or impair their understanding by gluttony or drunkenness. But they live in a genteel, regular sensuality, in an elegant Epicureanism, which does not hurt the body, but only destroys the soul, keeping it at a distance from true religion.[37]

He set out in detail his thinking about fasting in a sermon preached prior to 1748. Like Luther before him, he talked of the importance of good works following necessarily on faith and went on to discuss the nature of fasting, the reasons for it, how objections against it might be answered, and lastly, how it should be performed. In his approach he relied on and quoted the Anglican Church's Homilies. He took the meaning of fasting from the practice of the early church and accordingly it meant simply taking no food from morning to evening. Following Tertullian, he described as a half-fast, the omission of all sustenance until three in afternoon. He believed that what the church of his day meant by abstinence was simply to eat little, and described abstaining from pleasant food as the lowest kind of fasting. This, he thought, could be the reason for the ancient custom of abstaining from flesh and wine.[38]

The evolution of American Civil Religion

The Puritan tradition in America gave rise to a religious way of life for the family characterised by Scripture reading and instruction. This was not without its festal or para-liturgical ethos, despite the dismissal of church Feast Days, and was the origin of the Thanksgiving holiday, which was very much a celebration of family values. In a secularised society it remains that, despite the term 'Thanksgiving' and being ultimately derived from the Anglican Harvest Festival. It pre-dated by more than a century its official recognition in the Proclamation by President Abraham Lincoln (1809-1865) in October 1863 of a Day of Thanksgiving to be observed on the last Thursday of November. Even though the Civil War was still unfinished, he introduced the Harvest Festival note when declared that 'the year that is drawing to its close has been filled with the blessings of fruitful fields and healthful skies' and he attributed this to 'the ever-watchful providence of Almighty God'.[39]

Lincoln often referred to Divine Providence, perhaps unconsciously echoing Calvin's theology of Providence. He also recommended that a note of penitence be included 'for our national perverseness and disobedience' linking it to 'the lamentable civil strife in which we are unavoidably engaged'.[40] Joining penitence with thanksgiving reflects the essence of Puritan spirituality. The penitential mood of the times was similar to what had obtained some decades previously in England, when fears generated by the French Revolution and an outbreak of cholera (which had spread from France) caused Evangelicals to call for fasting and penance. 'King William issued a call to a national day of fasting and humiliation on 21 March 1832, on account of the cholera. ... Many country villages and some town churches kept the fast day with devotion and made collections to relieve the suffering and the poor.' [41] Queen Victoria appointed a national day of 'fasting, humiliation and prayer' in October 1857 at the time of the Indian Rebellion, the last decree of this kind in England.[42]

As well as decreeing the Thanksgiving Day in 1863, Lincoln had in August 1861 and in March 1863 signed Proclamations setting aside days for national prayer because of the Civil War. In each case, the call was for a day of national humiliation, prayer and fasting, all terms which had been in the writings, sermons and diary of Cotton Mather more than a century earlier and evoked also the sermons of Jonathan Edwards. However, 'Lincoln gave no definite impression that he belonged to any particular church or endorsed any special faith or doctrine'. Nonetheless, 'the President and his wife usually drove to the New York Avenue Presbyterian Church, but sometimes walked, accompanied by a guard'.[43]

Between the early eighteenth-century era of Cotton Mather, when Christians of various Protestant denominations shared Puritan beliefs and values, and the nineteenth-century regime of Lincoln, an important change had come in both the political and religious situations. The 1776 Revolution established the Unites States, of which Lincoln was President

Portrait of Abraham Lincoln (16th president of the United States)

from 1862 until his assassination in 1865. In addition to the political transformation influenced by the French Revolution and its promotion of liberty and equality, the religious climate had been transfused with Deist beliefs because of the intellectual movement, the Enlightenment, with its exaltation of reason. Deism held that reason and human experience determined belief rather than Christian dogma. Throughout the eighteenth-century, the founding fathers of the new America were influenced by a new critical approach to issues of authority in both politics and religion. How much each of the leaders was influenced by Deism is difficult to establish, because reference to Providence – in Lincoln's case, for example – could arise from Calvinist tradition inspired by Scripture or could, on the other hand, have the import of the terms used by Deists to refer to a governing principle. This could be called God, whose existence could be established by reason – and could serve to underpin the political establishment. Throughout his life, one of the founding fathers, Benjamin Franklin (1706-1790), remained independent of the ecclesiastical institution while referring – especially later in life – more and more to a Supreme Being. As a young man, he wrote *Articles of Belief and Acts of Religion* (1728). In it he

> measured the immensity of the universe against the minusculi-ty of the earth and the inhabitants thereof, and concluded from this that it was "great vanity of me to suppose that the Supremely Perfect does in the least regard such an inconsiderable nothing as man". Moreover, this Supremely Perfect had absolutely no need to be worshipped by humans. ... Yet if worship filled no divine purpose it did serve a human need. "I think it required of me, and my duty as a man to pay divine regards to *something*".[44]

He had a sense of duty and fairness throughout his life and already at that young age listed a set of cardinal virtues which he intended to practise, including frugality, justice and moderation. The first was 'Temperance. Eat not to dullness. Drink not to elevation'.[45]

There was a spectrum of religious belief running from non-Christian Deism to Christian Deism to Christian Orthodoxy among those founding fathers. Where the first President, George Washington came in this range is disputed by historians.

> Many of Washington's eminent contemporaries ... regarded him as a sincere believer in the Christian faith, and a truly devout man. Some of Washington's religious style probably reflected an Enlightenment discomfort with religious dogma, but it also reflected his low-key personal style. ... Simply as a matter of personal style, he would have refrained from the emotional language associated with Evangelical Christianity.[46]

When as a retired General he returned to his estate, Mount Vernon, in 1783 after the Revolutionary War, his attendance at the Protestant Episcopal Church was intermittent as he avoided Sundays when Holy Communion was celebrated, perhaps taking umbrage at being chided on a previous occasion by a minister for failing to do so, or it may be that he wanted to avoid being on public display.[47]

A rather reluctant President, he was a man of integrity, who promoted fairness - though he had three hundred slaves, many inherited through his wife's patrimony. In his will he decreed that they were to be freed after his wife's death. As President, he lived a life of simplicity and minimum ceremony.

> Once in each fortnight he gave an official dinner. Foreign ministers, officers of government, and other distinguished strangers were welcomed to the President's table. On these occasions there was neither ostentation nor restraint. Simplicity in the host and ease on the part of the guests was the order of the day.[48]

These dinners were held on every other Thursday at 4.0 p.m. 'If guests were even five minutes late by the hall clock, they found the President and his guests already seated. Washington would then explain curtly that the cook was governed by the clock and not by the company.'[49]

His Farewell Address to the American People in 1796, which is still read annually in Congress, included a reference to religion: 'Whatever may be conceded to the influence of refined education on minds of peculiar structure, reason and experience both forbid us to expect, that national morality can prevail in exclusion of religious principle.'[50] He expressed the wish that Heaven might show continued beneficence to his fellow citizens, and further on included the rhetorical question: 'Can it be, that Providence has not connected the permanent felicity of a Nation with its Virtue?'[51] Though this reference to Heaven and Providence seems only vaguely Christian, in his private life on Sunday evenings he read aloud passages from sermons or passages from Scripture.[52]

As he neared death in December 1799, he said he was not afraid to go but he 'never sought religious solace or offered any prayers'.[53] Instead of a lavish funeral, he had a simple military burial at his residence, Mount Vernon. Of the six pallbearers, five were Masons. The local Episcopalian minister led the service at the family vault, after which 'the Worshipful Master of the Masonic Lodge officiated over rituals performed by Masons garbed in their customary aprons'.[54]

Alexis de Tocqueville, who was sent by the French government in 1831 to study the American prison system, was fascinated by the fact that whereas the French Revolution led to the Terror and counter-Revolution, the American Revolution had brought forth liberal democracy. This led him to undertake his famous study of democracy in America. He was convinced of the importance of religion and concluded that the 'great utility of religion is still more obvious among nations where equality of conditions prevails than among others'.[55] Long before de Tocqueville's arrival, the religion of the many colonies was that of dissidents from English Anglicanism and even from the mainstream Protestant churches in Europe a century previously. The situation would change by mid-century with the influx of immigrants from Catholic countries like Ireland, but from the time of the Revolution onwards, America retained a Protestant ethos.

De Tocqueville observed 'the passion for physical well-being' felt by all in America, but believed that the taste for physical gratification did not lead a democratic people into excess. It was a tenacious passion but of limited range.

> To build enormous palaces, to conquer or to mimic nature, to ransack the world in order to gratify the passions of a man, is not thought of, but to add a few yards of land to your field, to plant an orchard, to enlarge a dwelling, to be always making life more comfortable and convenient, to avoid trouble, and to satisfy the smallest wants without effort and almost without cost. These are small objects, but the soul clings to them.[56]

He did not mention food in his description of the good life people sought, but it would be surprising if this desire for physical well-being, in general to get on in life, did not focus on such aspects of life as meals, and, in particular, meals for special occasions. In February 1862, when the Civil War was going in Lincoln's favour, his wife Mary invited a large number of guests - against the advice of the protocol officers at the State Department that the President's entertainment should be confined to soirees open to the public at large and to small private dinners.[57] Mary had already evoked the President's ire by her excessive expenditure on the renovation of the White House, but possibly wanted to let the elite of Washington see the results of her endeavours.[58] The five hundred guests arrived at nine and were presented to the President and First Lady by staff dressed in mulberry-coloured uniforms to match the new china table-ware, while the United States Marine Band played their repertoire.

> At midnight the doors to the dining room were opened to reveal a magnificent buffet concocted by Maillard's of New York, the most expensive caterer in the country. It displayed sugary models of the Ship of State, Fort Sumter and Fort Pickens flanked by mounds of turkey, duck, ham, terrapin and pheasant.[59]

The event, though not a seated affair, was much more a banquet than a reception, and the food provided was remarkably similar to that of the banquets which originated in sixteenth-century Italy, even to the music and the appearance of *trionfi* (though not called that, presumably) de-picting the symbols of victory. The extravagant affair did not receive the approval of all Washingtonians, especially those who had not received an invitation. A year after this event which harked back to the decid-edly non-Puritan banquets of Europe, Lincoln proclaimed the annual Thanksgiving festival and included a note of repentance; the inclusion of this typically Puritan note may have been influenced by the fact that the Civil War dragged on, but also by his grief over the death in the mean-time of his son, Willie.

Conclusion

The pattern of the Christian life established by the Church of England claimed a middle of the road or *via media* approach to how feasts and fasts were to be celebrated. This policy continued into the next centuries. But the dissenting parties did not decline with time and grew into other denominations with their own approaches to the balance between the elements necessary to maintain a steady pattern of Christian living. In general, the concept of freedom became a more important value among these diverse churches, as a non-hierarchical theology of church implicit in these denominations had its effects, and democracy in society made gains. Family life with the father at its head ensured that freedom did not mean licence, while preaching was relied upon to maintain discipline in congregations. There was much emphasis on compunction for sin, and fasting as a way of doing penance, but little regard for occasions of celebration and none at all for traditional church feasts. Such a disciplined way of life was not easily sustained and it is not surprising that two great but relatively short-lived 'awakenings' occurred in America in the course of a century.

The freedom from the requirements of formal worship in the Puritan communities did create opportunities to express other values such as the relationship between members – perhaps as a reaction against an overly individualistic religious sensibility. The Methodist tradition in its various embodiments provides an example of how this relationship can be expressed in a simple rite involving food and drink, though it is curious that such rites are of a meagre character through eschewing all but the most basic elements of nourishment, namely bread and water. It may be that there is a desire to maintain the distinction between the celebration of Holy Communion and the Love Feast, a distinction which Wesley himself upheld and has been reiterated by later writers.[60] For Wesley, the Holy Communion rite was that given in the 1662 *Book of Common Prayer* with its greater openness to the reception of the body and blood of Christ than in the 1552 edition, but the use of the rite in America was restricted initially by the lack of ministers and the refusal of an Anglican bishop to ordain men for the missions. This led to Methodism in America becoming more like the older Puritan denominations, Congregational and Presbyterian, with services consisting principally of Scripture reading and sermons. But perhaps more than other Protestant denominations, Methodism today looks to its traditions for guidance in the Christian life, in America and elsewhere, and the influence of the Wesley brothers, perhaps understated in contemporary worship, is still there. The rite for the celebration of Holy Communion has become revised as a result of ecumenically influenced liturgical studies, while retaining the warm sense of community evocative of the early Love Feasts.

The American colonies and the United States which emerged from them developed a culture pervaded by values described generically as Puritan, but with distinctive contributions from the main non-Anglican traditions, especially Presbyterian, Methodist and Congregational, which had created and developed their own institutions as churches in the seventeenth-century. Calvinist and Lutheran, but also Moravian influenced theologies, were present in them, but the advent of Deism created an American Protestant religious culture with a texture of its own. The fact of a uniquely unchallenged democracy, providing opportunity to explore and exploit vast prairies with constantly extending horizons, contributed to this uniquely American ethos. It became the land of the free. There was freedom but also hardship, intense labour and resulting prosperity, a sense of an over-arching guidance by a kindly but only vaguely defined power. Industrial development followed to supply new needs, and the ethos became more difficult to describe throughout this period; by now it differs little from secularism. It is often described as civil religion, implying that there are religious values underlying the culture of the nation, as appears from the retention (after a short lapse) of terms like 'In God we trust' on coinage and notes. Political campaigns use a rhetoric which exploits such sentiments, but as sociologists of religion have observed: 'Our rhetoric speaks in terms of another day, another age. It does not seem to express our present reality'.[61]

Given this judgment, it is worth observing also that the population of the United States attends church much more than is the case in other similar advanced countries. If, however, civil religion is the reality, in contrast with the Puritan influence which persisted certainly into the nineteenth-century, then in most denominational churches there can be little connection between the festive and religious dimension of life. Food and fast can have their reciprocal relationship of nourishment and diet, of indulgence and restraint, without an explicit involvement of religion.

ENDNOTES

1 John Wesley, *Letter to Susanna Wesley (1725). Works,* Vol. 25, Gerald Cragg ed. (Oxford: Clarendon Press, 1980) 170

2 Stanley Hauerwas, *Approaching the End. Eschatological reflectons on Church, Politics, and Life* (Grand Rapids MI: Wm B. Eeerdmans, 2013) 69

3 Rupert E. Davies, *Methodism* (Harmondsworth: Penguin Books, 1963) 27

4 Carlos M. Eire, *Reformations* (New Haven: Yale University Press, 2016) 556

5 David Grumett and Rachel Muers, *Theology on the Menu. Asceticism, Meat and Christian Diet* (London: Routledge, 2010) 31

6 Diarmuid MacCulloch, *Reformation. Europe's House Divided. 1490-1700* (London: Penguin Books, 2004) 530

7 Cf. Christopher Hill, *The World Turned Upside Down. Radical Ideas During the English Revolution* (Harmondsworth: Penguin Books, 1975) 406-7

8 Lewis Bayly, *The Practise of Pietie* (London: J. Hodges, 1613[3]) 163, cited in E. Glenn Hinson, 'Puritan Piety' in Frank G. Senn, ed. *Protestant Spiritual Traditions* (New York: Paulist Press, 1986) 165

9 Frank Mott Harrison, *John Bunyan. A Story of His Life* (London: The Manner of Truth Trust, 1964) 145

10 David Freeman Hawke, *Everyday Life in Early America* (New York: Harper & Row, 1988) 76

11 Samuel Eliot Morison, *The Oxford History of the American People,* Vol. One (New York: Meridian, 1994) 94-5

12 David Freeman Hawke, *Everyday Life in Early America* 89

13 Cited in E. Glenn Hanson, 'Puritan Piety' 171-2

14 Samuel E. Morison, *The Oxford History of the American People,* Vol. One, 117

15 Cotton Mather, *Diary* (Boston: Massachusetts Historical Society, 1911) 242

16 Samuel E. Morison, *The Oxford History of the American People,* Vol. One, 209

17 Cited in H. W. Brands, *The First American. The Life and Times of Benjamin Franklin* (New York: Anchor Books, 2002) 146

18 H. W. Brands, *The First American. The Life and Times of Benjamin Franklin* 34

19 Samuel E. Morison, *The Oxford History of the American People,* Vol. One, 211-2

20 Johanna Wesley, *The Complete Writings* (Oxford: O.U.P., 1997) 280, cited in David Grumett and Rachel Muers, *Theology on the Menu. Asceticism, Meat and Christian Diet* 61

21 John Pollock, *John Wesley* (Oxford: A Lion Paperback, 1989) 50

22 Idem

23 Richard P. Heizenrater, *Wesley and the People Called Methodists* (Nashville: Abingdon Press, 1995) 44

24 John and Charles Wesley, *Selected Writings and Hymns* (Mahwah N.J.: Paulist Press, 1981) 104

25 Rupert E. Davies, *Methodism* 125

26   John Pollock, *John Wesley* 103

27   Cited in Philip Tovey, *The Theory and Practice of Extended Communion* (Farnham: Ashgate, 2009) 40

28   P. Fintan Lyons, 'Conversion in the Benedictine and Methodist Traditions', in *Asbury Theological Journal,* Vols. 50 and 51, Fall 1995, Spring 1996, 87

29   Philip Tovey, *The Theory and Practice of Extended Communion* 43

30   Ibid. 44

31   Charles Wallace, 'On knowing Christ in the Flesh', in *Wesley and Methodist Studies,* Vol. 5 (2013) 71

32   www.methodist.org.uk/downloads/conf-holy-communion-in-methodist-church-2003.pdf

33   D. H. Tripp, 'Methodism' in Cheslyn Jones *et al., The Study of the Liturgy* (London: S.P.C.K., 1992²) 326

34   John Wesley, *Works 1829-31,* Vol. I (London: Mason, 1872) 469

35   'On Temperance' in *The Message of the Wesleys,* Compiled and with Introduction by Philip Watson (London: Epworth Press, 1964) 191

36   John Wesley, *Sermons on Several Occasions* Vol. V (Dublin: Methodist Book Room, 1804) 103

37   Ibid. 234

38   Ibid. 289-90

39   Abraham Lincoln, *Speeches and Letters of Abraham Lincoln, 1832-1865,* Merwin Roe, ed. (London and Toronto: J. M. Dent & Sons, 1907) 211-2

40   Ibid. 213

41   Owen Chadwick, *The Victorian Church. Part One 1829-1859* (London: S.C.M., 1971³) 37

42   Ibid. 490-1

43   Carl Sandburg, *Abraham Lincoln. The Prairie Years* and *The War Years.* One Volume Edition (New York: Harcourt, Brace and Company, 1954) 573

44   H. W. Brands, *The First American. The Life and Times of Benjamin Franklin* 95

45   Ibid. 97

46   Ron Chernow, *Washington. A Life* (New York: The Penguin Press, 2011) 131-2

47   Ibid. 470

48   James O'Boyle, *Life of George Washington* (London: Longmans, Green and Co., 1915) 328

49   Ron Chernow, *Washington. A Life* 580

50   Washington Irving, *Life of Washington* Vol. IV (London: Henry G. Bohn, 1859) 1683

51   Ibid. 1684

52   Ron Chernow, *Washington, A Life* 585

53   Ibid. 808

54   Ibid. 810

55   Alexis de Tocqueville, *Democracy in America,* Henry Reeve trans. (Ware: Wordsworth Editions Ltd, 1998) 182

56 Ibid. 238

57 David Herbert Donald, *Lincoln* (New York: Simon & Schuster, 1995) 335

58 Doris Kearns Goodwin, *Team of Rivals. The Political Genius of Abraham Lincoln* (New York: Simon & Schuster, 2005) 401-2

59 David Herbert Donald, *Lincoln* 336

60 Cf. Philip Tovey, *The Theory and Practice of Extended Communion* 44

61 Robert N. Bellah and Philip E. Hamilton, *Varieties of Civil Religion* (Eugene OR: Wipf & Stock, 2013) 18

CHAPTER FIFTEEN

The Orthodox World

The Baptism conferred on Saint Vladimir in Kiev was a key event in the evangelization of the world. The great Slav nations of Eastern Europe owe their faith to this event. ... In this perspective an expression which I have frequently employed finds its deepest meaning: the Church must breathe with her two lungs.[1]

The Byzantine feast

Only the Western world and its history of food, feast and fast have been considered in previous chapters. A very different view of these, and how they may be related, from that manifested by nineteenth-century America is to be found in the extensive world of Eastern Christianity. The commercial and political relations, and the religious conflict between Byzantium and the West since the Middle Ages, are well documented, but little information exists concerning such mundane domestic matters as the details of diet of the Eastern empire during its thousand years and more of existence, perhaps because its population was quite diversified. Within it there were Greeks and Jews, Armenians, Syrians and Macedonians and perhaps other cultural groups with their dietary traditions, while the imperial court had inherited Greco-Roman customs, which only gradually came under local influence.

A rare glimpse of eating in the imperial court was provided by Bishop Liutprand of Cremona and an embassy from the West in 968 to the Emperor Nicephoras Phocas. He was not hospitably entertained on his journey by the Greek bishops he encountered, but was received well and given a banquet by the emperor. He recorded his impressions: the food was 'fairly foul and stinking ... soused in oil like a drunkard's mess and sprinkled with some horrible fishy liquid.' He added that later 'the sacred emperor sent me one of his most delicate dishes, a fat goat ... richly stuffed with garlic, onions and leeks, and swimming in a fish sauce'.[2] The fish sauce was the old Roman *garum,* which was by then out of favour, even considered repulsive, in the West. Liutprand was there for the Christmas banquet, which must have been similar to one held in 912 and described in some detail by a Syrian prisoner of war. It was held in a large room in which there were a wooden table, an ivory table and, facing the door, a gold table.

> After the festivities, when the Emperor leaves the church, he enters this room and sits at the gold table. This is what happens at Christmas. He sends for the Muslim captives and they are seated at these tables. When the Emperor is seated at his gold table, they bring him four gold dishes, each of which is brought on its own little chariot. One of these dishes is encrusted with pearls and rubies, they say it belonged to Solomon. ...They are placed before the Emperor and one may eat from them. They remain there while the Emperor is at table: when he rises they are taken away. Then, for the Muslims, many hot and cold dishes are placed on the other tables and the imperial herald announces: 'I swear on the Emperor's head that there is no pork at all in these dishes!'. The dishes, on large silver and gold platters are then served to the Emperor's guests.[3]

As the meal continued, the guests were entertained by musicians, and to an extent, therefore, the tradition of the early Roman Empire banquets continued in tenth-century Byzantium. There was the difference, of course, that the emperor dined on leaving the church after the 'festivities'. The term would be particularly appropriate for the ceremonies of the Feast of Christmas, but in the Byzantine world worship was at that time much more elaborate than in the Western world, and has continued to be up to the present.

The Orthodox liturgy
Where there are church buildings proper to the tradition, the celebration of the Liturgy (where the capital letter indicates that the Eucharist

is intended) takes place in an architectural space which is replete with symbolism. To accommodate a dome, the building is square, unlike the typical rectangular shaped Western church. From the dome's apex:

> An image of Christ the Almighty looks down on the worshippers below. Round the drum supporting the dome there are prophets and apostles, and a procession of angelic deacons, while on the vault supporting the dome, and on the upper portions of the nave walls are depicted cherubim and seraphim, the four evangelists and scenes from Christ's life.[4]

This pattern of decoration is found throughout a typical Orthodox church and, together with votive lamps and a pervading scent of incense, make it for the worshippers a sacrament, a sign of saving grace, an introduction to the rituals of the Liturgy. Much of the ceremony is hidden from the people behind the icon screen and the chant is traditionally provided by a choir, yet worshippers experience a strong sense of participation. Strangely, from the perspective of now customary Western practice, the people do not generally receive Communion, but at the conclusion of the liturgy are regularly given small pieces which have been cut from the bread prepared for the offering at a table behind the icon screen. In the Russian Orthodox tradition, these pieces, along with un-consecrated wine, are sometimes given to communicants immediately after they have received the consecrated elements – as a way, it would seem, of linking participation in the sacrifice with sharing in a meal.

In general, the Orthodox Eucharist exhibits a sacrificial character, especially as the bread of offering is prepared by making an incision in the form of a cross with a lance, while the priest says, in the Greek rite, 'Like a lamb he was led to sacrifice, and was silent like a little lamb before its shearers'.[5] The texts used represent not so much the death on the cross – the primary signification of the action of the priest – as the Old Testament slaughter of the Paschal lamb and, above all, the incarnation and the birth of Christ.

Because of this representational approach, in the history of the Orthodox Eucharist allegedly miraculous events have occurred similar to and
even earlier than those recorded in the medieval West, such as the event
at Bolsena in 1263 (See Chapter Seven). According to Gregory of Decap-
olis (797-842), the conversion of a Saracen took place in the ninth-century during the rite of preparation of the bread. When the priest used the
lance this man saw him taking a little child in his hands and slaying it.[6]

> While the West was having its bleeding hosts and other Eucharis-
> tic wonders, the East had its visions of the infant Jesus bleeding on
> the *discos* (paten) as sacrificial lamb.[7]

In the East, these phenomena did not become as frequent as in the West,
as devotion to the Real Presence characteristic of the West from the second
millennium onwards was not emphasised in the East. There, as in the West,
at the conclusion of the Liturgy the Eucharist is reserved for the Communion
of the sick (and for the Liturgy of Good Friday) and in the eleventh-century
the practice developed of putting a drop of the Precious Blood on the Host
and allowing it to dry, so as to retain both elements of the Eucharist for the
sick. Reservation has always been in what is described as an ark, often shaped
like a boat and not visible behind the icon screen. Orthodox theology has not
focused on the Real Presence as happened in the West, because the doctrine
of the sacraments in the case of the Eucharist has avoided any suggestion of a
physical presence and considers the elements of bread and wine as symbols of
the body and blood of Christ, where 'symbol' has a profound meaning, one
that is very different from that implied when the term 'mere symbol' is used.
The use of symbolism for an in-depth understanding of the Eucharist will be
discussed in Chapter Eighteen.

The Orthodox Liturgy respects and upholds this depth of meaning,
yet also exploits representational imagery. The representational view developed over the centuries in the writings of commentators on the liturgy
and was applied to various stages of the celebration. The Great Entrance has
always been a very significant rite in that respect and at this point the peo-

ple are closely involved. The gifts are brought in procession out through a side door in the icon screen and then carried solemnly by one of the priests through the central doors in what is called the Great Entrance.

> As the procession appears the people cross themselves and bow, and many may kneel and prostrate themselves as the richly veiled chalice and paten are carried past.[8]

This suggests that for the faithful the symbolising function of the bread and wine is already operative, that Christ is already present in mystery. There is no obvious logic to this but through the centuries this procession has been seen to represent various aspects of the mystery of Christ's life and work: Christ being led away to his Passion, the revelation of the hidden mystery of salvation, his journey to Jerusalem on Palm Sunday and even the final coming of Christ. This multi-faceted symbolic *and* representational approach to the celebration, which relies on movement as much as on the text of the hymns, and involves a richly ornamented cover for chalice and paten and ornate vestments for the priest, enables the worshippers to experience a sense of mystery and be drawn into it in a way which is unique to the Eastern world. In the Liturgy of Basil the Great, which is used ten times a year in the Greek speaking church, a hymn sung on Holy Saturday during the Great Entrance has the sacrificial theme of Christ going to be slain but also that of a meal:

> Let all mortal flesh be silent, and stand in fear and trembling and harbour no earthly thoughts; for the King of Kings and Lord of Lords is entering to be slain and given as food to the faithful.[9]

The reference to Christ being slain and given as food while the bread and wine are being carried in procession, shows that the Eastern liturgy has had from earliest times a sense of sacrifice and of its commemoration in a Seder-like meal.

It is not therefore surprising that the early Christians in some places took this link to the level of imitating its Jewish origins by engaging in a rite of animal sacrifice, though now with the intention of making an offering to the God of the Christians. The evidence for this comes largely from the area in which Orthodox rather than Western Christianity predominates. It is likely that early Christians had a difficulty in finding meat for their consumption which was not the product of a pagan sacrifice, 'offered to idols', as St Paul recognised in I Cor 10:23-30. The universal availability of meat from sacrifices can be explained by the fact that 'the Greeks never failed to maintain relations with the divine powers through the ritualised killing of animal victims, whose flesh was consumed collectively according to precise strictures'.[10] A way around the difficulty for Christians could have been to find animals for themselves and slaughter them as an offering to the true God. This may be the explanation for what seems to have happened in various places as will be recorded below. They could also adopt the practice of meatless meals and some seem to have done so, using bread and water in a practice which, by stretching the words rather misleadingly, has been called 'ascetic Eucharists'.[11]

Animal sacrifices

The development of the Christian Eucharist tradition occurred about the time of the siege of Jerusalem in the year 70 by the future emperor Titus and the burning and destruction of the Temple, which brought an end to the Jewish sacrificial rites. Various pagan sacrifices existed also and the early Christians sought to distinguish their religious practice from both type of rites. It was only after Christianity was recognised as the official imperial religion that attempts were made to abolish the pagan rites as well as heretical Christian ones in such legislation as the *Theodosian Code* in 391, attributed to Emperor Theodosius. Anyone burning lights or offering incense, or suspending wreaths before 'senseless images', or sacrificing an animal would be guilty of high treason.[12] The Jewish religion was recognised but regarded as 'odious'.[13]

Distinguishing Christian practice from the pagan or Jewish rites did not of itself mean that Christians had no rites apart from the Eucharist proper and the *agapé* feasts which had become separate from it. The position is clearer with regard to the sacrifice of animals. There is evidence that in Armenia, at least, Christians continued to offer sacrifice to God through animal slaughter, and there is documentary evidence from the early fifth-century, from the twelfth, and even from the early twentieth-century, for the continuation of this practice in Armenia. The early evidence comes from the *Armenian Canons of St (Isaak) Sahak* (354-439), which reflect conditions prevailing in the Armenian Apostolic Church in the 5th century. It may incorporate in its initial section an Armenian translation of a Greek document made by the Armenian Church's first Patriarch, St. Gregory the Illuminator (301-325), in the 4th century.[14]

Gregory's success in converting King Irdat to Christianity left the priests of the pagan cult without a means of livelihood. They protested: 'we have no art or craft which may enable us to earn food or maintenance for ourselves and our children. For as long as we served the devils we were fed from their victims and fruits'.[15] To this, Gregory replied that if they abandoned the idolatrous cults they would 'receive fruits and firstlings according to the tradition the great prophet Moses received from the creator'.[16] He even specified the parts of the animals they would receive in addition to the tenths of the threshing floor and the wine vat. In effect, they could offer Christian sacrifice using the rites of the Jewish tradition. This rite was subsequently called *matal,* a name still used for today's rite.

In the fourth century, Epiphanius of Salamis (30-403) preached a homily in defence of the *matal* against accusations by Syriac Christians that the rite was fundamentally Jewish.[17] His response pointed to the fundamental differences: the Jewish rite required a male lamb one year old, whereas the *matal* used one a month old and no distinction was made between male and female. The Jewish practice had been to eat standing up and to include unleavened bread and bitter herbs, whereas now the Christians ate sitting down and used leavened bread without herbs. A fundamental difference was that the Jewish offering was for the living, the Christian one for the dead. His argument was repeated in a document of the twelfth-century by an Armenian Bishop, Nerses Schnorhali (1102-1173).[18]

In the early twentieth-century, an Anglican missionary and medical doctor concerned with the welfare of Syrian villagers, Archdeacon McLean, gave an account in a letter to a friend, F.C. Conybeare, of his experiences in a small area where Turkey, Syria and Iran meet. The towns he visited included Urumiah (modern Urmia in western Iran) and Qudshanis (probably modern Konak in eastern Turkey) and he witnessed sheep being slaughtered as an offering to God, but not considered a sacrifice by these Armenian Christians or as 'supplementing the sacrifice of Calvary'.[19] At Qudshanis, after three days fasting and the celebration of the Eucharist, the meat of the animal was distributed to the communicants as they left the church in the form of alms on behalf of the donor of the sheep, who in this case was seeking the favour from God of averting damage to crops by locusts. In some places, he reported, the offering could be on behalf of a dead person or for the repose of one, 'that the merciful promise made to the penitent thief may avail for him' – this rite being associated with Easter Monday.

The persistence of the 'sanctified slaughter' of animals in Greece has been chronicled in 1979 in an article in which it was made clear that these sacrifices are offered outside the church building, usually after the celebration of the Liturgy and are associated with particular feast days, such as that of St Elias (July 20) and St Athanasius (January 18).[20] After the slaughter, participants dip a finger in the blood and make the sign of the cross, and before the meal the priest or bishop blessed the meat stewing with various herbs and vegetables in a cauldron.[21] Clearly, such a celebration augments the experience of festivity on the feast day and adds a sacral character to what in other contemporary cultures would simply be a case of a religious feast being used as the occasion for a festive meal.

The writer, William Dalrymple, encountered the practice of animal sacrifice during a visit to the ruined town of Cyrrhus forty-five miles north of Aleppo in Syria in the early 1990s. A small mosque dating from the thirteenth or fourteenth century housed the shrine of a Sufi saint, named Nebi Uri, perhaps confusedly identified with Uriah the Hittite, who is honoured as a saint by Muslims, as his story is told in both the Quran and the Bible (2 Sam 11 and 12).

The guardian told the writer that many Christians as well as Muslims came regularly to the shrine, many seeking healing. He spoke of a recent incident:

> We had one Christian girl last week. She was sick for many months – her head was bad – and Nebi Uri appeared to her in a dream. So she came here and spent the night on the tomb. The next day she was healed. Last Friday she returned with a sheep, all covered with flowers and ribbons and with its horns died with henna. After prayers they cut its throat. Then they cooked it and everyone ate it.[22]

He didn't say if the girl shared in the Muslim meal. According to him, such visits by Christians were a regular occurrence. Dalrymple encountered a similar practice at the shrine of St George at Beit Jala in the Christian quarter of Jerusalem. The Greek Orthodox custodian, Fr Methodius, told him that as many Muslims as Christians came there with their offerings, including sheep, which - in his own words - he sacrificed, keeping only a small portion for himself while the rest went to the poor. The donor took the blood and smeared it on the doorpost, in what he described as the 'tradition'. 'It was all very curious: Orthodox priests merrily slaughtering sheep, and doing so in homage to St George.'[23]

Comparison with the early Roman liturgy

In earlier centuries, similar practices were not unknown in the Western world. Pope Gregory the Great was concerned about the pastoral treatment of the indigenous Angli and their practice of sacrificing animals, an inheritance of their pagan past. As noted in Chapter Five, he wrote to Abbot Mellitus, a missionary in England and later Archbishop of Canterbury, about the sensitivities of the situation and the need to divert this practice to Christian usage by instructing them to do so 'to the praise of God for their own eating and return thanks to the giver of all for their fullness'.[24]

In the century leading up to Gregory's pontificate, the Roman cultural values, patterns and institutions exerted a remarkable influence on the liturgy in the West in both its ritual aspects and its theology. 'Simplicity, sobriety and practical sense are deeply etched in the rites, while the formularies are marked by restraint, brevity and directness.'[25] As noted earlier, the status of the church after its recognition by the Emperor Constantine was such that the formalities of the upper ranks of society became part of the private and public life of the papacy.

> The entrance rite has the appearance of an imperial court ceremonial, but thereafter the native Roman quality of sobriety prevails. Thus the nucleus of the Eucharistic liturgy, namely the word and the sacrament, remained practically untouched by the drama and pomp of the imperial court.[26]

In successive centuries, a Latin liturgical language of great beauty was developed, marked by a lapidary conciseness, though appealing more to the intellect than to the heart of the listeners.[27] This is in contrast with the devolution of the ritual moments of the Orthodox Liturgy described above, where the sense of mystery increases with each stage of the ceremonies and actions are as important as the formularies used. Compared with the sense of mystery evoked by the actions and hymns, even the more solemn celebrations of that Latin Roman liturgy seem to have lacked elements conducive to a deep level of participation.

Orthodoxy and fasting

It is not surprising that the spirituality of the East tends to be of a markedly mystical nature compared with that of the West, but it also has a very practical dimension in that fasting has traditionally been taken quite seriously, whereas religiously motivated fasting is not widely practised in Western Christianity. In the Orthodox world, as elsewhere, fasting may be undertaken for various reasons. These can range from the ascetic, which has to do with a perception of the need to control bodily desire in the interest of some superior good, to the penitential, to the simple dietary approach with a view to experience better health and wellbeing. Because of the concentration of Orthodox populations in Eastern Europe and further to the east, the diet natural to this population, as will be seen below, is what is now recognised internationally, as conducive to good health.

Fasting has always been associated with liturgical seasons, and therefore with the Christian mysteries, and thus can have an eschatological perspective, the fast which marks the life of the Christian waiting for the return of the Bridegroom (Mt 9:15). Orthodox fasting is of that liturgical kind, though other motivations are not necessarily excluded. In contrast to the West, in the season of Advent the Orthodox world engages in fasting and abstinence from meat in the period of what is called the Nativity Fast, which runs for 40 days, mid-November to December 24th. For churches that follow the original Julian calendar, the fast does not begin until November 28th (in our calendar) and continues until the Epiphany.

But the Orthodox world is far from being monolithic in its observances and so the actual fasting regime can show wide variations. The contemporary practice has been described in some detail in the case of one branch, the West Assyrian Church. The days of fast are:

> All Wednesdays and Fridays except the holidays for seven weeks after Easter; Nineveh Fast, three days beginning Monday of the third week preceding Lent (St Ephrem the Syrian devoted seven homilies to it); Lent, a fast of 48 days; fast of the Apostles Peter and Paul three days before the feast (This is in honour of the Holy Spirit who enabled the apostles to preach the gospel of salvation.); Fast of the Assumption of Mary five days before the feast; Advent, fifteen days before the Nativity. The total varied (as some fasts may coincide) between 133 and 143 days.[28]

On days of fast some do not eat anything at all or drink even a drop of water until after a church service at 11 a.m.

> Fasting means restriction to a vegetarian diet, with emphasis on the inclusion of lentils and various kinds of beans. Potatoes and bread are included as well as seasonal vegetables and fruit. Folk knowledge over the centuries has ensured that there are no negative effects from the exclusion of animal products and makes 'the

fasting menu rich, attractive and truly healthy. For almost one third of the year Assyrians are absolute and real vegetarians'.[29]

How representative of the Orthodox world this West Assyrian practice is would be difficult to say and in fact historically, 'there has not been a general consensus among church leaders on exactly which foods were permitted during particular fasting days'.[30] While fasting is still a common practice among Greek Orthodox Christians, surveys have shown that since the 1980s the length of periods of fast observed is less than that of previous decades. It has also emerged that fasting practices differed according to the economic environment; people in poor mountainous regions (at least on the island of Chios) fasted for longer periods than those in the towns, and the data indicate that now 'a rather small portion of the Greek population complies with the traditional fasting regime of the Orthodox Church'.[31] It is true, nonetheless. that the diet of this part of the world, if not characterised by fasting, appears more restricted, but also healthier than that of the Western world and there is an environmental reason for this.

> The Eastern Mediterranean dietary reliance on plant food sources is dictated by the dry climate and mountainous landscape, which can only support small-scale husbandry.[32]

Conclusion

It was noted above that the practice of receiving Communion is not widespread among participants in the Orthodox liturgy. In consequence, the relationship between food, feast and fast becomes less clear and more complex. During the era of the Byzantine Empire there may have been a more integral relationship between the liturgical festivities attended by the emperor and his court and the banquet which followed, but as the empire came to an end with the Turkish occupation of Constantinople in 1453, the link between food and feast became less easy to celebrate. The long established custom of having communicants receive bread and wine after the Eucharist could then be seen as an attempt to maintain the link between the Eucharistic feast and food. The sacrifice of animals in some parts of the Eastern world - and in the West for some centuries – could be said to represent an instinctive desire not only to bring out the sacrificial nature of Christian worship but also the age-old link between worship and eating, especially since the rite of the Eucharist itself had become less evidently a meal shared by all the community.

The linking of fasting with the liturgical seasons is a significant verification of the perception of the Eucharist as a celebration of the whole mystery of Christ, his life death and resurrection leading to his second coming. His return is anticipated by the adoption of fasting. Even when the reception of Communion is infrequent, a profound, eschatologically meaningful connection with the feast is expressed by the practice of fasting. This, the most profound meaning of Christian fasting, is not always to the fore in fasts undertaken by people in the Orthodox world because today's emphasis on the link between diet and health so characteristic of Western society inevitably affects their perception of fasting, though there can be encouragement to continue traditional practices when it is realised that because of the nature of the indigenous diet this usage is conducive to health.

ENDNOTES

1   Pope John Paul II, Encyclical *Ut Unum Sint, no. 54*

2   *The Works of Liutprand of Cremona,* T.A.Wright trans. (London: Routledge, 1930) 247, 254, cited in Roy Strong, *Feast* 41

3   Andrew Dalby, 'Christmas Dinner in Byzantium' in *Food on the Move, Proceedings of the Oxford Symposium on Food and Cookery 1996,* Harlan Walker ed. (London: Prospect Books, 1997) 80

4   Hugh Wybrew, *The Orthodox Liturgy. The Development of the Eucharistic Liturgy in the Byzantine Rite* (Crestwood NY: St Vladimir's Seminary Press, 1996) 3

5   Hans-Joachim Schultz, *The Byzantine Liturgy,* Matthew J. O'Connell trans. (New York: Pueblo, 1986) 66

6   idem

7   Robert Taft S.J., Foreword to Hans-Schultz, *The Byzantine Liturgy* xi

8   Hugh Wybrew, *The Orthodox Liturgy* 7

9   Hans-Joachim Schultz, *The Byzantine Liturgy* 37

10   Andrew McGowan, *Ascetic Eucharists. Food and Drink in Early Christian Ritual Meals* (Oxford: Clarendon Press, 1999) 60-1

11   Cf. the title of the work in the preceding note.

12   *The Theodosian Code and Novels, and the Sirmondian Constitutions,* Clyde Pharr, Theresa Sherrer Davidson, Mary Brown Pharr eds. (Union, N.J.: Lawbook Exchange, 2006) 473

13   S. Zeitlin, 'The Theodosian Code' in *The Jewish Quarterly Review* Vol. 43, No. 4 (April,1953) 392-394

14   Published in English translation in *The American Journal of Theology* Vol. II, 1898, 828-48.

15   Ibid. 847

16   Ibid. 848

17   Epiphanius, *In Sanctam Resurrectionem* 3 PG 43:466-470

18   Text in *Rituale Armenorum*, Frederick C. Conybeare, Arthur John Maclean eds. (Oxford: Clarendon Press, 1905) 78

19   Frederick C. Conybeare, 'The Survival of Animal Sacrifices inside the Christian Church' in *The American Journal of Theology* Vol. 7, No. 1 (January 1903) 62-90, at 83

20   Stella Georgoudi, 'L'égorgement sanctifié en Grece moderne' in Marcel Detienne et Jean-Pierre Vernant, *La Cuisinne du Sacrifice en Pays Grec* (Paris: Editions Gallimard, 1979) 279

21   Ibid. 284

22   William Dalrymple, *From the Holy Mountain. A Journey in the Shadow of Byzantium* (London: HarperCollins, 1997) 166-9

23   Ibid. 339-41

24   Gregory the Great, *Epistle* LVXXI in *Nicene and Post Nicene Fathers* Series II, Vol.13, Part II, Philip Scharf, Henry Wace eds. (New York: Christian Literature Co., 1890) 84-5

25   Anscar J. Chupungco, 'History of the Liturgy until the Fifteenth Century' in *Handbook for Liturgical Studies* Vol. 1, A. J. Chupungco ed. (Collegeville, The Liturgical Press, 1997), 136

26   Ibid. 137

27   Ibid. 139

28   Michael Abdalla, 'The Way the Contemporary Western Assyrians take Food in the Middle East during Fasts and Church Holidays' in *Fasting and Feasting (Proceedings of the Oxford Symposium on Food & Cookery, 1990),* Harlan Walker, ed. (London: Prospect Books, 1991)

29   Ibid. 20

30   Antonia-Leda Matalas et al., 'Fasting and Food Habits in the Eastern Orthodox Church' in Harlan Walker, ed., *Fasting and Feasting* 192

31   Ibid. 200-1

32   Ibid. 202

CHAPTER SIXTEEN

Food and Feast

Let us fast, then - whenever we see fit, and as strenuously as we should. But having gotten that exercise out of the way, let us eat. Festally, first of all, for life without occasions is not worth living. But ferially, too, for life is so much more than occasions, and its grand ordinariness must never go unsavoured. But both ways let us eat with a glad good will, and with a conscience formed by considerations of excellence.[1]

In the relationship between food, feast and fast, food becoming feast implies a festive atmosphere, an enhanced and shared experience. Food and fast, on the other hand, makes sense, and perhaps especially so, on the individual level. In contrast, the term 'food and famine' indicates a multiplicity of people and is an important issue in itself, though not dealt with here, except for the following brief comment. When relief agencies distribute food parcels at a time of famine or natural disaster, often from the back of a truck, the scene can be very chaotic as desperate people jostle each other to acquire a sack of essential food, a container of life-saving water. The scene can bring to mind animals eating or drinking at a trough, jostling for access, marginalising the weaker ones. With humans, however, it is not necessarily a case of individuals: it is more often a case of desperate attempts to get food for a family, and of strenuous efforts and sacrifices to ensure that children are fed.

The shared meal
Food and family go together even though the family today, in Western, prosperous society, rarely dines together. And this is a much lamented development, often explained in terms of careers of both parents, and TV programmes and computer games dictating the timetable of chil-

dren - who in any case belong to a cyber-community rivalling that of the family. In effect each member has a personal schedule. A shared meal, on the other hand, whether in a family or among friends, brings into prominence the bonds there are between those who participate, and people realise there is something missing from family life when each personal timetable leads to eating alone. There may be an instinctive attempt to humanise solitary eating – making it seem less like animal activity – by reaching out to a cyber-community in the social media or even by vicarious sharing in the life of well-loved characters in a 'soap opera' on TV.

But there is a perceptible difference between the act of eating and the human activity of actually sharing a meal. The loss to human flourishing which has resulted from the decline of the family meal is to some extent made up by the increasingly popular custom of eating out – provided it is done as a family. Restaurants recognise this lucrative trend by providing for children. But there is an obvious difference between food from a restaurant kitchen and that which has been seen evolving from raw ingredients to the dish on the table. Up to recent decades. Homes for the middle classes were built with separate kitchen and dining room, partly because of the expectation that there would be someone not of the family employed there, but also because of a desire to keep the unattractive aspects of food preparation hidden from view. More recently, open plan kitchen and dining has been favoured, not only because hired help is a rarity but also because of a more realistic approach and interest in food in all its aspects. The fruit of the earth provides the food, the work of human hands the preparation and sharing makes the meal.

The word 'companion' indicates a bond and mutual support in some situations and its Latin source - bread together - indicates the role of a meal in expressing or augmenting or even creating this bond. Sharing a meal implies relationship and is generally indicative of a positive development in people's lives, even a reconciliation. But as has been evident throughout history, the motivation, the deep, human dimension of sharing, can vary from the noble to the ignoble, from the transcendent to the secular, the *agapaic* to the malicious. It can range from eating food with glad and generous hearts, as the early Christian community is reported to have done (Acts 2:46), to cynically observing the effects of poison on a guest, as countless historical examples from Nero to Pope Alexander VI have shown. Human behaviour throughout history has often been a dissipative force destroying rather than augmenting the human values a shared meal should express. When values are not thus distorted, a shared meal has in itself a festive character, even if the occasion is 'ferial', as Robert Capon pointed out (in the quotation at the head of this chapter). Each participant who is open to others brings to it the warmth and the strengths of their personality, and thus enhances the others' dignity and sense of self-worth.

> Food is not merely something you put in your mouth and digest. Food is an occasion for a social act. It's an occasion for meeting. It's an occasion for conversation.[2]

Of the dinner party, Robert Capon, the author of a theologically undergirded and humour-filled cookbook, says: 'try your best to summon guests who will enhance each other as persons'.[3] Warmth or empathy generates a corresponding response in table companions; recognised strengths of personality in a participant generate in the others the desire to emulate such characteristics as optimism, benevolence, a feeling that life – as well as the present encounter – is worthwhile. These psychological processes begin to function when people gather. Preliminary formalities have varied over a considerable range in the course of history from hand washing to formal ordered procession (even genuflecting when passing the *nef*), and culminate in the physical activity of eating. Ideally, there is the preparatory condition of hunger, a body drive which recurs in all human beings in a regular cycle; without it, it is difficult to create the atmosphere of a shared or festive meal.

Hunger and appetite

Hunger has to be distinguished from appetite, which is also a necessary component. Appetite is basically a state of mind, a mental awareness of desire that heightens anticipation, brings eagerness to be involved in the event of the meal. It can vary from one person to another at a meal. If eager, then it can communicate a sense of anticipation among the others; if lacking it puts a damper on enjoyment for all. That is why shared meals often begin with discussion of likes and dislikes; a person with a sense of sharing will show enthusiasm for some dish in an effort to bring all participants to an increased feeling of enjoyment of the occasion.

At this point, the issue of control arises. The relationship between hunger and appetite is a psychological one, sometimes referred to as the appestat - a term corresponding to thermostat – and indicating the need for the appetite to be set at a level corresponding to physiological need.[4] (When its setting is defective, it contributes to the creation of the extreme conditions of bulimia or anorexia, though in these cases the appestat is an effect rather than a cause.) The psychological perception requires a rational basis – an awareness of the menu and its sections and the distinctions involved, along with choices to be made and perhaps some guidance. The great strength of the shared meal of festive character is interaction, the recommendations, the conversation, the pauses which mark such an event. In the great banqueting tradition already described from Roman times up to Louis XIV, musical interludes, dramas, jugglers and fools filled these intervals, while a *scalco* hovered in the background.

The Fork

The custom of small portions in large numbers taken by the hand was standard in the early centuries before the knife and fork setting arrived and changed eating habits forever. Historical evidence for the introduction of the fork was not easy to establish and relied on contributions from art history as well as recipe books, but it seems that in the sophisticated surroundings of Byzantine Court life in the tenth-century small gilt ones began to be used to pick up sweetmeats. These forks were known in Greece for some centuries before arriving in Italy, where a French traveller noticed them admiringly at a ducal banquet in Venice in 1518.[5]

Feast in the House of Levi. Paolo Veronese, 1573

At a session of the Inquisition Tribunal in Venice in 1573, the painter Paolo Veronese was questioned about a large painting, over four metres wide and nearly two high, a representation of the Last Supper commissioned for their refectory by the monks of SS Giovanni e Paulo in the city. As it was so large he had been able to include many figures including local notables, and as the Inquisitors put it: 'buffoons, drunkards, Germans, dwarfs and other scurrilities'.[6] It also included the monk who had paid him not enough for the picture. He is placed under the left arch, with knife and fork and napkin and ready to dine.[7] All of these surround Christ and his apostles shown in the format typically used for the Last Supper, but St Peter seated beside Christ is engaged in carving a piece of meat. When asked what a figure to the right of Christ was doing he replied that he was cleaning his teeth with a toothpick (*piron*).[8] To the Inquisitors, the painting presented this sacred event in a decidedly worldly mode; they felt it was copying the practice obtaining in places infected with heresy, such as Germany, to mock the sacred rites of the Catholic Church.[9] In fact, despite the terms of his commission, Veronese had never called it a Last Supper, and when asked what the picture actually was he replied that it was a painting of Christ and his disciples in the house of Simon, though he later changed it to the *Banquet in the House of Levi*, its present title.

The instinct of these officials was that the commensality he portrayed, involving so many 'vulgarities' such as the toothpick and the fork, was completely unacceptable in a sacred context. Whether his contemporaries shared this dissociation between the sacred and the 'modern' or simply retained traditional ways is not clear but, in any case, until after 1800 and the transition from the great banqueting tradition to the more intimate suppers, already noted, most northern Europeans continued to eat with fingers and knives, or spoons and large slabs of bread called trenchers on which individual servings were placed. At a formal banquet in Russia in 1606, a Bavarian guest found that there was neither spoon nor plate provided.[10]

Food rituals have always been important for sailors as their companionship can be so important for their survival, whether in commercial vessels or in the fraught conditions of naval battles. Nineteenth-century British navy gun-crews apparently ate their meals at tables slung between their weapons, taking turns to serve food from the galley.

> The natural camaraderie of the table was thus transferred directly to the fighting effectiveness of the ship: men who ate their meals together worked better as a team and would more readily die together.[11]

Perhaps that is the explanation for an otherwise strange Navy rule:

> Even as late as 1897 the British Navy was forbidden the use of knives and forks, which were considered prejudicial to discipline and manliness. In America, however, nineteenth-century etiquette manuals were so severe about people who ate peas off their knives that those with better manners went to the other extreme – with the result that America became a nation of dedicated fork-eaters.[12]

The introduction of the fork radically changed eating habits and had a significant effect on the humanising potential of the shared meal, its festive character, for a reason not overtly connected with the British Navy's disciplinary concerns - but ultimately perhaps not totally unconnected. The use of the fork in addition to the knife made eating a more efficient operation and consequently conducive to eating more quickly and in greater quantity. The two are in fact linked, as an increased pace of consumption interferes with the physiological process that registers fullness. This is a fundamental cause of over-eating. Clearly, such a practice has a negative effect on the atmosphere of sharing – even if plenty is available – as companions are likely to register feelings of unease, though probably silently.

A more fundamental situation also resulted from the introduction of that 'momentous innovation', the fork.[13] As the Venetian officials seem to have realised, for the first time in Christian history there was now only indirect contact between the person and the food. A fundamental change had occurred in an activity which has the character of ritual. The implications for the ritual at the centre of the Christian liturgy, the 'breaking of the bread', will be discussed in a further chapter.

Wine

Attention needs also to be given to the issue of the use of wine in that ritual, given the question of whether any intake of alcohol can avoid injury to health, as some modern studies have held. A 2017 report in the *British Medical Journal* concluded: 'Alcohol consumption, even at moderate levels, is associated with adverse brain outcomes including hippocampal atrophy'.[14] Including wine or other forms of alcohol at a shared meal is almost always a subject of discussion and an issue where views can diverge considerably today, unlike the era of the great banquets when its exclusion would have been inconceivable. St Benedict, who in the sixth century restored human values to the shared meal by relating it to the Christian faith, would seem to side with the report just mentioned, but in effect had somewhat ambivalent views on the subject and looked back to a supposedly golden age of monasticism.

We read that monks should not drink wine at all, but since the monks of our day cannot be convinced of this, let us at least agree to drink moderately, and not to the point of excess, 'for wine makes even wise men go astray' (Sir 19:2) (*RB*:40.6)

Benedict in Italy assesses the situation in terms of summer heat and the need there may be for a greater amount in those conditions, but is totally unaware of a potential role for wine in fostering what a modern study calls 'connectedness', or bonding, to be considered below.[15] This is understandable in that monastic meals were taken in silence, but Benedict seems to have had no sense of the place of feasting, of simple enjoyment of food – or drink – in monastic life. In the view of one monastic commentator on the *Rule*: 'It would have been good if Benedict had made provision for festive meals'.[16] The life of a monk, he believed, ought to be a continuous Lent (*RB* 49.1) and the restrictions on food, drink, sleep, etc. of the season were to enable him to look forward to Easter with joy and spiritual longing (49.7), making it clear that spiritual joy was the fundamental value to be cherished.

In history, drink as a social bonding resource has for the most part gone unquestioned outside ascetic circles, but, as a powerful influence on people's lives, it has of course been regulated by state authorities. The case of seventeenth-century Russia illustrates the state's approach. When home-brewing gave way to the newly imported drinks, brandy and vodka, where production would require capital investment and technology, an opportunity arose for state control. The most obvious motives were the mixed ones: the elimination of abuses and creation of a source of revenue for the state.

As a result, the old inns and taverns soon gave way to the state drink shops, which sold no food but only state-produced or state-licensed drinks...; the whole atmosphere of drinking became more purposeful, less social.[17]

Purposeful drinking clearly led to excessive drinking, with no food to mitigate the effects and in 1652 these drink shops were abolished in favour of a kind of off-license, the 'pot house', with only one allowed in each town and restrictions on how much could be sold to each customer. Clerics and monks were not allowed to purchase drink, and this could reveal a hidden motive behind regulations that had first introduced and then eliminated the drink-shops: not so much anti-clericalism as the fear that as influential people clerics might foster social discontent. The social dimension of alcohol consumption was recognised and discouraged.

Why humans drink

In a 2018 article on why humans drink, Robin Dunbar, the professor of evolutionary psychology at Oxford University, concluded that the reasons humans drink (alcohol being understood here) are both simple and complex. Humans are social animals and rely on bondedness to maintain social coherence. They know that a shared bottle of wine helps in this process. There is more to it, however:

> It isn't just because alcohol causes people to lose their social inhibitions and become over-friendly with our drinking chums. Rather, the alcohol itself triggers the brain mechanism that is intimately involved in building and maintaining friendships in monkeys, apes and humans. This mechanism is the endorphin system.[18]

The opiate-like effect of the system, according to the author, 'seems to be crucial for establishing bonded relationships that allow individuals to trust each other'. It needs to be noted that this article was concerned only with the function and effects of neuro-transmitters in the brain and not with the long-term consequences of the use of alcohol to stimulate this activity, while the *British Medical Journal* study involved 550 participants over a 30 year follow-up period and included those whose alcohol consumption was 'moderate'.

Decades before Dunbar's article, Robert Capon in his book perceptively and humorously discoursed – 'glass in hand' - on the good things of God's creation; God's creative activity, he said, is necessary to an unnecessary world:

> God makes wine. For all its difficulties, there is no way round the doctrine of creation. But notice the tense: he *makes*; not *made*. He did not create *once upon a time*, only to find himself saddled now with the unavoidable and embarrassing result of that first rash decision…. Wine *is*; the fruit of the vine stands in act, outside of nothing, because it is his very present pleasure to have it so.[19]

Further on, he explained:

> Only the ungrateful or the purblind can fail to see that sugar in the grape and yeast on the skins *is* a divine idea, not a human one. Man's part in the process consists of honest and prudent management of the work that God has begun. Something underhanded has to be done to grape juice to keep it from running its appointed course.[20]

That may not be enough to overturn the results of a scientific study, but it probably resonates with people who are more attuned to the history of human culture and the wisdom of the ages than to the undoubtedly important need to reflect on what science says about a potentially hazardous future. For such people the witness of the scriptures may come to mind: 'wine to cheer man's heart' (Ps 104:15).

Laughter and singing
In itself, triggering the endorphin system is not necessarily a harmful process; other activities which cause it range from laughter to singing and even dancing. That would indicate that the shared meal can be successful with the help of these others and without alcohol. As in the case of Renaissance or Versailles banquets, the event today, at least in larger

gatherings, would benefit from entertainment being provided by professionals rather than the participants. But alcohol has always had a place; humans have consumed alcohol over a very long period of time. There is archaeological evidence to this effect going back more than eight thousand years in China, so it is not surprising that despite medical evidence shared meals in most cultures typically include alcohol.

The food itself has a central role in the shared meal and from the banquets of Roman times to today those who have charge of arrangements use both imagination and ingenuity to make the event both an enjoyable and memorable experience. In big catering events, the demanding role of the catering manager is still something like that of the *scalco* described earlier, but in small-scale gatherings, the main concern will be the guiding of the diners' choices, or actually providing the appropriate dishes in the case of the family.

The most significant addition to the food comes from the words spoken, the address which sets the tone and brings out the underlying meaning and significance of the event. A testimonial dinner is a case in point. The speaker builds a picture of the person being honoured by evoking memories of achievements and invokes a blessing, or wishes good fortune, for the years ahead. The person being honoured is at the centre of the event, with a presence and profile enhanced by seating arrangements, surrounded by guests while glasses are raised in a toast. At a wedding banquet, evocation is likely to be more light-hearted and invocation more thoughtful. These factors of evocation, invocation and presence will be considered in more detail when the Eucharistic feast is considered in Chapter Eighteen.

Babette's Feast

A short story by Isak Dinesen (Karen Blixen), 'Babette's Feast', in her collection, *Anecdotes of Destiny,*[21] centres on the remarkable effects which both choosing and cooking the food had on the twelve participants in a celebratory meal in a small Norwegian town, Berlevaag, in the nineteenth-century. The occasion was the centenary of the birth of an unnamed Lutheran pastor, the Dean, who had founded a Pietistic com-

Scene from the Gabriel Axel directed drama, 'Babette's Feast.'

munity of his own among the simple fisher-folk there. A charismatic figure of rigorous views, the community which gathered around him was inevitably small and intensely loyal. After his death his two unmarried daughters continued to pastor the aging group of his followers, who were becoming fewer in number every year, 'whiter or balder and harder of hearing, … even becoming somewhat querulous and quarrelsome'. The members renounced the pleasures of this world 'for the earth and all that it held was to them but a kind of illusion'.[22] Their clothing and diet reflected this unworldliness. The two sisters, who had been beautiful in their youth, never had an article of fashion and always dressed in grey and black; the standard diet was split cod and an ale-and-bread soup. The age-old sumptuary laws had no need of being imposed.

Into this secluded world came a refugee who made her way to this remote place following the defeat of the Paris Commune in 1871, a woman named Babette, who offered to cook for the two sisters in return for her

302

keep. Frightened by this intrusion of a presumed Papist into their austere world, the ladies agreed that the example of a good Lutheran life would be the best way of converting their servant and they impressed upon her that their food must be as plain as possible.

Babette's presence gradually had a transformative effect on their lives and it had something to do with how her cooking not only saved money but also added zest to the food that the sisters ate and distributed to the poor and the sick. The whole group of believers observed how contented the two sisters were and in turn found their own troubles and cares became less of a weight in their lives.

The Dean's centenary had been intended to be a quiet affair, perhaps some special readings and prayers when they gathered in the sisters' house, where the evocation of the past would in some way show that the Dean still presided. But a sensational event broke in suddenly on their quiet lives. Babette won the French lottery and offered to cook a French dinner for the small group from her own resources. This caused panic among the believers, who met and resolved that for the sisters' sake

> they would on the great day be silent on all matters of food and drink. Nothing that might be set before them, be it even frogs or snails, would wring a word from their lips. ... 'On the day of our master we will cleanse our tongues of all taste and purify them of all delight or disgust of the senses, keeping and preserving them for the higher functions of praise and thanksgiving'.[23]

The 'day of our master' became the evening of the 'French dinner'. The little group of believers fortified themselves spiritually by singing one of the Dean's hymns as they crossed the threshold, and then struck up another: 'Take not thought for food or raiment, careful one...'. The oldest member had got permission to bring her visiting nephew, a French General, and so the participants numbered twelve.

After grace, they raise a glass to their lips, the believers doing so gravely 'in confirmation of their resolution'. But the General, uninformed about the origin and nature of the dinner, is startled to find he is sipping a very fine Amontillado. He is more perplexed by what follows, which he realises is turtle soup – 'and what a turtle soup'.

> Usually in Berlevaag people did not speak much while eating. But somehow this evening tongues had been loosened. An old brother told the story of his first meeting with the Dean. Another went through that sermon which sixty years ago had brought about his conversion.[24]

The General wished to contribute, but was reduced to silence by the next course. Incredibly, it was Blinis Demidoff. His fellow eaters went on quietly eating without any sign of surprise or approval. The serving boy now poured them a sparkling drink; it must be lemonade, they thought. 'The lemonade agreed with their exalted state of mind and seemed to lift them off the ground into a higher and purer sphere.'[25] The General set down his glass and said to his neighbour: 'But surely this is a Veuve Cliquot 1860', but the neighbour only smiled and made a remark about the weather.

> The convives grew lighter in weight and lighter of heart the more they ate and drank. ... It was, they realised, when man has not only altogether forgotten but has firmly renounced all ideas of food and drink that he eats and drinks in the right spirit.[26]

The General, however, was concentrating more and more on the food. He was astounded to find himself tasting Cailles en Sarcophage, which he had experienced once before in Paris, where he had learned that it had been invented by the chef at the Café Anglais, the greatest culinary genius of the age. Transported to another realm by this extraordinary feast – and intoxicated by 'the noblest wine of the world' - the General felt compelled to make a speech. The words that came were not what he would have planned; he seemed a mouthpiece for a message 'meant to be brought forth'. It was a case of a transformative word. His hearers did not altogether understand him but the sound of well-known and cherished words about grace and gratitude had seized and moved all hearts.

None of the guests later on had any clear remembrance of it. 'They only knew that the rooms had been filled with a heavenly light, as if a number of small haloes had blended into one glorious radiance.' Time had merged into eternity and the old believers were transformed physically and spiritually. Old wrongs were forgotten, ancient loves rekindled and a mystical redemption of the human spirit settled over the table.

Conclusion

Such were the effects of Babette's feast, Babette the former chef of the Café Anglais. Even if it is not always the outcome of a shared meal, this story provides compelling witness to how food can be transformed into a feast. The old believers had set their hearts on not commenting on, not enjoying what they believed might be the sinful products of the devil's kitchen, but with the help of the 'lemonade' and obviously the excellence of the food – the General is there to underline that fact – their inhibitions melt away, and the meal creates fellowship. The General's words had also something to do with the transformation of the intended simple commemoration into a feast.

The exotic dishes were not of course vegetarian; there is a vivid reminder of this when on the day before the feast the serving boy places what seems a strange greenish black stone on the kitchen floor and one of the sisters shrinks back in horror as a snake-like head shoots out from it, weaving slightly from side to side;[27] it is really an advance notice to the reader that turtle soup will be on the menu. Today, such dishes remain a part of *haute cuisine,* but the supremacy they once had does not go unquestioned. There is now a vast body of literature not only promoting vegetarianism but also questioning the ethical status of meat-eating. Vegetarianism is no longer the fad of some marginal elements in society. Rather it is expressive of a way of life to which sectors of the population are turning because of the serious conclusions of environmental studies, especially research on the detrimental effects of meat production on an industrial scale. For people strongly attached to the traditional culture of meat-eating such a choice is a rather 'unpalatable' one. This issue will be discussed further in the next chapter.

It could hardly be otherwise than that alcohol would have a role in the feast, given that it was a 'French dinner', and it is certainly presented as having a part in the transformative effect. Robert Capon would no doubt approve and the Dunbar article already cited would add credence to this belief, whatever the BMJ report might hold counter-intuitively.

However, alcohol remains a problematic issue in all considerations of the shared meal, not perhaps in the case of the participants in Babette's feast as they appear to have been accustomed to ale - though not to champagne. They were, it can be presumed, descendants of the Vikings and drink was at the heart of Viking feasts, which seem in fact to have been more about drink than food.[28] Their religious beliefs are important to the story in showing how far they have to travel from their settled convictions to a situation which mainstream Christianity – and secular society – would recognise as the transformative nature of an excellent shared meal. The story does not delve into the details of the little community's life of worship, but it could be imaginatively extended to take note of the fact that without the Dean, there would no longer be any sacramental celebrations, but only gatherings to remember his proclamation of the Word. Babette's feast used food to bring the group together into grace-filled, reconciled unity, such as a mainstream Lutheran celebration of the Eucharist as well as - it is to be hoped - a Catholic one could achieve for believers. Chapter Eighteen will explore the difference the Christian context makes to the shared meal.

ENDNOTES

1   Robert Farrar Capon, *The Supper of the Lamb. A Culinary Reflection* (Garden City, N.Y.: Image Books, 1974²) 32

2   Robert Disch, *The Ecological Conscience. Values for Survival* (Upper Saddle River, NJ: Prentice Hall, 1970) 96

3   Robert Farrar Capon, *The Supper of the Lamb* 151-2

4   Stephen Mennell, *All Manners of Food. Eating and Taste in England and France from the Middle Ages to the Present* (Oxford: Basil Blackwell, 1985) 21

5   Reay Tannahill, *Food in History* (London: Headline Book Publishing, 1988²) 188

6   Pietro Caliari, *Paolo Veronese. Sua Vita e Sue Opere* (Roma: Forzani e C.,1888) 104

7   Ibid. 100, note 1

8   Ibid. 104

9   James Hall, *A History of Ideas and Images in Italian Art* (London: John Murray, 1981)106

10 Reay Tannahill, *Food in History* 250

11 Carolyn Steel, *Hungry City. How Food Shapes Our Lives* (London: Chatto & Windus, 2008) 213

12 Reay Tannahill, *Food in History* 188

13 John Bossy, *Christianity in the West* 121

14 Anya Topiwala, et al.,'Moderate alcohol consumption as risk factor for adverse brain outcomes and cognitive decline: longitudinal cohort study', *British Medical Journal* 2017;357:j2353

15 Robin Dunbar, 'Humanity's drinking game', *Financial Times,* Life and Arts, 11 August 2018, 1-2

16 Terrence Kardong O.S.B., *Benedict's Rule. A Translation and Commentary* (Collegeville: Liturgical Press, 1996) 324

17 Reay Tannahill, *Food in History* 249

18 Robin Dunbar, 'Humanity's drinking game' 1

19 Robert Farrar Capon, *The Supper of the Lamb* 79

20 Ibid. 83

21 Isak Dinesen, *Anecdotes of Destiny* (London: Michael Joseph, 1958) 27-65

22 Ibid. 27

23 Ibid. 47

24 Ibid. 55

25 Ibid. 56

26 Idem

27 Ibid. 46

28 Roy Strong, *Feast. A History of Grand Eating* (London: Jonathan Cape, 2004) 58

CHAPTER SEVENTEEN

Food and the Ethics of Feasting

> I do not want to know how my everyday eating habits make
> me complicit with cruel treatment of animals. I do not want
> to know that the way I have learned to eat contributes to
> the ongoing degradation of the land. I do not want to know
> how the way my food is produced puts an unjust burden on
> people who have no food to eat at all.[1]

The quotation is from the Foreword a distinguished U.S. professor of
ethics contributed to a book on the theology of eating. His stirrings of
conscience provide a summary of the issues which Christians and people
of no religious belief need to address in face of the environmental crisis
to which the world is perceived to be heading. The reliance on meat as a
stable part of the contemporary Western diet and the quantity consumed
are cited in many reports as major issues.

Questions arise as to whether the 'feast' in which meat in abundance
has a central role can any longer be considered authentic. Even in finger food amounts, can it uphold genuine human values, since meat and
meat products in general have their origin in a mass-production process
that implies ethical ambiguity rather than deriving from the work of the
skilled and sensitive hands of a Babette? A fundamental issue is whether,
in addition to environmental concerns, cruelty is endemic to a large-scale
process for the slaughtering of animals in order to provide meat for humans. The nub of the case against industrialised slaughtering is that the
scale of the operation makes human involvement remote, reducing it to
a mechanical process in which human sensitivity to the infliction of pain
is eliminated. In earlier times in the towns of Europe, animal slaughter
for food was carried out at the point of sale, or even domestically, and
consumers had to be aware of the cost in suffering to another creature the
nurturing of their human lives required. The portion of meat they took

away from the market had an association with life as well as death, the life given up so that they could continue to live. Instead of causing qualms of conscience in most cases, it would instead have helped humans to realise their dependence on the resources of nature and as a result mitigate an arrogance and sense of independence and autonomy that fails to reflect the real status of humanity in the grand scheme of things.

Age-old tradition could certainly have had the effect of making people of normal sensitivity accept that this arrangement was a law of nature; sustaining life for humans meant the losing of life for other creatures. In the original marketplace practice of slaughter, according to a modern study of the abattoir system, the violence involved in taking life remained with the butchers 'who were credited with possessing a violent and brutal character'.[2] Consumers witnessing the slaughter might in that case react with feelings of unease, but in fact familiarity may well have led them to associate any destructive feelings with the butchers rather than themselves and so register only an interest in the nourishment the meat would provide. Vegetarians have never accepted this as a justification for the practice of eating meat.

The satisfaction of the consumers was always a priority of those who provided them with meat, while their health and wellbeing was the concern of civil authorities. In the nineteenth-century, medical discoveries relating to infectious diseases - rather than the desire to shield people from the reality of butchering - led to standards of hygiene being introduced that led to slaughterhouses being removed from public places. The gradual industrialisation of the process came with the need to provide for an increasing population, along with the realisation that mass production resulted in greater profitability. This certainly has had the effect of allowing consumers to see meat in a different light, giving the impression, one shared by the providers, that it is simply a commodity, the subject of a transaction.

Animal welfare issues
But investigation today of the meat production and processing industry has led to concern on the part of activists in animal welfare movements regarding conditions obtaining there, but also with regard to the psychological and physical wellbeing of those who work in abattoirs. The

310

priority in interest is often accorded to animal welfare, as the mass production system seems open to physical abuse when animals are crowded
into the facility, and more obviously because the mechanised nature of
the process means that human intervention is in stages and no one has
direct responsibility for killing. In the killing process there is dissociation
between the individual actors and the individual acts[3] and the issue of
whether it can be a humane act becomes irrelevant. The counter-argu-
ment on the side of industry relies on questioning whether individual
butchering was generally a humane process, given the possibility of im-
precision or carelessness or sheer cruelty - if the opinion of historians is
correct that butchers of old were of a brutal nature. Nonetheless there is a
growing perception that greater cruelty is endemic to the production-line
slaughtering of animals. However, investigation of whether animals experience panic on smelling blood as they enter the abattoir has not been
conclusive. The welfare of the workers is also an issue. In the view of two
present-day theologians:

> In the context of mechanised mass slaughter, the alienation of the
> workers from the product of their activity and the annihilation of
> their compassion, sensitivity and imagination are essential means
> of conditioning them to perpetuate slaughter willingly.[4]

Environmental issues and human health

An issue separate from the slaughtering process arises from investigation
of the industry in environmental studies. The need for new thinking in
relation to animals being used as a food resource has come with the findings of recent decades concerning atmospheric pollution and the threat
it poses to the entire eco-system. According to a study in 2017 of the
effects of cattle farming, 'the livestock sector contributes 14.5% of global
greenhouse gas (GHG) emissions, driving further climate change'.[5] A Report of the Intergovernmental Panel on Climate Change for the decade
2000-2010 concluded that GHG emissions from the production of beef
and beef products were more than ten times that from other agricultural

Sustainable diet guidelines

14g of red meat a day - half a rasher

No more than 29g of poultry a day

One and a half eggs a week

A big reduction in potatoes

More fruit and nuts

sectors, such as rice and cereals.[6] A report entitled *Food in the Anthropocene: the EAT–Lancet Commission on healthy diets from sustainable food systems*[7] was issued by an international commission in January 2019, with the aim of defining global dietary targets that will help to ensure that the UN Sustainable Development Goals (SDGs) and Paris Agreement targets are achieved. It found that because of disparities of lifestyle between developed and under-developed economies more than 820 million people have insufficient food. Many more consume low-quality diets that cause micronutrient deficiencies and contribute to a substantial rise in the incidence of diet-related obesity and diet-related non-communicable diseases, including coronary heart disease, stroke, and diabetes.

It established what it called a 'healthy reference diet', one that needs to obtain universally in order that the burgeoning world population may be fed without further degradation of the eco-system. The diet consists largely of vegetables, fruits, whole grains, legumes, nuts, and unsaturated oils, a low to moderate amount of seafood and poultry, and includes no or a low quantity of red meat, processed meat, added sugar, refined grains, and starchy vegetables. The finding with regard to red meat has been severely criticised by farming lobbies, while media summaries of it accurately present it as implying a very meagre 'half a rasher' a day - to many consumers a finding which invites derision.

Climate change poses a major threat to the sustainability of all life, human, animal and plant, as the average global temperature continues to rise. Whatever natural climatic cycles occur, there is scientific consensus that human activity is the main cause for this and meat eating a major contributory factor.

Interconnectedness and theology

The two issues of possible animal cruelty and the degradation of the environment coalesce as the greater one of the failure to realise the interconnectedness of all creation, and the consequent rupture of the connection between humanity and the rest of creation which sustains it, the land, the plants, the animals. The failure has its origin in the dominant role humans have endeavoured to exercise from earliest times in the world over plants, animals, land and sea.

Many are now more aware than in the past that a malaise affects humanity in relation to its place in the world. The reasons for this will be understood differently according to whether there is belief in a creator or not. Christians look to the Book of Genesis for an explanation.

The account of humankind's doings over the course of several chapters of the Book of Genesis represented an acknowledgement and explanation of the situation which actually existed at the time of the compilation of the text (which included more than one literary tradition). It also was an attempt to reach back into pre-history to a world where harmony was thought to have existed. The first account of creation in Genesis 1:28, where the Creator gave humankind its place in creation in relation to other creatures, is one which in all translations establishes humankind's supreme role. It states:

> Be fruitful and multiply, and fill the earth and subdue it; and have dominion over the fish of the sea and over the birds of the air and over every living thing that moves upon the earth.

However, the next verse, 1:29 adds:

> See, I have given you every plant yielding seed that is upon the
> face of all the earth, and every tree with seed in its fruit; you shall
> have them for food.

As scripture presents it, in the beginning, humans were meant to rely
on the regenerating resources of plants and trees. That was the situation
in the ideal conditions of the beginning. The end of that account has God
resting on the seventh day, not from a feeling of need but of delight in
all he had created - and there is no mention of humankind sharing this
rest. The account of God resting is in fact peculiar to the author of the
first account of creation and elsewhere in the Old Testament, as well as in
the New, God's creative activity is continuous. When the Jews persecuted
Jesus for working a miracle on the Sabbath, he replied: 'My father goes
on working and so do I' (Jn 5:17). Accordingly, the second account of
creation (Gn 2:5-25) gives the detail of how God continues to deal with
humankind: 'The Lord God took the man and put him in the garden of
Eden to till it and keep it' (Gn 2:15). Humankind was not meant to live
a life of indolence but work would be a sharing in God's creative activity.
Later in Genesis, after the expulsion of sinful humanity from the garden,
work was described as a frustrating and painful task. The earth would
yield brambles and thistles and work involve toil and sweat (Gn 3:17-19).

As the generations succeeded one another, 'the Lord saw that the
wickedness of humankind was great in the earth' (Gen 6:5) and sent
the great deluge to clear away the evil civilisation which had developed.
Noah, who was a man who 'walked with God', was chosen to inaugurate
a new epoch after he and the survivors emerged from the ark and he had
offered burnt offerings from the clean animals and birds; their fragrance
was pleasing to the Lord (Gen 8:21) and led to his making a covenant
with Noah and succeeding generations. The new epoch thus inaugurated
presumed the existence of the disorder caused by sin and the continuing
need for sacrifice. The compilers of the text in effect defended the legit-

imacy of the religious institution and its laws that existed in their day regarding the religious rites, which from the time of the covenant with Moses included sacrifices of well-being (or peace) where the flesh of the animal was eaten, though without its blood, after parts had been made a burnt offering. This had been part of the covenant with Noah:

> Be fruitful and multiply, and fill the earth. The fear and dread of you shall rest on every animal of the earth, and on every bird of the air, on everything that creeps on the ground, and on all the fish of the sea; into your hand they are delivered. Every moving thing that lives shall be food for you; and just as I gave you the green plants, I give you everything. Only, you shall not eat flesh with its life, that is, its blood. (Gn 9:1-3)

The dominant role of humankind was asserted, but, fundamentally, the way the narrative developed involved recognition that life as lived was still marked by restrictions. It was not fulfilled because humans yearned for a life they could not have, that which was signified by the picture of the original garden and by God's rejoicing at the work of his hands in the Sabbath rest on the seventh day. The ideal for humanity would have been to enter into his Sabbath rest. The Psalmist spoke of how things actually turned out, of how God was wearied of humankind. 'They are a people whose hearts go astray, and they do not regard my ways. Therefore in my anger I swore, "They shall not enter my rest." ' (Ps 95:10-11)

The Old Testament established a culture in which the eating of meat had association with sacrifice and would be based on what was normal dietary practice. As a result, eating meat was not an ethical problem for the developing Judeo-Christian community. Some of the first Christians even continued animal sacrifice, though now with a different meaning as already noted, while others simply repudiated the Jewish rites. They retained the meat (and fish) eating culture, and Peter's experience recorded in the Acts of the Apostles 10:13 established greater freedom for them with the elimination of the classification of clean and unclean. In the gospels, Jesus is often depicted at meals with others and even described by his critics as a glutton and a drunkard (Mt 11:19). He served breakfast of bread and fish to the disciples after his resurrection, and there is the unique and mysterious event of him in his glorified state eating a piece of broiled fish in their presence – prompting the Venerable Bede to ask what in those circumstances became of the fish.

Despite acceptance by the Christian community, in monastic tradition and in ascetical circles generally there has been a settled conviction about the need to abstain from meat – a restriction imposed on all Christians during Lent and at all times on Fridays. But such restrictions were seen against a background of the need to do penance and of suspicion that the eating of meat inflamed the passions. Those who abstained were not concerned with what some today would call 'animal rights' – a rather infelicitous term as 'rights' is a concept which correlates with 'duties' and is not really appropriate in relation to animals. As it developed, Christian tradition did not extend the idea of 'right' to animals. St Augustine, for example, in his argument against Faustus, who held the Manichean view that animals had souls, discussed the incident where Christ sent demons into a herd of pigs (Mt 8:32) and held that Christ was indifferent (literally cruel, *crudelis*) to those brute beasts because they had no souls.[8] He elaborated on this in his *On the Morals of the Manicheans*: 'For we see and hear by their cries that animals die with pain, although man disregards this in a beast, with which, as not having a rational soul, we have no community of rights'.

In religious terms, the issue is not a potential community of rights but the relationship between humans and the rest of creation and this has begun to be studied anew in light of the environmental factors mentioned, but also from a new interest in the nature of the human person inspired by studies of biological evolution, physical cosmology's predictions concerning the future and neuroscience's findings.[9] This involves re-visiting previously unquestioned theological positions derived from scripture and centuries of theological development.

Some kind of restriction is needed to express a new vision of humankind's relationship with other creatures. In fact, something to this effect has been there, at least seminally, in the Judeo-Christian tradition. Animals serve as humankind's food but only to the extent of being the container of life, not life itself which is identified with the blood and must still be honoured. When Old Testament religion was established, this restriction was observed; in the sacrificial rites, the blood was sprinkled on the altar, giving it back to God, though also sprinkled on the people as a sign of the covenant. In the Acts of the Apostles this restriction was respected when at the Council of Jerusalem (15:20) a letter was sent to new converts telling them to refrain 'from (ingesting) blood' and from 'the meat of strangled animals' - where blood remains life is there also.

This restriction on the eating of animals can be seen in the Celtic world, according to the *Canons of Adomnan,* who was abbot of Iona in Scotland in the seventh century (though there appears to be 'no substantial evidence to link these canons with Adomnan').[10] The canons almost all deal with alimentary regulations including the prohibition of carrion as food.

> Canon 2: Cattle that fall from a rock, if their blood has been shed, are to be taken; if not, but if their bones are broken and their blood has not come out, they are to be rejected as if they were carrion. Canon 3: (Animals) that have died in water are carrion, since their blood remains in them.[11]

In the contemporary world there is a felt need to re-discover harmony with the rest of creation, to revive the vision of an ideal environment in an attempt to reverse the malaise which increasing pollution inflicts on the planet. Writers and reports such as those from the United Nations focus on a reversal of the deteriorating climate. From the perspective of world history the plans are necessarily short-term, stated in terms of a crisis before the end of this century, rather than the remaining life-span of the planet of about four-and-a-half billon years.

A theology of eating

Among the studies of this situation from a theological standpoint is *Food and Faith. A Theology of Eating*, by Norman Wirzba.[12] He approaches the question of harmony of humankind with the rest of creation by drawing on the idea of the original garden. His aim is to establish the ethical principles by which people need to live in order to experience some anticipation of an eventual return to this garden where they might share God's Sabbath contentment. This will require a disciplined existence. Continuing to call humankind by the name Adam, he states:

> To eat, Adam must garden rather than simply shop. Food is not simply a 'resource' to be mined or a commodity to be purchased. Adam's work, and the insight that comes from gardening discipline, enables him to eat with a deep appreciation for what he is eating. It is this appreciation that enables him to experience the Garden of Eden as a 'garden of delights'.[13]

In his view, the issue of vegetarianism versus meat-eating does not then arise. Humanity enjoys the rights accorded by the covenant with Noah. In fact, he begins his work by referring to a memorable meal which 'included some of the freshest and best-tasting greens, tortillas, salsa, and chicken I had ever tasted'.[14]

He does recognise the importance of the text of Genesis 1:28 from the first account of creation and that the prophets Isaiah and Hosea suggested a vegetarian diet will also mark God's future peaceable kingdom. But he then asks if it follows that all consumption of meat is wrong and whether there are theological considerations that can be brought to bear on 'this very complex and important issue'. His argument depends on the idea of sacrifice. His thinking is in accord with that articulated by Edward Kilmartin, in a pioneering work, *The Eucharist in the West. History and Theology*. Kilmartin summed up his thinking on sacrifice:

Sacrifice is not in the first place an activity of human beings directed to God and, in the second place, something that reaches its goal in the response of divine acceptance and bestowal of divine blessing on the cultic community. Rather, sacrifice in the New Testament understanding – and thus in its Christian understanding – is in the first place, the self-offering of the Father in the gift of his Son, and in the second place the unique response of the Son in his humanity to the Father, and in the third place the self-offering of believers in union with Christ by which they share in his covenant relation with the Father.[15]

Wirzba says that the movement of sacrifice that characterises God's life also characterises created life:

Creation understood as God's offering of creatures to each other as food and nurture, reflects a sacrificial power in which life continually moves through death to new life. … Because there is no life without sacrificial love, and no love without surrender, the destiny of all creatures is that they offer themselves or are offered up as the temporal expression of God's eternal love.[16]

As stated here, there is a mutuality implied, but clearly 'offering themselves' is proper only to rational creatures. This is a principle fundamental to the Christian life and is exercised in many ways, sometimes heroic. It falls to other creatures, such as animals, to 'be offered' and tradition from Old Testament times on has considered that this is God's will. In accordance with that argument, one can see that Buddhists or Hindus could argue that it would be appropriate for humans to offer themselves for the protection of other creatures and so avoid all harm to them – as exemplified in avoiding treading on an insect. It is interesting that Jesus did not give any teaching of that sort. Wirzba does not discuss a non-Christian scenario but does consider whether a vegetarian can avoid concerns about sacrifice and the life-and-death character of life. He points out that a strictly vegetable diet cannot avoid the death of a great number of creatures ranging from microorganisms in the soil to rodents and other small animals above the ground, all of which are constantly feeding on one another. 'How does one compare the death of a microbe with the death of a cow?'

> Considering vegetarianism, however, enables us to think more deeply about the nature of eating as an act that leads us into the life and death of creation. It invites us to think more carefully about how human eaters are best to approach and consume the gifts of plant and animal life.[17]

He grants that vegetarians have grounds for arguments against meat-eating and summarises three general forms: the findings of academic studies to the effect that people who eat a heavy animal-based diet suffer greater incidence of chronic diseases compared with those who have a plant-based diet; second, the abuses which are endemic in the meat-producing industry and third, an animal-based diet requires that precious soil, water, plant and fossil fuel resources be converted into animal feed before they can provide food for humans. He concurs with the various reports that 'the health of humans, animals, fields and waterways would be better served if people ate less meat, particularly the sort of meat raised and slaughtered according to industrial models of production'.[18] He does not go so far as to say, as some vegetarians would, that industrial slaughtering is tantamount to offering sacrifice to the idol of profitability. Overall, he holds that the Genesis texts which taken together indicate that God gave both plants and animals as food is an indication of 'the self-offering that characterises God's creative and sustaining life from the beginning'.[19]

> This does not mean that eaters are to take lightly the death of creatures given by God as food. ... But it does suggest that we must – through care-full and compassionate living – learn to accept and honour the gift of the death of others as God's means of provision and salvation for the world.[20]

Wirzba believes that instead of 'care-full and compassionate' treatment, what takes place in industrial farming and food systems is a violation rather than the care of each other. He holds that a 'reconciliation deficit disorder' exists which obstructs God's reconciling way with the world. To counter it, Christians need to be supporters and champions of local economies in which distance, blindness and ignorance can be overcome and replaced with knowledgeable participation and honest celebration.[21] His experience is that local church communities are creating such economies, to the extent even of developing church community gardens – a reminder of his basic vision of today's Adam called to 'garden rather than shop'.

Overall, he develops cogent arguments for meat-eating in his theology of God's self-giving, and his general principles accord well with those of Pope Francis, in his Encyclical, *Laudato si'* (2015) 'On the Care of our Common Home'. The pope addressed the issue of the global ecological crisis, exemplified by global warming, and the thinking needed to counteract degradation of the environment. His approach continued that of recent popes, who have applied Catholic Social Teaching to this issue. After an analysis of the economic and social problems which have given rise to potential disaster for people and planet, he developed a theme based on the three terms, interconnected, interrelated and interdependent. His concern was to provide principles for 'Ecological Education and Spirituality' (Chapter Six), using those concepts theologically. His teaching was well summed up in one paragraph:

> The human person grows more, matures more and is sanctified more to the extent that he or she enters into relationships, going out from themselves to live in communion with God, with others and with all creatures. In this way, they make their own that Trinitarian dynamism which God imprinted in them when they were created. Everything is interconnected, and this invites us to develop a spirituality of that global solidarity which flows from the mystery of the Trinity. (no. 240)

When our hearts are authentically open to universal communion, this sense of fraternity excludes nothing and no one. It follows that our indifference or cruelty towards fellow creatures of this world sooner or later affects the treatment we mete out to other human beings. We have only one heart, and the same wretchedness which leads us to mistreat an animal will not be long in showing itself in our relationships with other people. (92)

Conclusion

Pope Francis rightly speaks of the need for open hearts, that is, for the full involvement of our humanity in attitudes and actions in relation to the rest of creation and not just cold reasoning, which will be sure to meet with counter-arguments and alternative sets of facts. Acting in that way must not at the same time descend into an irrational sentimentality that Wirzba warns against. By his logic it would be sentimental and romantic to oppose the fate of that extraordinary animal, the turtle, belonging to a lineage of two hundred and twenty million years, offered up to the guests by the fictional Babette in the form of soup. But equally, sensitivity to humankind's place in creation must cause humans to take pause in asserting the right to use animals as food; there are situations where humans need to be conscious of the precious heritage the long history of creation has provided. In fact, many species of turtle are endangered, or very endangered.

This sensitivity along with the reasons for avoiding meat-eating given above – health risks from a meat-heavy diet, animal welfare considerations and environmental degradation – has led to the recurrence of vegetarian movements in recent history. The term 'vegetarian' itself is not an old one, going back only to the decade up to the founding of the British Vegetarian Society in 1847 and the corresponding one in America in 1850. John Wesley had been a proponent of fasting and abstinence from meat in the eighteenth century but by the nineteenth Methodism was part of mainstream church life in England and it was radicalism in religion as well as radical social and political movements in the nine-

teenth-century that gave rise to this dietary movement, as its popularity
with Quakers, Unitarians and some Baptists demonstrated.

Two journals promoting vegetarianism were founded in America in
the mid-eighteen hundreds and were influential in introducing whole-
meal bread and crackers as a substitute for the pork, bean, and pie break-
fasts which were the typical breakfast for the stockyard and railway workers of the time. Out of this new breakfast diet came the invention of
cornflakes, a cereal which was accidentally discovered by John H. Kellogg
through leaving rolled flakes of corn to rest for a few hours, whereupon
they became the now well-known crispy flakes.[22]

The new approach to breakfast in America made people more conscious of the need for a balanced diet but that that did not in the end
reduce the amount of meat eaten. In the history of the past almost two
centuries, other factors have had greater influence on lifestyle, in particular several wars – two in Europe but two more for the United States,
the Korean and Vietnam conflicts. These and the industrial development
which preceded them, and was sometimes both cause and effect, created
a new world order. Humankind was coerced into being efficient oper-
atives of a great machine which had to be maintained at that level by
the best possible nourishment. The urgency of this showed itself in the
introduction of food immediately available, notably in the McDonald
franchise which began in the U.S. when in 1954 Ray Kroc bought the
rights of producing food according to the system used by two McDonald
brothers in their diner in California.[23] The chain he founded has had
such an impact on eating habits as to lead to the idea of 'fast food' and
discussion of the 'Mcdonaldization of society'.[24] Serious study of the 'philosophy of food' has introduced the idea of misrepresentation:

> By appealing to universal features, a food style can gain dominance as
> the healthy one, the profitable one, and so on; and then other food
> styles cannot exert their power. ... In the Western world, fast food
> has an enormous advantage, both in marketing and advertising and
> also in research and even cooking. This misrepresentation means that

everything is biased towards fast food, even though the consumer never asked for fast food, … for mealtimes eight times a day.[25]

As mentioned earlier in this work, this process of changing the role of food in daily life began to be seen in early modernity, with the printer, Froschhauer, in Zürich under pressure to meet his deadline for the Frankfurt book fair. But all of this has led over the centuries to an ecological crisis and the urging of today's international experts that a reverse process is needed. One obvious reaction to fast food is the phenomenon of 'slow food', a movement begun in Italy as a protest against 'the fast, quick way to cook everything and the neglect of quality, enjoyment, health, the environment and the landscape'.[26]

Quite recently, as a result of scientific reports, civil authorities in various places are taking note of the challenge posed by various sources of pollution by introducing remedial measures in relation to meat consumption in addition to other micro-level initiatives, such as controlling emissions from traffic. In 2009 Ghent became the first city on earth to have an official weekly vegetarian day. Introduced by the city authorities, it has led to ninety hotels and restaurants in the city offering vegetarian meals on Thursdays, which has come to be called Donderdag Veggiedag - Thursday Veggie Day. It had been found that people were willing to reduce consumption of meat, but were not well informed on how to create meatless meals.

It cannot be claimed that the mainstream Christian churches, which in the past called for fasting and abstinence from meat for penitential reasons, have up to now addressed the issue of meat-eating in an ecological context.

In 2003, representatives of the 'Veg4Lent' campaign, wrote to nearly sixty Anglican and Roman Catholic bishops in Britain inviting them to support its initiative by abstaining from meat for Lent. Only one quarter of the bishops contacted responded, and just one third of these considered that the campaign raised significant ethical or spiritual issues. The most prominent bishop to respond positively was Richard Chartres, the (then) bishop of London , who later became a vegetarian.[27]

It is true, however, that the predecessors of Pope Francis, Pope St John Paul and emeritus Pope Benedict XVI had responded to the ecological crisis in their teaching with forcefulness and clarity. It is true too that scientific evidence had sounded the alarm about the ecological crisis and led to the Kyoto Protocol by 1997, but this was concerned with establishing targets for the limiting of harmful emissions rather than identifying the actual emissions caused by, for example, the agricultural sector. It was a case of declaring principles and establishing targets. It provided the basis for the investigations which have more recently focused in on such detailed items as meat consumption.

For the Christian way of life a set of principles has always existed to regulate how life in the world should be lived. The extent to which the Christian is 'at home' in the world has been perceived differently throughout the centuries, especially with regard to the place of ascetical practices. The way St Jerome saw it differed considerably from the view of Pope Leo X, while the Protestant Reformers asserted the freedom of the Christian. Throughout the Middle Ages and beyond, church authorities endeavoured to maintain a discipline seeking to balance fast against feast, while the faithful looked for compromise between them, relying on the availability of dispensations.

The present era has led to new perspectives and new urgencies with regard to lifestyle, in effect an enlargement of the vision of the Christian life, where tradition has to find a new voice. Support for the Christian life needs to look anew at resources such as food regimes, including fasting and, above all, the place of the Eucharist as the supreme source of nourishment. The subject of the Eucharistic feast will be the topic of the next chapter.

ENDNOTES

1 Stanley Hauerwas, 'Foreword' to Norman Wirzba, *Food and Faith. A Theology of Eating* (Cambridge: C.U.P., 2019[2]) ix
2 Noelie Vialles, *From Animal to Edible* (Cambridge: C.U.P., 1994) 77
3 Ibid. 45

4   David Grumett and Rachel Muers, *Theology on the Menu. Asceticism, Meat and Christian Diet* (London: Routledge, 2010) 123

5   M. Melissa Rojas-Downing, 'Climate change and livestock: Impacts, adaptation, and mitigation', *Science Direct*, Vol. 16, 2017, 145-163

6   IPCC, *Climate Change 2014. Mitigation of Climate Change .Working Group III Contribution to the Fifth Assessment Report of the Intergovernmental Panel on Climate Change*, 2014, 87

7   *The Lancet*, Vol. 393, Issue 10170, February 2, 2019, 386-7

8   Augustine, Contra Faustum Manichaeum 6.5, *Sancti Augustini Opera Omnia V* (Paris: Paul Mellier, 1842) 273

9   See, for example, Oliver Davies, 'Neuro, Self and Jesus Christ' in Lieven Bove et al., *Questioning the Human. Towards a Theological Anthropology for the Twenty-First Century* (New York: Fordham Press, 2014) 79-100

10   Hugh Connolly, *The Irish Penitentials* (Dublin: Four Courts Press, 1995) 35

11   *Medieval handbooks of penance: a translation of the principal Libri Poenitentiales and selections from related documents*, John Thomas McNeill ed. (New York: Columbia University Press, 1938) 131

12   Norman Wirzba, *Food and Faith. A Theology of Eating* (Cambridge: C.U.P., 2019²)

13   Ibid. 89

14   Ibid. xi

15   Edward Kilmartin S.J., *The Eucharist in the West. History and Theology* (Collegeville: Liturgical Press, 1998) 382

16   Norman Wirzba, *Food and Faith* 174

17   Ibid. 178

18   Ibid. 178-9

19   Ibid. 181

20   Ibid. 182

21   Ibid. 230

22   David Grumett and Rachel Muers, *Theology on the Menu* 63-67

23   Carolyn Street, *Hungry City. How Food Shapes our Lives* (London: Chatto & Windus, 2008) 134

24   Cf. Eric Schlosser, *Fast Food Nation. What the All-American Meal is Doing to the World* (London: Penguin Books, 2002); George Ritzer, *The Mcdonaldization of Society* 6 (Thousand Oaks CA: Sage Publications, 2010)

25   David M. Kaplan ed., *The Philosophy of Food* (Berkeley CA: University of California Press, 2012) 114

26   Ibid. 115

27   David Grumett and Rachel Muers, *Theology on the Menu* 70

CHAPTER EIGHTEEN

The Eucharistic Feast

Christ remains with us in the Eucharist, making his presence in meal and sacrifice the promise of a humanity renewed by his love'.[1]

'Do you believe in the Eucharist?', Cranley asked. 'I do not', Stephen said. 'Do you disbelieve, then? 'I neither believe in it or disbelieve in it', Stephen answered.[2]

The celebration of the Eucharist throughout Christian history, as outlined in earlier chapters, evolved from a rite which was incorporated into a shared meal - and in the early texts not easily distinguished from that context - to a rite consisting of a set of texts accompanying an act of eating and drinking, the consuming of material elements in remembrance of Christ's sacrifice. It was to be continued in history until its fulfilment, Christ had said, in eating and drinking at his table in the banquet of the kingdom (Lk 22:30).

Sacrificial Meal

From the beginning of the church, it was understood to be a sacrificial meal in which Christ's body and blood were consumed. Worship practice was based on Christ's own teaching in John 6: 'Unless you eat the flesh of the son of man and drink his blood, you will have no life in you'. His initial hearers had reacted in disbelief at this saying, and perhaps particularly at the mention of drinking blood, as the Temple sacrifices, which involved eating of flesh, never included the drinking of the blood of the lambs. The blood, the symbol of life, was sprinkled on the altar to indicate that the life was being offered to God. As stated earlier, the Christian community retained the dietary practice of not ingesting blood and the letter from the Jerusalem council to the converts from paganism in Acts 15:20 included the regulation among others that they abstain from blood.

327

During the centuries up to the end of the first millennium the rite was understood to be a recalling and re-presenting of Christ's sacrifice in anticipation of his return, in the course of ingesting food and drink, echoing to an extent the manner of participating in the sacrifices of the pre-Christian era. The rite which was directly mandated by Christ himself at the Last Supper as a memorial of his sacrifice used bread and wine from the beginning. The action was understood to be a sacrifice, as John Chrysostom (347-407) emphasised in his day:

> Do not we offer every day? We offer indeed, but making a remembrance of His death, and this [remembrance] is one and not many. How is it one, and not many? Inasmuch as that [Sacrifice] was once for all offered, [and] carried into the Holy of Holies. This is a figure of that [sacrifice] and this remembrance of that. For we always offer the same, not one sheep now and tomorrow another, but always the same thing: so that the sacrifice is one.[3]

When some Christians did offer animal sacrifices, as noted earlier about the practice in Armenia, they made it clear that their rite was a way of worshipping God to be distinguished from the Jewish one. The emphasis in the case of animal rites was clearly on sacrifice, while in the rite using bread and wine, the conception of a meal was more obvious and it was considered bodily nourishment, as Justin Martyr (100-165) took for granted in his day:

> And this food is called among us Εὐχαριστία [the Eucharist], of which no one is allowed to partake but the man who believes that the things which we teach are true, and who has been washed with the washing that is for the remission of sins.... For not as common bread and common drink do we receive these; but in like manner as Jesus Christ our Saviour, having been made flesh by the Word of God, had both flesh and blood for our salvation, so likewise have we been taught that the food which is blessed by the prayer of His

word, and from which our blood and flesh by transmutation are nourished, is the flesh and blood of that Jesus who was made flesh.[4]

Eucharist as food

Justin made clear that the Incarnation made possible this assimilation of the Christian to Christ's body and blood, just as Irenaeus in his argument against the Gnostics, who held a dualistic view which made the body evil, asserted that it was the nature shared by humanity and the Word that made possible the nourishment for eternal life of the human body by consuming Christ's body and blood. The visible elements were ingested as food, food which fortified and built up the substance of human flesh, flesh capable of receiving God's gift of eternal life.[5]

The relationship between the visible elements and the body and blood of Christ was not a matter for theological speculation in the early centuries. For the Eastern Fathers, there was an overwhelming sense of mystery generated by the rituals of the celebration of the Eucharist, and this approach is still emphasised in the Orthodox Church's liturgy today. In the West, Augustine (like Chrysostom in the East) used the technical language of 'figure', which he drew from Neo-Platonism, and spoke of Christ delivering to his disciples at the Last Supper the 'figure' (*figuram*) of his body and blood. [6] He could use the simple expression that the sacrament of Christ's body was 'in a certain way' the body of Christ, and the sacrament of his blood 'in a certain way' the blood of Christ.[7] But as noted in an earlier chapter, he could also speak of Christ being really present in the Eucharist - saying, for example that Christ's body was offered and served to the participants in the Eucharist.[8] He could also be upset by the way the Eucharistic celebration at the tombs of the martyrs involved drunken excess.

But like other commentators in those early centuries, he endeavoured to maintain a balance and used the terms 'table' and 'altar' interchangeably. The celebration of the Eucharist was a meal; on the one hand it was not a phantasm or, on the other, a gross act of grinding the body of Christ with the teeth, which would be tantamount to returning to Old Testaments sacrificial rites.

Pope St John Paul II in his Encyclical *Ecclesia de Eucharistia* of 2003 expressed concern about contemporary interpretations of the Eucharistic rite: 'At times one encounters an extremely reductive understanding of the Eucharistic mystery. Stripped of its sacrificial meaning, it is celebrated as if it were simply a fraternal banquet' (no. 10), though he sought to maintain a balance by linking meal and sacrifice: Christ remains with us in the Eucharist, making his presence in meal and sacrifice the promise of a humanity renewed by his love.

Christ's presence in the celebration

The issue of Christ's presence was dealt with in Catholic tradition in the West from the time of St Augustine under the heading of sacramental theology. The sacraments in the Christian life, those rites which created grace in the recipients, were spoken of in terms of 'signs'. A sign, Augustine explained, 'leads to knowledge of something other than itself'.[9] A sacrament had come to be seen as a visible 'sign' of invisible grace; there was an inner and an outer aspect to the sacramental rite, with the priority given to the inner - the real but invisible presence of Christ in the Eucharist, for example. The focus was on Christ's presence through the conversion of the elements into his body and blood. Ambrose had explained how this came about: 'when it comes to the consecration of the venerable sacrament, the priest no longer uses his own language, but he uses the language of Christ. Therefore, the word of Christ consecrates this sacrament'.[10] Ambrose's explanation in terms of a formula of words applied to the elements of bread and wine by one empowered to do so by ordination provided the basis for the subsequent development of the idea of the priest as the one who offered on behalf of the people rather than the people co-offering with him.

Thomas Aquinas sought to explain the result of this formulaic approach in relation to the sacrament of the Eucharist by using philosophical concepts. 'Substance' was the underlying nature of a thing, 'accident' its external appearance. In the Eucharist, the substance of the bread was changed into the body of Christ, while the external appearance of bread remained. 'Sight, touch and taste in thee are each deceived', he wrote in his hymn, *Adoro te devote*. His theology continued to be the support for Catholic doctrine at the Council of Trent and beyond. The doctrine was rejected by the Protestant Reformation and became almost the defining issue between Catholicism and the Protestant world.

Ecumenical dimension

Fortunately, the desire for Christian re-union, which emerged at the beginning of the twentieth century, occurred at a time when Catholic theology was already seeking another way than that of such philosophy to articulate a theology of the Eucharist by returning to the early reliance on the concept of symbol. As the Orthodox theologian, Alexander Schmemann explained:

> (T)his is precisely the heart of the matter: the primary meaning of "symbol" is in no way equivalent to "illustration". In fact it is possible for the symbol *not* to illustrate, that is, it can be devoid of any similarity with that which it symbolises. ... This is because the purpose and function of the symbol is *not* to illustrate (this would presume the *absence* of what is illustrated) but to *manifest* and to *communicate* what is manifested. We might say that the symbol does not so much "resemble" the reality that it symbolises as it *participates* in it, and therefore it is capable of communicating it in reality. ... (I)n the original understanding it is the manifestation and presence of the *other* reality – but precisely as *other*, which, under given circumstances cannot be manifested and made present in any other way than as symbol. [11]

Because the reality is *other* and, in the case of the Eucharist the body and blood of Christ, the symbol is inseparable from faith, faith being the evidence of 'things unseen' (Hebr 11:1), and both East and West have always described the Eucharist as the 'mystery of faith'. The symbols bread and wine are not, on the face of it, illustrative of 'body and blood'.

In the modern discussion of symbolism in the West, starting from the concept of sign in sacramental theology, symbol is taken to mean more than sign in that in signifying it also brings about sharing in something beyond itself. A classic example is the piece of coloured paper of which a currency note consists; it is a sign of gold held in reserve somewhere, but more than a sign, it also gives access to it. The more distinctive it is, the more likely it is to be genuine. Unfortunately, in common usage the term 'symbol' often connotes superficiality and has the epithet *mere* attached, when as understood in early centuries it was a term of depth. The symbolic approach to the Eucharistic rite indicates a return to the language of Justin and Irenaeus for whom the ingestion of the physical elements was seen as food; they were symbols leading to a reality beyond themselves. Justin and Irenaeus were both second-century writers; by the end of the fourth-century, however, Ambrose (d. 397) saw the Eucharist as spiritual food only: 'in that sacrament is Christ, because it is the Body of Christ, it is therefore not bodily food but spiritual'.[12]

It is interesting that the only clear case where the text of today's Eucharistic rite acknowledges the twofold nature of the nourishment received in the sacrament occurs in the Prayer over the Gifts of the Eleventh Sunday in Ordinary Time:

> O God, who in the offerings presented here provide for the twofold needs of human nature, nourishing us with food and renewing us with your Sacrament, grant, we pray, that the sustenance they provide may not fail us in body or in spirit. Through Christ our Lord.

While some within the Catholic Church would find unacceptable a shared approach to the perception of the Eucharist by Catholics and any other denomination, the approach to describing the sacraments in general and the Eucharist in particular in terms of symbolic words and actions has proved a fruitful way of establishing common ground with Christian denominations such as the Lutheran and the Anglican, which give priority to sacramental life. And it is significant that in these churches rituals are not perfunctory but involve language and ceremonial which emphasise symbolism in the celebration of the sacraments.

Common ground with other Christian traditions is now more feasible because of a converging approach to the theology of sacrifice as applied to the Eucharist. As stated in the last chapter, the initiative lies with God who wishes to bring humanity into communion with himself in Christ through the power of the Spirit. Sacrifice in Christian understanding 'is in the first place, the self-offering of the Father in the gift of his Son'. The liturgy employs symbolic words and actions to give access to the reality of this relationship between God and humanity; symbolism has essentially to do with relationships.

Symbolism

The words of Scripture have this symbolic function of conveying this offering of the Father, and so does the breaking of the bread in the Eucharistic rite, where the specific effect is the creation of communion with Christ's body and blood. In the understanding of liturgy set out in the Constitution on Liturgy of the Second Vatican Council, the faithful are nourished both at the table of the Word and the table of the Eucharist. In the two parts of the rite, ritual words, actions and material things are employed to express the symbolism of the rite.

> An object, word or gesture is a symbol only to the extent that it can be immediately understood as vehicle of a meaning greater than its own reality, or more accurately, as being something more and other than it appears to be. It is this material density, this concrete value attached to a thing that gives symbols their realism and ensures their validity. ... It is therefore important to preserve the material density of the elements used in the liturgy. ... The Eucharistic meal implies that the participants eat real bread and that, unless there is some serious obstacle, they drink from the cup. [13]

This reference to eating 'real' bread may shock those who hold that only the appearance of bread remains after the Narrative of Institution (the Consecration), but it is a physical fact that if someone who drank from the chalice at Communion were breathalysed soon after, the result would be positive. (It has been remarked that many crumbs must have been left lying about when Christ broke bread for the Apostles at the Last Supper.) As the theologian, Kallistos Ware, pointed out, the Orthodox Church takes material things and makes them a vehicle of the Spirit:

> Orthodoxy rejects any attempt to diminish the materiality of the sacraments, the human person is to be seen in holistic terms, as an integral unity of soul and body, and so the sacramental worship in which we humans participate should involve to the full our bodies along with our minds. ... At the Eucharist leavened bread is used, not just wafers.[14]

Transignification and Transfinalisation

Two months before the conclusion of the Second Vatican Council in 1965, Pope St Paul VI issued an Encyclical, *Mysterium Fidei,* in which he reacted against the literature that had emerged on the concept of symbolism as a way of expressing the theology of the Eucharist. He stated that:

> (I)t is not permissible ... to concentrate on the notion of sacramental sign as if the symbolism—which no one will deny is certainly present in the Most Blessed Eucharist—fully expressed and exhausted the manner of Christ's presence, ... or to discuss the mystery of transubstantiation without mentioning what the Council of Trent had to say about the marvellous conversion of the whole substance of the bread into the Body and the whole substance of the wine into the Blood of Christ, as if they involve nothing more than "transignification," or "transfinalisation" as they call it. (no. 11)

He acknowledged that 'the Fathers and the Scholastics had a great deal to say about symbolism in the Eucharist' (40), but continued:

While Eucharistic symbolism is well suited to helping us understand the effect that is proper to this Sacrament—the unity of the
Mystical Body—still it does not indicate or explain what it is that
makes this Sacrament different from all the others. (no. 44)

These reservations about symbolism underlie the *Credo of the People of
God*[15], issued by the pope in 1968, which appears to have been influenced by
the publication of the *Dutch Catechism* in 1966. It was based on a document
produced by the Thomist philosopher, Jacques Maritain. In the *Credo* it is
stated that

> Every theological explanation which seeks some understanding of this
> mystery must, in order to be in accord with Catholic faith, maintain
> that in the reality itself, independently of our mind, the bread and
> wine have ceased to exist after the Consecration, so that it is the ador-
> able body and blood of the Lord Jesus that from then on are really
> before us under the sacramental species of bread and wine.[16]

The document was issued on June 31th, 1968: the fact that the Encyclical *Humanae vitae* followed on July 25th, and became immediately the
centre of controversy, explains why it received little attention. This way of
formulating the doctrine of transubstantiation in terms of the dissapear-
ance of the earthly elements has to be considered more evocative of magic
than of mystery, and it is not surprising that for many of the faithful today
there is no point in speculation about this fundamental doctrine.

The agnostic statement by Stephen Daedalus of neither believing
nor disbelieving quoted in James Joyce's 1916 novel may well have expressed an attitude beginning to take hold among educated Catholics in
the twentieth-century. Unfortunately, reluctance to engage thoughtfully
with the mystery of Christ's presence in the Eucharist could well be true
of some regular churchgoers and it allows people who are indifferent to
the obligations of religion to receive the Eucharist on occasions such as
weddings or funerals in an un-reflecting way. That is not at all the same as

Calvin's preference to experience Christ's Eucharistic presence rather than to understand it, quoted in Chapter Ten. On the other hand, today some return constantly to the term transubstatiation as the necessary underpinning of Eucharistic doctrine, an attitude reflected in calls for revision of theology generally and the promotion of the 1570 Lation rite.

The concept of symbol has proved very fruitful in avoiding such agnosticism , while not purporting to 'explain' the mystery of the Eucharist. It does have its limits and theologians since Paul VI have looked at ways of harmonising symbolic thinking with tradition. The usefulness of the terms 'transignification' and 'transfinalisation' was discussed in the years after Vatican II. It was summed up in 1980 by Ghislain Lafont, using the term transignification in relation to the meal rather than the elements:

> Recent theological research has rightly tended to speak here of a 'transignification of the meal': the signification of covenant inscribed in every exchange of food is here totally designated.[17]

Much discussion of the theology of the Eucharist has tended to focus on the kind of issue raised by Pope John Paul II, the need to present a balanced consideration of it as meal and sacrifice. In the symbolic approach, interpretative words and acts give to the food shared a meaning which includes the concept of sacrifice.

> The ceremonial breaking of the bread in the celebration of the Eucharist is already a symbolic act signifying the fellowship created by the meal. But symbolic interpretations of the Lord's Supper also see the fraction pointing to the sacrifice of Christ, the benefits of which are conveyed to the communicants.[18]

Transformation
The richness of the symbolic acts and words needs to be asserted as something going beyond the simplest form of symbol. The currency note which gives access to gold reserves is an example of a symbol. It has per-

manence and does not require a repeated voice promising to pay – that is permanently engraved on it. In that sense it is not a dynamically functioning symbol; it is not a symbolic word or act. When considering the shared meal, however, the testimonial dinner or the wedding reception, for example, symbolic value is added by the words spoken, the evocation and the invocation. (Cf. Chapter 16.) In the case of the Eucharist, the words spoken, the ritual acts, are central to the conferring on the shared meal the fullness of its meaning. Being the celebration of the Paschal mystery, the memory of Christ's sacrifice is *evoked*, while the words of the Eucharistic prayer *invoke* for the community the blessing of a share in this mystery by the power of the Spirit. The community is the Body of Christ on earth and looks forward to participation in the Supper of the Lamb when history reaches its culmination in the Kingdom.

> In the earthly liturgy we take part in a foretaste of that heavenly liturgy which is celebrated in the Holy City of Jerusalem toward which we journey as pilgrims. (*Constitution on the Sacred Liturgy,* no.8)

In the Eastern Church's tradition, the Eucharistic rite was always seen as a symbolic action where the fullness of meaning came from the power of the Holy Spirit. Chrysostom emphasised this when he said:

> That table at that time was not of silver, nor that cup of gold, out of which Christ gave His disciples His own blood; but precious was everything there, and awful, for that they were full of the Spirit. [19]

'Full of the Spirit': he seems to imply that in the subsequent celebrations bread and wine too were full of the Spirit and that the result was the transfer of the bread and wine, as well as of the communicants, to another order of existence, so that all become one in Christ. It is hard to see how this transfer to another order of existence could leave the elements unchanged from the point of view of their final state. In the previous chapter, the view of Norman Wirzba was noted that 'the destiny of all creatures is that they offer themselves or are offered up as the temporal expression of God's eternal love'.[20] From that perspective the bread and wine would appear to have an intrinsic connection with Christ's sacrifice in the rite empowered by the Spirit and to enter substantially into union with his body and blood. Ghislain Lafont was attracted by this perception of the sacrificial dimension of all creation as it applies to the Eucharist:

> The Eucharistic story addressed to God celebrates the plenitude of his gift to us and of our giving it back in Jesus Christ. It says that in Jesus all this 'substance' of the world and of human beings is really taken up into the ultimate dynamic of exchange between God's generosity and the pure offering made in response.[21]

Transubstantiation
Lafont believed that there was a role for the term 'transubstantiation' in the description of this exchange.

> In this marvellous and unique exchange, transubstantiation correctly says and effects an aspect of the mystery: the passage from a human reality into the divine-human reality that humans have sought, from the beginning, to attain and that is given to them in the Eucharist so that they can in turn offer it back.[22]

Consequently, when the food, as part of the substance of the world, receives its full symbolic meaning in uniting the communicant with the body and blood of Christ, reverence is called for in how it is to be treated.

Augustine, some decades after Chrysostom, spoke of the role of the food in the Eucharist, its assimilation into the body and thereby the assimilation of the body into Christ. In the Eucharist the believer does not assimilate the body of Christ, but is assimilated into him: 'I am the food of grown men; grow, and you shall feed upon me; nor shall you change me, like the food of your flesh, into yourself, but you shall be changed into me'.[23] Clearly, the bread and wine form an essential part of that process of assimilation. How they are transformed in the process is worthy of much reflection.

Pastoral Concerns

The full meaning of the Eucharist as a shared meal is impeded for people today by the form the rite takes in most situations. The setting is often one which makes the idea of altar architecturally prominent and that of table obscure; the sharing in many cases does not include the cup; the opportunity to pause for reflection after the distribution - which could contribute to a sense of sharing - not availed of. The bread used, ordinary bread in the early centuries and in Orthodox Christianity today, is now reduced to an unleavened wafer, giving little impression of food to be eaten. The term 'Host', derived from the Latin for victim, is an appropriate reminder of sacrifice, but the regular 'particles', resulting from the method of production, take away from the sense of broken bread shared .

As noted earlier, consuming food in daily life involves the use of cutlery which has the effect of rendering remote the connection between the food and the consumer; the introduction of the fork in history was decisive in this regard. All of this makes unfamiliar the immediacy of taking and breaking bread and sharing with others, the fundamental symbol of the unity of the community in Christ.

Other factors enter into consideration of the extent to which the Eucharistic rite of today is effective as a symbolic presentation of the whole Christian mystery – the life, death and resurrection of Christ and the participation of believers in it. Celebration in the morning may be inevitable but the festive nature of the rite is more easily brought out in the evening and makes more evident its origin in the Last Supper.

This question of timing is a part of the larger one of how people actually live in time – at least in the Western world. The 'weekend' is a relatively new idea and contrasts with the older one of 'Sunday and weekday', which had its origin in the way of life of most people. There were six days of work and one day of rest, the original Jewish Sabbath having been effectively transferred to Sunday in the Christian centuries. That could and did for many people make Sunday a festive day, and in impoverished communities of the past the festive dimension could at least be hinted at where Sunday worship was held in magnificent cathedrals with elaborate ceremonies to the accompaniment of good music. As noted earlier, this could and did inspire the carrying out of celebrations in the streets of medieval towns. Paradoxically, there was little popular understanding of the meaning of the liturgy as the celebration of the Paschal Mystery, but stark images of the crucified Christ and the prevailing substitutionary theory of the atonement, according to which Christ took on the punishment due to the sins of humankind, gave people a sense of relief. This was very important in a religious culture where heaven was as real as earth, and death was a daily prospect.

> Culture is central to every aspect of human life. It is the taken-for-granted air of meaning that structures our behaviour, what we feel and experience and how we relate to each other interpersonally. It is the material through which we create webs of meaning.[24]

Up to relatively recent times a religious culture provided this material, creating a web of meaning to uphold daily living. But in today's secularised culture – where heaven can hardly be said to be as real as earth - Christians are affected by the levelling down of the traditional difference between Sunday and weekday. There is a continuous drift towards conforming to secular patterns, as one English commentator noted:

> Holy days of obligation are celebrated on the nearest Sunday so as to avoid inconvenience or the interruption of secular patterns of living. Sunday Mass can be heard on a Saturday to make way for a day's work or cleaning the car or a morning in bed with the papers, like our pagan neighbours.[25]

Sunday is no longer perceived as a festive day, with the result that everyday becomes potentially a day for a feast, with special emphasis usually on Friday and Saturday nights. A commentator on life in the Netherlands has observed:

> Through various measures, such as reduction of working hours and early retirement, everyone's share in the work process is reduced, and free time has increased considerably. Leisure is no longer primarily intended to recoup one's strength for work, but has become an end in itself, defining our lifestyle to an ever greater degree. [26]

With the decline of a religious culture to give meaning, the meaningless nature of the weekend celebration quickly becomes evident and efforts are made to enhance it by excess; binge drinking is a symptom of this desperate attempt. From the standpoint of people caught up in such a downward spiral, the Sunday Feast can seem not liberating but an expression of reproof, of obligation and control. Various commentators have pointed to perception of the church's liturgy by many as an expression of a hierarchical world, denoting exclusion of the non-ordained, despite the clear thrust of the Constitution of the Liturgy towards inclusion, participation.

This is a great challenge for the Christian Sunday – to be truly one of celebration where participants can find true freedom and cope with the gamut of emotions intrinsic to a memorial of the death and resurrection of Christ. If it begins with a penitential exercise, the outcome is meant to be the conferring of a commission to bring good news to the world. Entering fully into that trajectory can only come when there is acceptance that the unity which the shared meal expresses is meant to embrace not only those participating but also all those who are excluded from community in society and throughout the world; this was what Jesus wished to be the result of his being 'raised up' on the cross. Properly celebrated, the Sunday feast gives back true meaning to everyday life and the challenges and possibilities it brings.

It can only do this if the everyday is not kept captive to forces of dehumanisation, the treadmill of the economic machine, to which the individual is enslaved (with 'parole' for the 'weekend'). The way to freedom from this condition is for people to be members of a church that is truly itself, a leaven in society, and an agent of transformation of the world towards its destiny as God's kingdom, 'an eternal and universal kingdom, a kingdom of truth and life, a kingdom of holiness and grace, a kingdom of justice, love and peace'.[27]

As John Zizioulas pointed out, if it is to be the 'local church', the embodiment locally of the universal church, it must be both localised and church. For the church to be local, Christ's saving action must root itself in the lives of the believers of all cultures and ethnicity in that place. To be church its celebration of the Eucharist must transcend all the divisions which a multi-cultural community might bring. It must find the culmination of its liturgical life in a rite that even now anticipates the banquet of the Kingdom, the Supper of the Lamb, by the lifting up of hearts to join the chorus of praise of the angels and saints.[28] If it does this, inclusiveness will be its keynote and it will proclaim a message of hope for a world in which there is so much exclusion for some, and lack of meaning for others.

This gives an indication of how the church must relate to the state, where that state embraces secularism and regards the church as a social body coterminous with it territorially and a lobbyist organisation. Such a state configures the borders of the church on the grid of a two-dimensional nation state and eliminates the dimension of time, as William Cavanaugh points out.[29] But relations of the ecclesial body with the state cannot be considered under the heading of shared space or timelessness. The state is in time in terms of political epochs and programmes; the church is in history because of the incarnation of the Word. The Christ event brought salvation and the church exists therefore as its record in time, in the interval between the first and second comings of Christ, or as some passages in the New Testament suggest, the time until the upward movement of creation reaches its fulfilment, one which is anticipated and made possible by Christ's resurrection. Zizioulas deals with the roles of Christ and the Spirit in the church:

Now if becoming history is the particularity of the Son in the economy (of salvation), what is the contribution of the Spirit? Well, precisely the opposite: it is to liberate the Son and the economy from the bondage of history. If the Son dies on the cross, thus succumbing to the bondage of historical existence, it is the Spirit that raises him from the dead. The Spirit is the *beyond* history and when he acts in history he does so in order to bring into history the last days, the *eschaton*.[30]

Zizioulas applies this theology of the Spirit to the specific case of the Eucharist. The invocation and presence of the Spirit in the celebration means that the being of the church is not founded simply on its historical and institutional base, as if it were an institution like others within the state. Instead, the Spirit's action dilates history and time to the infinite dimensions of the *eschaton*.[31]

This means that the church must create its own 'space' and 'time' in relation to other cultural groups in society and the state. The shared Eucharist transforms the partakers into a body with social dimensions; its anticipation in time of the banquet of the kingdom urges the participants to work for inclusiveness among the peoples of the world, transcending cultural and national perspectives, engaging with the unfinished task of becoming truly 'catholic' or universal.

> (T)he task of the church is to 'domesticate' the world, to heal the homelessness and anomie of the modern condition by extending the 'community of persons' that exists in the family – and that mirrors the Trinitarian life - to the whole world.[32]

The church must also have its own 'times and seasons' and these must continue to be lived through, when Sunday is effectively secularised and the great seasons of Advent, Christmas, Lent and Easter have secular meanings assigned to their rituals.

When robbed of their transcendent symbolism, celebrations such as the pre-Lent carnivals (while retaining the name 'goodbye to the flesh') suffer the same descent into excess as the regular weekends. Shrove Tuesday, with a name derived from penance, becomes Pancake Tuesday. Brueghel's famous painting shows what life was like before secularism eliminated the tension inherent in the Christian life lived in the world.

Where it is lived authentically, the shared meal of the Eucharist, seen as anticipation of the kingdom, works towards a gradual transformation of humanity in all its activity towards true fulfilment. It addresses the real needs of the participants and motivates them to address the needs of others. The secular state is not necessarily indifferent to need; human nature has an empathetic constituent and states do provide a range of services for the disadvantaged; in the effectively capitalist economy of the Roman Empire, the banquets of the great included provision for the poor from the left-over food.

One could speculate whether social services of the contemporary secular state are influenced by values inherited from a Christian past. At the same time, it is true that when the state over many centuries manifested Christian values more explicitly, the practice of social justice was often less than could be desired. Over a long period, beginning with the guest facilities provided by monasteries, the care of the deprived devolved largely to communities of religious. As noted in a previous chapter, monasteries provided a wide range of social services and in more recent centuries religious communities were founded for the specific purpose of providing education and health care for the poor and for many who were marginalised by society, for example, those with special needs.

From Communal to Indivual Offering

At their best these communities in their celebration of the liturgy were motivated by Christ's self-sacrificing love; at their best their sharing at the table of the Lord motivated them to draw others into community, to extend the idea of community outside their walls. But the spirituality mainly promoted in devotional works was focused principally on the idea of sharing in an individual way in the sufferings of Christ; participation in the sacramental life sought an increment of grace in the soul.

In the early church, the celebration of the Eucharist was, as its name implied, an act of thanksgiving to God for Christ's work of redemption more than a petitioning of grace. It was performed by a community over which a leader presided as in the case of Justin's community mentioned above. It included the bringing of gifts over which the prayer of thanksgiving was offered and the surplus was distributed to the poor. This aspect of the celebration gradually gave way over the centuries to one in which the bishop (or in time the priest) became the one who offered the sacrifice to God on behalf of the people. The material gifts, which had been gradually substituted by money offerings became a symbol of the people's self-offering with the expectation of spiritual blessings to be received from the celebration. The offerings could be made on behalf of the living and the dead.

> Seen as a unified act accomplished by the priest, the Mass was offered upon request. Gifts were given with a view to a special remembrance by the celebrant of the liturgy. During the seventh and eighth centuries, the gift was not considered to obligate the priest in a special way even if each donor expected to be named in the great petition.[33]

The offering for a particular intention, which continues to the present time, brought the concept of the rite into the area of individual offering and need, and made the connection between the liturgy and social issues less obvious. The recovery of the idea of the shared meal strengthens not only the realisation of the church as a community whose members care for one another and are sharers in the graces received, but also brings a global view when the universal nature of Christ's sacrifice, in which the faithful's self-offering shares, is taken into account.

A church that 'awaits the joyful hope and the coming of the Saviour' will be aware of the provisional nature of the feast. It takes place in a world where evil stalks the land and remains impenetrable to explanation, where social justice for all has not been achieved, where the participants are aware that their unity is impaired by sin and that they have to express themselves unworthy that the Lord should enter under their roof. They will know that there is a place for penance and for fasting while the Bridegroom is absent. That way of life will be the subject of the final chapter of this work.

Conclusion

It was suggested in earlier chapters that the religious feast embraces more than the Eucharistic feast with bread and wine. There can be other celebrations also marking a Feast Day: a feast for the eyes and ears in a solemn Vespers, the musical tropes once performed in the sanctuary, the overspill on to the streets in the medieval mystery plays with *al fresco* meals to finish. The possibilities for celebration gripped the imagination of medieval people when freed from the restrictions church authority could impose; performance was not limited to the elite, and should not be limited to an elite group today. There is an appetite for such celebrations as is evident from the popularity of the 'Street Feast' introduced in Ireland some ten years ago by private individuals and now linked with a government initiative called the Big Hello, which has the aim of creating community, of rescuing people from isolation and loneliness. According to Street Feast's website, 'since its small beginnings 400,000 neighbours have joined in the fun'. It has spread to Minnesota and is due to arrive in Australia.[34] It is not a religious movement, and is in some ways an alternative to religion in a society where attendance at Sunday worship has radically declined. But it differs from the street feasts of Revolutionary France, which were intended to celebrate the freedom, the equality, the fraternity which rejection of religion was thought to bring.

It can be asked whether the church can satisfy the appetite for such celebrations. It would be a mistake to think that the Corpus Christi procession could fill that role today, as it did once through the 'social miracle' of the Eucharist in a society where it was almost impossible not to believe in God, where membership of the community of the church was taken for granted and the theology of the Real Presence

346

made people rejoice at the presence of the Lord among them. A Eucharistic procession at a time when this meaning of the Eucharist is not strongly perceived by many is problematic in that those who witness it (as opposed to those who take part in it) may react indifferently or even disrespectfully. A celebration of the Eucharist which took account of its nature as a shared meal could, however, provide motivation for street feasts in which the atmosphere would be one of desiring to continue the sense of unity in Christ already achieved. A street feast lasts only as long as it does and in the end people disperse, some to a solitary life, but the joy of belonging can be continued in what St John Paul II called 'the intimate converse with Jesus ... in a prayerful moment of Eucharistic adoration apart from Mass'.[35]

ENDNOTES

1   Pope St John Paul II, *Ecclesia de Eucharistia* 20

2   James Joyce, *Portrait of the Artist as a Young Man* (Ware, Herts: Wordsworth Editions, 1992) 184-5

3   Chrysostom, *Homily on Hebrews* 17.6 (Hebr 10:2-9) in *Homilies on the Gospel of St. John and the Epistle to the Hebrews, Nicene and Post-Nicene Fathers, Vol. XIV* (Buffalo: The Christian Literature Co., 1886)

4   Justin Martyr, *Apologia* 1.66 in *First Apology; Second Apology in Ante Nicene Fathers, Volume 1: Apostolic Fathers*. With Justin Martyr and Irenaeus (Grand Rapids MI: Eerdmans, 1988)

5   Irenaeus, *Libri quinque adversus Haereses*,Tom. II, W.W. Harvey ed. (Cantabrigiae: Typis academicis, 1857) 204-5

6   Augustine, *Enarratio in Ps. 31* in Augustine, *Expositions on the Book of Psalms*, Vol. I:Psalm I - XXXVI (Oxford: John Henry Parker, 1847)

7   Augustine, *Epistola* 98.9 in *Augustine: Letters - Volume II* (83 - 130) (Washington D.C.C. U. A., 1966)

8   Augustine, *City of God* 17.20 (New York: Image Books, 1958)

9   Augustine, *De Doctrine Christiana* 2.1 in *Sancti Augustini Opera apologetica IV* (Paris Paul Mellier, 1842)

10   Ambrose, *De Sacramentis* IV.14.4, in *On the Mysteries and the Treatise on the Sacraments*, Translated and Edited by T. Thompson, with Introduction and Notes by J.H. Strawley (New York: Macmillan, 1919).

11   Alexander Schmemann, *The Eucharist* (Crestwood N.Y.: St Vladimir's Seminary Press, 1987) 38

12   Ambrose, *De Mysteriis*, 9.58. See Note 9.

13   I. H. Dalmais, 'The Theology of the Liturgical Celebration' in A.G. Martimort, ed., *The Church at Prayer*, One Volume Edition (Collegeville: Liturgical Press, 1992) 236

14   Timothy Ware, *The Orthodox Church* (London: Penguin Books, 19932) 274-5

15   Issued in the form of a Motu Proprio, *Solemni hac liturgia* (30 June 1968)

16   Pope Paul VI, *Credo of the People of God* 1968, no. 25

17   Ghislain Lafont, *Eucharist. The Meal and the Word* (Mahwah NJ: Paulist Press, 2014) 142

18   Frank C. Senn, *Christian Liturgy. Catholic and Evangelical* (Minneapolis: Fortress Press, 1997) 5

19   Divi Joannis Chrysostomi, *Homilia in Matthaeum* 51 in *Opera Omnia Tomus 2* (Paris, 1588) 371.

20   Norman Wirzba, *Food and Faith. A Theology of Eating* (Cambridge: C.U.P., 20192) 174

21   Ghislain Lafont, *Eucharist. The Meal and the Word* 143-4

22   *Ibid.* 155

23   Augustine, *Confessions VII*, 10 (London: Sheed and Ward, 1944) 113; PL 32. 742

24   Tom Inglis, 'Church and Culture in Catholic Ireland' in *Studies*, Vol. 106, No. 421, 2017, 24

25   Eamon Duffy, 'To Fast Again', *First Things*, March 2005

26   Louis Van Tongeren, 'The Squeeze on Sunday. Reflections on the Changing Experience and Form of Sundays' in P. Post et al., *Christian Feast and Festival. The Dynamics of Western Liturgy and Culture* (Leuven: Peeters, 2001) 706

27   Preface of the Mass for the Feast of Christ the King

28   John Zizioulas, *Being as Communion. Studies in Personhood and the Church* (Crestwood NY: St Vladimir's Seminary Press, 1993) 253ff

29   William Cavanaugh, *Theopolitical Imagination* (London: T & T Clark, 2002) 91

30   John Zizioulas, *Being as Communion* 130

31   *Ibid.* 22

32   David L. Schindler, 'Homelessness and the Modern Condition: The Family, Evangelisation and the Global Economy' *Logos* 3, No. 4 (Fall 2000) 34-56, cited in William Cavanaugh, *Theopolitical Imagination* 93

33   Edward Kilmartin, 'The Sacrifice of Thanksgiving and Social Justice' in Mark Searle ed., *Liturgy and Social Justice* (Collegeville: Liturgical Press,1980) 60

34   www.streetfeast.ie

35   Pope John Paul II, *Ecclesia de Eucharistia* 61

CHAPTER NINETEEN

Food, Feast and Fast

The whole rationale of symbolic gestures requires that they disrupt and disturb the secular order. Their power to witness—not only to others but to ourselves—comes precisely from their awkwardness. The abolition of such observances (as fasting) strikes at the heart of tradition, the distinctive language of belief. ... Spiritual needs are expressed in physical needs.[1]

Current considerations

Previous chapters have described the history of fasting from food in general, and abstinence from meat in particular, over the centuries. The broadest definition of fasting is that it is the voluntary denial of the otherwise normal function of eating and drinking, for some chosen aim. The motivation for such practices has until recent times been largely religious. It could arise because of prescription by authority and this kind of fasting has had a long and rather troubled history. It would quite often be inspired by the liturgical seasons. It could simply be voluntarily undertaken, as part of a penitential programme to accompany prayer and almsgiving, especially in Lent. Today, it is often undertaken for health reasons. In early centuries it was likely among monks to lead to prayer rather than follow from it. 'Bodily abstinence was the necessary preparation for one's real prayer.'[2] Religious fasting can be motivated by, or accompanied by, the desire to give alms; it can also be put in abeyance because of the demands of charity, as many examples from the lives of the Desert Fathers attest, for example:

> Once two brethren came to a certain elder whose custom it was not to eat every day. But when he saw the brethren, he invited them to dine with him, saying: 'fasting has its reward but he who

eats out of charity fulfils two commandments, for he sets aside his own will and refreshes his hungry brethren'.[3]

There can be mixed motives, as is evident from the fact that fasting and abstinence continue today in diverse communities, Christian and non-Christian and among non-religious people. It is somewhat remarkable that in Western Christianity, Catholic and Protestant, the tradition has gradually declined and almost disappeared. Previous chapters have tracked this decline and associated it with changing perceptions of the human condition, brought about in some cases by changes in religious thought, for example, the assertion of the freedom of the Christian which marked the rise of the sixteenth-century Reformation, and in the Catholic tradition by the development of a spirituality for people in the lay state, in the writings of St Francis de Sales, for example, and the emergence of a Christian humanism which sought to liberate the spiritual life from the heritage of Jansenism.

The Second Vatican Council was a watershed event for the Catholic Church and the new spiritual ethos which developed included change in perception of the traditional fasting regime. The documents of the Council put less emphasis on the institutional nature of the church and its prescriptive rules and more on its spiritual dimensions as the Mystical Body of Christ. The spiritual aspects of life were intended, however, to be manifested in external practices, including penance. The *Constitution on the Sacred Liturgy* - in the only reference to Christian fasting in the Council's documents - stated:

> During Lent penance should not be only internal and individual, but also external and social. The practice of penance should be fostered in ways that are possible in our own times and in different regions, and according to the circumstances of the faithful. ... Nevertheless, let the paschal fast be kept sacred. Let it be celebrated everywhere on Good Friday and, where possible, prolonged throughout Holy Saturday, so that the joys of the Sunday of the resurrection may be attained with uplifted and clear mind. (no. 110)

The reference to the paschal fast lasting through Holy Saturday evokes the Byzantine Church's early tradition, according to which fasting had a central role:

> Originally, the only liturgy of the Paschal Triduum, if we exclude the Easter Vigil itself ... was fasting, 'the fast in the Bridegrooms' absence', Tertullian calls it. So the primitive Triduum was a time of sober readiness; there is no wine until it is drunk again in the Messianic Banquet of the Kingdom. ... It was a time not of liturgical pomp, but of expectant meditation, while the body of the Lord reposes in the tomb, the final Sabbath rest before the fulfilment, the dawn of the eschatological 'Eighth Day'.[4]

In Rome at the end of the sixth century, this fast was, it seems, rigorously observed. Pope Gregory the Great (r590-604) was unable to observe it one year because of painful spasms of intestinal pain, which his monks relieved at frequent intervals with food. 'When I could not fast on Holy Saturday, a day on which even young children fast, I felt worse, more through grief than through sickness.'[5]

The *Catechism of the Catholic Church* misses the opportunity to highlight the special character of the observance of the two days, Good Friday and Holy Saturday, when in No. 1438 it simply refers to the 'seasons and days of penance in the course of the liturgical year (Lent and each Friday in memory of the death of the Lord)', a text repeated in a Pastoral Letter of the Irish Catholic Bishops in 2010.

Prior to the reform of the liturgy of the three days, Holy Thursday to the Holy Saturday Vigil, the Lenten regulations ended at noon on Holy Saturday as the Easter Vigil had been celebrated on that morning, so the present Lenten regime should in principle extend to the current celebration of the Vigil on Holy Saturday night, but in practice the rule of fasting and abstinence, which is limited to Good Friday, leaves uncertainty about Holy Saturday and does not echo the ancient tradition linking Good Friday and Holy Saturday, or take account of the Constitution on the Liturgy.

The Vatican Council's programme of updating theological perspectives to take account of modern conditions extended also to a desire to return for inspiration to the sources of the church's tradition, but not in an uncritical way. Research inspired by the Council has cast light on the asceticism of the early Christian centuries and has recognised that at its best it represented an idyllic Christian existence lived by heroic figures in the primitive conditions of the deserts of the Middle East (with their particular climate). It could appear at its worst to have shown, in those times, signs of Manichean rejection of the body. Those ascetical practices were already being reassessed in the changing cultural situation by the time of St Benedict, for example. He considered the fasts of earlier times idyllic but not feasible in his own day, the sixth-century. But as the church went through periods of decline and renewal in the transition from the first millennium to the second, fasting regulations became more reflective of institutional authority and more severe. By the sixteenth-century in Pre-Reformation Germany, 'there were as many as 161days of fasting or abstinence - over one third of the year'.[6] A present-day historian, commenting on centuries of legalistic approaches to regulating the ascetical and essentially inner aspects of the Christian life has noted:

> The authoritarian narrowing of the tradition to, in essence, a body of doctrines to be believed and orders from above to be obeyed, was a decisive factor in desensitising ordinary Catholics, clerical as well as lay, to the beauty and independent value of their inherited observances—matters over which no authority has or ought to have absolute control.[7]

It is no surprise then that attempts to avoid or minimise restrictions became increasingly part of the Christian culture.

At the same time, centuries in which humanism became influential, brought about changes in the perception of the human condition through advances in medicine, in education and in labour-reducing technology - a process which has more recently included even food science. Scientific and technical advances favouring health and psychological well-being have tended to challenge a religious perception that places more emphasis on the spiritual than on the physical condition.

The Enlightenment philosophical movement, in asserting the supremacy of reason, placed great emphasis during several recent centuries on progress in all areas of life, making any deprivation appear counter-progressive and negative. As noted earlier, the era of industrial development imposed such demands on the workers serving its progress that the need to maintain physical energy at maximum level made a fasting regime an illogical and even impossible way of life. In the post-industrial age of the knowledge and digital economies, work of a less obviously physical but sedentary kind has been found to be equally tiring; instead of exhausting physical effort, the minimal effort associated with work deprives the worker of the exercise the body needs and in so doing affects brain function negatively also. The tendency in this situation is to use stimulants, such as coffee or even opioids, in order to improve the sense of well-being, and this affects the normal psychological balance of the appetite for food, leading to the excesses of over-eating in some cases and food deprivation in others. The high rate of obesity in Western society does bear witness to lack of discipline on the part of people who lack religious motivation for fasting, but it is also due to cultural factors which entrap people in unhealthy lifestyles.

In retrospect, it is surprising that the regime of fasting which had been established in the Middle Ages remained unquestioned for Catholics from the era of modernity up to the twentieth century. But it did come to be perceived as involving considerable hardship and to be ill-adapted to the needs of people in today's working conditions. This was especially true in those environments where two World Wars gave people little choice except that of eating whatever they could procure.

With the coming of the Second Vatican Council in the twentieth-century radical change occurred. Much more discretion was now left to the individual – as well as to national Bishops' Conferences – with regard to fasting and abstinence. In many cases, national regulations did not require abstinence from meat, while still calling for penance on Friday. The decision of the Catholic Bishops' Conference of England and Wales in 1967 to prorogue the regulation of Friday abstinence was noted for its 'total absence of any attempt to explain the power and meaning of the traditional observances'.[8] It led to scathing comments from the sociologist of religion, Mary Douglas, who questioned the removal of a ritual characteristic of Catholicism on the basis, she claimed, of ritual conformity not being considered 'a valid form of personal commitment and … not compatible with full development of the personality'.[9]

> (A)ny anthropologist knows that public forms of the symbolic expression are not to be despised. The reformers who set low values on the external and symbolic aspects of Friday abstinence and who exhort the faithful to prefer eleemosynary deeds are not making an intellectually free assessment of forms of worship. They are moving with the secular tide along with other sections of the middle classes who seek to be justified in their lives only by saving others from hunger and injustice.[10]

This criticism was made more than forty years ago and presumably was not the reason why the Bishops' Conference reversed its decision in 2011. In a brief statement the bishops declared:

> Every Friday is set aside by the Church as a special day of penance, for it is the day of the death of our Lord. The law of the Church requires Catholics to abstain from meat on Fridays, or some other form of food, or to observe some other form of penance laid down by the Bishops' Conference. … Respectful of this, and in accordance with the mind of the whole Church, the Bishops' Conference wishes to remind all Catholics in England and Wales of the obligation of Friday Penance. The Bishops have decided to re-establish the practice that this should be fulfilled by abstaining from meat. Those who cannot or choose not to eat

meat as part of their normal diet should abstain from some other food of which they regularly partake.[11]

Quite apart from regulations prescribed by church authorities, many people of no religious affiliation observe some restrictions on their way of life when Lent comes. This may be because of an atavistic instinct or simply an acknowledgment that an annual assessment of one's way of life is appropriate and Spring a good time to undertake it. Reform is likely to centre on what people recognise as their bad habits, in the sense of unhealthy practices, and as the civil powers tend to make suggestions such as abstaining from smoking, there can be a general acceptance of the need to make some changes.

Those who recognise the importance of both diet and exercise accept that this involves control of food and drink intake. Such an approach is still to an extent counter-cultural in that much media content extols the desirability of various dishes and the culture of fine dining, and gives little attention to vegetarian alternatives to meat. The Sunday Supplements as well as TV shows bear colourful witness to this, and if some recognition is given to the fact of Lent it is usually by way of anticipating the good things to be enjoyed at Easter. Considerable creativity is often evident in the development of recipes, and undoubted excellence in the dishes resulting from skilful preparation.

Gluttony

To enjoy these can be an acknowledgement of God's goodness, as previous quotations from the writing of Robert Capon made clear, but it can also lead to entrapment in gluttony, which is often described as one of the seven deadly sins, though more accurately in the Christian tradition it is described as one of the capital sins, because, according to Gregory the Great, it propagates other sins, such as scurrility and dullness of mind.[12] Gluttony is an abuse of the natural and legitimate passion for food or drink but can, if limited in its extent, be simply a case of eating more than is necessary or desirable for health. Augustine struggled with the difficulty of keeping a balance.

> I strive daily against greediness in eating and drinking. ... For the reins of the throat are to be held somewhere between too lightly and too tightly. Who is he, Lord, who is not carried somewhat beyond the limits of the necessary?[13]

Because a glutinous act is connected with the need for nourishment, but satisfied in what is not an appropriate or necessary measure, it may not be a serious perversion, and only to be considered a serious sin if it turns a person away from God and his commandments.[14]

In the early monastic tradition, various aspects of gluttony were identified, such as gorging oneself, anticipating eating with preoccupied, eager longing, eating expensively, seeking after delicacies, paying too much attention to food.[15] In monastic life these faults would have implications for relations with the community, but it is true too of people today that disordered relations with food may reflect disordered relations with oneself, with others, with the earth and with God, and not necessarily to do with excess in quantity of food.[16] *The Screwtape Letters* has an account which makes that point with searing precision. In a letter to Wormwood, his nephew, Screwtape describes an elderly lady:

> She is a positive terror to hostesses and servants. She is always turning from what has been offered her to say with a demure little sigh and a smile 'O please, please ... *all* I want is a cup tea, weak but not too weak, and the teeniest weeniest bit of really crisp toast'. You see? Because what she wants is smaller, less costly than what has been set before here, she never recognises as gluttony her determination to get what she wants, however troublesome it may be to others. At the very moment of indulging her appetite she believes she is practising temperance.[17]

Quantity, more or less, is not ultimately the issue affecting a person's tendency to gluttony; the issue is a self-centred obsession with food. People can address this problem motivated by the desire to overcome self-centred-ness and become truly Christian, in a life centred on Christ and lived in accordance with his commandments. In the desire for conversion, penance in the form of fasting may then be undertaken for a variety of particular reasons such as in memory of the passion and death of the Lord, as a sharing in Christ's suffering, or as a form of reparation for sin.

It then becomes a question of the nature and extent of the fasting undertaken. The fasting undertaken by the monks of the Egyptian desert is not a myth but a fact of history and so can appear as an ideal but not one considered feasible or even desirable for people who do not live apart from society and in primitive living conditions to the extent these solitaries or small communities did. To emulate them could well pose a health challenge, especially in harsh climates, though it is true that Celtic monks did survive in unfavourable climatic conditions.

To Love Fasting

A modern attempt to live as a hermit and follow a fasting regime inspired by the *Rule of Benedict* has been chronicled by a French monk, Adalbert de Vogüé, who lived in a hermitage near his monastery of La Pierre-qui-Vire, in Burgundy, from 1974 until his death in 2011 at the age of 86. In this context, fasting does not mean significant reduction in the daily amount of food but the timing of eating to give a long period daily without food, and only a single meal. His book, entitled *To Love Fasting*, records his personal experience and includes an account of the nature and history of Christian fasting as well as polemical comments, typical of his writings, on the state of fasting observance in contemporary monasticism. His vindication of fasting as a monastic practice, whether for hermits or those who live in community, can only have limited relevance to people 'in the world', but is nonetheless of interest, as it shows how a return to a regime of dining which was common for all in the ancient world is still possible in appropriate circumstances. He notes the 'tenacious legend that today blocks the path of every attempt at the true fast, namely modern man's incapability to fast as the ancients did.'[18]

The key to his success in arriving at his one meal a day regime was the gradual way in which it developed. From the usual monastic practice of three meals a day, he began by cutting down on breakfast and transferring to the other two meals what he took from it. By the end of two years, breakfast had disappeared and yet he found himself in good shape. He then turned his attention to supper. 'Progressively, and in about the same length of time, I reduced it to the point where I could do without it.'[19] In settling on the resulting one meal a day pattern, he was actually diverging from the *Rule* he was endeavouring to follow, as St Benedict's arrangement provided for two meals a day at some times of the year. His next step was to decide on the hour of the daily meal, and here again he diverged from the tradition which allowed for different times according to the season, while he chose the fixed hour of 6.30 p.m. However, he reported that to his surprise his arrangement was extremely satisfying and avoided the heaviness that a mid-afternoon meal would have produced for the rest of the day.

> Those afternoon hours are the best of the day. They consist of two and a half hours of intellectual work, the office of None, an hour of manual work, an hour of walking and meditating in the forest. Although fasting since the previous evening, I am at my best. One could say that the further I get from the one meal of the day, the better is my whole tone of being. My mind is at its most lucid, my body vigorous and well disposed, my heart light and full of joy.[20]

By consulting a medical confrère, he got an explanation for this state of wellbeing in terms of his own ability to eat a large amount of food at one time, as well as operative hormonal mechanisms and the effects of a long rest for the digestive system.

His experience can be helpful for those who are simply dieting for health reasons as well as for those who undertake fasting as a spiritual exercise, though caution is needed in drawing conclusions from it. His principal conclusion was that contemporary Benedictine monasteries have almost all laid aside a fundamental observance laid down by St Benedict by adopting the three-meal a day practice of the contemporary world. [21] However, he also admitted that the regime he adopted was one which was more feasible for a hermit than for those who continued to live in community. Applying this insight to people who are not monastics, it does seem that someone in the workplace favouring a diet with long periods without food in the hope of some purifying, de-toxing effects, would need to separate somewhat from work colleagues to pursue such a routine.

The author also focused on the issue of work itself. He asked himself where the energy once devoted to ascetical practices such as fasting in monasteries was now invested, and concluded that the work on self, ascesis, 'had passed to work on things that was so exclusive and so demanding that it left no energy available for another effort'.[22] In an earlier book, he had spoken of

> the extroversion of human dynamism, which, having cast aside effort on self, has invested itself wholly in working on things. ....
> Work mobilises all energies, and by its implacable rhythm and demand for productivity, imposes the eating schedule and physical conveniences which are conditions for such work.[23]

His comments in both citations refer to monastic life in community, but again they have relevance for people in all walks of life. As noted earlier, the demands of the world of work can cause people to adopt unhealthy practices in regard to food and lead to attempts to free themselves from these by undertaking dieting.

Dieting by Intermittent Fasting

At the level of practice, though not necessarily of motivation, there is a contemporary dieting regime which corresponds to an extent to that described by De Vogüé about thirty years ago, in that it requires significant periods of fasting, usually rather more than his practice of a twenty-three hour fast. It requires intermittent fasting and is one of the more popular but demanding types of dieting at present. Intermittent fasting consists of having regularly scheduled periods of time when a normal pattern of eating is maintained, alternating with periods of restricted eating or total fast.[24] It amounts to skipping meals for a day or more on a regular basis or taking only light snacks. Intermittent dieting is in fact similar to the fasting regime at the beginning of his monastic life of one of the Egyptian monks, Pachomius (292-348), whose mentor Palamon introduced him to the practice of eating each day in summer, but only every other day in winter. Palamon's diet consisted of bread and salt and he never took oil or wine.[25] When Pachomius founded his own community, he did not try to impose such a regime on his followers, recognising that different individuals had different needs. Similarly, today the one who engages in intermittent dieting will find it difficult to do so in a family or even workplace environment, so it can result in a certain amount of isolation which would be counterproductive to the overall objective of promoting one's health.

In all dieting that is more than a passing attempt at controlling weight, the calorie count, the balance between fat and carbohydrate content and the release of toxins (which occurs when the fat in which the body had stored them has been used up), have to be taken into account. Fasting as part of a modern desire for health maintenance and improvement is therefore a complex process needing careful management and even professional guidance.[26]

Motivation

This is all at the level of practice, but the issue of motivation is the fundamental one, as De Vogüé held in relation to monastic life. In the Christian tradition or at least in that part of it where asceticism was not extreme and damaging to health, the motivation for fasting was liturgical or simply part of an overall motivation to maintain control over all inordinate desires.

> The appetite for nourishment is only one of the desires emanating from the human heart. ... Its incessant compelling urgency sets it aside from other desires. Some, like sexuality, are not less natural, but none of them is as immediately essential (as the desire for physical nourishment). From this results its key position and its value as a test for the whole moral effort.[27]

The implication of putting fasting in this spiritual context is that it helps to avoid the backsliding and ultimate dishonesty that have often been evident in the history of outward conformity to the fasts imposed by church authorities. In medieval and later times, the Lenten regulations which forbade the use of certain foods caused little hardship when ingenious methods were found to present others such as fish in many tasty forms – enough to satisfy a glutton quite often. Undertaking fasting for less than spiritual reasons - physical health or even a desire to improve one's self-esteem resulting from a more attractive appearance - is not likely to achieve lasting success, because to do so does not respond to the real need of the human person. There are many possible motivations which ultimately have to do with obsession with the self rather than a desire to live a life in conformity with God's law as revealed in Christ's teaching and example. In his Apostolic Exhortation, *Evangelii gaudium* (1993), Pope Francis spoke of the spiritual worldliness which can lurk behind 'an obsession with programmes of self-help and self-realization' (no. 95).

Islam

Lenten penance in the Christian tradition, inspired by Isaiah (58:1-12), puts fasting in its necessary spiritual context and it is worth noting that this perspective is shared by writers of the Islamic tradition, as exemplified by a Muslim physician, Muhammad Salim Khan, commenting on the fast from dawn to sunset during the annual season of Ramadan:

> Complete fasting is one institution that combines spiritual, physical, individual and community needs in a most harmonious way. The spiritual aspect of an individual is developed and enhanced in the most potent and sublime manner. *Taqwa* – God consciousness, discipline and empathy with the poor and needy – is the main emphasis behind fasting. Fasting as a devotional process and internal purification enables the person to transcend his gross physical needs.[28]

The community dimension of the observance of Ramadan is made prominent by 'empathy with the poor and the needy' as it is in Christianity by the practice of almsgiving undertaken as a contribution to social justice. For Muslims, the community dimension is especially evident in the celebration that concludes the fast, the *Eid al-Fitr*, which can be translated as the Feast of the Fast-Breaking. It is meant to be as a much a spiritual feast as one involving food.

> So Muslims begin three days of festivities with prayer. … (L)arge numbers of Muslims, who may not normally pray together at their mosque, gather for *Eid al-Fitr*.… After their prayer, Muslims break their month-long Ramadan fast with family and friends.[29]

As Muslims in the Western world are generally minority communities, the community dimension can be expected to be prominent in such an important feast – often an open-air one in that one mosque may not be large enough to accommodate all the Muslims in a city. The corresponding Christian celebration is Easter, and this raises the issue of the extent to which that is in practice a community celebration. There may well have been a sense of coming together in a parish during Lent through some shared initiative for charitable purposes, but this does not necessarily merge into a community celebration of Easter, especially as for some it is a time for a vacation spent elsewhere, while family celebrations are hardly as festive as the corresponding one at Christmas. Clearly, Easter Sunday will be a festive climax only if the Triduum from Holy Thursday to the Holy Saturday Vigil has realised its potential to be a community celebration.

Conclusion

This consideration returns the whole issue of fasting to its connection with the liturgy, the fast in anticipation of the Bridegroom's return. Fasting in Christianity is an ascetical exercise in the sense of purification with a purpose that is not inward looking, self-regarding, but one of preparation for the consummation of this age heralded in the Book of Revelation as the marriage supper of the Lamb celebrated with his bride the Church (19:9; 21:10). Jesus had indicated that the period of preparation for his return as the Bridegroom would be an indefinite one in history and marked by fasting, yet whenever it is celebrated, the Eucharistic meal in which the community has communion with his body and blood anticipates the sharing of the church in his wedding feast. The Eucharist transfers the offering the church makes to the altar on high, as the Roman Canon (Eucharistic Prayer One) puts it.

The daily life of the Christian is lived, however, 'in the bondage of history'[30] with its restraints and its challenges. To appreciate, as far as human consciousness can, the other order of existence, the wedding feast of heaven, requires a purification process well exemplified by fasting. The solemn fast of the Paschal Triduum referred to above, had its correlate in the fast from midnight when the Eucharist was celebrated only in the morning. The current regulation requiring a fast of one hour must from that perspective be regarded as no more than a token. Yet it has to be admitted that fasting is just one aspect of the purification needed in order to prepare for participation in the celebration of the Eucharist. But as Mary Douglas warned (in relation to abstinence), the symbolic acts, the rituals, characteristic of traditional religious practice are not to be despised. Fasting has had too important a place in the Christian life for its value to be questioned. The challenge for Christians is to experience a desire and find a place for it in today's living conditions, without having to isolate themselves noticeably from society. Given that some undertake quite radical fasting regimes in the interest of health both physical and psychological, to undertake moderate fasting for religious reasons is hardly an unhealthy option.

ENDNOTES

1   Eamon Duffy, 'Fasting – our lost rite', *The Tablet*, 31 January 2004, 7

2   Tomáš Špidík, S.J., *The Spirituality of the Christian East. A Systematic Handbook*, Anthony Gythiel trans.(Collegeville: Liturgical Press, 1986) 224

3   *The Wisdom of the Desert. Sayings of the Desert Fathers of the Fourth Century*, No. 141, Thomas Merton trans. (New York: New Directions Publishing, 1970) 77

4 Robert Taft, *The Liturgy in Byzantium and Beyond* (Aldershot: Variorum, 1995) V 71

5 Gregory the Great, *Dialogues* III, Fathers of the Church Vol. 39, John Zimmerman trans. (Washington: C.U.A Press, 2002) 172

6 Steven Ozment, *The Reformation in the Cities* (New Haven: Yale University Press, 1975) 94

7 Eamon Duffy, 'Fasting - our lost rite', 7

8 *Idem*

9 Mary Douglas, *Natural Symbols* (London: Barrie and Jenkins, 1973) 22

10 *Ibid.* 25-6

11 Text in *Catholic Herald,* 16 May 2011

12 Gregory, *Moralia on Job* 39.25 in *Morals on the Book of Job,* Library of the Fathers (Ante Nicene), (Oxford: John Henry Parker, 1850) 490

13 Augustine, *Confessions* X.31, Frank Sheed trans. (London: Sheed and Ward, 1954) 193

14 Denis Okholm, 'Gluttony: Thought for Food', *American Benedictine Review* 49.1, March 1998, 38-9

15 *Ibid.* 42

16 *Ibid.* 43

17 C. S. Lewis, *The Screwtape Letters* (New York: The Macmillan Company, 1948) 86-7

18 Adalbert de Vogüé O.S.B., *To Love Fasting* (Petersham: St Bede's Publicatins, 1989) 2

19 *Ibid.* 7

20 *Ibid.* 6

21 *Ibid.* 67

22 *Ibid.* 69

23 Adalbert de Vogüé, *The Rule of St Benedict. A Doctrinal and Spiritual Commentary,* J.B. Hasbrouck trans. (Kalamazoo, Cistercian Publications, 1983) 230

24 Many books on this topic have appeared in recent times, often privately published.

25 *The First Greek Life of Pachomius,* Armand Veilleux trans., CS 45 (Kalamazoo: Cistercian Publications, 1980) 301

26 Cf. Leon Chatow, *Principles of Fasting* (London: Thorsons,1996) 29

27 Adalbert de Vogüé, *The Rule of St Benedict* 241-2

28 Muhammad Salim Khan, *Islamic Medicine* (London. Routledge, Kegan and Paul, 1980) 78, cited in Leon Chatow, *Principles of Fasting* 102

29 Carole Garibaldi Rogers, *Fasting. Exploring a Great Spiritual Practice* (Notre Dame: Sarin Books, 2004) 143

30 John Zizioulas, *Being as Communion* (Crestwood NY: St Vladimir's Seminary,1985) 130

CHAPTER TWENTY

General Conclusion

Looking back to people and dynasties, periods and events, through the centuries has been for the purpose of establishing how eating habits affected Christians in their lives and even in their worship. For Christians, religious motives can inform going without food on the one hand, and feasting both religious and material on the other. Clearly, in a secularised society other motives can exist for both fasting and feasting. It has been interesting to observe how important or unimportant the food itself and the fundamental daily practice of eating have been for Christians. There have been periods when 'they shared their food gladly and generously' (Ac 2.47), with sharing a significant feature of the eating and drinking, but in that same period in the Roman Empire a different food culture existed among a decadent upper class. Food shared was an expression of class division rather than of unity, a way to flaunt riches, dispose of enemies and indulge in gluttony – though the *vomitorium* was more myth than reality.

To what extent an emerging Christian upper class was prone to excess is not clear, though stories linger around people such as Pope Damasus. He had a puzzling relationship with St Jerome; it is as if he wished to deal with personal and institutional failings by employing a scholar who would introduce the respectability of scholarship along with personal austerity as a compensatory mechanism in the life of the Christian establishment. And it is true that Jerome proved very influential in the lives of some. Why his followers turned out to be women must have some explanation in gender roles as they were at the time, but there were also examples of Christian senators who embraced an austere way of life.

Fasting inevitably came to be characterised by a solitary rather than a shared life. Initially a reaction against excess in life generally, which naturally showed itself in eating, it could obviously be best practised in desert regions where food was in any case scarce. It soon became a powerful way

365

of achieving control of one's life, in face of all the temptations that these solitaries identified and fought against. St Ambrose was one in a long line of authors, pagan and Christian, who associated food with sexual temptation - he held that luxury was the mother of lust.[1] Going apart from a society that was corrupt by Christian standards, gave rise to the remarkable and often extreme ascetical practices of the early monks. As pointed out earlier, if asceticism was appropriately expressed by fasting in desert regions, this could not have been the case for monks like those of Skellig Michael in Ireland, where mere survival required adequate nourishment.

Fasting was also part of the mainstream Christian community as the papal and diocesan structures established norms for the celebration of feasts and their anticipatory fasts, following to an extent the lead of the earlier Jewish norms. Fasting was mainly connected with the liturgical cycle of feasts and it needs to be emphasised that for Christians, whose lives are nourished by the liturgy, this remains the principal role for fasting. Fasting as part of an ascetic lifestyle makes sense in the context of an authentic human life, but from a Christian perspective, it is regarded as purification in preparation for a feast, an external manifestation of a more fundamental inner attitude, rather than simply part of an ascetical lifestyle. Thus purified, the Christian can enter joyfully into the feast, in both liturgical and culinary mode.

The Carolingian period in Europe marks a transition from a tribal culture of excess in food–fuelled aggression and general excess to a culture where the Christian liturgy brought a new understanding of feasting. The ceremonial surrounding the rite of Communion in the body and blood of Christ according to the Roman observance had a subtle effect on the way in which earthly food was consumed - if the way of life of Charlemagne depicted in his biography is accepted as corresponding to reality. There is evidence that this might be the case in the fact that he gave due importance to both the liturgy and civilised behaviour at the table. He was also influenced by the monasticism of the time.

Monastic practice was no longer that of the desert but a tradition established by St Benedict, where food was substantial if measured, frugality was given more emphasis than fasting, and the fact that some needed more food, some less, was a governing principle when it came to food as well as other needs. Benedict's admiration for the monks of old did cause him to think that the monk's life should be a continuous Lent but he was realistic about his community's perception of basic needs in regard to wine, for example. Failure on his part to recognise that a predominantly spiritual feast has to be celebrated by people of flesh and blood in some bodily way probably laid the ground for the attempts in later monasticism – as Gerald of Wales observed – to dodge the implications of the rule of abstinence from meat in ingenious ways. The consumption of food became in this way an unfortunate concomitant of falling standards in the Christian life.

The growth of religious life in the early centuries of the second millennium, among women especially, brought a new understanding of the role of food in relation to the central mystery of the church's life, the Eucharist. A theological development that emphasised the sacrificial character of a rite which needed completion simply by the priest's communion, along with emphasis on the Real Presence of Christ in the celebration, caused the consumption of the elements of the Eucharist to give way to simple contemplation in the lives of many. This mystical, non-physical, communion was a relationship with Christ that sometimes even manifested itself in physical sensations, but departed in a fundamental way from the physical reality of the sacrament. In a new way, food was in an uneasy relationship with the spiritual life and the Eucharist was not seen as a shared meal.

Monasticism went through periods of decline and renewal as one millennium gave way to another and there was a close correlation between levels of observance and food regimes. This had become very evident when, in the sixteenth-century, Erasmus in his *In Praise of Folly* used the weapon of satire to show how ineffective food regulations were as a measure and promoter of Christian living. Where fasting could now be a chosen exercise rather than endemic to the economic circumstances, it became more and more a resented imposition on people's Christian freedom. The Protestant Reformation's espousal of the principle of the freedom of the Christian could have established a balanced approach to the discipline of fasting as a force for the renewal of the Christian life, but in practice the reduction of the authority of the clergy in face of this new-found freedom meant that exhortation in such documents as the Anglican Homilies had little effect.

It was a time when the Renaissance culture gave the banquet a prominence reminiscent of the days of the Roman Empire and now it had strongly ecclesiastical connotations because it was a feature of life of ecclesiastics recruited among the upper classes. The banquet was an example of refinement that covered up disregard for truly human values when a shared meal could have its meaning contradicted by the administration of poison, and blood lust could ignore any concern for animal welfare in the provision of food for the table. The values of sharing and self-giving sacrifice enshrined in the liturgical feast could have little echo in a culture typified by such banquets.

It was a time when the Council of Trent reaffirmed the theology of the Eucharist that emphasised its sacrificial character. It would still require several centuries of theological progress to produce a liturgical theology of the Eucharist, that is, a theology derived from the liturgical celebration itself of the whole mystery of Christ, from incarnation to death and resurrection and anticipation of the end-time. In this understanding, the Mystical Body joined with its Head in the worship of the Father through communion with him and one another – as the Second Vatican Council-would in time say. This communion is with the risen Christ and requires transformation of a shared meal using bread and wine to a new order of existence, though for the earth-bound communicants an existence not released from the restraints of time. The rubrics of the present Order of Mass have not highlighted the importance of presenting the celebration as a shared meal centred on real bread and wine, so it is not surprising that the faithful generally do not perceive it in this way. In contrast, Kallistos Ware has pointed out that 'Orthodoxy rejects any attempt to diminish the materiality of the sacraments'.[2]

But the neglect of the food dimension of the liturgy has a long history. The gap between eating habits and the liturgical feast showed itself as much in the developing Protestant tradition as in the Catholic past, particularly when Puritanism adopted an ascetical way of life that emphasised fasting, while holding with an understanding of the Eucharist that emphasised the spiritual, non-bodily, encounter with Christ in the celebration. For someone like Bishop Bayley 'the extraordinary practice of piety consists in either fasting or feasting'.[3] Fasting was what the name implies, but feasting for him meant only observing the days laid down by Royalty as days for church services consisting of prayers and long sermons. That approach contrasts with the convivial delight expressed by Robert Carron in leaving aside fasting for feasting: 'Let us fast, then - whenever we see fit. ... But having gotten that exercise out of the way, let us eat. Festally, first of all, for life without occasions is not worth living. But ferially, too...'[4]

It would be unjust to label Robert Capon's approach as hedonistic because his love of food is in the context of deep appreciation of the goodness of creation and the generosity of the Creator who has provided humankind with such delights as wine – though in the form of the grape and with the challenge to take it from there. Norman Wirzba's theology of eating, summarised earlier, defends the eating of meat on the basis of creation being understood as God's offering of creatures to each other as food and nurture, reflecting a sacrificial power in which life continually moves through death to new life.[5] Both authors have lived and worked in a prosperous Western world now only gradually becoming aware of the larger context – the wastefulness of the culture, a rapidly expanding world population with aspirations to the Western lifestyle and a growing environmental crisis. That must curb enthusiasm on the part of the Western population for eating both 'festally and ferially'. The Catholic Church persisted with its canonical regime of fasting long after other churches had ceased to make such demands on their members, but in quite recent times it relaxed the ancient rules on fasting, turning instead to exhortations to broader notions of penance. In light of present-day environmental issues, it may be opportune for the church to preach restraint in eating practices once more.

For many centuries exploitation of the planet's resources of food and water, of minerals and metals, has made no apparent difference to the world itself. Quite recently it has come to be recognised that in fact it always did, from the time the plough first cut into the earth's virginal surface, but the damage to the planet was not up to recent times deemed to be irreversible; it was able to recover using its own resources. The stress on the idea of the planet's ability to right itself came in the proposal of a hypothesis by the scientist, James Lovelock (1919-). It was given the name Gaia by a neighbour and entered the Oxford Dictionary with the description: 'the global ecosystem, understood to function in the manner of a vast self-regulating organism, in the context of which all living things collectively define and maintain the conditions conducive for life on earth'. Further reflection on his part led to his warning that human activity could lead to devastation and the possible disappearance of the human race (*The Revenge of Gaia*, 2006), as the ecosystem moves to protect itself. While not everyone would agree with his attributing such healing ability to the ecosystem, all his work was based on scientific study. As reported in the present work, international studies have now quantified the increasing dangers to all life on earth caused by human activity. Humans' food culture cannot be blamed completely for the looming crisis, but the fundamental action of eating is the basic preparation for human activity.

When Christians become aware of all this as a challenge to their faith and life, the question arises of what they can do about it. In the end is it all about their carbon footprint? They can of course, like non-believers, make serious adjustments to their lifestyle, but it does seem that the Christian Community can play a part even more radical than just taking to heart the teaching of Pope Francis in *Laudato Si'*, with its many insights and recommendations for environmentally sensitive Christian living, but with little emphasis on the Christian's belonging to a world that is to come - in theological terms, the eschatological dimension of Christianity.

There is need for the church as community to become more aware of its identity as a harbinger of the end-time, as a body which is not simply tied down to a role of witnessing to kingdom values in its teaching or in lobbying the state, but one which in the shared meal of the Eucharist experiences anticipation of the kingdom, and from this empowerment works towards a gradual transformation of humanity in all its activity towards true fulfilment.

In the end, the role of food, feast and fast in the Christian life must include addressing the looming environmental crisis from the perspective of the coming reign of God.

ENDNOTES

1   Ambrose, *Letters* 63:26 in *Nicene and Post Nicene Fathers*. Second Series, Vol. X, P. Schaff, H. Wace eds. (New York, The Christian Literature Co., 1896) 460

2   *The Orthodox Church* 274

3   *The Practice of Pietie. Directing a Christian how to walke that he may please God* (London: J. Hedges, 1613) 215

4   Robert Farrar Capon, *The Supper of the Lamb. A Culinary Reflection* 32

5   Norman Wirzba, *Food and Faith* 174

Bibliography

Early Christian Works and Documents

Ambrose, *De Mysteriis, Nicene and Post-Nicene Fathers*, Second Series, Vol. 10. P. Schaff, H. Wace eds. (Buffalo, NY: Christian Literature Publishing Co., 1896.)

— *De Sacramentis*, in *On the Mysteries and the Treatise on the Sacraments*, trans. T. Thompson, ed. with Introduction and Notes by J.H. Strawley (New York: Macmillan, 1919).

— *Letter* 63.26, *Nicene and Post-Nicene Fathers*, Second Series, Vol. 10.

Athanasius, *Life of Anthony*, Cistercian Studies 45 (Kalamazoo: Cistercian Publications, 1994)

Augustine, *Confessions* (London: Sheed and Ward, 1954)

— *Contra Faustum Manichaeum, Sancti Augustini Opera Omnia* V (Paris: Paul Mellier, 1842)

— *De Doctrine Christiana. Sancti Augustini Opera Apologetica* IV (Paris Paul Mellier, 1842)

— *Enarratio in Ps. 31*.Augustine, *Expositions on the Book of Psalms, Vol I: Psalm I - XXXVI* (Oxford: John Henry Parker, 1847)

— *Epistola* 98. Augustine: Letters - Volume II (83 - 130) (Washington D.C. C. U. A., 1966)

— *Letter* 22.1.3, J. G. Cunningham trans., *Nicene and Post-Nicene Fathers, First Series*, Vol. 1, Edited by Philip Schaff (Buffalo, N.Y: Christian Literature Publishing Co., 1887)

— *On the Usefulness of Fasting.* Treatises on Various Subjects. The Fathers of the Church, Vol.14 (Washington: Catholic University Press, 1952)

— *Sermon 205, Sermons on the Liturgical Seasons,* Vol. 38 (New York: Fathers of the Church, 1959)

— *The City of God*, Marcus Dodds trans. (New York: the Modern Library, 1950) Bede, The Venerable, *A History of the English Church and People,* Translated with an Introduction by Leo Sherley-Price (Harmondsworth: Penguin Books, 1965[2])

Benedict, Saint, *Rule of Benedict,* Timothy Fry ed. (Collegeville: Liturgical Press, 1982)

Cassian, John, *The Institutes,* Ancient Christian Writers 58, Boniface Ramsey O.P. trans. (New York: The Newman Press, 2000)

Chrysostom, John, *Homilies on the Gospel of Matthew*, in *Nicene and Post-Nicene Fathers*, Vol. X

— *Homilies on the Gospel of St. John and the Epistle to the Hebrews, Nicene and Post-Nicene Fathers*, Vol. XIV

Clement of Alexandria, *Paedagogus* 2.1 trans. Simon Wood (Washington: Catholic University of America, 1951)

373

Didache. Text and Commentary in Thomas O'Loughlin, *The Didache: A Window on the Earliest Christians* (London: S.P.C.K., 2010)

Epiphanius, *In Sanctam Resurrectionem* 3, in Migne, *Patrologia Graeca* 43:466-470

Gregory the Great, Pope, *Dialogues* III, Fathers of the Church Vol. 39, John Zimmerman trans. (Washington: C.U.A Press, 2002)

— *Epistle* LVXXI in *Nicene and Post-Nicene fathers,* Series II, Vol.13, Part II

— 'Letter to King Ethelbert', in *Bede's Ecclesiastical History of England. Anglo-Saxon Chronicle,* Chapter XXXII, J.A. Giles ed. (London: Henry Bohn, 1849²)

— *Moralia on Job* 39.25 in *Morals on the Book of Job,* Library of the Christian Fathers (Ante Nicene), (Oxford: John Henry Parker, 1850)

Irenaeus, *Libri quinque adversus Haereses,* Tom. II, W. W. Harvey ed. (Cantabrigiae: Typis academicis, 1857)

Jerome, *The Letters of Saint Jerome. The Latin Text.* Edited with Introduction by James Duff (Dublin: Browne and Nolan, 1942) Letter 107

Justin Martyr, *First Apology; Second Apology* in *Ante Nicene Fathers*, Volume 1: Apostolic Fathers. With *Justin Martyr and Irenaeus* (Grand Rapids MI: Eerdmans, 1988)

Leo the Great, *Sermon XVII, Sermon XLII, Nicene and Post-Nicene Fathers.* Series II, Vol.12

Liber Pontificalis (The Book of Pontiffs), Translated with an Introduction by Raymond Davis (Liverpool: Liverpool University Press, 1989)

On the Apostolic Tradition, Translation with Introduction and Commentary by Alistair Stewart-Sykes (Crestwood N.Y.; St Vladimir's Seminary Press, 2001)

Origen, *Contra Celsum* in *Ante Nicene Fathers*, Vol, 4. *Tertullian; Minucius Felix; Commodian; Origen,* Alexander Roberts and James Donaldson eds. (New York: Christian Literature Publishing Co., 1885)

Ratramnus, *Ratramni Opera Omnia*, (Paris: J.P. Migne, 1852) 121. 146. XLIV

— *De Corpore et Sanguine Domini,* 2. English translation in *Of the Body and Blood of Christ* (Oxford: J.H. Parker, 1838)

Rituale Armenorum, F. C. Conybeare, A.J Maclean eds. (Oxford: Clarendon Press, 1905)

Sahak, Saint Isaac, *Armenian Canons of Saint Isaak Sahak,* English translation in *The American Journal of Theology* Vol. II, 1898

Tertullian, 'Apology' in *The Fathers of the Church* Vol. 10 (Washington: C.U. A., 1950)

— *De oratione,* Edited and translated by Ernest Evans (London: S.P.C.K., 1953)

— 'On Fasting' in *The Writings of Tertullian* Vol. III, *Ante-Nicene Christian Library Vol. XVIII* (Edinburgh: T & T Clark: 1871)

The First Greek Life of Pachomius, Armand Veilleux trans., CS 45 (Kalamazoo: Cistercian Publications, 1980)

Theodoret of Cyrrhus, *A History of the Monks of Syria,* R. M. Price trans. (Kalamazoo: Cistercian Publications, 1985)

The Theodosian Code and Novels, and the Sirmondian Constitutions, Clyde Pharr, Theresa Sherrer Davidson, Mary Brown Pharr, eds. (Union, N.J.: Lawbook Exchange, 2006)

The Wisdom of the Desert. Sayings of the Desert Fathers of the Fourth Century, No. 141, Thomas Merton trans. (New York: New Directions Publishing, 1970)

Later Works and Documents

Abdalla, Michael, 'The Way the Contemporary Western Assyrians take Food in the Middle East during Fasts and Church Holidays' in *Fasting and Feasting (Proceedings of the Oxford Symposium on Food & Cookery, 1990)*, Harlan Walker, ed. (London: Prospect Books, 1991)

Anderson, Bernhard W., *The Living World of the Old Testament* (London: Longmans, 1967²)

Aquinas, Thomas· *Summa Theologiae*, III, q. 80, a. 12

Bainton, Roland H., *Erasmus of Christendom* (London: Collins, 1970)

— *Here I Stand. Martin Luther* (Oxford: Lion Books, 1978)

Bayly, Lewis *The Practice of Pietie. Directing a Christian how to walke that he may please God* (London: J. Hedges, 1613)

Bellah Robert N. and Philip E. Hamilton, *Varieties of Civil Religion* (Eugene OR: Wipf & Stock, 2013)

Benedict XVI, Pope, *General Audience,* Wednesday, 9 December 2009

Benham, Hugh, *Latin Church Music in England 1460-1575* (London: Da Capo Press 1977)

Boissonnade, P., *Life and Work in Medieval Europe,* Eileen Power trans. (New York: Dorset Press, 1927}

Bossy, John, *Christianity in the West 1400-1700* (Oxford: O.U.P.,1982)

Bouwsma, William J., *John Calvin. A Sixteenth Century Portrait* (New York: O.U.P., 1988)

Bradshaw, Paul , *Early Christian Worship* (London: S.P.C.K., 2010)

Brands, H. W., *The First American. The Life and Times of Benjamin Franklin* (New York: Anchor Books, 2002)

Brillat-Savarin, Jean, *The Physiology of Taste: Or Meditations on Transcendental Gastronomy* (Scotts Valley CA: CreateSpace Independent Publishing Platform, 2017)

Brown, Peter, *Augustine of Hippo. A Biography* (London: Faber and Faber, 1967)

— *The Body and Society. Men, Women and Sexual Renunciation in Early Christianity* (New York: Columbia University Press, 1998)

— *The Making of Late Antiquity* (Cambridge, Mass: Harvard University Press, 1978)

Burckhardt, Jacob, *The Civilization of Renaissance Italy* (London: Phaidon Press, 1995³)

Burton, Robert, *The Anatomy of Melancholy* (1621) cited in Herbert M. Vaughan, *The Medici Popes*

Bynum, Caroline, *Holy Feast and Holy Fast. The Religious Significance of Food to Medieval Women* (Berkeley: University of California Press, 1987)

Byrne, James, *Glory, Jest and Riddle. Religious Thought in the Enlightenment* (London: S.C.M. Press, 1996)

Byron, Lord George, *Letter 12,* October 1821 (Oxford: Oxford Dictionary of Humorous Quotations, 2008)

Caliari, Pietro, *Paolo Veronese, Sua Vita e Sue Opere* (Roma: Forzani e c., 1888)

Calvin, John , *Commentary on Matthew 4:1* in *A Harmony of the Gospels. Matthew, Mark and Luke,* Vol. I, A. W. Morrison trans. (Edinburgh: St Andrew's Press,1972)

— *Confession of Faith Concerning the Eucharist (1537),* in *Calvin Theological Treatises,* J.K.L. Reid ed. (Philadelphia: Westminster Press, 1964).

— *Forme des priéres et chants ecclésiastiques., avec la manière d'administrer les sa-crements et consacrer le mariage selon la coutume de lÉglise ancienne.*

— *Institutes of the Christian Religion,* Vol. 2, Ford L. Battles trans. (Philadelphia: Westminster Press, 1960)

— *Sermon I Cor 10,* in *Joannis Calvini opera quae supersunt omnia,* Vol. XLIX (Brunsvigae: C.A. Schwetschke, 1892)

Cameron, Euan, *The European Reformation* (Oxford: Clarendon Press, 1991)

Capatti, Alberto and Massimo Montanari, *Italian Cuisine. A Cultural History* (NewYork: Columbia University Press, 1999)

Catholic Bishops' Conference of England and Wales, 'Statement on Friday Penance', *Catholic Herald,* 16 May 2011

Cavanaugh, William, *Theopolitical Imagination* (London: T & T Clark, 2002)

Chadwick, Owen, *The Victorian Church. Part One 1829-1859* (London: S.C.M., 1971³) 37

— *The Reformation* (Harmondsworth: Penguin Books, 1964)

Chatow, Leon, *Principles of Fasting* (London: Thorsons, 1996) 29

Chazelle, Celia, 'Figure, Character and the Glorified Body in the Carolingian Eucharistic Controversy', *Traditio,* Vol. 47 (1992)

Chernow, Ron, *Washington. A Life* (New York: The Penguin Press, 2011)

Chupungco, Anscar J., 'History of the Liturgy until the Fifteenth Century' in *Handbook for Liturgical Studies* Vol. 1, A. J. Chupungco ed. (Collegeville, The Liturgical Press, 1997)

— 'History of the Liturgy until the Fourth Century' in *Handbook for Liturgical Studies* Vol. 1

Cicero, *De senectute,* 13.45, Andrew Peabody trans. (Boston: Brown and Company, 1884)

Connolly, Hugh, *The Irish Penitentials* (Dublin: Four Courts Press, 1995)

Conybeare, Frederick C., 'The Survival of Animal Sacrifices inside the Christian Church' in *The American Journal of Theology* Vol. 7, No. 1 (January 1903) 62-90

Coulton, G.G., *The Medieval Village* (New York: Dover Publications, 1989)

Cragg, Gerald R., *The Church in the Age of Reason* (Harmondsworth: Penguin Books, 1966)

Cranmer, Thomas, *A defence of the true and Catholic doctrine of the sacrament of the body and blood of our saviour Christ.* Focus Christian Ministries Trust, 1987

Cuming, G. J., 'The Office in the Anglican Communion' in Cheslyn Jones *et al., The Study of the Liturgy* (London: S.P.C.K., 1992²)

Dalby, Andrew, 'Christmas Dinner in Byzantium' in *Food on the Move, Proceedings of the Oxford Symposium on Food and Cookery 1996,* Harlan Walker ed. (London: Prospect Books, 1997)

Dalmais, I. H., 'The Theology of the Liturgical Celebration' in A.G. Martimort, ed., *The Church at Prayer,* One Volume Edition (Collegeville: Liturgical Press, 1992)

Dalrymple, William, *From the Holy Mountain. A Journey in the Shadow of Byzantium* (London: HarperCollins, 1997)

Davies, Oliver, 'Neuro, Self and Jesus Christ' in Lieven Bove et al., *Questioning the Human. Towards a Theological Anthropology for the Twenty-First Century* (New York: Fordham Press, 2014)

Davies, Rupert E., *Methodism* (Harmondsworth: Penguin Books, 1963)

de Montaigne, Michel, *The Essayes of Michael Lord of Montaigne,* Vol. I, John Florio trans. (London: Grant Richards, 1904)

de Tocqueville, Alexis, *Democracy in America,* Henry Reeve trans. (Ware: Wordsworth Editions Ltd, 1998)

de Vogüé, A., *To Love Fasting* (Petersham: St Bede's Publicatins, 1989)

— *The Rule of St Benedict. A Doctrinal and Spiritual Commentary,* J.B. Hasbrouck trans. (Kalamazoo, Cistercian Publications, 1983)

Deissmann, Gustav, *Paulus: Eine Culture und religionsgeschtliche Skizze* (Tübingen: Mohr, 1911)

Dinesen, Isak, *Anecdotes of Destiny* (London: Michael Joseph, 1958)

Disch, Robert, *The Ecological Conscience. Values for Survival* (Upper Saddle River, NJ:- Prentice Hall, 1970)

Documents Illustrative of the Continental Reformation, B. J. Kidd, ed., (Oxford: Clarendon Press, 1911)

Donald, David Herbert, *Lincoln* (New York: Simon & Schuster, 1995)

Douglas, Mary, *Natural Symbols* (London: Barrie and Jenkins, 1973)

Duffy, Eamon, 'Fasting - our lost rite ', *The Tablet,* 31 January 2004

Dunbar, Robin, 'Humanity's drinking game', *Financial Times,* Life and Arts, 11.8.2018

EAT–Lancet Commission, 'Food in the Anthropocene', *The Lancet,* Vol. 393, Issue 10170, February 2, 2019

Edwards, John, *The Roman Cookery of Apicius, Translated and Adapted for the Modern Kitchen* (London: Random House, 1984)

Einhard and Notker the Stammerer, *Two Lives of Charlemagne* ,Einhard, *The Life of Charlemagne* (Harmondsworth: Penguin, 1969) Bk III,

Eire, Carlos M., *Reformations. The Early Modern World, 1450-1650* (New Haven: Yale University Press, 2016)

Eliade, Mircea et al., eds, 'Development' in *The History of Religions. Essays in Methodology* (Chicago: Chicago University Press, 1959)

Epstein, Morris, *All About Jewish Holidays and Customs* (New York: KTAV Publishing House, 1970)

Erasmus, Desiderius, *A Book called in Latin Enchiridion Militis Christiani and in English the Manual of the Christian Knight* (London: Methuen & Co. 1905)

— *In Praise of Folly* (Harmondsworth, Penguin Classics, 1966)

— *The Essential Erasmus,* With Introduction and Commentary by John P. Dolan (New York: The New American Library, 1964)

Farrar Capon, Robert, *The Supper of the Lamb. A Culinary Reflection* (Garden City, N.Y.: Image Books, 1974²)

Feeley-Harnik, Gillian, *The Lord's Table. The Meaning of Food in early Judaism and Christianity* (Washington: Smithsonian institution Press, 1994²)

377

Francis, Pope, *Evangelii gaudium*, Apostolic Exhortation, 2013

— *Laudato si', Encyclical Letter 2015*

Freeman Hawke, David, *Everyday Life in Early America* (New York: Harper & Row, 1988)

Freisenbruch, Annelise, *The First Ladies of Rome. The Women Behind the Caesars* (London: Jonathan Cape, 2010)

Gäbler, Ulrich, *Huldrych Zwingli. His Life and Work,* Ruth Gritsch trans. (Edinburgh: T.&T.　　　 Clark 1986)

Garibaldi Rogers, Carole, *Fasting. Exploring a Great Spiritual Practice* (Notre Dame: Sarin Books, 2004)

Gawain and the Green Knight, Sir, Translated with an Introduction by Brian Stone (Harmondsworth: Penguin Books: 1974²)

George, Timothy, *The Theology of the Reformers* (Nashville: Broadman and Holman, 1988)

Georgoudi, Stella, 'L'égorgement sanctifié en Grece moderne' in Marcel Detienne et Jean-Pierre Vernant, *La Cuisinne du Sacrifice en Pays Grec* (Paris: Editions Gallimard, 1979) 279

Gerald of Wales, *The Autobiography of Gerald of Wales,* ed. and trans. H. E. Butler (Woodbridge: Boydell & Brewer, 2005)

Gontard, Friedrich, *The Popes,* A. J. and E.J. Peeler trans. (London: Barrie & Rockliff, 1959)

Grimm, Veronika, *From Feasting to Fasting. The Evolution of a Sin* (London: Routledge, 1996)

Grumett, David, 'Dynamics of Christian Dietary Abstinence' in Benjamin Zeller, *et al.* eds. *Religion, Food and Eating in North America* (New York: Columbia University Press, 2014)

Grumett, David and Rachel Muers, *Theology on the Menu. Asceticism, meat and the Christian diet* (London: Routledge, 2010)

Hall, James, *A History of Ideas and Images in Italian Art* (London: John Murray, 1981)

Hallinger, Cassius, *a cura, Corpus Consuetudinum Monasticarum,* Tome 1, (Siegburg: Franciscum Schmitt, 1963)

Hare, Augustus, *Walks in Rome,* Vol, I (London: George Allen, 1903¹⁶)

Harrison, Frank Mott, *John Bunyan. A Story of His Life* (London: The Manner of Truth Trust,1964)

Harvey, Barbara, *Living and Dying in England 1100-1540. The Monastic Experience* (Oxford: Clarendon Press, 1993)

Hauerwas, Stanley, *Approaching the End. Eschatological Reflections on Church, Politics, and Life* (Grand Rapids MI: Wm B. Eeermans, 2013)

— 'Foreword' to Norman Wirzba, *Food and Faith. A Theology of Eating* (Cambridge: C.U.P., 2019²)

Heizenrater, Richard P., *Wesley and the People Called Methodists* (Nashville: Abingdon Press, 1995)

Henisch, Bridget Ann, *Fast and Feast. Food in Medieval Society* (University Park PA: Pennsylvania State University Press, 1976)

Hibbert, Christopher, *The Rise and Fall of the House of Medici* (Harmondsworth: Penguin Books, 1979)

Hill, Christopher, *The World Turned Upside Down. Radical Ideas During the English Revolution* (Harmondsworth: Penguin Books, 1975)

Hillerbrand, Hans, ed., *The Reformation in its Own Words* (London: S.C.M. Press, 1964)

Hinson, E. Glenn, 'Puritan Piety' in Frank G. Senn, ed. *Protestant Spiritual Traditions* (New York: Paulist Press, 1986) 165

Höpfl, Harro, *The Christian Polity of John Calvin* (Cambridge: C.U.P., 1982)

Horn, Walter, Jenny White Marshall, Grellan D. Rourke, *The Forgotten Hermitage of Skellig Michael* (Berkeley, University of California Press, 1990)

Inglis, Tom, 'Church and Culture in Catholic Ireland' in *Studies,* Vol. 106, No. 421, 2017

International Panel on Climate Change, *Climate Change 2014. Mitigation of Climate Change.* Working Group III Contribution to the Fifth Assessment Report of the Intergovernmental Panel on Climate Change, 2014

Irving, Washington, *Life of Washington* Vol. IV (London: Henry G. Bohn, 1859)

Izbicki, Thomas, *The Eucharist in Medieval Canon Law* (Cambridge: C.U.P., 2015)

Jackson, Pamela, 'Eucharist' in Allan D. Fitzgerald O.S.A., *Augustine Through the Ages. An Encyclopedia* (Grand Rapids: William B. Eerdmans, 1992)

Jackson, Wes, *New Roots for Agriculture* (Lincoln: University of Nebraska, 1985[2])

Jasper, R.C.D. and G.J. Cuming, eds., *Prayers of the Eucharist: Early and Reformed* (New York: Oxford University Press, 1980[2])

Jedin, Hubert ed., *History of the Church,* Vol IV, Vol. V (London: Burns & Oates, 1980)

John Paul II, Pope St, *Ecclesia de Eucharistia,* Encyclical Letter, 2003

— *Ut Unum Sint,* Encyclical Letter, 1995

Jones, A. H. M., 'The Economic Life of the towns of the Roman Empire' in Jean Virenne, ed., *La Ville,* (Brussels: Libraire Encyclopédique, 1955)

Joyce, James, *Portrait of the Artist* (Ware, Herts: Wordsworth Editions, 19920

Jungmann, Joseph, *The Early Liturgy. To the Time of Gregory the Great* (London: Darton, Longman and Todd, 1960)

— *The Mass of the Roman Rite. Its Origins and Development,* F.A. Brunner trans. (London: Burns & Oates, 1959[3])

Kaplan, David M., ed., *The Philosophy of Food* (Berkeley CA: University of California Press, 2012)

Kardong O.S.B., Terrence, *Benedict's Rule. A Translation and Commentary* (Collegeville: Liturgical Press, 1996)

Kearns Goodwin, Doris, *Team of Rivals. The Political Genius of Abraham Lincoln* (New York: Simon & Schuster, 2005)

Kelly, J. N. D., *Jerome. His Life, Writings and Controversies* (London: Duckworth: 1975)

— *The Oxford Dictionary of the Popes* (Oxford: O.U.P., 1986)

Kilmartin S.J., Edward, 'The Sacrifice of Thanksgiving and Social Justice' in Mark Searle ed., *Liturgy and Social Justice* (Collegeville: Liturgical Press,1980)

— *The Eucharist in the West. History and Theology* (Collegeville: Liturgical Press, 1998)

— 'The Eucharistic Cup in the Primitive Liturgy', *Catholic Biblical Quarterly,* Vol. 24, No. 1, 1962

Kingdon, Robert M., *Adultery and Divorce in Calvin's Geneva* (Cambridge, Mass.: Harvard University Press, 1995)

Kirk, Martha, 'Liturgical drama', in *The New Dictionary of Sacramental Worship,* Peter Fink, ed. (Dublin: Gill and Macmillan, 1990)

Kirtio, Leah, 'The inordinate excess in apparel': Sumptuary Legislation in Tudor England', in *University of Alberta* Student *Journal* 3 (1) (2012)

Lafont, Ghislain, *Eucharist. The Meal and the Word* (Mahwah NJ: Paulist Press, 2014)

Lamb, Charles, 'A Dissertation on Roast Pig' in *Essays of Elia and Elana* (London: Bell and Dandy, 1871)

Lane Fox, Robin, *Pagans and Christians* (London: Penguin, 1986)

Langland, William, *Piers Plowman.* A New Annotated of the C-text by Derek Pearsall, Passus IX, 85 (Exeter: Exeter University Press, 2008)

Lançon, Betrand, *Rome in Late Antiquity* (Edinburgh: University Press, 1995)

Lavelle, Des, *Skellig. Island Outpost of Europe* (Dublin: The O'Brien Press, 1977²)

— *The Skellig Story. Ancient Monastic Outpost* (Dublin: The O'Brien Press, 1976)

Leon-Dufour, Xavier, *Dictionary of Biblical Theology* (London: Geoffrey Chapman, 1973²)

Lewis, C. S., *The Screwtape Letters* (New York: The Macmillan Company, 1948)

Lincoln, Abraham , *Speeches and Letters of Abraham Lincoln, 1832-1865,* Merwin Roe, ed. (London and Toronto: J. M. Dent & Sons, 1907)

Liutprand, *The Works of Liutprand of Cremona,* T.A.Wright trans. (London: Routledge, 1930)

Luther, Martin, *On the Freedom of a Christian* in *Martin Luther's Basic Theological Works,* Timothy Lull, ed. (Minneapolis: Fortress Press, 1989)

— 'Preface to the Wittenberg Hymnal' in *Luther's Works,* Vol. 53, Ulrich Leupold ed. (Philadelphia: Fortress Press 1965)

— *Table Talk,* William Hazlitt trans. (London: Fount, Harper Collins, 1995)

— *The Babylonian Captivity of the Church* in *Martin Luther's Basic Theological Works*

— *Tischreden 1531-46,* 3392b in *D Martin Luthers Werke* (Weimar, 1883-1929)

Lyons, O.S.B, Fintan, 'Church Music and the Reformation' in Helen Phelan ed., *Anáil Dé. The Breath of God* (Dublin: Veritas, 2001)

— 'Conversion in the Benedictine and Methodist Traditions', in *Asbury Theological Journal,* Vols. 50 and 51, Fall 1995, Spring 1996/7

MacCulloch, Diarmaid, *Thomas Cranmer. A Life* (New Haven: Yale University Press, 1996)

Macy, Gary, *The Banquet's Wisdom. A Short History of the Theologies of the Lord's Supper* (Mahwah N.J.: Paulist Press, 1992)

Matalas et al., Antonia-Leda, 'Fasting and Food Habits in the Eastern Orthodox Church' in *Fasting and Feasting,* Harlan Walker, ed. (London: Prospect Books, 1991)

Mather, Cotton, *Diary* (Boston: Massachusetts Historical Society, 1911)

McBrien, Richard, *Lives of the Popes. The Pontiffs from St Peter to John Paul II* (San Francisco: Harper One, 1997)

McGowan, Andrew, *Ascetic Eucharists. Food and Drink in Early Christian Ritual Meals* (Oxford: Clarendon Press, 1999)

McGrath, Alister, *A Life of John Calvin. A Study in the Shaping of Western Culture* (Oxford: Blackwell, 1990)

McKitterick, Rosamond, *The Frankish Church and the Carolingian Reform 789-895* (London: Royal Historical Society, 1977)

— Charlemagne. *The Formation of a European Identity* (Cambridge: C.U.P., 2008)

McManners, John, *Church and Society in Eighteenth Century France*. Vol. 1: *The Clerical Establishment and its Social Ramifications* (Oxford: Clarendon Press,1998)

Medieval handbooks of penance: a translation of the principal Libri Poenitentiales *and selections from related documents,* John Thomas McNeill ed. (New York: Columbia University Press, 1938)

Meeks, Wayne, *The First Urban Christians* (New Haven: Yale University Press, 1983)

Mennell, Stephen, *All Manners of Food. Eating and Taste in England and France from the Middle Ages to the Present* (Oxford: Basil Blackwell, 1985)

Merrony, Mark, *The Plight of Rome in the Fifth Century* (Abingdon, Oxon: Routledge, 2017)

Messisbugo, Cristoforo, *Banchetti compositioni di vivande et apparecchio generale 1549* (Delhi: Gyan Books Pvt. Ltd., 2016)

Morison, Samuel Eliot, *The Oxford History of the American People,* Vol. One (New York: Meridian, 1994)

Moss, H. St. L. B., *The Birth of the Middle Ages 395-814* (Oxford: O.U.P., 1963)

Moyer, Johanna B., 'The Food Police. Sumptuary Prohibitions on Food in the Reformation', in *Food and Faith in Christian Culture,* Ken Albala and Trudy Eden eds. (New York: Columbia University Press, 2011)

Mullins, Michael, *Called to be Saints. Christian Living in the First Century* (Dublin: Veritas,1991)

O'Boyle, James, *Life of George Washington* (London: Longmans, Green and Co., 1915)

Obelkevich, James, *Religion and the People, 800 -1700* (Chapel NC: University of North Carolina Press, 1979)

Okholm, Denis, 'Gluttony: Thought for Food', *American Benedictine Review* 49.1, March 1998

One Hundred Grievances. A Chapter from the History of Pre-Reformation Days, C.H. Collette, ed. (London:Partridge,1869)

Ozment, Steven, *A Mighty Fortress. A New History of the German People* (New York: Harper Perennial, 2005)

Paul VI, Pope Saint, *Mysterium fidei*, Encyclical letter, 1965

— *Solemni hac liturgia (Credo of the People of God)*, Motu Proprio, 1968

Parker, T.H.L., *John Calvin* (Berkhamsted: Lion Publishing 1975)

Pastor, Ludwig, *The History of the Popes,* Vols. VII ff, (London: Kegan Paul, 1924ff)

Paul VI, Pope Saint, *Credo of the People of God,* 1968

Pelner, Cosman, Madeleine, *Medieval Holidays and Festivals* (London: Piatkus, 1984)

Peters,Greg, *Reforming the Monasteries* (Eugene OR: Cascade Books, 2014)

Petri, C., *Roma Christiana: Recherches sur l'Église de Rome organisation, sa politique, son idéologie de Miltiade a Sixte III(311-4)*

Pettazoni, Raffaele, 'The Supreme Being: Phenomenological Structure and Historical Development' in Mircea Eliade et al., eds, *The History of Religions. Essays in Methodology* (Chicago: Chicago University Press, 1959)

Pliny the Younger, *Letters* (http://www.attalus.org/old/pliny10b.html)

Plutarch, 'Cicero' in *The Fall of the Roman Republic*, trans. Rex Walker (London: Penguin,1958)

Pollock, John, *John Wesley* (Oxford: A Lion Paperback, 1989)

Reardon, Bernard M. G., *Religious Thought in the Reformation* (London: Longman, 1981)

Rilliet, Jean, *Zwingli. Third Man of the Reformation*, H. Knight trans. (London: Lutterworth Press 1964)

Ritzer, George, *The Mcdonaldization of Society 6* (Thousand Oaks CA: Sage, 2010)

Rojas-Downing, M. Melissa, 'Climate change and livestock: Impacts, adaptation, and mitigation', *Science Direct,* Vol. 16, 2017, 145-163

Roscoe, William and Luigi Bossi, *Vita e pontificato di Leone X., di Guglielmo Roscoe. Tradotta e corredata di annotazioni e di alcuni documenti inediti dal conte cav. Luigi Bossi,* Vol. 5 (Lexington: Ulan Press, 2012)

Rubin, Miri, *Corpus Christi. The Eucharist in Late Medieval Culture* (Cambridge: C.U.P., 1991)

Salim Khan, Muhammad, *Islamic Medicine* (London. Routledge, Kegan and Paul, 1980)

Salisbury, Joyce E., *Church Fathers. Independent Virgins* (London: Verso, 1991)

Sandburg, Carl, *Abraham Lincoln. The Prairie Years* and *The War Years.* One Volume Edition (New York: Harcourt, Brace and Company, 1954)

Sartore, D. et al., a cura di, *Liturgia* (Cinisello: Edizioni Paoline, 2001)

Schaff, Philip, *History of the Christian Church, Vol. VII, Modern Christianity. The German Reformation* (Oak Harbor WA: Logos Research Systems, 1997)

Schindler, David L., 'Homelessness and the Modern Condition: The Family, Evangelisation and the Global Economy' *Logos* 3, No. 4 (Fall 2000)

Schlosser, Eric, *Fast Food Nation. What the All-American Meal is Doing to the World* (London: Penguin Books, 2002)

Schmemann, Alexander, *The Eucharist* (Crestwood N.Y.: St Vladimir's Seminary Press, 1987)

Schultz, Hans-Joachim, *The Byzantine Liturgy,* Matthew J. O'Connell trans. (New York: Pueblo, 1986)

Senn, Frank, *Christian Liturgy. Catholic and Evangelical* (Minn: Fortress Press, 1997)

Shaver, Stephen, 'A Eucharistic Origins Story', Part 2, in *Worship,* Vol. 92, July 2018

Shipley Duckett, Eleanor, *Alcuin, Friend of Charlemagne* (New York, Macmillan, 1951)

Smart, Ninian, *The Religious Experience of Mankind* (London: Fontana Library, 1969)

Smith, Dennis E., *From Symposium to Eucharist. The Banquet in the Early Christian World* (Minneapolis: Fortress Press, 2003)

Špidík, S.J., Tomáš, *The Spirituality of the Christian East. A Systematic Handbook* , Anthony Gythiel trans.(Collegeville: Liturgical Press, 1986)

Steel, Carolyn, *Hungry City. How Food Shapes Our Lives* (London: Chatto & Windus, 2008)

Stephens, W. P., *Zwingli: An Introduction to his Thought* (Oxford: Clarendon Press, 1992)

Strong, Roy, *Feast. A History of Grand Eating* (London: Jonathan Cape, 2002)

Suetonius, *The Twelve Caesars,* Robert Graves trans. (London: Guild Publishing,1990)

Tacitus, *The Annals of Imperial Rome,* trans. Michael Grant (London: Penguin Classics,1989²)

Taft, Robert, *The Liturgy in Byzantium and Beyond* (Aldershot: Variorum, 1995)

Tannahill, Reay, *Food in History* (London: Headline Publishing, 2002³)

The Book of Common Prayer and the Administration of the Sacraments of the Church of England (Oxford: O.U.P., 1910)

The Confession of Augsburg XXVI, 1- 40 in *Concordia. The Lutheran Book of Confessions* (St Louis MO: Concordia Publishing, 2007)

Thurston, Herbert, *Lent and Holy Week* (London: Forgottten Books, 2018)

Tierney, Brian, and Sidney Painter, *Western Europe in the Middle Ages: 300-1475* (Boston: McGraw-Hill College, 1999⁶)

Topiwala, Anya, et al.,'Moderate alcohol consumption as risk factor for adverse brain outcomes and cognitive decline: longitudinal cohort study', *British Medical Journal* 2017;357:j2353

Torrance. Thomas F., *Space, Time and Incarnation* (Edinburgh: T & T Clark, 1969)

Tovey, Philip, *The Theory and Practice of Extended Communion* (Farnham: Ashgate, 2009)

Trevor-Roper, Hugh, *Religion, Reformation and Social Change* (London: Macmillan, 1967)

Tripp, D. H., 'Methodism' in Cheslyn Jones *et al., The Study of the Liturgy* (London: S.P.C.K.,1992²)

Van Tongeren, Louis, 'The Squeeze on Sunday. Reflections on the Changing Experience and Form of Sundays' in P. Post et al., *Christian Feast and Festival. The Dynamics of Western Liturgy and Culture* (Leuven: Peeters, 2001)

Vaughan, Herbert M., *The Medici Popes, Leo X and Clement VII* (London: Methuen & Co., 1908)

Vialles, Noelie, *From Animal to Edible* (Cambridge: C.U.P., 1994)

Wallace, Charles, 'On knowing Christ in the Flesh', in *Wesley and Methodist Studies* Vol. 5 (2013)

Ward, Benedicta, trans. *The Desert Fathers* (Oxford :O.U.P., 1975)

Ware, Timothy, *The Orthodox Church* (London: Penguin Books, 1993²)

Wesley, Johanna, *The Complete Writings* (Oxford: O.U.P., 1997)

Wesley, John and Charles Wesley, 'On Temperance' in *The Message of the Wesleys,* Compiled and with Introduction by Philip Watson (London: Epworth Press, 1964)

Wesley, John, *Letter to Susanna Wesley (1725) . Works,* Vol. 25 , Gerald Cragg ed. (Oxford: Clarendon Press, 1980)

— *Sermons on Several Occasions* Vol. V (Dublin: Methodist Book Room, 1804)

— *Works 1829-31,* Vol. I (London: Mason, 1872)

Wesley, John and Charles, *Selected Writings and Hymns* (Mahwah N.J.: Paulist Press, 1981)

Wilken, Robert, *The Spirit of Early Christian Thought* (Newhaven: Yale University Press, 2003)

Wirzba, Norman, *Food and Faith. A Theology of Eating* (Cambridge: C.U.P., 2019[2])

Wybrew, Hugh, *The Orthodox Liturgy. The Development of the Eucharistic Liturgy in the Byzantine Rite* (Crestwood NY: St Vladimir's Seminary Press, 1996)

Zeitlin, S., 'The Theodosian Code' in *The Jewish Quarterly Review* Vol. 43, No. 4 (April,1953)

Zizioulas, John, *Being as Communion. Studies in Personhood and the Church* (Crestwood NY: St Vladimir's Seminary Press, 1993)

Zwingli, Huldreich, *Selected Works of Huldreich Zwingli (1484-1531. The Reformer of Switzerland,* Edited and Introduction by S. M. Jackson (Philadelphia: University of Pennsylvania, 1901)

INDEX

Want to keep reading?

Columba Books has a whole range of books to inspire your faith and spirituality.

As the leading independent publisher of religious and theological books in Ireland, we publish across a broad range of areas including pastoral resources, spirituality, theology, the arts and history.

All our books are available through
www.columbabooks.com
and you can find us on Twitter, Facebook and Instagram to discover more of our fantastic range of books. You can sign up to our newletter through the website for the latest news about events, sales and to keep up to date with our new releases.

columbabooks

@ColumbaBooks

columba_books

columba
BOOKS